A DISTANT WAR COMES HOME

A DISTANT WAR COMES HOME

MAINE·IN·THE CIVIL·WAR·ERA

DONALD W. BEATTIE · RODNEY M. COLE

CHARLES G. WAUGH · *EDITORS*

ILLUSTRATIONS BY JOHN L. OGDEN

DOWN EAST BOOKS · CAMDEN · MAINE

TO OUR THREE VERY PATIENT WIVES

LORRAINE BARTLETT BEATTIE,

LOIS WIGHTMAN COLE,

AND

CAROL-LYNN RÖSSEL WAUGH

Copyright © 1996 by Charles G. Waugh, Donald W. Beattie, and Rodney M. Cole
"John Wilkes Booth Won Hearts in Portland," © 1988 by the *Maine Sunday Telegram*
"The Late, Great Medal of Honor Caper," © 1981 by *Down East* magazine
"The Confederate Raid on Calais," © 1966, renewed 1992 by Mason Philip Smith
All articles have been double-checked in the Catalog of Copyright Entries (Copyright Office,
the Library of Congress), and, except as noted above, are in the public domain.
ISBN 0-89272-393-9
COVER DESIGN BY LURELLE CHEVERIE/GARY RIDSDALE
INTERIOR DESIGN BY LURELLE CHEVERIE/KARIN WOMER
Color separation and image modification by Phil Schirmer
Printed and bound at Bookcrafters, Inc.

2   4   5   3   1

Down East Books, P.O. Box 679, Camden, ME 04843

LIBRARY OF CONGRESS CATALOGING-IN-PUBLICATION DATA

A distant war comes home : Maine in the Civil War era / edited by
    Donald W. Beattie, Rodney M. Cole, and Charles G. Waugh ;
    illustrated by John L. Ogden.
        p.   cm.
    Includes bibliographical references and index.
    ISBN 0-89272-393-9
    1. Maine—History—Civil War, 1861–1865. I. Beattie, Donald W.
II. Cole, Rodney M., 1932– . III. Waugh, Charles.
E511.D57   1996
974.1'03—dc20   96-33329
                                                                   CIP

Contents

BATTLES, CAMPAIGNS
AND EVENTS
★ 77 ★

PERSONAL EXPERIENCES

AFTER THE WAR

INTRODUCTION

More than 108,000 books have been written about the Civil War.[1] That's more than any for other war.[2] You would have to read four books a day for seventy-four years to finish them all. Indeed, a publishing executive once quipped, "Today, there is no question as to who won the Civil War—the book publishers."[3]

Why is this "Great Rebellion" such a popular subject?

The Civil War is one of four watershed events in United States history.[4] We would not be a world powerhouse today if the South had won.[5] First, it was a clash over ways of life: a rural, class-conscious South fought an industrial, democratic North over conflicting visions of the future.[6] It was also a clash over principles: Southerners thought secession was morally justified; Northerners held slavery to be morally wrong. The Union's victory resolved these issues. Since 1865, the United States has thought of itself as a nation, not a union, and slavery has been condemned by virtually all.[7]

The Civil War was also a watershed event because it changed the nature of warfare. Romantic elements gave way to modern ones. Soldiers still wore bright uniforms, used horse borne cavalry, and carried swords, but this was the conflict that saw the beginning of aerial reconnaissance, the development of repeating rifles and machine guns, the launching of ironclad ships and submarines, and the inauguration of mass warfare against civilians.[8]

The Civil War involved a tremendous cost to the nation. Fatalities totaled 620,000: 360,000 Northerners and 260,000 Southerners.[9] That represents nearly 4% of the United States male population in 1860, and almost totals deaths from all our other wars combined.[10]

The Civil War was internecine. Neighbors fought neighbors, friends fought friends, and family members fought one another. For example, Woodrow Wilson, president during World War I, was the "southern-born son of a pro-Confederate Ohioan and an English mother, with uncles who served in the Union. . . ."[11]

★

Finally, the Civil War took place in our hometowns. Battle-grounds dot Eastern roadmaps. Maryland, New Jersey, and New York experienced draft riots. Even Maine and Vermont were invaded. Farmers still occasionally plow up artifacts from Civil War battles.

Maine was a major Civil War player. Famous personages such as Governor John Fairfield and Harriet Beecher Stowe helped provoke the war. To fight it, Maine raised "32 infantry regiments, [two] cavalry regiments, one regiment of heavy artillery, seven batteries of mounted artillery, [two regiments of sharpshooters] seven companies of coast guards, and six for coast fortification."[12] Maine sent more troops (72,117) per military-aged population than any other state.[13] Nine Maine regiments fought in more than twenty battles each.[14] The 1st Maine Cavalry took part in more battles (42) than any other Union regiment.[15] The 1st and 2nd Maine Sharpshooters killed more Confederates than any other Union regiment.[16] The 5th Maine regiment captured more prisoners than it had men.[17] The 20th Maine was responsible for turning the tide of the war at Gettysburg.[18] And the 1st Maine Heavy Artillery suffered the greatest battle casualties of any Union regiment. After the war, the first National Solders' Home for disabled Civil War veterans was established at Togus, in Hallowell (now Chelsea), Maine. Maine politicians James G. Blaine and Thomas Reed helped the Republican party maintain prominence, and Maine native Adelbert Ames became the longest-lived Civil War General.

This book presents an overview of Maine's Civil War involvement, the first such survey to be published.[19] Events leading to the war are discussed in the chapters of Section I. Notable Maine figures in the war are profiled in the second section. In Section III, Civil War battles, campaigns and events are discussed. Personal experiences during the war are presented in Section IV, including fascinating accounts from soldiers, spies, escaped slaves, and prisoners of war. Finally, postwar events are chronicled in Section V, including the participation of Maine figures in events surounding the assassination of President Lincoln and the attempt to impeach Andrew Johnson, Lincoln's successor. Except for Section II, Famous Sons and Daughters, all chapters are arranged chronologically.

Our book is designed to be reader friendly. It presents fascinating information in well-written articles that, for the most part, have never before been reprinted. You will learn, for example, more about how *Uncle Tom's Cabin* came to be written in Maine. You will read how an Old Town private who enlisted at eighteen

won promotion to general three years later; about a prominent one-armed Maine general who founded many of the nation's most prestigious Black colleges; about how the men of the 27th Maine, which never saw combat, were *all* awarded the Congressional Medal of Honor. You will be surprised to learn that, on the day he assassinated Lincoln, John Wilkes Booth had been in the custody of Union troops led by a Maine man—until a senior officer ordered Booth's release.

Virtually all the articles are unfamiliar. Three are original; the reprints come from ten different sources. About 60 percent are three-quarters of a century old. Many were published thanks to decades of research and writing by Lewiston, Maine, journalist L. C. Bateman.

Finally, you will find the articles in this book well written. Accessibility has been a major goal. From more than seven hundred reprint candidates, we chose just forty-three. Most originally were newspaper articles. When necessary, we have straightened out problems of organization, removed irrelevancies, and corrected typographical substantive mistakes that appeared in the original versions.

Every organization and person contacted about this book, with one nameless exception, have been extremely helpful. Thanks go to: Representative Herbert Adams, the Bates College Library, Professor Jay Hoar, the Kansas State Historical Society, the *Lewiston Sun-Journal*, the Maine State Historical Society, the Maine State Library, the Portland Public Library, the Rockland *Courier-Gazette*, the libraries at the University of Maine at Augusta and Farmington, and the Department of Veterans Affairs Medical and Regional Office Center at Togus.

We alone, of course, are responsible for any mistakes. Any additions, observations, or corrections should be sent to Charles Waugh, 5 Morrill St., Winthrop, ME 04364.

—C. G. Waugh and D. W. Beattie

NOTES

1. Patricia L. Faust, ed., *Historical Times Illustrated Encyclopedia of the Civil War*, New York: Harper & Row, 1986, p. xix. (Number of Civil War books written through 1996 is estimated at 108,060, based on an average publication rate of 806 books per year.—C. G. W.)

2. James M. McPherson, *Ordeal by Fire: The Civil War and Reconstruction*, New York: Alfred A. Knopf, 1982, p. 487.

3. Esther E. Wood, "Maine has Proud History to Recall in Civil War," *Lewiston Journal Illustrated Magazine,* 12 August 1961, p. 7.

4. The other three watershed events are, in our judgment, the Revolutionary War (which determined our nationhood), World War II (which saved the world from tyranny and turned the U.S. into a superpower), and the Vietnam War (which shattered our illusions of invulnerability and cast a pall of cynicism and distrust of government across the land).

5. For some ideas about what the world might have been like if the South had won, see MacKinlay Kantor, *If the South had Won the Civil War,* New York: Bantam Books, 1961, and Ward Moore, *Bring the Jubilee,* New York: Farrar Straus, 1953.

6. James M. McPherson, op cit., pp. 6, 9–19, 23–31, 181–83.

7. James M. McPherson, op cit., pp. 488–489; and Leon L. Bram, Robert S. Phillips, and Norma H. Dickey, eds., *Funk & Wagnalls New Encyclopedia,* 26, New York: Funk & Wagnalls, 1983, p. 306.

8. Ashley Halsey, Jr., *Who Fired the First Shot?,* New York: Hawthorn Books, Inc., 1963, pp. 65–73, 76–81.

9. James M. McPherson, op cit., p. 488.

10. Ashley Halsey, Jr., op cit., p. 15.

11. Ashley Halsey, Jr., op cit., p. 13.

12. Marjorie Wight Farrand, "Maine's Great Part in the Civil War," *Lewiston Journal Illustrated Magazine,* 12 December 1959, p. 2.

13. William B. Jordan, Jr., *Maine in the Civil War: a Bibliographic Guide,* Portland, Me.: The Maine Historical Society, 1976, p. 72; and Esther E. Wood, op cit., p. 2.

14. William B. Jordan, Jr., op cit., pp. 59-61, 63-64, 66-67, & 69.

15. Henry Ernest Dunnack, *The Maine Book,* Augusta, Me., 1920, p. 6.

16. William B. Jordan, Jr., op cit., p. 69.

17. Marjorie Wight Farrand, op cit., p. 2.

18. Thomas A. Desjardin, *Stand Firm Ye Boys from Maine,* Gettysburg, Pa.: Thomas Publications, 1995, pp. xii, 154–159.

19. To date our three closest rivals have been: William E.S. Whitman and Charles H. True, *Maine in the War for the Union, a History of the Part Borne by Maine Troops in the Suppression of the American Rebellion* (1865); Ruel H. Stanley and George O. Hall, *Eastern Maine and the Rebellion, being an Account of the Principal Local Events in Eastern Maine During the War, and Brief Histories of Eaastern Maine Regiments, Contains Accounts of Mobs, Riots Destruction of Newpapers, War Meetings, Drafts, Confederate Raids, Peace Meetings, Celebrations, Soldier's Letters, and Scenes and Incidents at the Front, Never Before in Print* (1887); and Donald M. McCormick, *A Cross-Section of Maine History During the Civil War Period* (1934). The first looks only at military events, the second only at a portion of the state's involvement, and the last only at in-state events. The first two lack some historical perspective and access to more recent information. None is easily found (the latest is an unpublished dissertation).

BEFORE THE WAR

With the enactment of the Missouri Compromise in 1820, Maine became a "free" state and an active participant in ante-bellum interests of national importance. Brunswick, Maine, in particular, seemed to be a center of the new state's circle of social reformers who focused on feminist, temperance, and human dignity issues). Key individuals with Maine roots (by birth or choice), such as Elijah Parish Lovejoy and Harriet Beecher Stowe, contributed significanty to the momentum that drove the Union to war against the fledgling Confederacy in 1861.

Abolitionism was a social movement dedicated to ending slavery. Though not widely embraced, it was a major cause of the Civil War. It gained national recognition and force from the dramatic murder of Elijah Parish Lovejoy, an abolitionist newspaper editor, in Alton, Illinois, in 1837. Ironically, during Lovejoy's childhood in Maine, his uncle Abiel Lovejoy, of Sidney and Vassalboro, owned several slaves who worked as sawyers in his lumber business.

An "underground railroad" developed to smuggle slaves north to freedom. (Canada became a favorite destination after the Fugitive Slave Act of 1850 established that escapees could legally be retrieved from "free" states.) In Portland, Maine, Lydia Dennet, Charlotte Thomas, and her brother George were engaged in this often risky activity. But aiding the escaped slaves was looked down upon, even in Maine. Indeed, former governor John Fairfield lost the 1844 Democratic vice-presidential nomination because years earlier he had not helped Southern courts extradite two Maine citizens accused of smuggling a slave out of Georgia.

Harriet Beecher Stowe was perhaps the woman most hated by Southerners. She wrote *Uncle Tom's Cabin* (1851), a wildly popular anti-slavery novel, while living in Brunswick with her husband, a Bowdoin College professor. Uncle Tom, her central character, was American literature's "first fictional Christ figure," and her book lucratively tapped the ideological convictions

of a nationwide audience. Stowe was a popular hostess while in Brunswick, and Bowdoin undergraduate Joshua L. Chamberlain was a sometime attendee at the discussion groups and teas held at her home.

"Kansas Fever" seized many emigrant Mainers after the Kansas-Nebraska Act of 1854. Kansas fever was spread by organizations such as the New England Emigrant Aid Society. Their idea, which was ultimately successful, was to pack Kansas with Northerners so that its citizens would vote to enter the Union as a free state. But as Cole's article indicates, this strategy was resisted by Southern sympathizers, and led to seven years of bloody conflict.

Maine may not have founded the G.O.P., but it was deeply involved with the Republican party's successful emergence during the mid-1850s, and it did elect the nation's first Republican Governor: Anson P. Morrill (1855–56). Foremost in their platform, Republicans resolved to oppose slavery as a national policy and to prevent the expansion of slavery into any current or future nationally held territories. Symbolically, Maine was a natural place to strike out against slave-state/free-state compromises, as the Maine itself had been granted statehood in the first effort to create a balance between free and slave states.

Maine's Bowdoin College produced many famous and effective Union Generals, such as Joshua L. Chamberlain and O. O. Howard. However, in 1858, it also granted Jefferson Davis, the future president of the Confederacy, an honorary doctorate. What a paradox, one could argue, to place such an honor on a man who was politically juxtaposed against the ideas of Lovejoy and Stowe and Maine Senator William Fessenden (profiled in the article beginning on page 259), who also received an honorary doctorate at the same ceremony. However, there was no war then, and ivory-tower minds have historically maintained an openness to personal competency and worthiness which outweighs personal bias and partisanship. (Apparently, Davis also narrowly escaped serious injury or death during his visit, when a Mainer prevented him from falling down a set of stairs.)

Lincoln's assassin, John Wilkes Booth, may be America's biggest villain. His postwar connections with Mainers, while surprisingly plentiful, are rather conventional. But his pre-war connections to Maine are unusual, and may even include a love affair with a young Portland actress, Helen Western, whom he apparently remembered longingly.

Elijah Parish Lovejoy—
A Martyr to the Liberty of the Press

LOUISE HELEN COBURN

There are many kinds of freedom over which our starry banner waves. Freedom from kings and lords, freedom of person and property, freedom of religion, freedom of speech and of the press, freedom of the slave—all these have been fought for and toiled for and won at great price. They are implanted in the Constitution of the United States, and are the shining foundation stones of free government. These great freedoms ought to be cherished by all Americans, for Americans in every generation have died for them. The people of Maine should always remember and honor the name of the Maine country boy, born and educated in our state, who shed the first blood for the freedom of the slave, and who was the champion and martyr of the freedom of the press.

Elijah Parish Lovejoy was the son of a Congregational minister, and was born in the town of Albion, Maine, November 8, 1802. His home was on land which had been cleared out of the wilderness only twelve years before his birth, so his boyhood was that of the pioneer. The ax, the plow, and the scythe were familiar to his hands, but every spare hour was devoted to reading and study. Like many another famous man, he learned to read at his mother's knee, asking her for the name of each letter, and learning in this way the letters and the words, so that at four he could read the Bible easily. He was always first in school, and had a remarkable memory. He could repeat long passages from the Bible, and a great deal of poetry of which he was especially fond. His brother remembered having heard him say from memory a hundred and fifty hymns at one time. But he was also a leader in all kinds of boyish sport, such as swimming in the pond beside which he lived. The boys used to practice deep diving, sometimes going down twelve or fifteen feet, and bringing up mud or clams to prove they had touched the bottom. At one time Elijah swam across the pond, three-quarters of a mile, and back again.

When he was eighteen he became eager for more education than the district school could give him, and went to Monmouth Academy, where, though he had studied Latin for only a few weeks previously, he read the whole of Virgil and parts of Cicero and Sallust in a single term. He also attended China Academy for a while, and entered Waterville (now Colby) College as a sophomore, and was graduated from it with first honors in 1826. In college he especially liked languages, and was a fine classical scholar. He had been in the habit from childhood of writing verse, and his Commencement part was a long and well-written poem, called "The Inspiration of the Muse." After teaching for a few months, he heard, as did so many of the young men of those years, the call of the West, and stirred with the spirit of adventure left home and parents and native state for the great Mississippi valley, and what was then the frontier town of St. Louis. Here he taught for a while, writing a few poems and prose articles for the papers, and then became editor of a political newspaper which was supporting Henry Clay for the Presidency.

The prospect of a political career, doubt-

Originally published in *Lewiston Journal Illustrated Magazine*, 6 December 1924.

less a brilliant one, was opening before this talented young man, when at some revival meetings the religious impressions of his childhood were renewed, and the direction of his life was changed. He decided at once that it was his duty to be a minister, and came east in the spring of 1832 to study in Princeton Theological Seminary in New Jersey. While there he was able to make a visit—his only one—to his parents and brothers and sisters in the old home in Maine. After a year of study and a few months of preaching in Newport, R. I., and New York City, he returned to St. Louis. Some of his friends, who were anxious that his ability and literary talent should be used to the best purpose, provided the money for starting a religious weekly paper in St. Louis, of which he should be the editor. The first number of the *St. Louis Observer*, as it was called, was issued in November, 1833.

Now one would think that the stirring part of Lovejoy's life was over, for nothing would seem more likely to be calm and unexciting than the career of an editor of a religious paper. But a brave man can be a hero in any calling, as he can in any place, and Lovejoy had in him the stuff of which heroes and martyrs are made.

Missouri was a slave state, and the more intolerant because it neighbored the great free state of Illinois. The soul of the young man from Maine was deeply moved by the wrongs of the slave, and the crime of slavery, as he saw it, and as he saw he spoke and wrote. He printed in the *Observer* a series of editorials, describing and condemning the evil of slavery, and pleading for freedom for the slave. Great Britain had just passed the act abolishing slavery in her colonies. The north of the United States was agitated with this subject, and abolition sentiment was rapidly spreading. Lovejoy was in favor of gradual emancipation, which should be carried out by the slave states and the slave owners themselves, and for this he argued and entreated.

Of course he soon made many enemies who did all they could to injure him, until even his friends were afraid to take his part. His printing-office and his life were frequently threatened. During an absence of the editor from St. Louis, the owners of the paper printed the statement that no more slavery articles would be published until his return, and that when he came back he would no doubt follow the course they wished. At the same time nine prominent citizens sent the editor a personal letter, urging him so far to change the character of the *Observer* as to pass over in silence everything connected with the subject of slavery.

They found they had mistaken their editor. When Lovejoy returned to the city, he printed his famous Appeal, in which he said: "I cannot surrender my principles, though the whole world besides should vote them down—I can make no compromise between truth and error, even though my life be the alternative." and added, "I do therefore as an American citizen and Christian patriot, and in the name of Liberty and Law and Religion, solemnly PROTEST against all these attempts, howsoever or by whomsoever made, to frown down the liberty of the press, and forbid the free expression of opinion. I declare it to be my fixed purpose to submit to no such dictation. AND I AM PREPARED TO ABIDE THE CONSEQUENCES. I have appealed to the constitution and laws of my country; if they fail to protect me, I APPEAL TO GOD, and with Him I cheerfully rest my cause. I CAN DIE AT MY POST, BUT I CANNOT DESERT IT."

At this crisis an unexpected friend rose up who took over the ownership of the paper, and Lovejoy continued for a number of months longer to publish the *Observer* in St. Louis, and to speak his mind about slavery and anti-slavery.

Finally he decided that it was best for him to leave Missouri, and in July, 1836, he moved to Alton, Illinois, a city about twenty-five miles from St. Louis, and also on the shore of the Mississippi River, upon its other side, where he had the promise of the support of friends. A few days before he left St. Louis his printing office was partly wrecked by a mob, and he himself narrowly escaped.

The press was sent to Alton by boat and landed on the bank on Sunday morning, and on Monday morning, July 31, 1836, it was destroyed by unknown hands and thrown into the river.

Lovejoy set up a new home in Alton with his wife and baby son. Some people of the city furnished money for a new press, and the *Alton Observer* was issued for something less than a year. The editor continued to urge the abolition of slavery, helped in organizing a state Anti-slavery society in Illinois, and was one of its officers. He often preached on Sunday, always speaking frankly about slavery. But here in a free state, he was still repeatedly threatened, and knew that his press and his home were in danger. However, he felt only more strongly that he had a duty to God and humanity to perform, to hold up the cause of freedom in the borderland of slavery. He wrote in August, 1836, "The cry of the oppressed has entered not only into my ears, but into my soul, so that while I live I cannot hold my peace."

As the months went by the hostility to Lovejoy and the *Observer* became more furious. He was waylaid on the street in the evening by armed men, and threatened with death, but finally allowed to go. When he was on a visit to his wife's mother in St. Charles, Missouri, a mob entered the house, and he was only saved by his wife's throwing her arms around him, and by friends aiding him to escape. His second printing-press was destroyed August 21, 1837, by men who entered the office of the *Observer* and wrecked everything. The third press, which was sent for immediately, was taken from a warehouse near the river on the night of its arrival, September 21, 1837, broken to pieces, and thrown into the Mississippi. A few days after this, Lovejoy wrote, "By the blessing of God I will never abandon the enterprise so long as I live, and if I die it cannot be in a better cause." And a little later he wrote, "I have sworn eternal opposition to slavery, and by the blessing of God I will never go back."

On November 3, when the fourth press was expected very soon to arrive, a meeting of citizens of Alton was held, at which resolutions were passed demanding that Lovejoy should no longer be connected with any newspaper in the city. Lovejoy made a speech —the last appeal of his life—in which he broke down weeping and moved many who heard him to tears. He said in closing: "If I am not safe in Alton, I shall not be safe anywhere. I have no more claim upon the protection of any other community than I have upon this; and I have concluded after consultation with

ELIJAH PARISH LOVEJOY

my friends and earnestly seeking counsel of God, to REMAIN AT ALTON, and to insist on protection in the exercise of my rights. If the civil authorities refuse to protect me, I must look to God, and if I die, I have determined to make my grave in Alton."

There was no police force in Alton, so a volunteer company was formed of sixty men, who were opposed to mob violence, to protect the new press when it should come. It was organized with a captain, and acted under the direction of the mayor of the city. The expected boat arrived in the night of November 6, and the press was taken to the upper floor of a stone warehouse that stood beside the river. The Mississippi runs at this point nearly east. The warehouse was a double building having two stories on the street and three on the river, and with windows and doors in the gable ends north and south, but no windows on the east or west sides, which faced vacant lots. The following night, as there had up to that time been no disturbance, most of the guard had gone away, but twenty men remained, including one of the owners of the warehouse. About ten o'clock in the evening a mob arrived, armed with stones and guns and pistols, and demanded the press. Those in the building replied that they were ready to defend it with their lives. The attacking party threw stones and tried to batter down the stout north door. Shots were fired and returned by the defenders, and one man of the mob was killed. The mayor commanded the mob to disperse, and when he was laughed at for his pains he carried back and forth the demands of the mob and the answers of the defenders. He told the men in the building that they had a perfect right to defend their property, but refused to call upon the citizens for help.

By this time the city bells were ringing, and the citizens in large numbers were standing around and looking upon the scene. A new method of attack was now adopted. A ladder was raised on the east side of the building, where there were no windows, and a man was sent up to set fire to the wooden roof. Upon this, several of the defenders went out of the south door and around the corner of the warehouse, fired at the man on the ladder, and came in again to reload. Then Lovejoy and two or three others again stepped out of the same lower door on the river side. Lovejoy stood a moment, a little ahead in the light of the full moon, when two or three men who had concealed themselves behind a pile of lumber near the river fired, and Lovejoy received five shots. He turned quickly, ran through the door up a flight of stairs into the counting room, and, with arms across his breast, fell, crying, "Oh God, I am shot," and died without another word. His companions surrendered the press and made their escape.

So died the son of Maine, the bold defender of human freedom and a free press. This was November 7, 1837, the day before what would have been his thirty-fifth birthday.

In appearance Lovejoy was of medium height, broadly built, had a dark complexion, and piercing black eyes, with a sort of twinkle in them. He had a round, pleasant face full of good humor and beaming with kindness. He was always calm when others were excited, and had no bitterness in his heart, no venom on his tongue, no fury in his voice. So mild and so gentle is described to us this high-hearted apostle of freedom.

The death of Lovejoy moved the entire country, as it had not been moved since the death of Washington. John Quincy Adams said that it had given a "shock as of an earthquake throughout this continent, which will be felt in the most distant regions of the earth." Sermons were preached about it in cities and country towns all through the north, and a number of them were printed. Newspaper editorials in many states paid honor to the man, who, as one of them said, "fell a martyr to the liberty of the press and to the cause of the slave in the land of the free."

Public meetings were held in the cities of the north, with resolutions and speeches denouncing the crime, and pledging loyalty to the great principles of freedom. At an indignation meeting held in Faneuil Hall, Boston, the Attorney General of Massachusetts spoke of Lovejoy's "imprudence," and said, "He died as

the fool dieth." Then a young lawyer of the city sprang to his feet, and made on the spur of the moment a speech that thrilled his audience, for this was Wendell Phillips' first speech for freedom, the beginning of his life work as an anti-slavery orator.

George William Curtis said at Phillips' funeral that there had been three great speeches in the history of our country—the one of Patrick Henry that closes with "Give me liberty or give me death." Lincoln's Gettysburg address, and this of Wendell Phillips at the meeting held in Faneuil Hall to denounce the murder of Lovejoy—"These three," said Mr. Curtis, "and there is no fourth."

Twenty years after Lovejoy's death, and four years before the great conflict that gave freedom to the slave, Abraham Lincoln said, "Lovejoy's tragic death for freedom in every sense marked his sad ending as the greatest single event that ever happened in the new world."

Thirty years after Lovejoy's death, and two years after the Civil War, Wendell Phillips visited Alton, and wrote in a letter, "How prudently most men creep into nameless graves, while now and then one or two forget themselves into immortality."

Sixty years after Lovejoy's death the state of Illinois, citizens of Alton, and others erected a stately monument over his grave. It is ninety-three feet high, and entirely of granite, except for the bronze statue of Victory upon its summit, and bronze panels on the four sides of the square die, from which the round column rises. Each of these panels carries an inscription, one in honor of the hero, the others quotations from his speeches or writings. The panel on the north side pictures the old press, beneath which are Elijah Parish Lovejoy's historic words: "As long as I am an American citizen, and as long as American blood runs in these veins, I shall hold myself at liberty to speak, to write, and to publish whatever I please on any subject, being amenable to the laws of my country for the same."

ALSO SEE

"Elijah Parish Lovejoy, Colby's Most Famous Graduate, to be Honored at the Centennial of the College," *Lewiston Journal Illustrated Magazine*, 6 March 1920, pp. 1–2.

"A Maine Martyr to the Cause of Liberty— Elijah Parish Lovejoy," *Lewiston Journal Illustrated Magazine*, 12 January 1918, p. 1.

PORTLAND AND THE
ANTI-SLAVERY MOVEMENT

L. C. BATEMAN

It is a long stretch of time since the old anti-slavery agitation days, and the memories of that mighty struggle have well nigh faded from the minds of men. The present generation can have but a faint conception of what it meant to denounce the curse of slavery in the early forties. True, the cause of humanity was gaining with mighty strides in the North, but much prejudice yet remained to be overcome. Even the assassination of Elijah Lovejoy in Alton, Illinois, as early as 1837 had but faintly aroused the nation from the moral lethargy into which it had fallen, but the burning philippies of Garrison and the eloquent denunciations of Wendell Phillips were slowly burning their way into the hearts of the American people. Here and there in nearly every community were a few brave men and women who dared to face the scorn of their fellows by defending the cause of the hound-hunted slave. It was their bold words and deeds that came like the first ray of sunlight to scatter the despair of centuries. Any man can defend a system that is hoary with antiquity and bolstered up with great names, but it is only given to the immortal few to incur the hostility of the multitude by defending a just and righteous, though unpopular cause. It is to such men and women, however, that posterity always builds its noblest monuments, and to whose inspired words the pen of the historian is ever attuned.

Unfortunately for the credit of our State, Maine lagged far in the rear during this mighty contest. A few noble spirits were here to uphold the banner of freedom, and as usual they were obliged to face the vituperation and abuse of their fellows. Prominent among these were a few of the old and aristocratic families of Portland. In this connection the names of Lydia Dennett, General Samuel Fessenden, Newell A. and Stephen Foster, Nathan Winslow, the Southwicks and above all the Thomas family will stand out in the memory of the older generation. They were the pioneers of the movement here, and to them belongs a credit that has never yet been fully rendered.

The relevant history of the Thomas family begins with Elias Thomas, who was born here January 14, 1772. During the war with England, and while yet a very small child, he was removed from the city by his mother who feared that the place might be captured and pillaged by the British.

At the close of the Revolutionary war the family returned, and here the child grew to manhood, and here he continued to reside until only a few years ago when he died at the age of 101 years.

In 1802, Elias Thomas was married to Elizabeth, daughter of Judge William Widgery of New Gloucester. This was one of the oldest and proudest family names in Maine, and the union was a singularly happy one. They were both possessed of strong individualities and made their mark upon the generation in which they lived. The mother was a woman of rare wit and unflinching courage. It required courage in those days to befriend and defend the slave, but in this duty neither she nor her husband for one moment hesitated.

The original home of the Thomas family

ORIGINALLY PUBLISHED IN *LEWISTON JOURNAL ILLUSTRATED MAGAZINE*, 2 JANUARY 1904.

was on India street, and it was here where most of the old anti-slavery agitators were received and entertained. This historic mansion was burned in the great Portland fire of 1865, and no picture of it is known to be extant. The present family residence, built in 1800, was purchased shortly afterwards, and here in later years have been entertained some of the most famous men in the nation. Here came Wendell Phillips, Garrison, Parker Pillsbury and Fred Douglass to do honor to the family that had been their mainstay in Maine during the darkest days of the anti-slavery struggle, and hither they brought the tributes of their affection to the surviving members.

To Elias Thomas and Elizabeth Widgery no less than eight children were born, all of whom became distinguished in one direction or another. But the two that have always been the most conspicuous in the public eye are George A. and Charlotte J. Thomas. Neither brother nor sister has ever married, but together have lived in the old homestead and kept up all the traditions of the family—including the great virtue of hospitality and, most markedly, an uncompromising and fearless advocacy of great reforms.

Striking personalities indeed are George A. Thomas and his sister, Charlotte. Known and loved by nearly every person in Portland, and with a circle of friends reaching all over the State, it is indeed singular that so few of the present generation recall their names in connection with the great struggle for the slave. In the noble old mansion, and surrounded with friends, their lives are now flowing smoothly on with but little to remind them of that far-off time when howling mobs were thundering at their doors.

But a few days since it was the good fortune of the writer to be entertained at the Thomas residence and listen to the thrilling story of the slave as it fell from the lips of dear Aunt Charlotte. And Uncle George was there, too, with now and then a word when the memory of his sister might be at fault. In the cozy library we sat and talked of the old days when to be a philanthropist and a reformer was sufficient to cost even the proud family of Thomas its social prestige. Aunt Charlotte is not old. No matter what her years may be, the heart is still young and the eye is bright. Her voice was pitched in tender cadence as the wrongs of the slave were recalled, but when the seared conscience of the North was mentioned her eye would flash and ever and anon the voice ring out in tones of scorn and contempt.

"My mother," said Miss Thomas, "and father were both connected with all the great reforms of their day. They were with Neal Dow in the temperance movement, but it was in the anti-slavery agitation that they did their most effective work.

"Lydia Dennett was the first actual mover in this reform in Portland. She was a magnificent woman in all that the name implies. Of fine intellect, great force of character and the highest social standing, it was a great shock to Portland when she espoused the cause of the slave. The Southwicks, Nathan Winslow, Mrs. Peter Morrill and Neal Dow were all in the movement a little later, and together with my father's family it made a strong working force. My mother was always anti-slavery, and it was but natural that she should become a living force and an inspiration in the cause.

"My first recollection of that struggle was when we helped runaway slaves through to Canada. They reached Portland by what was then known as the underground railroad. Stretching from the Ohio river there was a chain of men and women of the same stamp as those in Portland, whom I have already named, and when once a slave could reach Ohio soil he was well nigh certain to be spirited through to a place of safety. They would be secreted by day and after being furnished with food and money pushed on to the next place by night. It might take them months to get through, but it was seldom that they were caught by their masters when once well on the road.

"After the famous, or rather the infamous Dred Scott decision by the Supreme Court [1857], there was no longer any safety for a slave even after reaching Maine, and it then became necessary to run them through to Canada. In this work Lydia Dennett and my mother were deeply interested and usually successful. It is a shame to reflect that liberty could only be found under the British flag from which we had rebelled only a half century before, and this fact should make us more modest in speaking and boasting of our institutions today.

"I well remember one famous case that Mrs. Dennett and my mother had on their hands. A slave named Ellen Crafts, and her husband, had worked their way through from Kentucky by the underground railway and reached Portland. The woman was almost white, and her color showed only too plainly the double crime that had been perpetrated against her mother. The woman was dressed as a man, and wore a tall silk hat such as were worn by a valet to a gentleman in those days. They were hungry and tired as well as being

ELLEN CRAFTS, THE ESCAPED SLAVE

badly frightened when they reached Portland, and Mrs. Dennett at once sent them to our house. After staying at our house one night mother took them to the Grand Trunk Railway, which had just been opened up, and started them for Canada. It was midnight when she did this, and the risk of being detected was very great, but she never stopped to consider that danger. General Samuel Fessenden aided her in this matter.

"There were not more than half a dozen houses in town that dared to harbor a slave in those days. Newell A. Foster, who owned the Press, and his brother Stephen came near being tarred and feathered for helping us in other slave cases. As the slaves were coming and going all the time we were all kept busy in the work, and so we didn't notice the social ostracism very much. We had to work all sorts of dodges. In the case of Ellen Crafts we put her right arm in a sling for fear that someone might ask her to write. As a slave she could not do this, and had that fact become known it would have aroused suspicion. With her arm in a sling we knew no one would make

such a request, and even if they did she would have a good excuse for not complying. She was a very intelligent woman, however, and a credit to her race and sex.

"Mrs. Lydia Dennett was a cousin of John Neal and also to Neal Dow. She was highly connected, but that didn't save her from being turned out of the Quaker church for aiding the escaped slaves. That didn't change her course in the slightest degree, and no one among us did more for the cause than she.

"Of course you will want to know something about our being mobbed in Portland. That was in 1847, and William Lloyd Garrison with a freed slave by the name of Charles Lennox Remond, and Fred Douglass came here to lecture in the old Quaker church. The party first reported to Mrs. Dennett, and then came over to our house to tea.

"About half past seven o'clock we all started for the church at the corner of Pearl and Federal streets. There we found a mixed audience, but very few of whom were sympathizers. None of the fashionable people were present, but we expected that condition of affairs. Nathan Winslow presided and at once introduced Mr. Garrison. Garrison began in clear, distinct tones and quiet but dignified manner. He was a wonderfully convincing speaker. There was nothing of the ranter about him, but in simple language he stated the awful curse of slavery, and dwelt on its injustice. He referred to the Declaration of Independence as a living lie and during all his terrible arraignment everyone listened with breathless attention.

"Then the escaped slave, Remond, came on the stage to speak. No sooner had he made his appearance than the trouble commenced. A mob had gathered on the outside and began to throw stones at the building. In less than five minutes every window in the church was smashed out and several persons in the audience had been hit by the flying missiles. A panic at once occurred and the meeting was broken up. The mob were trying to get at Garrison and the Negro who still remained on the stage. Then the rotten eggs began to fly and scores of them were hurled at the speakers. They were hit in several places but continued to stand their ground. As I turned around to look at the mob one of the eggs struck me squarely in the forehead and spattered its contents all over my face. It didn't hurt me in the least, but it made a much stronger abolitionist of me.

MISS CHARLOTTE J. THOMAS

"Of course the meeting was broken up. When the racket commenced the mayor was notified and he sent the militia to guard the speakers. Garrison and Douglass were taken out of the building between two women, but even that did not protect them from the curses and insults of the mob. The militia had hard work to save them from personal assault. Mr. Garrison walked out first between Mrs. Dennett and my mother, while Douglass and Remond followed behind with the rest of us around them. It was a fearful tumult outside, but I was too angry to be frightened in the least. Mr. John Spear, editor of the *Prisoner's Friend,* who was to have been one of the speakers was very badly injured by the rocks that struck him and had to be carried to Mrs. Dennett's house. A long and severe sickness followed, during which time Mrs. Dennett nursed him with the greatest care. He finally recovered and soon plunged into the fight with greater enthusiasm than ever.

"Lucy Stone used to come to our house before she was married to Blackwell. She was young then, but an able and fearless speaker. Parker Pillsbury, of New Hampshire, was here often

in the same work. One time they came here together and we gave them a great reception. They had been to Brunswick to lecture but couldn't find a place in town for a long time where they could get put up. At last a gentleman took them into his house, but the next morning he told them that had he known who they were he wouldn't have allowed them to remain under his roof. That was the sort of treatment that we all had to put up with in those days.

"Lucy Stone was a splendid type of woman. She looked very much like a Quaker. She had brown hair and red cheeks and was altogether a lovely woman as well as a very talented one. Her voice was sweet and her manner winning and graceful. She spoke here several times, and only her sex prevented her from being mobbed. None of the aristocracy would go to hear her.

"Fred Douglass, you know, married a white woman in later years. She was here only three years ago, but no one but us wanted to entertain her. You see it is the same old spirit.

"Susan B. Anthony is another of the noble band of reformers. She has been at my house and has spoken here. We have always entertained her, and no guest has been more welcome. Then there is Elizabeth Cady Stanton; a noble woman is she. She is a welcome guest beneath this roof. These women were not in the thickest of the anti-slavery fight, but have been more fully identified with the later suffrage movement. Cady Stanton was a fine and fascinating speaker in her younger days. Miss Anthony was earlier in the fight, but the two have always been warm admirers of each other.

"Wendell Phillips? Ah! What shall I say of him? He visited us when we lived in the old India Street house and we knew him well. He was witty, sarcastic and convincing. Eloquence in a marvelous degree was his, but his talk was always concentrated. It was like Mosaic work in its clearness and beauty. His voice was like a flute, deep and sweet in tone. He was calculated to remind you of the high-bred courtier, handsome, and brave. In those days no anti-slavery advocate had any fear, and Phillips was the most fearless of the lot. He lectured here several times and was received a little better than they received Garrison. They knew that he stood so high socially that they attempted no cut-throat business with him. It later years he lectured here on the Lost Arts and was royally received.

"Portland was never anti-slavery until the close of the war, and then circumstances forced it to be. By the word 'war' I mean the political war that raged over the slavery question. The later Civil War was not started to aid the slave, but simply because our flag was pulled down and insulted. There was no thought of freeing the slave when that began. That war might have been averted very easily. Lincoln deserves great credit for his share in that contest, but it is only from a political basis and not as an anti-slavery advocate. While the rest of us were fighting, Lincoln did nothing. It was only when the flag was struck that he came to the rescue. The future historian has got some corrections yet to make.

"Oh, yes, I am still in the reform harness and so is Brother George. Slavery is settled, but the woman suffrage battle is now on. We are in that fight, but it is an easy battle compared with the other. The fact is nearly everyone believes in the justice of that cause and

triumph is almost here. Of course the timid and the fossils are lagging in the rear, but the reform is rolling majestically on and as usual those who oppose will soon be sunken into oblivion. Their puny efforts are about on a par with trying to stay an Atlantic tide with a mop.

"Then there is a theological fight on the docket. The only danger I can see to this republic lies in the apathy of the people. There are only a few who care to go ahead and do the work. It will be done, however, and one by one these great questions will be settled and reform will come. This is an age of scientific but not of moral progress, but even this will come in time."

Certainly Aunt Charlotte has given us an interesting and graphic interview. It is a vivid portrayal of the times that tried men's souls, only in this instance it was woman's soul that at times proved the stronger of the two. Whether in the anti-slavery cause or the woman suffrage movement Miss Thomas has proved a tower of strength and she will doubtless live to see the later triumph as she already has the former. Her home in Portland is the abode of peace, prosperity, happiness and good cheer. Here she and her good brother are gliding down the pathway of life with hearts and souls as fresh and pure as when the voice of humanity first called them to strike for God and their country's honor.

Also See

"Abolitionists Organize: The Maine Antislavery Society," Maine Historical Society Newsletter, 9, 1969/1970, pp. 33–38, 73–78.

"The Anti-Slavery Movement in Maine," Sprague's Journal of Maine History 1, April 1912, pp. 38–39.

"Garrison at Close Range," Lewiston Journal Illustrated Magazine, 16 December 1905, pp. 2–3.

"The 'Harper's Ferry' of Maine," Lewiston Journal Illustrated Magazine, 28 March 1920, p. 13.

"Looking Backward to Days Before the War," Lewiston Journal Illustrated Magazine, 28 April, 1906, pp. 8–10.

"Rufus King, Maine's Brilliant Young Advocate of Prohibition of Slavery in the Country's Early Days," Lewiston Journal Illustrated Magazine, 25 July 1903, p. 10.

Harriet Beecher Stowe, The Little Lady of Brunswick Who Started the Great War

MIRIAM STOVER THOMAS

The novel which precipitated one of the most disastrous wars in the United States history and resulted in the physical emancipation of the colored race was written in Brunswick, Maine.

Abraham Lincoln named Harriet Beecher Stowe, "the little lady who started this great war."

Harriet Beecher Stowe was most certainly going down to Washington to see President Lincoln who was procrastinating again. All the Beechers believed in pushing the issue whether it be suffrage, temperance, or abolition. She would see, for one thing, what his stand was on Emancipation.

"The time has come," she thundered in her column, "when the nation has a Right to demand, and the President of the United States to Decree freedom for the slave. . . . How many plagues must come upon us before we will hear the evident voice, 'Let my people go?' When the Army of Virginia retreated and lost its supplies to Stonewall Jackson, Harriet asked her fellow countrymen "to turn to prayer to make Lincoln 'obey the voice of the Lord.'"

In the *Tribune* Lincoln had declared "my paramount object in the struggle is to save the Union and is not to either save or destroy slaver," Harriet answered back "My paramount object in this struggle is to set at liberty them that are bruised and not either to save or destroy the Union."

So Hattie put on her bonnet and best hoops to visit the White House. She took her little son, Charley, dressed in his finery, stopped over in Brooklyn to see her brother, Henry Ward Beecher, who protested that Lincoln had no constitutional right to free the slaves, but Harriet said she intended to see him and see what his attitude was anyway.

She hurried on to Washington to take Thanksgiving with her oldest son, Frederick, of the 1st Massachusetts Volunteer Infantry.

Senator Henry Wilson of Massachusetts had been engaged to present Mrs. Stowe at the White House. As she stood, clasping little Charley by the hand, on the threshold of the small room where the President was to receive her, all the anger which she so recently aimed in his direction melted away.

Mr. Lincoln sat hunched in his favorite rocking chair, wrapped in his old black shawl, with his feet on the mantel. He sat back to the little delegation, but Harriet, who had so recently been feted by the nobility of Europe, sent her heart out to him.

She was not at that moment the woman who had tasted the sweetness of fame. She was again humbled as when years ago, she had written of herself, "I am a little bit of a woman, somewhat more than forty, about as thin and dry as a pinch of snuff; never much to look at in my best days, and looking like a used up article now."

Mr. Lincoln, hearing footsteps, hastily re-

Originally published in *Lewiston Journal Illustrated Magazine*, 15 August, 1964.

moved his long, gangling legs from the mantel, walked sadly, but calmly, to the little woman and laid his big, gnarled hand in hers and said, "So this is the little lady who made this big war?"

Embarrassed, he turned toward the smoldering fire and added, "I love a fire in a room. I suppose it's because we always had one to home."

Little Charley, son of a Bowdoin professor, said wide-eyed, "Ma, why does the President say 'to home' instead of 'at home'?"

Completely ignoring the youngster, Mrs. Stowe and the President continued their discourse for an hour, she telling him of her reply to the affectionate and Christian address (of our English sisters) and Mr. Lincoln assuring her of his intentions to sign the Emancipation Proclamation on New Year's Day.

President Lincoln to the contrary, ensuing generations have questioned whether this little lady actually did start the War. One group considers the tremendous effect of *Uncle Tom's Cabin* to be one of perfect timing. It was given into the hands of the *National Era* at the exact time when the Fugitive Slave Law was upheld in the North by word, but not by deed.

Calvin and Harriet Stowe's home in Cincinnati had at least once been a way station for fugitive slaves. Her brother Edward's home in Boston had been so many more times—Edward who had been a friend of Elijah Lovejoy.

Hundreds, if not thousands, of Northerners were saying with Senator William Seward of New York, "There is a divine law of justice and freedom which compels us through conscience not to obey the order of government."

Into this intense feeling of opposition dropped *Uncle Tom's Cabin* of which Montgomery's *History of the United States*, written 40 years afterwards says, "It meant to be truthful, to be fair, to be kind. No arguments, no denials could shake the influence of the story. People laughed with Topsy and they cried with Uncle Tom."

Rufus Choate, the brilliant lawyer, read

HARRIET BEECHER STOWE

Uncle Tom's Cabin, as all learned men read the latest fiction discussed over the dinner table. At the end, Mr. Choate slammed it down and said, "There, that will add 2,000 more to the ruff-scuff abolitionists."

His estimate was a moderate one. If it did not actually start the war, it startled the world. Eight thousand copies sold the first day. The second edition came out the next week and the third in two weeks.

In Great Britain and her colonies, where Harriet failed to take out her patent rights, 1½ million copies were sold. Countless plays, which Harriet's Calvinistic background allowed her to attend only incognito, played to packed houses. In four months, Mrs. Stowe's royalties were $10,000.

A few practical-minded among us might easily believe that *Uncle Tom's Cabin* was written not to start a war, or even to free the slaves, but to see Harriet Beecher Stowe free from the pitiful $1,000 a year salary Bowdoin College was paying her husband. Hattie wanted a silk dress like young Mrs. Phoebe Upham's (Ed. Note: The portrait of beautiful Phoebe Lord Upham, as a young girl, was done by the great Gilbert Stuart and for years has been probably the most admired of all the Stuart portraits that hang in Bowdoin College's Art Museum, which is noted for its outstanding Gilbert Stuart collection.)

A more critical school takes rather a more involved and psychological view that Harriet Beecher wrote the impetuous novel to free her soul from the slavery of Calvinism and the incessant drudgery of poverty housework. Slater Catherine, studious and sedate, was a true daughter of Lyman Beecher, but not Hattie, pretty with dancing curls and gleaming eyes, who read Lord Byron in secret and rebelled at her father's sermons on "The memory of the wicked shall rot."

Try as she might she could not find any deep-seated evil in her small self, whereupon her father feared for the future of her soul.

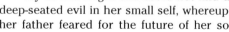

She rebelled at her father's antidote for all ills, good hard work, and with Calvin Stowe she found plenty of the latter. Bald-headed, bearded, phantom-seeing Calvin Stowe was hardly the subject for romance. Was *Uncle Tom's Cabin* a release for Harriet's own religious and cultural suppression?

Perhaps it was in some small degree, but largely it was a book written from the heart to the heart. Channing's famous Baltimore sermon was written when Harriet was only eight years old, but she scarcely could have lived in Boston without hearing it discussed. Was this then her break with Calvinism? She was the daughter of a minister, wife of a minister and sister of five others, and moreover she was a Beecher. She was born to preach.

Channing preached the humanity of Jesus. Harriet Beecher preached in terms children could understand. She preached the brotherhood of man. "There is no one so lowly, God will not take his hand." "The slaveholder and the slave," she said, "are alike our brethren whom God commands us to love as our own."

When Brother Edward's wife wrote to her: "If I could use a pen, Hattie, as you can, I would write something that would make the whole nation feel what an accursed thing slavery is." Harriet crushed the letter in her hand and cried, "I will write something. I will if I live."

She had no thought of style or literary touch. The house was on fire and the children were dying. She called on her fellow countrymen to help her. She had little thought of the consequences.

When she took up her pen she little dreamed that a war would be fought on this issue: perhaps never dreamed that she would see the slaves freed in her lifetime. Despite Henry's admonitions, she did not see what a disaster sudden franchisement of a large, un-trained class of people would bring.

She had merely a vision and at odd moments while nursing the baby or preparing a meal she set down a few sentences at a time. This woman, who was forbidden to read novels in her youth, wrote one that has been classed with those of the Brontës and George Eliot. She had kept her adolescent resolution: "I do not mean to live in vain. He has given me talents and I will lay them at his feet, well satisfied, if He will accept them."

At Harriet Beecher Stowe's last public appearance, John Greenleaf Whittier spoke these words:

And when, with sins and follies past
Are numbered color, hate and caste;
White, black and red shall own as one,
The noblest work by woman done.

Also See

"The 'Bad Book' Which Made Good," *Yankee* 20, March 1956, pp. 41–46.

"Brunswick, Birthplace of 'Uncle Tom's Cabin,'" *Lewiston Journal Illustrated Magazine*, 23 April 1938, p. 9.

"The Little Lady Who Is Said to have Started the Civil War," *Lewiston Journal Illustrated Magazine*, 3 September 1983, pp. 4–5.

"New Book, *Building of Uncle Tom's Cabin,* Tells How Harriet Beecher Stowe Came to Write Her Book," *Maine sunday Telegram*, 13 August 1978, p. 7D.

"Phoebe Upham had Role in Writing of Famous Book, *Uncle Tom's Cabin*," *Lewiston Journal Illustrated Magazine*, 10 November 1973, p. 3.

"*Uncle Tom's Cabin* and the Brunswick Church," *Maine Christian Pilgrim*, 28 February 1941, pp. 3–6.

KANSAS FEVER

RODNEY M. COLE

In January 1854, Illinois Senator Stephen Douglas reported for the Committee on Territories with the Kansas-Nebraska Bill. Outrage in New England was immediate. Northern politicians who supported such a scheme were labeled "Nebrascals" and "doughfaces" (for molding themselves to Southern interests). Although Douglas and his colleagues may have been more interested in developing railroads, most saw the issue as pure sectionalism.

Douglas's bill called for the repeal of the Missouri Compromise's geographic limitation on slavery (under which Maine was granted statehood in 1820) and urged "popular sovereignty." Each territory's populace would vote on whether to seek statehood as a free or slave state. With Missouri, a slave state, abutting Kansas on the east, the movement of pro-slavery interests into the territory was a foregone conclusion. Nebraska, on the other hand, would probably enter as a free state, and a Missouri Compromise–style balance would be maintained.

Although Maine was more than 1500 miles to the east, it became a player in these events. The idea of organized emigration came into being under the sponsorship of New England industrialists like Boston's Amos Lawrence; educators such as Eli Thayer, of Worcester, Massachusetts, and A. S. Packard, of Maine's Bowdoin College; and clergy led by Edward Everett Hale. With the New England states in the vanguard, a "Kansas Fever" approach was proposed; that is, free states would promote emigration, thus flooding Kansas with free-soilers.

When President Franklin Pierce, a Bowdoin College graduate and archetypical doughface, signed the Kansas-Nebraska Bill on May 30, 1854, the first emigration parties were ready to go. The contest for Kansas was on; before long, the territory would be called Bleeding Kansas.

The instruments for moving free-soil emigrants were often "emigrant aid companies." Agents scouted the territory and set up town sites and facilities, arranged transportation, and served as a source of information about emigration. The largest of these companies, The New England Emigrant Aid Company advertised itself as a chartered profit-making venture and sold stock. Although it effectively bowed out of the business and sold its interests at a loss in 1858, major subscribers were still pleased. Their goal of creating a free state was succeeding. Lawrence (named for Amos Lawrence), Topeka, Manhattan, and many surrounding villages were centers of free-state settlement.

With New England Emigrant Aid Company support, the ten-day journey to Kansas cost about $25, and parties left every few weeks. Less affluent travelers were sometimes sponsored by churches or civic groups. The trip generally began with a tedious train ride to the Mississippi River. At that point things became much more hazardous as the emigrants boarded steamboats for the journey to Kansas City and Leavenworth.

Letters back to the emigrant aid company officers complained of the predations of the "levee sharks" in the St. Louis area. Joseph Simpson, one of the three East Corinth, Maine, natives in an eastern party, was robbed of all his funds in St. Louis. He managed to borrow enough from a fellow traveler to continue. But when an outbreak of cholera on their Missouri River steamboat killed sixteen of the eighty remaining emigrants, Stephen Dexter, another of the East Corinth men, had seen enough. He jumped ship and hiked back to St. Louis. (Later that year he bought a farm in East Corinth.)

The details of one such journey are indicated by the following letter to a family in Waterville, Maine, from Charles Gray (born in St. Albans, Maine, and a founding settler of Topeka). Like many others, he went to Kansas, built a rudimentary home, and then returned to Maine to fetch his bride. Their route west was one of several that were recommended at the time. (The spelling is Mr. Gray's.)

Topeka May 16 1858

Dear Brother and Sis. Bailey

I ought to have written before but have neglected it. I have bin very buisly. We started from Lewiston April 6. Lois Cook and her children went with us as far as it was on thare way. We went by the way of Montreal arived thare the 7 two o'clock. At this place had quite a time gitting across the river. The ice was running in the river at the time. Went about half a mile afoot on the ice, after waiting too ours then took a large canoe managed by about half a dozen French men, our bagage had to be carried across in the same way, we with the bagage all got across safe at last. It was a cold day and I cought some cold the rest stood it well & arrived at St Lewis the 10th two o'clock, at Jefferson City that night by the Cars. The same night toock the boat up the river up to this place. I had rather a bad time of it not being well having cought cold riding night and day. It about used me up, but on the river I improved the oppertunity well in lying in bed most of the time. Got rested and felt much better on ariving at Leavenworth. Arived thare the 13 at midnigh. We had a short and pleasant trip up the river [the Kansas River this time]. We arived at Topeka Friday night the 15. Next Tuesday the 20th commenced to keep house in my house just two weeks from the day we left Lewiston. So here we are. Mary J. stood the journey well her health is good with the exception of a bad kold. She likes here much better than she expected to. She sendes her love to you and intends to write to you soon, wee want to hear from you very much. We are getting along very plesantly. I have had my house lot plowed and fenced. I have sat out some trees and planted it. Jane has sowed some flower beds and have sat out some grape and hop vines about the house. Times are very hard here no money. I have done no work yet excepting for one day for anyone except for myself. . . . Considerable excitement here in Politicks. The bridge across the Kansas river a well finished. Thare is crossing on it now (a steamboat was up to this place a week ago) . . . Plese write to us on reception of this from your brother.

C. N. Gray

The reasons for emigration from Maine were varied. Some, like Dr. James Blunt, were ardent abolitionists, but many others were not. The New England Emigrant Aid Company vehemently rejected the label of abolitionists (whom they portrayed as irrational and unpatriotic rabble-rousers). Instead they emphasized two major reasons why Mainers did make the journey: self-improvement through homesteading, and the opportunity to establish new business enterprises. A few, including C. N. Gray, wanted to spread prohibition, or "Maine Law," through which Portland's Neil Dow and his followers sought to ban alcohol consumption. Some Kansas free-staters were even anti-black, unsuccessfully advocating "Black Laws," like those in early Illinois, which would bar all Negroes, slave or free, from entering the territory.

About a third of the Maine emigrants from the early parties stayed in Kansas. A total of 728 native Mainers were counted in the final territorial census of 1860. Added to those who moved directly from Maine in the 1850s, were many who had progressed west over the years as new territories opened and now joined their fellow Yankees in this new land.

In spite of emigrant aid company efforts, life was hard. The towns improved slowly but were still primitive. Lawrence's *The Herald of Freedom*, a free-state newspaper, printed the following nostalgic poem, "The Kansas Emigrant's Lament," on October 13, 1855. (Missouri raiders wrecked *The Herald*'s presses seven months later, in May 1856.)

I left my own New England,
The happiest and the best,
With a burning Kansas fever
Raging in my breast.
Oh that fair New England!
Oh that lovely home!

If I ever live to reach you, surely
I never more will roam.

I came to Lawrence city,
A place of great renoun,
Alas! what disappointment
To find so small a town.
The houses were unfinished,
The people had no floors,
The windows had no glass in,
And sheets were used for doors.

For those settling in the country, conditions were usually more severe. Rural life in a sod cabin was harsh and often lonely. Infants and young children frequently died of a malaria-like infection termed Kansas Fever. "Proving up" to claim a 160-acre homestead took resolve, capital, and luck.

Although many problems occupied the minds of Kansas emigrants, a reign of terror surged to the foreground as 1855 ended. Lane's Army of the North and The Kansas Red Legs made "jayhawking" raids into Missouri. John Brown, with a loyal band of followers, added his own abolitionist raiding and mayhem to the mix. (Among "Old Brown's" raiders were two Mainers: Charles Plummer Tidd, of Palermo, and William H. Leeman, of Hallowell.)

On May 21, 1856, came the Southern retaliation. Lawrence was sacked by a posse of about eight hundred "border ruffians," including Colonel Harry Titus, and five cannon appropriated from a federal armory. Printing presses were thrown in the river (shades of Lovejoy), the fortlike Free State Hotel was battered and burned, homes were looted and torched, and one citizen was killed. It was a grim foreshadowing of Quantrill's more devastating raid seven years later.

Major Jefferson Buford, of Alabama, traveled through the South organizing an "army" of four hundred to ride to Kansas to defend Southern interests. Fortunately for the free-staters, much of Buford's money was stolen as he traveled from St. Louis to Kansas City by riverboat. with their funding gone, many recruits returned South, some joined other groups like the Kickapoo Rangers, and others chose to settle into the territory independently.

Fifty-six-year-old Hannah A. Ropes, of New Gloucester, Maine, landed right in the thick of the "war" when she journeyed to Kansas to serve as a nurse. For six months she carried out her duties "with loaded pistols and a bowie knife on my table at night," then returned to Maine and wrote a book, *Six Months in Kansas* (1856), about her experiences. (She would later die while working as a field nurse in the Civil War.) Her letter to Senator Charles Sumner is a vivid description of Bleeding Kansas:

Lawrence, K. T., Nov., 1855

HON. CHARLES SUMNER:

MY DEAR SIR, — Waiting to-night in my cabin, for L—— and C—— to come in their supper, L—— surprised me, coming alone to ask if he might bring home Judge S. to tea; which of course was only a pleasure to me, if it added at all to the comfort of any one engaged in the wearisome work of taking care of this "Yankee" settlement.

While sitting at the "board," L—— explained to me the necessity of sending some person immediately to Washington; and, would I write to you, or any other person I knew there? so that all the light possible to throw upon our present position might be given? I can hardly refuse; and yet I feel wholly unequal to, and quite out of place on a subject of so much importance.

Judging from my own impressions, I fear you Eastern people hardly do justice to the patient forbearance and long suffering of Kansas immigrants. Here in Lawrence, no week has ever passed without more or less insult and contumely thrown at our people by our nearest neighbors, the Missourians. We never ride, even within our own territory, and meet them, but our ears are pained with words too wicked to repeat. And they shoot at defenceless people with as much cool indifference as they would at partridges or prairie chickens.

My poor womans'-head does not pretend to sift, or unravel this state of things. I am only cognizant of the present sad and dangerous condition in which, as a town, we find ourselves. You who are wise and benevolent should be able to help us who are so defenceless, and so far removed from the ordinary means of helping ourselves. Perhaps, like many other "wise men," you may have imbibed the impression that Lawrence is a good-for-nothing fellow, always putting himself in the way disagreeably, or treading upon his neighbor's corns; if so, I wish I might be able to disabuse you of any such injustice. Lawrence is a hard-working, money-loving, mind-your-own-business sort of person; who, if it would not pay a good profit, probably would not take the time or trouble to look at or travel into his nearest neighbor's inhospitable domain. Through the most of this month, there has been more quiet and freedom from annoyance, than for many a week previous. Elections were over; the Free-State people had shown themselves three to one, and the question seemed to be at rest. But it was a mere seeming, a lull before a storm. There is not, there has not been, a single cabin safe from outrage anywhere in the territory for the two past weeks. Without the slightest provocation, men are cut down, leaving families in lone places without any protection; our cattle are taken; teams of freight stopped on the public way, and all the merchandize handled over, to see what it contains. Ammunition withdrawn, and then the luckless wagoner sent on his way. Market-men, too, coming to bring us apples, and potatoes, and flour, are forbidden to proceed. Gentlemen whom I know and honor, some of them simply visitors, riding in their own carriages up from Kansas City, find their horses' heads seized, while beastly, half-drunk Missourians demand their business, and a pledge that they will not tell Lawrence people how near armed men are camping around them.

It gives me pleasure to be able to affirm that I have known of no outrage exciting to this on the part of these poor, hard-struggling immigrants. I can but believe it to be wholly the result of bitter opposition to Eastern people, having the prospective chance of a fee simple [a type of real estate holding] in the fair and beautiful hills and plains of Kansas. I see and believe that this feeling has been strong enough to lead Missouri to put forth her mean and treacherous hand, with the will to tear up by the roots every settlement where the southern mark is not stamped upon its inhab-

itants. O, men of Congress! where is the use of your assembling together, if not for the good of those who are in need of your aid?

Last night a strong and noble specimen of a man passed close by our cabin on his watch. I heard his cheerful voice, and the slow tramp of his horse, as though he did not wish to disturb our sleep, but only to assure us of safety. To-day, while off of duty, he is cut down as a butcher would an ox. Long before this reaches you, other victims will sleep their last sleep. Our houses are no protection. There is hardly a cabin which a strong man could not tear down.

Let me add, as a relief to myself, that I am proud of Kansas and Kansas men and women. They live in cabins; wear shabby clothes, and rusty boots; their whole appearance offends my intuitive love for whatsoever is beautiful, orderly, and graceful; but the energy, courage, good judgment, and noble magnanimity shown in these nights and days of danger, sweep away all antecedents. I see them in the majesty and power of a true and noble manhood.

H. A. R.

Some immigrants, however, were attracted to Kansas precisely because of its turmoil. They were just plain spoilin' for a fight. For example, most members of the "lumbermen's colony" recruited by William Crosby, a merchant from Hampden, Maine, already engaged in Kansas business and politics, were drawn by the promise of action. The colony left Maine on the coastal passenger ship *Eastern City* with Mr. J. C. Dunn, of Bangor, in charge. They were encouraged, by Thomas W. Higginson and Calvin Cutter, of Massachusetts, to travel without wives or family. Each was provided with a rifle, or if they had their own rifle, with a revolver.

Upon their arrival in Boston they made an impressive appearance, as Higginson recalled in his book *Cheerful Yesterdays* (1898): "[T]he party was formed largely of Maine lumbermen recruited in a body for the service. I never saw thirty men of finer physique, as they strode through Boston in their red shirts and rough trousers . . . this was really a rehearsal in advance of the great enlistments of the Civil War. . . ."

Their search for adventure was attested

to by the "worthy Congregational clergyman" charged with guiding the party to Kansas by train. He drolly wrote Higginson that, "if I had any doubts of the doctrine of total depravity, I had better organize another party of Maine lumbermen and lead them to Kansas."

Within a few months one of the party was a fugitive with a price on his head. Charles H. Calkins, of Haynesville, was captured, along with over eighty other free-state men, by a United States marshal after a skirmish at Hickory Point. He was charged with murder, escaped, and on November 15, 1856, Territorial Governor Geary offered one hundred dollars for his recapture.

A number of Maine emigrants remained to fight, and some became prominent players in the Kansas "war." For example, a group of eastern free-soilers, led by Frederick Law Olmstead and Horace Greeley, smuggled a small wheelbarrow-sized brass cannon, nicknamed Old Sacramento, into the area. Later, Portland, Maine, machinist and sometime artilleryman Capt. Thomas Bickerton used it to batter down the walls of Fort Titus, a proslavery stronghold located a few miles west of Lawrence. Bickerton reported in a letter that he had the cannon "brought up, and planted forty rods from the fort. It was loaded with balls run from the type metal of *The Herald of Freedom* press, which Col. Titus had destroyed last May. When the first shot was fired the Lawrence boys shouted, '*The Herald of Freedom* is issued again!' The cannon was fired six times. At the sixth fire they surrendered. One of their men was killed, and Col. Titus badly wounded. We took nineteen prisoners and a quantity of arms and ammunition."

(During the Civil War, Bickerton served as a Captain in the Union Army with the Kansas artillery. To this day, Old Sacramento is still displayed by the Kansas Historical Society.)

The battle for Kansas ended on January 19, 1861, when word reached Lawrence that statehood had been granted under a free-state constitution. An estimated two hundred lives had been lost, and some historians argue that it was really the first stage of the Civil War, which began in earnest some three months later with the firing on Fort Sumter.

Many Mainers stayed in Kansas to farm, run businesses, and play an active part in their new state. (Rufus H. Crosby, of Hampden, and James Emery, of Industry, had served among the thirty-four members of the first free-state Topeka Constitutional Convention in October 1855, and eight Maine natives were numbered among the hundred and one members of the first State Legislature in 1861.) Some even continued to fight under Captain Bickerton and General Blunt in Kansas units during the Civil War.

General James G. Blunt was probably the highest-ranking Mainer who fought in the Kansas theater. Born and raised in the Ellsworth area, Blunt ran away to sea at age fourteen, and became a physician in Ohio in 1845. An active abolitionist and John Brown

GENERAL BLUNT

supporter, he was drawn into Kansas affairs in 1856. He rode with Lane's Army of the North and led raiding parties into Missouri. A Falstaffian figure, he was notorious for camp debauchery, graft, and a portly bearing, which earned him the nickname Fat Boy. Blunt, as a military leader, was best at cut-and-slash guerrilla tactics. Confederate partisan William Quantrill was his most persistent enemy.

Soon after the start of the Civil War, old comrade-in-arms James Lane, now a United States Senator from Kansas, succeeded in having Blunt commissioned Major General. Early on, Blunt defeated Confederate General Marmaduke and chased General Cabell back to Arkansas. Then disaster fell. Quantrill and his raiders, disguised as Federal soldiers, staged a bold ambush. Most of Blunt's staff, along with all of his unarmed military band, were killed. Blunt escaped by riding for his life, but was thereafter relegated to minor tasks such as keeping Indians on reservations or recruiting them for the Union. (After the Civil War, he was declared insane and died in an eastern asylum.)

The New England Emigrant Aid Company continued on as a small, almost fraternal, organization, meeting intermittently for nearly fifty years. Its only remaining asset— an uncollected claim against the United States government for damages to the Free State Hotel by federal cannons in 1856—was given to the University of Kansas. Since the original campus site had been purchased for that purpose by company officer Amos Lawrence, that seemed reasonable. But the University collected nothing. In 1897, the company's last two active members met to petition for a ten-year charter extension, which was granted. By 1907, the New England Emigrant Aid Company, once so active in creating Kansas Fever, was no more.

ALSO SEE

"50th Anniversary of John Brown's Execution," *Lewiston Journal Illustrated Magazine*, 1 December 1909, pp. 8–9.

"Maine Man in John Brown Raid," *Lewiston Journal Illustrated Magazine*, 12 January 1935, pp. 1, 4.

"Maine's Admission to the Union," *Sprague's Journal of Maine History*, 8 June 1920, pp. 8–18.

Did the G.O.P. Begin in Maine?

CHARLES G. WAUGH

This article was written with strong assistance from the 1954 Maine Council of Young Republican Clubs. Sizable chunks of their public domain document, The Maine Origin of the Republican Party, *form the heart of this piece.*

The Republican Party burst to life in 1854. It was mainly a response to the Kansas-Nebraska Act's supercession of the Missouri Compromise of 1820. The Missouri Compromise had geographically limited slavery, but the Kansas-Nebraska Act threatened to extend it by granting territorial residents popular sovereignty. That is, they could vote on how to enter the Union: as slave state or free. Stephen Douglas, an Illinois senator, had initiated the bill to draw people and railroads to the Midwest. But as he brought the bill out of committee and Senate debate began, it became apparent this Act was shattering old alignments.

However, the G.O.P. ascendancy also involved other factors, both national and local. For example, abolitionists such as Harriet Ward Beecher wanted freedom for all slaves. Temperance advocates, such as Mainers Anson P. Morrill and Neil Dow, splintered Democratic and Whig constituencies. Angry "Know Nothings" hoped to disenfranchise and exclude Catholics and foreigners. And Northern industrialists wanted high tariffs for protection, while Southern agrarians preferred low tariffs to facilitate trade.

As a name for the new party, "Republican" was a good choice. It brought to mind pioneering days of the Republic to those striving "to restore the government to the principles of Washington and Jefferson." As half the Democratic Party's original name (Democratic-Republicans), it conciliated Free-Democrats. It was short and easier to handle than the cumbersome "Anti–Missouri Compromise Repeal" under which some coalitions were then laboring. It was more comforting than the short, but science-fictional sounding "fusionist" alternative. Indeed, "Go West" Horace Greeley wrote, "Call it Republican—no prefix, no suffix, but plain Republican."

Precisely when the Republican Party's natal moment occurred remains controversial, and dependent primarily upon your choice of definition. Partly this is due to the spontaneous, bottom-up nature of the movement: "Many new local groups appeared to demand repeal of the Kansas-Nebraska Act, as well as the Fugitive Slave Act of 1850. These groups soon coalesced into state organizations. . . ."[1]

However, Wisconsin's and Maine's importance is indicated by the fact both claim several potential firsts. Wisconsin held the first political meeting in which it was suggested a new "Republican" party be formed. Prominent Whig A. E. Bovay called a public meeting in Ripon, Wisconsin, to discuss the pending Kansas-Nebraska Bill on February 28, 1854. Attendees resolved that if it passed, they would throw out old party organizations and organize anew. Three weeks later at a second meeting, they voted to dissolve both Whig and Free-Soil town committees, and Bovay suggested calling the new party "Republican," but counseled against the hubris of such a small body adopting the term. (Later Bovay related his idea to Horace Greeley, who embraced it—privately in an April letter and publicly in a June 16 *New York Tribune* editorial.)

Wisconsin also elected the first Republican Congressmen in 1854 and chose the first Republican Senator in 1855. On July 13, the anniversary of the Ordinance of 1787 (which forever dedicated the Northwest Territory to freedom), Wisconsin held its first statewide gathering in Madison. No names had been signed to the call, but it invited "all men opposed to the repeal of the Missouri Compromise and the extension of the slave power." Several thousand attended, and by November the movement had become strong enough to elect the first Republican Congressmen—two of three candidates—and choose a legislature which, when seated in 1855, elevated to the U. S. Senate the first Republican distinctively chosen as such.

In Maine, prior to 1854, anti-slavery forces vented their feelings by flooding Congress with petitions, by flocking to anti-slavery societies, and by similar agitation. The temperance forces had passed "the Maine Law" (1851) but were not politically united and could not advance a positive program. The previous September, these reformers had cast a large enough vote for Anson P. Morrill, their gubernatorial candidate, to prevent the regular Democratic candidate from gaining a majority at the polls. The contest was thrown into the Democratic legislature early in 1854. As all segments maneuvered to block each other, Morrill was defeated by Whig candidate William G. Crosby, and William Pitt Fessenden, also a Whig, was chosen United States Senator over the orthodox Democratic candidate. But despite this success, Maine's Whig Party was dying, and its Democratic Party, long in the ascendancy, was also in decline. Down East party lines were being split by slavery and temperance.

In Washington, the Senate vote on Kansas-Nebraska came at five o'clock on the morning of March 4, and it passed 37 to 14. Nevertheless, Maine's two senators, Democrat Hannibal Hamlin and Whig William Pitt Fessenden, both voted "nay," in a portent of the future. During the House battle, even more determined opposition was encountered, but the Democratic Pierce administration was able, by persuasion and patronage, to whip most dissenters into line. On May 22, after several delays, the House passed the Kansas-Nebraska Act by a vote of 113 to 110, with all but one of Maine's six representatives voting against it.

That same day, a Maine Congressman called the first congressional meeting to discuss forming a new Republican party:

The day that the [Kansas-Nebraska] Act passed the House of Representa-

tives, [Israel] Washburn [a 40-year-old representative from Maine] called a meeting of the anti-slavery members of the House. They agreed to meet again the next day [at Mrs. Crotchett's boarding house on Sixth Street], and at that session Washburn made a speech in which he urged the formation of a new party to resist the slave power controlling the government. He suggested that all men who felt the need for such a party unite under the label Republican.[2]

This suggestion, however, does not seem to have been immediately enacted. McLaughlin's "painstaking search" of subsequent Congressional debate records found no mention of "Republican."[3]

When the Kansas-Nebraska Act became law, on May 30, 1854, popular protest flared. And a sensational fugitive slave case helped fan New England's flames. On May 24, federal marshals seized Anthony Burns, a runaway from Virginia, in Boston. He was chained and dragged to the harbor. Many began to feel that their political parties no longer reflected popular stands on the major issues of the day; many considered starting a new party to replace old alignments. In Maine, the Democrats ran the popular but elderly Parish for governor without a platform. But Maine's old parties could no longer successfully evade or offer only limited commitments concerning the burning issue of slavery. The coalitions achieved by those opposing slavery's extension during the debate on the Kansas-Nebraska Bill became even more united.

The people of Maine never had much use for men who followed one code on Sundays and another on weekdays. They had few close commercial ties with the Southern States, and their small rural farms buffered them from serious counter-forces. They voted strong anti-slavery resolutions in their church conferences, and some eight to ten thousand cheered Harriet Beecher Stowe when she spoke at a Fourth of July appearance in Livermore. In Oxford County, two temperance Democratic state senators who had broken with their party in 1853 were renominated nonetheless. And, according to contemporary W. H. Vinton, their rebellion "spread with lightning rapidity throughout the whole state...."[4]

In neighboring Franklin County, a momentous step was taken when three parties fused into a political group calling itself Republican and nominated the first Republican slate. (On July 6, 1854, A Michigan state convention, meeting in Jackson, may have been the first political group to formally declare itself "Republican."[5] Franklin's Whigs, Morrill (temperance) Democrats, and Free-Soilers all published calls for nominating conventions to be held August 7, 1854, in the picturesque little town of Strong (Farmington, the county seat, was suffering a smallpox epidemic). The Whigs met in the Congregational Church, electing as president O. L. Currier, of New Sharon.[6] The Morrill (or Maine Law) Democrats met in the Methodist Church and elected Colonel Benjamin F. Eastman, of Phillips. The Free-Soilers met in Porter Hall, electing Cyrus G. Morrill, of Wilton. Committees chosen by each convention then met in the law office of Judge P. M. Stubbs to compare notes and consider fusion. On the two great issues of the day—the slavery issue in the nation, and the temperance issue in Maine—they found they saw eye-to-eye and could work together.

Then, according to long-time resident W. L. Daggett's eyewitness account, the joint convention resumed in Porter Hall with Colonel Eastman presiding. On the question of what name they should take, Major John H. Willard, a farmer and hotel keeper from Wilton, proposed "Republican," and his motion was accepted by acclamation. It was a name that was popping up everywhere by midsummer of 1854. The convention proceeded to name a county committee, adopt a platform, and nominate candidates—opposed to the introduction of slavery into the territories and committed to the temperance cause—to run as Republicans. Their work finished, the delegates adjourned "to the beautiful lawn of the Methodist church where a sumptuous dinner had been prepared by the ladies beneath the overspreading tent, and where post-prandial speeches added another chapter to the enthusiasm of the day."

Maine's campaign that year was rather short. Election day was September 11, the second of several states holding elections that fall. The ticket nominated at Strong won, bringing another distinction to Maine: these were the first nominated Republican candidates to be elected in the nation.

Though no attempt was made to organize the new party on a statewide basis until the following February, fusion tickets were spontaneously assembled in five of Maine's six congressional districts, and in every instance

defeated what was left of Maine's old-time Democratic Party. These representatives took their seats in Augusta as Republicans, markedly changing the house tone toward reformation. (Perhaps because, as the *Portland Advertiser* remarked, lawyers had decreased and clergymen increased.) Though there was no majority vote for governor at the polls once again, the fusion forces were finally successful in winning Anson P. Morrill the office. He became, in 1855, the nation's first Republican governor.

But beyond origin issues, Maine, when totalities of influence are considered, clearly contributed more to the young party than any other state.

Maine's new legislators quickly passed resolutions with national implications:

[They condemned] slavery as a moral wrong, the fugitive slave act of 1850 as unconstitutional, and the repeal of the Missouri compromise as the violation of a solemn compact. The legislature instructed Maine's senators and requested its representatives to act to end slavery in the District of Columbia, repeal the fugitive slave act, end slavery in the territories, and oppose the admission of any new slave state. Going beyond pious declarations, the legislature passed a personal liberty law which required county attorneys to act as counsel for all persons arrested as fugitive slaves. This act also made it illegal to use jails or other public buildings to retain such prisoners, and it forbade police, judges and justices of the peace from taking cognizance of any cases relating to fugitive slaves.[7]

Maine Republicans also gained two powerhouses when Maine senators Hannibal Hamlin (1856) and William Pitt Fessenden (1855) independently decided to switch allegiances to the new party.

Hannibal Hamlin was one of five Democratic senators to cross party lines and vote against the Kansas-Nebraska Act. He helped shape the Republican platform of 1860, and was chosen to run with Lincoln, becoming the nation's first Republican Vice-President.

The platform adopted in 1860 went beyond the free-soil declarations of 1856, indicating a tendency to extend the appeal of the party to a broader segment of the electorate. Planks dealing with the following issues gained acceptance: opposition to disunion; maintenance of states' rights in domestic affairs; denunciation of the Buchanan administration for its treatment of Kansas; denial of the authority of Congress, or of a territorial legislature, to make slavery legal in a territory; immediate admission of Kansas as a free state; advocacy of a protective tariff; protests against alienation of lands held by actual settlers; demands for a free homestead policy; approval of easy naturalization laws; appropriations for river and harbor improvements; a demand for a railroad to the Pacific Ocean and support for its construction; and the prompt establishment of a daily overland mail.[8]

But, to the South, the Republican platform was anathema. Lincoln carried just the Northern states, California, and Oregon. His victory in a four-way race, with only 40 percent of the vote, led eleven Southern states to secede, and started the Civil War.

Hamlin's Whig colleague, William Pitt Fessenden, served as Republican chairman of the Senate's finance and appropriations committees. Then Lincoln drafted him to serve as Secretary of the Treasury during the most critical war years, where, through a series of brilliant maneuvers, he cleaned up Salmon P. Chase's mess, and staved off bankruptcy almost single-handedly. Upon returning to the Senate, he headed the joint committee on reconstruction and, with incredible political courage, saved the Republican party from a disastrous blunder in 1868, by voting against the impeachment of President Johnson.

Nationally, the Republican Party remained dominant until the depression, holding onto the presidency for "all but 16 years between 1860 and 1932."[9] Maine's James G. Blaine and Thomas Reed were two reasons why.

James G. Blaine moved to Maine from Pennsylvania in 1854 at the age of twenty-four and quickly bought into Augusta's *Kennebec Journal*, which became the Republican's quasi-official mouthpiece. Soon he was an force in the party: holding the chairmanship of the Republican state committee for more than twenty years, acting as speaker of the national House of Representatives from 1869 to 1875, and serving as secretary of state in 1881 and from 1889 to 1892. In 1884 he ran for president on the Republican ticket, losing by a whisker. (Or maybe by a whiskey, since he was defeated by a rumor that he had called Democrats the party of "rum, Romanism, and rebellion.")

Portland-born Thomas Reed became an extremely influential representative from 1877 to 1899, when he resigned in protest of the administration's policy on the Spanish-American War. He served as Speaker of the House from 1889 to 1891 and 1895 to 1899, and unsuccessfully sought the Republican nomination for president in 1896, a contest he lost to Ohio governor William McKinley, who won the election only to be assassinated.

It is truly a grand old record of inauguration and support for the Grand Old Party by Maine, one of the most isolated and least populated states in our country.

Also See

"The Birthplace of the Republican Party," *Lewiston Journal Illustrated Magazine,* 11 August 1906, pp. 8–10.

"First Maine Republican Meeting Held in Portland 1856," *Portland Sunday Telegram*, 30 October 1904, p. 15.

"1st Slate of Candidates to bear the Republican Party Label," *Portland Press Herald,* 27 July 1954, p. 20.

"The Founding of the Republican Party," *Sprague's Journal of Maine History* 12, October–December 1924, pp. 223–24.

"The Governors of Maine: Second Series, No. 13 — Anson P. Morrill," *Lewiston Journal Illustrated Magazine,* 26 May 1906, pp. 10–11.

"The Maine Senate of 1854," *Lewiston Journal Illustrated Magazine,* 5 August 1905, p. 5; 12 August 1905, p. 3.

"Maine Showed Way to Infant GOP," *Portland Sunday Telegram*, 4 September 1966, p. 9A.

"One Hundred Years Ago a Maine Man was Nominated as Lincoln's Running Mate by Republicans," *Portland Sunday Telegram*, 31 July 1960, p. 9A.

Notes

1. *Collier's Encyclopedia* 20, 1985, p. 9.
2. From: Richard Wescott, *History of Maine Politics 1840–1856,* dissertation from the University of Maine, 1966, pp. 235–36.

3. "The Governors of Maine: Second Series, No. 13—Anson P. Morrill", *Lewiston Journal Illustrated Magazine,* 26 May 1906, p. 11.

4. The Maine Senate of 1854," *Lewiston Journal Illustrated Magazine*, 5 August 1905, p. 5.

5. *Collier's Encyclopedia* 20, 1985, p. 9.

6. Two eye-witnesses conflict over where the Whigs and Free-Soilers met: the Congregational Church or Porter Hall. I have accepted Benjamin Eastman's recollections. He was more involved in the event than was W. L. Daggett, and his recollections were recorded twenty-six years earlier than Daggett's.

7. Richard Wescott, *History of Maine Politics 1840–1856,* dissertation from University of Maine, 1966, pp. 259–60.

8. *Collier's Encyclopedia* 20, 1985, p. 10.

9. *Encyclopedia Americana* 23, 1989, p. 433.

When Bowdoin College Conferred the LL.D. Degree on Jefferson Davis

CAROLINE E. VOSE

Notable among the Commencements of Bowdoin College is that of 1858—just before the Civil War—when an honorary LL.D. Degree was conferred upon Jefferson Davis, future president of the Southern Confederacy.

Davis, who with his family was spending the summer in Maine, was at the time senator from Mississippi and had won distinction as Secretary of War under President Franklin Pierce—a Bowdoin graduate. Even so, in those high-tension days, fraught with strong feeling about the right of secession and the whole slavery question, it is interesting that Bowdoin college, which has never indiscriminately handed out honorary degrees, should have chosen Jefferson Davis, of all men, upon whom to bestow such a great honor. It is especially significant since Bowdoin is situated in Brunswick, Maine, the very New England village in which Harriet Beecher Stowe had written *Uncle Tom's Cabin*, the celebrated anti-slavery novel, just a few years before.

Judging from contemporary newspaper accounts, the entire 1858 Bowdoin Commencement was a successful affair. It began Monday, August 2, and ended on Thursday, August 5. "On Wednesday, Commencement proper took place," to quote *The Portland Transcript* of August 14, 1858. "The same old hat on the same dignified Presidential head entered the church at the usual hour surrounded by the dignitaries of the day and the young aspirants for baccalaureate honors. The ordinary amount of fine orations, elegant bouquets, and smiling and chatting friends— with music to match—filled the hours appropriated to the commencement services.

"The degree of LL.D. was conferred upon the distinguished Senators, Fessenden of Maine and Davis of Mississippi. . . . The services of the week, as a whole, are reported as more than usually interesting."

On August 5, The Portland Advertiser—a strongly partisan Republican newspaper— said: "Notwithstanding the unpropitious state of the weather yesterday, the attendance at the Commencement exercises was quite as large as usual. The performances of the graduating circus was considered very creditable; the music was excellent, and everything seemed to pass off in a manner satisfactory to all concerned.

"The degree of LL.D. was conferred on Hon. Wm. Pitt Fessenden, of this city, and Hon. Jefferson Davis, U.S. Senator from Mississippi."

The next day, the paper reported that "the number of people present (Wednesday) was very large—and by many thought to be greater than it has been for several years."

And on August 8, it closed comments on the Bowdoin graduation with: "And thus ended the most brilliant commencement festivities Bowdoin has enjoyed for several years."

That the "festivities" included the giving of an LL.D. Degree to Senator William Pitt Fessenden also made the circumstances even more dramatic. The two men were miles apart in their political aims, views and ideals. They were usually on opposite sides of a question in Washington and often engaged in heated debates with each other.

Originally published in *Lewiston Journal Illustrated Magazine*, 18 April 1925.

Fessenden was a Northerner, a Bowdoin alumnus, a Republican leader, an abolitionist. Not surprising, then, that his own Maine college should bestow a degree upon him in recognition of his worth and work. But it does seem surprising for the college to have granted at the same time the same degree to Davis, a Southerner, a West Point graduate, a Democratic leader, and a violent anti-abolitionist.

Interestingly, however, William Pitt Fessenden's son, Frances Fessenden, has said: "The two senators were very much alike in some of their mental and physical characteristics, resembling each other in appearance. They both had slender figures and intellectual faces, were high-strung in spirit and prompt to resent attack. Senator Davis was eloquent in debate and sharp in reply."

Two weeks later *The Portland Advertiser* revisited the Commencement in a long editorial expressing surprise and bitter indignation: "it was quite natural, nay inevitable, that a part of the proceedings of the Trustees and Overseers (of Bowdoin) at their recent annual meeting should be received by a large number of friends of Bowdoin college with extreme chagrin and mortification," namely "giving an LL.D. Degree to Jefferson Davis and withholding it from Judge Nathan Clifford."

(It may be noted that Bowdoin—two years afterward in 1860—did give Judge Nathan Clifford an LL.D. Degree.)

The editorial characterized the presentation as "a prostitution of the honors and degrees of one of our first literary institutions," a "public grievance" demanding "stern reprobation," and a "most extraordinary circumstance," necessitating an explanation. Davis was declared "destitute of those peculiar acquisitions" which merit an LL.D. Degree, and was scored on account of his extreme sectionalism, and termed an "enemy to the Union." The editorial concluded that if Bowdoin's desire was to balance Fessenden's degree by awarding one to a Democrat, Nathan Clifford should have be chosen because of his distinguished services and ability, and that he probably would have been but for "sinister influences which were set to work."

And on the next day *The Portland Advertiser* reprinted an item from the Charleston South Carolina, *Mercury,* which intimated that the Bowdoin degree must mean Davis had not been loyal to the South, and must be appearing in the North as an abolitionist. The *Adver-* tiser followed this reprinted article by the comment that the "efforts in New England to popularize Davis were hurting him in the South."

But *The Argus,* a Democratic newspaper, condemned these attacks and called attention to the fact that *The Portland Advertiser* was a strictly Republican newspaper. In an article defending Davis's degree, it affirmed that "universal gratification" was felt over the "justly bestowed" compliment to Davis, who "is not only a distinguished statesman and soldier, but a thorough scholar."

Finally, a few days later, *The Argus* published a letter by "Bowdoin," lamenting *The Portland Advertiser*'s "attack" on Senator Davis and warmly commending the bestowal of the degree.

Apparently the two articles cited—which were probably nothing more than political flurries—were practically the only protests about Davis's degree, and there the matter dropped. All through his subsequently stormy career, Jefferson Davis was honorably entitled to the degree of LL.D. from Bowdoin College. And even today, his name stands on the official records and in the directory of that college, though strangely enough few people seem to be aware of it.

ALSO SEE

"Auburn Man Led Orchestra in Georgia Celebrating Capture of Jeff Davis," *Lewiston Journal Illustrated Magazine,* 27 May 1933, p. 2.

"Bangor's Veteran Mail Clerk Remembers Jefferson Davis," *Lewiston Journal Illustrated Magazine,* 14 February 1914, pp. 8–9.

"Face to Face with Jeff Davis in '64," *Lewiston Journal Illustrated Magazine,* 16 May 1908, p. 11.

"How Jefferson Davis Captured Maine," *Maine Sunday Telegram,* 31 July 1988, pp. 1, 32.

"Jeff Davis's Guard Lives in Auburn at Age of 84 Years," *Lewiston Journal Illustrated Magazine,* 22 December 1928, p. 3.

"A Lion's Welcome for a Man Who Became South's No. 1 Rebel," *Maine Sunday Telegram,* 28 January 1979, p. 3D.

"Jefferson Davis and Wife Seriously Considered Adopting Portland Girl," *Portland Sunday Telegram,* 30 July 1939, p. 11C.

"When Jeff Davis Was in Washington County," *Lewiston Journal Illustrated Magazine,* 19 October 1907, p. 2.

John Wilkes Booth Won Hearts in Portland

HERBERT ADAMS

Portland had seen nothing like it, that uneasy spring of 1861: The young actor under the stage lights roared, soared, shattered shields, struck sparks and swung his sword like a demon. To the footlights he strode at last, eyes flashing, washed again and again in the waves of applause that swept audience and actor away in a spell of glory.

It was March 1861. Seven states had seceded from the Union. Lincoln had been president just two weeks. War clouds were rumbling over Fort Sumter, and John Wilkes Booth, that charmed son of the South, had captured Portland, Maine, without a shot.

Fresh from four weeks at the Gayety Theater in Albany, N.Y., Booth was making Portland one of his first stops on his first swing through the North as a major star of the American stage.

A flamboyant secessionist, Booth came with misgivings. But Yankeedom's doors opened for him everywhere—even in Puritan Portland, where Saturday night shows were still outlawed.

Down East audiences rose as one, wrote a Portland paper in a "rapturous reception for one of the brightest ornaments on the American stage."

Philadelphia's papers agreed: "The star of his destiny is set in blood."

Gallant and gifted, the son of the great British tragedian Junius Brutus Booth, at age 23 John Wilkes was heir to a family tradition both brilliant and strange.

Although remembered as a villain, young Booth was in fact a loyal friend and boon companion whose presence was oddly radiant. "His dark eyes glowed, fascinating as a snake's eyes," wrote his adoring sister. "His teeth flashed an actor's smile. He was devastatingly ambitious."

And devastatingly handsome. Booth's swashbuckling success with women broke hearts from Richmond to Portland, onstage and off, a fact he enjoyed to the fullest.

"Good heavens!" sighed one actress long after, "As the sunflowers turned upon their stalks to follow the beloved sun, so, young and old—our faces smiling—we turned to him."

And yet a strain of strangeness ran through all the Booth family, like a flaw in fine oak. Booth's father died insane; brother Edwin was a melancholic, and John Wilkes burned with a bold, fierce ambition: "I lust for fame!" he declared. "I shall have glory!"

"Yes, [John] was a queer fellow; had strange ways," wrote Walt Whitman, who saw all the Booths on stage. "It took some effort to get used to him. But now and then he had, I thought, flashes of real genius."

To John's chagrin, it was "Edwin Booth, the young Tragedian" who Portland papers announced would open at William English's Portland Theatre on Monday, March 18: "We bespeak for Mr. Booth a warm reception."

In fact it snowed, but Booth's red-hot rendition of *Richard III* left frosty Portlanders roaring. And despite a second train-stopping snowstorm that week, eager audiences packed Portland Theatre (in present day Monument Square) nightly for Booth's thundering *Othello, Hamlet* and bloody *Macbeth.*

Originally published in
Maine Sunday Telegram, 17 April 1988.

JOHN WILKES BOOTH

"He throws his whole soul into his sword!" gasped the *Eastern Argus,* repeating the rhapsodies of the Albany papers. "No such fighting has ever been seen in this city. The last scene of the fifth act was truly terrible. . . . At the end of the tragedy; three cheers were proposed for *Richard the Third;* they were given with a power that almost took the roof off."

Spring had never come in like such a lion. At week's end William English boasted that "at much expense, [due to] the great desire manifested to witness Mr. Booth . . . he has induced him to remain another week" and the one week soon became four.

What was Booth like on stage? More athletic than artistic, spoiled by good looks and good luck, Booth embraced quick success in blood-and-thunder melodramas—not that Mainers minded.

Eager Portlanders flocked to watch Booth run *Richard III* three times, *Hamlet* twice, and two different productions of *Macbeth* in two months—each replete with Booth's ringing voice, sweeping stage leaps, and stunning swordplay.

Besides the Shakespearian standards, Booth traveled with several tailor-made plays he carried, like a costume trunk, from stage to stage.

In four weeks Booth performed 16 plays in Portland, including *The Apostate* (a play his father made famous), the Pygmalion-like *The Marble Heart* (which Lincoln would watch him perform at Ford's Theater in 1863) and swashbuckling twins in *The Corsican Brothers.* Many

were stock wheezers; no matter. It was Booth, bounding, boyish Booth, the people came to see.

Forty years later Portland patron Nathan Goold still remembered Booth in *The Corsican Brothers*: "He was dressed in a loose white shirt and black pants. He stood with a rapier in his right hand raised up, and his left arm about the same position. He was to be slid across stage under an illumination of red fire. I suppose he stood on a plank which had not been properly greased, for it would stop, then start, [with] a sympathetic movement of head and shirt each time, which destroyed the scene. I shall never forget it while I remember such things."

Portland papers printed no real reviews, and Booth needed none. "We cannot speak too highly of Mr. Booth's merits as an actor," said the *Portland Advertiser.* "All who remember his distinguished father will find it easy to trace the resemblance in the son. We saw Mr. Booth in *Evadne,* and thought it by far the best piece of real acting we have witnessed in this city."

There are hints, however, that this southern cavalier made more than theatrical conquests in Portland.

HELEN WESTERN

From the opening night of *Richard III,* Booth had been supported by William English's actress step-daughters, Lucille and Helen Western, billed as "The Beautiful Star Sisters." Lucille made a formidable Lady Macbeth, but Helen, remembered Nathan Goold, "was a brunette, one of the handsomest women on stage," and just a blushing 19.

Playbills show that Helen was soon Lady Ann to Booth's Richard III, Desdemona to his Othello—and Juliet to his Romeo. Booth's much-ballyhooed "Farewell Performance" of March 29 (he intended to return in a week) was also Helen's, and the two names drop out of print for the first week of April.

In the real world, meanwhile, real tragedy kept pace with Shakespeare.

Far to the South, Portland papers reported, Fort Sumter was besieged in Charleston Harbor, and Maine Governor Washburn grimly proclaimed April 11 as "Fast Day, for Humiliation, Public Fasting and Prayer," amid the lilies of Easter and the rumblings of war.

On Fast Day itself Booth was back, as William Tell and the bloody Macbeth, sharing the boards—one can imagine his thoughts—with Portland's patriotic tribute, "Brother and Sister, or The Soldiers of Fort Sumter."

On April 12, at the very hour Booth was uttering Hamlet's immortal words about treason, indecision and death, the Confederacy fired on Fort Sumter. On April 13 Fort Sumter surrendered, while Booth was acting [in] *Raphael, The Reprobate*—the last play he would ever perform, four years later, at Ford's Theater.

Civil War had come at last, and perhaps Booth learned the news from the roaring rally held in Monument Square that night, or from Portland's papers on the railroad back to Albany.

Few noticed his departure, other than the outraged *Portland Advertiser,* for Booth left without paying his printing bill. "Our experience with him shows he lacks the requisites of a gentleman," growled its editor. "He was extremely liberal in his offers, and not sparing of promises. Just before his departure we called on him for the amount of his indebtedness, but were referred to his agent, who referred us to his principal . . . : to cut the story short, we have not seen; the color of the gentleman's money."

Four years later to the very day, April 14, 1865, Booth played his last and strangest role offstage at Ford's Theater during "Our American Cousin."

The news that he had assassinated President Lincoln amazed Mainers, remembered Nathan Goold in 1902, for "[Booth] was a man well known in Portland. . . . Men looked in each other's eyes and wondered what it all meant."

For Maine, Booth's brief visit Down East meant an ironic touch with the great events of the Civil War era. But for Booth, perhaps, it meant much more. For in Booth's battered wallet were found photographs of several beautiful women. The most lovely of all was a handsome brunette—Miss Helen Western, of Portland, Maine.

ALSO SEE

"John Salvador, Hallowell Civil War Veteran, Saw Wilkes Booth's Body Pass Harpers Ferry in 1865," *Lewiston Journal Illustrated Magazine,* 25 May 1929, p. 2.

Famous Sons and Daughters

Some Southerners have argued that if Maine had not taken part in the military campaigns of the War, the South might have won. This has been said especially of Hiram G. Berry, O. O. Howard, and Joshua L. Chamberlain. Other Mainers, such as Dorothea Dix, Lew Estes, and Hannibal Hamlin provided similar, if not equivalent, service to the Union cause.

Hiram G. Berry, a Rockland native, was, before the war a banker and Democratic legislator in the Maine House with Nelson Dingley and William Fessenden. During the war he became one of Maine's famous Civil War generals, saving the Union army from defeat three times. Had he not been killed at Chancellorsville, it is possible that he, not Grant, would have been appointed Commander of the Army of the Potomac.

Joshua L. Chamberlain, a Brewer native, may be the man most singularly responsible for saving the Union, defending Little Round Top during the battle of Gettysburg. After running out of bullets, Chamberlain and his 178 surviving troops from the 20th Maine fixed bayonets and charged down the hill, shattering the attack and capturing more than 300 Confederate prisoners. After the war, he served as governor of Maine for four terms and president of Bowdoin College for more than a dozen years.

Dorothea Lynde Dix, a Hampden native, was a feisty reformer for most of her life. Her particular interests were education, prison reform, mental health reform, and nursing. During the Civil War, she created and directed a women's nursing corps for the Union, an action for which she neither asked nor received compensation. Due to her efficient practices thousands of soldiers' lives were saved.

Llewellyn G. Estes, an Old Town native, is perhaps the most remarkable of all Maine's Civil War Generals. He enlisted as a private in 1861 by lying about his age. He was very active in all the campaigns of the Army of the Potomac until joining the Army of the Mississippi in April 1864. In Sherman's struggle for Atlanta (August 30, 1864), then Captain Estes was asked by Major General O. O. Howard if his squadron "could keep the enemy in mo-

tion" so that Howard and Kilpatrick could secure the Flint River Bridge, near Renfro Place and Jonesboro. According to Howard, Estes "gave a sanguine reply, and galloped off at the head of his men" to complete the task, an action for which Estes was later to receive the Congressional Medal of Honor. At war's end in 1865 he was mustered out a Brigadier-General at the age of 21.

Hannibal Hamlin, a Paris Hill native, may be best remembered today as a character in a famous short story, "The Stranger and the Fried Pies." (See C. A. Stephens, *Stories from the Old Squire's Farm*, 1995.) In real life, however, he served as Maine's governor, as a senator, and as Lincoln's first Vice-President. After being cast aside for Andrew Johnson, the vigorous Democratic military governor of Tennessee, before the election of 1864, Hamlin returned home and served briefly with the Norway Company in Fort McClary at Kittery point. There he met young L. C. Bateman, an experienced newspaperman. Bateman later recounted their meeting in a few of the many Civil War interviews and articles he wrote over the next sixty years.

Oliver Otis Howard, a Leeds native, graduated from both Bowdoin College and West Point. A deeply religious man, General Howard fought in many Civil War battles and continued in the army for much of his life. After the South surrendered, General Howard joined Edwin M. Stanton's War Department for seven years as Commissioner of the Bureau of Refugees, Freedmen, and Abandoned Lands. Under President Grant, he settled numerous problems with American Indian Tribes in the Southwest. During the Spanish-American War, though now a civilian, he volunteered to visit and speak at army camps. However, his most significant accomplishment is one for which he is little known: He founded many of the nation's most prominent Black Colleges such as Fiske, Hampton, and Howard.

While most Mainers were Yankees, a few fought for the South. General Danville Leadbetter, a Leeds native, was one of the chief engineering officers of the Confederacy. Unlike most of their generals, it appears he was never captured and never surrendered. General Zebulon York, an Avon native, graduated from the University of Louisiana Law School. By the beginning of the Civil War, he and his partner were probably the largest slave owners in the South.

Maine's Greatest Soldier— Major General Hiram G. Berry, Who Three Times Saved the Day

GEORGE LORING WHITE

In the Preface to his biography of General Hiram G. Berry, E. K. Gould calls him "Maine's greatest soldier," marshalling abundant testimonial proof from Berry's peers.

Comparisons are odious, and it is always safer to say "one of the greatest," instead of the greatest. But during the Civil War my father's family continually mentioned the name of General Berry in such a way that it was always my impression that he was one of the bravest and most skillful generals in our army. My perusal of this biography has confirmed my lifelong impressions. Three times he arrived on the field of action just in time to save the day. At Williamsburg he saved Hooker and won "fighting Joe's" everlasting friendship, so that when Hooker was elevated to the command of the Army of the Potomac, he placed Berry over his fighting corps. At Fair Oaks, Kearny's division, of which Berry's brigade formed a part, came on to the field just in time to save the day, and it was his brigade that bore the brunt of the battle. Finally, at Chancellorsville, when Stonewall Jackson was on the cusp of annihilating Hooker's army by his famous flank movement, Berry was on hand with his division to stay the oncoming tide of rebel victory. Such timely arrivals had to be due to Berry's soldierly alertness, not just to good fortune.

Berry's courage was unsurpassed. He always led his troops into action and by conspicuous bravery inspired his troops— whether regiment, brigade or division—with such a determined spirit and such courage that it was often the proud boast of the usually modest Berry, that his men had never taken a backward step when face-to-face with the foe.

Yet bravery was but a small part of Berry's military genius. The leader who inspires his men with unconquerable determination to win is possessed of one form of military genius. No commander was ever better loved by his soldiers than General Berry. He cared for his men as mothers care for their children. He never sent an aide on a perilous mission but took it upon himself, and he was on such a mission at Chancellorsville when a sharpshooter got him. In arranging for a battle he placed his men with consummate strategic skill. Just before his death, there was talk in high quarters that he, though but 38 years of age, would yet be the choice of the Government for the command of the Army of the Potomac.

Hiram G. Berry was born in the eastern part of Thomaston, now Rockland, Me., August 24, 1824. His grandfather, Thomas Berry, was an officer in the Revolutionary war and his father, Jeremiah Berry, took part in the war of 1812. So he came honestly enough by his fighting propensities. Still, it was only a sense of duty that urged him into the war and to be aggressive as a fighter.

At 26 he entered heartily into business in Rockland, becoming one of three incorpora-

ORIGINALLY PUBLISHED IN *Lewiston Journal Illustrated Magazine*, 24 May 1930.

tors of the Rockland Steam Mfg. Co., and at 29 was elected a director of the Limerock National Bank, an office he held until resigning to enter the army in 1861.

At the age of 29 he was also appointed Inspector of the Fourth Division of Militia, with the rank of lieutenant-colonel. The next year, 1854, he and several others organized a light infantry company, called the Rockland City Guards. Here was a chance for intensive military training which helped to educate him for the severe tasks that devolved upon him during his two years of service in the Civil War.

He naturally loved politics, for there is a militant aspect to politics which pleased his military instincts. At 28 he was elected to represent his town in the State Legislature. Here he met William Pitt Fessenden and Nelson Dingley. In 1856 he was re-elected.

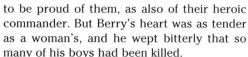

Major General Hiram Berry

In 1856 he also became the second Mayor of the new city of Rockland. But being a Democrat, he failed to secure a second term in 1857 as pre-war politics raged with unusual fury.

In 1861, four companies of the 4th Maine were raised in Rockland, with Hiram G. Berry the Colonel of the regiment. On the way to Washington, Colonel Berry determined to march through Baltimore. The rough usage given a Massachusetts' regiment in that city led Berry to prepare his men to resist any foolishness via paving stones and brick-bats, and the march was made without disturbance.

The 4th Maine regiment was a part of Howard's brigade, which formed a portion of Heintzelman's division. The division began fighting at the first battle of Bull Run, and soon men were falling, shot to death or sorely wounded. Major Stephen H. Chapman was the first victim, pierced in the heart by a rifle ball and his last words were, "Tell my wife I am shot—God bless her!" Others soon followed and all was excitement and turmoil. The thunder of artillery, the rattle of officers' sabers, the whistle of bullets, the shriek of shells, the shouts of combatants, the cries of wounded, made a chaos of excitement as though Hell itself had broken loose. Men became wild with

excitement, discharging their guns into the air, ramming several charges into their rifles before attempting to discharge them and thus doing more damage to themselves than to the enemy. But the 4th Maine withstood this murderous fire most gallantly.

Colonel Berry manifested great coolness and bravery amidst all this excitement, encouraging and cheering his men, and directing their movements with judgment and discretion. When the color-bearer was shot down, he seized the fallen standard and bore it aloft through the fray. His stalwart figure was a conspicuous mark for the foe, and his clothing was riddled with bullets and his horse shot from under him. The Fourth Maine was the last to leave the field and the men had behaved so gallantly that the people of this state had reason to be proud of them, as also of their heroic commander. But Berry's heart was as tender as a woman's, and he wept bitterly that so many of his boys had been killed.

In a letter home he describes how he felt in his first battle: "Never was a braver set of men than those who went into battle under my command. They were perfectly cool, did exactly as I wanted, obeyed all my orders and behaved nobly. . . . As for my poor self, I tried to do my duty. Strange as it may seem to you, I was no more excited than ordinarily when in earnest. I did not believe I should be hit in any way, and I did not think of it at all. My mind was occupied by my command entirely. Men fell all around me, killed and wounded. The ground was covered with men and horses, some mine and some of other regiments, who had passed over the same ground. Chapman left me only one minute before he was shot. He came for orders to my post by the Regimental colors; asked for orders with a smile, I gave them, he extended his hand, we exchanged blessings, he cautioned me against unnecessary exposure, and we parted for the last time. He was shot through the heart immediately on resuming his post. I shall come out all right I have no doubt; shall do my

whole duty, and I never again, probably, shall be placed in such a position, should the war last for years as that at Bull Run."

In recognition of Colonel Berry's gallant services at Bull Run, President Lincoln promoted him March 20, 1863, to the rank of Brigadier-General of Volunteers. The fourth Maine regretted their loss, and the sergeants presented him with a beautiful sword, made expressly for him, the mountings on the hilt being of solid silver, the blade of Damascus steel, and flowered one third of its length. The other officers, not to be outdone, presented him with an elegant service of silver plate costing about $1,000. Few commanders ever enjoyed greater love and devotion from men and officers under them than Hiram Berry.

Williamsburg

After Bull Run came the campaign of the Peninsula, and Berry's first battle there was at Williamsburg. His Brigade consisted of four regiments, three of which were from Michigan and one from New York, an Irish regiment, the 37th. They all displayed remarkable courage and tenacity under Berry's leadership and became famous for their discipline and battling qualities. I have no space to recite in detail the battle of Williamsburg, but when Hooker was hard pressed and his troops began to falter, Berry passed impetuously through other and slower brigades, reaching Hooker just in time to turn defeat into victory.

Phil Kearny (whose division was under attack), Heintzelman, and the *New York Herald* and *New York Tribune* credited Berry for saving the day. The *Tribune* said in part: "But now Brigadier Berry of the stout State of Maine, wading through the mud and rain at such speed that he actually overtook and passed three other brigades—came in sight. . . . A wild hurrah went up from the army, and, with a yell that was electric, three regiments of Berry's brigade went to the front, formed a line nearly half-a-mile long, and commenced a volley firing that no troops on earth could stand before, then at the double-quick dashed with the bayonet at the rebel army and sent them flying from the field."

Kearny said in his report: "General Berry was ever on the alert, and by good arrangements and personal example influenced the ardor all around him. His regiments fought most desperately."

General McClellan sent for him and in the presence of Heintzelman thanked and congratulated him. He told him that he and his brigade had won the fight. Berry was showing the world that he was a mighty fighter.

But Berry, in typical fashion, gave his troops primary credit in an address he gave to them: "Soldiers! You have won by your bravery the hearts of all your commanders— brigade, division, corps, and even those higher in command. Soldiers! I thank you; my superiors thank you; your country thanks you, and will remember you in history."

Fair Oaks

At Fair Oaks, Berry saved the day once more. The rebels had massed their men and made so fierce an onset that disaster seemed to stare the Federals in the face when Kearny arrived, and Berry's brigade pitched into the fight with their usual ardor. I haven't the space to tell of specific troop movements that day, but his Irish regiment distinguished themselves, fighting like tigers. Over half Berry's men were lost, and he remained in the saddle all the day, a conspicuous object for sharp-shooters.

The *New York Tribune*'s correspondent praised highly the Michigan regiments of Berry's brigade, saying: "I would covet the honor, if usage could confer it, of adoption into either of the Michigan regiments whom I saw on the leap through shot and shell infested wood . . . so that when asked 'To what service do you belong.' I could proudly reply, 'I belong to Berry's brigade.' Cromwell never had better troops than those, who, under the command of this good officer, swept with fire and steel the whole rebel force from Casey's camping ground and earthworks, piling it with monuments of their terrible marksmanship." And four generals: McClellan, Heintzelman, Kearny and Hooker personally complimented General Berry for his skill and bravery in this action.

It was at Fair Oaks, however, that many union officers lost enthusiasm for their leader, "Little Mac." Though the Federal Army was close enough to clearly see Richmond's church spires, McClellan decided to retreat. Kearny, Hooker, Heintzelman, Berry, and other brigade commanders were indignant, visiting headquarters to remonstrate with McClellan and urge the taking of Richmond. Spokesman Kearny urged the case with his accustomed vehemence, and when McClellan was not moved by their united arguments, Kearny "denounced him in language so strong, that all who heard it expected that he would be placed under arrest until a general court-martial could be held."

Fredericksburg and Chancellorsville

Just before the battle of Fredericksburg, the 17th Maine was added to Berry's brigade and the 35th New York was joined with the 37th.

It is needless to say that Berry added to his laurels in the Fredericksburg fight. Under a flag of truce to care for the wounded after the battle, the aide of General A. P. Hill asked what brigade came up after their heavy artillery fire, the answer was "General Berry's brigade." "General A. P. Hill sends his compliments to General Berry," said the Confederate officer, "and say to him that it was the best behaved brigade that he ever saw under fire."

Berry had once taken Birney's place as commander of a division and soon the gallant general was promoted to that position. General Hooker wrote Major-General Halleck warmly recommending that Brigadier General Berry be promoted to a Major-general of Volunteers. Heintzelman wrote Lincoln in the same vein. And, old friend Hannibal Hamlin, Lincoln's Vice-President, was always ready to lend Berry all the help he could. On March 7, 1863, at the age of 38, General Berry received this merited and distinguished honor.

At the famous battle of Chancellorsville, Stonewall Jackson had turned Hooker's right, after completely deceiving Hooker and his generals as to his intentions, and come in upon Howard with such suddenness and force that a rout would have ensued, had not the tide been met and turned by General Berry, in command of Hooker's old division.

Berry was near the Chancellor house acting as a reserve when the 11th Corps was attacked by Jackson. First there was noise and tumult, then panic-stricken fugitives came pushing their way through Berry's steady ranks. Hooker hurried up to his friend Major-General Berry, shouting, "General, throw your men into the breach—receive the enemy on your bayonets—don't fire a shot—they can't see you."

The last night Berry spent on earth was a night of toil, trouble, danger and watchfulness. The battle was prolonged throughout most of it and although the moon shone brightly, and the night was beautiful and clear, in the heavy forest, shade cast gloom around the fiercely fighting combatants.

In the morning hours the battle by spells continued and, at about 7 A.M., General Berry decided to communicate with General Mott. He performed the errand himself instead of sending an aide as most commanders do, and in spite of warnings about sharpshooters in the trees.

"Reaching General Mott, they conversed for a short time; then [Berry] started to return. He had gained the Plank road, crossed it, and had nearly reached the place where the staff officers were standing, when from the trees in which the North Carolina sharpshooters were posted came a wreath of smoke, followed by the sharp crack of a rifle, and Major-General Hiram G. Berry had fought his last battle." As his staff bent over him, he murmured, "My wife and child," adding, "Carry me off the field." At 7:26 on that beautiful Sunday morning of May 3, 1863, Berry died, and there passed from earth one of the gentlest, most affectionate, and heroic spirits ever gracing this mortal sphere.

When General Hooker rode up and was told Berry had fallen, he sprang from his horse and approached the prostrate form, weeping bitterly. Kneeling reverently, he kissed the cold forehead, murmuring sadly: "My God, Berry, why was this to happen? Why was the man on whom I relied so much to be taken away in this manner?" Then turning to the sympathetic group of officers, he said that he had lost one of his best officers and warmest friends.

On October 31, 1865, Rockland honored him with appropriate ceremonies and a beautiful statue in the Achorn cemetery. Still, the rest of Maine has never seemed to me to honor General Berry as much as his great merit deserves, for no officer ever tried harder to do his whole duty to the end of his brief life than did General Hiram G. Berry.

ALSO SEE

"Prominent Rockland Citizen Became Renowned General in Union Army," *Lewiston Journal Illustrated Magazine,* 27 April 1963, pp. 6–8.

"The Rise and Fall of Fortune's Son," *Maine Sunday Telegram,* 15 March 1981, pp. 1D, 3D.

"Sketch of Major-General Hiram G. Berry," *Northern Monthly* 1, March1864, pp. 6–11.

Joshua Chamberlain Still Ranks As One of Maine's Greatest Men

ISABEL WHITTIER

When I was a young girl, my mother took me to hear this great Civil War General speak in the Court Room in the old town hall in Brunswick. Some little time later I attended his funeral services in the First Parish Church, the Church-on-the-Hill, in Brunswick. More recently I have read John J. Pullen's *The Twentieth Maine* and William M. Wallace's *Soul of the Lion.* I have also read much by Chamberlain and about him in the manuscript division of the Library of Congress and even more recently have talked with Catherine Smith, who was his secretary in his later years when he was Surveyor of the Port of Portland.

Maine has every reason to be proud of this man. Well informed historians feel that by his presence of mind and prompt heroic action in his defense of Little Round Top on July 2, 1863, Chamberlain was a big factor in bringing victory to the Union forces at Gettysburg, 101 years ago.

Historic Stand

At Gettysburg in the late afternoon of that terrible July 2, 1863, the first day of the historic Battle of Gettysburg, Chamberlain's Maine men found themselves outnumbered nearly three to one. For hours they had been in the midst of desperate fighting, and now, suddenly, on them depended the all important job of holding, at all costs, the left flank of the Union Line.

The Confederate troops, concentrating on that position, planned to swing the left flank and get behind the long Union line. Hitting the Union line from the front and back, they could break it quickly and then the road was clear to Washington.

Fresh Southern troops were poured into the Confederate line that late afternoon to get Chamberlain's outfit. As those fresh troops, spearheaded by Hood's Texans, swept across the field, Chamberlain found all his superior officers were either dead or seriously wounded. Ammunition was almost gone. His men, out on their feet, were looking at him for command.

Unhesitatingly he gave the famous order: "Fix bayonets" and the Maine men, led by Chamberlain, went down the hill to meet the fresh Southern troops in hand-to-hand fighting in the memorable and historic stand at Little Round Top.

Chamberlain, by taking the pressure from the Union on the west side, contributed to the defeat of the hard fighting Confederate force under John Bell Hood of Longstreet's Corps. For this gallant action Chamberlain was subsequently awarded the Congressional Medal of Honor.

If the Confederates had secured Little Round Top, the Union would have lost the battle at Gettysburg and Robert E. Lee's invasion of the North might well have led to the capture of Washington. Certainly a Southern victory would have given strength to the peace-demanding groups in the North and might have influenced many in France and England to reconsider recognizing the Confederacy.

Here one may recall the words of Alexander Pope, "The child is father of the man." Throughout his life and from a very early age

ORIGINALLY PUBLISHED IN *LEWISTON JOURNAL ILLUSTRATED MAGAZINE*, 4 JULY 1964.

Chamberlain displayed courage, an iron will, clear-sightedness, a sense of personal responsibility, and perseverance. These qualities are shown in his early life on a Maine farm, in his courtship, in his position as teacher at Bowdoin, as general in the Civil War, and as governor of Maine.

Born in Brewer

Joshua—known in his early days as Lawrence—was born on Sept. 8, 1828, in Brewer, Maine. He was a descendant of a Richard de Tankerville, grandson of a Norman knight, who became Chamberlain to King Stephen of England in the 12th century. Lawrence's father, also named Joshua, was a farmer, an active citizen who had commanded the militia regiment sent out by Governor Fairfield at the time of the Aroostook War. Lawrence's great-grandfather had fought in the French and Indian War and in the American Revolution.

On his father's side of the family there was a tradition of military service. On his mother's side he was also descended from men who had seen service in the colonial wars with France and in the American Revolution. Through his mother, Lawrence was descended from a Jean Dupuis. Dupuis was a Huguenot who had come to Boston from La Rochelle on the Bay of Biscay when Louis XIV, in 1685 revoked the Edict of Nantes, which for approximately a hundred years had given religious toleration to Calvinists in France.

Our Lawrence was named after Captain James Lawrence, the American naval captain of the frigate *Chesapeake* who, when mortally wounded in the War of 1812, cried out, "Don't give up the ship!" Lawrence, years later, showed the same tenacity as this man whom his father had so much admired.

Lawrence's father was a quiet, serious man. His mother was lively and very industrious, and though she had five children was particularly fond of her eldest. While her husband wanted Lawrence to adopt a military career, she wanted her firstborn to become a Calvinist minister.

Good Student

As a boy Lawrence was busy with all kinds of chores on the farm. He learned to sail the sloop *Lapwing*. He became a good swimmer and learned to shoot and handle a broad sword. He enjoyed visiting the Indians at Old Town and listening to their weird stories. He early became interested in music. In his teens he attended a military academy at Ellsworth, as his father wanted him to go to West Point. He did some "teaching of school" to add to the family's resources. Through his mother's influence he became a member of the Congregational Church in Brewer, and at this period he thought he might become a missionary. He applied for admission to Bowdoin, found he did not have sufficient Greek, but set about learning it with dogged persistence. He entered Bowdoin in 1848, conditioned in Greek, but with "advanced standing" in other subjects.

Chamberlain had a very good record as a student at Bowdoin, achieving an enviable record in many subjects; in Greek, French, mathematics and astronomy, and was an assistant in chemistry and in the library. He was one of seven to present English oration at his commencement in August 1852. He became a member of Phi Beta Kappa.

While at Bowdoin Chamberlain lived at 21 Maine Hall, was a member of the Peucinian Society and composed poems for it, and became a member of Alpha Delta Phi Fraternity. He taught Sunday School at a church two miles outside of the town in his first two years at college, and was leader of the choir of the First Parish Church-on-the-Hill, in his junior and senior years.

Meets "The Girl"

It was while he was pursuing his studies at Bowdoin and active in the choir at the Congregational Church that he became very much interested in Fanny Adams, the minister's daughter, who played the church organ.

William M. Wallace, the History Professor at Wesleyan University who wrote *Soul of the Lion*, the biography of General Joshua L. Chamberlain, has several very well-written pages on this part of Lawrence's life.

He reminds the reader that while Chamberlain was studying at Bowdoin, Harriet Beecher Stowe's husband, Calvin Stowe, was teaching at Bowdoin and Harriet was writing a book that was going to rouse strong sentiment against slavery, a factor in causing a war in which Chamberlain won distinction.

Chamberlain decided to enter Bangor Theological Seminary on graduation from Bowdoin. Fanny Adams, an adopted child of the Rev. George E. Adams, was a very attractive vivacious young woman. She was two years older than Chamberlain. Dr. Adams apparently had no great regard for the young

Bowdoin graduate, who had three more years of study ahead of him before he would be in a position to support a wife, and he probably thought Fanny wasn't mature enough for marriage. But Chamberlain remained persistent, and so did Fanny, with the result that the Rev. Adams gave his consent to an engagement.

In the chancel in back of the pulpit of the First Parish Church in Brunswick there is a handsome stained glass window given years later by Joshua L. Chamberlain in memory of his father-in-law.

Enters Theological School

In the fall of 1852 Chamberlain entered Bangor Theological Seminary. During his three years he supervised schools in his native town of Brewer, led the choir, played the organ, and often taught in Sunday School. In vacations he took trips into the Maine woods with his father, who was a surveyor and appraiser of timber. He also acted as an interpreter in his father's business transaction with French Canadians.

Chamberlain had presented a paper on Law and Liberty to his alma mater hoping for a Master of Arts degree. As a result he was offered a position at Bowdoin for 1855–6 to teach logic and natural theology, subjects that Calvin Stowe had taught at Bowdoin back in 1852. Chamberlain accepted the offer. On Dec. 7, 1855, he was married to Fanny Adams at the altar of the First Parish Church in Brunswick by the bride's father, the Rev. George E. Adams, pastor of the church.

By 1862 Chamberlain while teaching at Bowdoin became very much concerned about the secession of the South. Hoping to prevent his going to war, for which his colleagues considered him ill prepared, the college in August 1862 offered him a two-year leave of absence to travel and study in Europe. This he tentatively accepted, but he went to Augusta to see Governor Israel Washburn. The governor and the attorney-general were trying to raise troops asked for by President Lincoln. On Aug. 8, 1862, the governor offered Chamberlain a commission as lieut. Colonel of the 20th Regiment Infantry, Maine Volunteers. Soon Chamberlain was at Camp Mason in Portland.

The 20th Maine

The 20th Maine was composed of volunteers between 18 and 45 who had enlisted for three years. The 20th Maine left Portland by train for Boston Sept. 3rd and boarded the *Merri-mac,* reaching Alexandria, Virginia, Sept. 6th and then moved on to Washington, D.C. The 20th Maine was present at Antietam, but did not participate. The company spent Oct. 1862 training near Antietam. Chamberlain worked hard to master the art of war. He wrote Fanny that he was often in the saddle 12 or 15 hours a day. The 20th Maine took an active part at Fredericksburg.

Chamberlain came to be considered a severe disciplinarian, but one who was just. He had a well-trained and loyal command and believed in preserving the dignity of the individual. He rested his men frequently on long marches.

Had the 20th Maine never partaken in any other battle, its fighting and great stand on July 2, 1863, at Little Round Top would have given it enough glory for all time. On that day —the turning point of the Civil War, so it was to develop—Colonel Strong Vincent ordered the 20th Maine to hold Little Round Top at all costs.

Chamberlain's biographer, Wallace, says that Chamberlain had an intuitive grasp of where the Southern attack would come, based on his observance of the terrain, weapons, and soldiers. He had the faculty of improvisation for emergencies, the mark of a good officer.

During the fight on July 2nd, his men ran out of cartridges, but that did not deter Chamberlain. As the battle grew desperate he decided to counterattack. He ordered Capt. Ellis Spear to take the bent-back left wing and sweep down the hill to the right. Chamberlain saw to it that his men could not be surprised by a flank attack in the desperate fight of muskets and bayonets. The men who served under Chamberlain at Little Round Top revered him the rest of their lives.

Decisive Action

Oates, the Confederate leader, attacked in front and rear, gave the order to retreat. Chamberlain ordered the 20th Maine, bayonets drawn, to pursue the Confederates. He stopped his men when he had cleared the front of assailants and reached the front of the 44th New York. Colonel Rice of the 44th New York was one who considered this a very critical point in the battle. Colonel Oates of the 15th Alabama later said that Chamberlain's skill and the bravery of his men were the factors that saved Little Round Top and the Army of the Potomac. After this Chamberlain and his men with bayonets fixed went on and secured Round Top. The 5th Corps Commander, Sykes, considered Chamberlain's achievement, securing Round Top and protecting the left flank of the long Union line, one of the most important accomplishments of July 2nd, 1863.

In June of 1864 Chamberlain was badly wounded at Petersburg. A Minié ball hit his right hip joint, passed through his body, and came out behind the left hip joint. He was carried to a field hospital at the rear, where his life was despaired of. Fortunately, several very competent surgeons were at hand, and Chamberlain was a very cooperative patient with a strong will to live. This is the wound from which Chamberlain was to suffer, from time to time, for the rest of his life. It was soon after this battle that Chamberlain was made a brigadier general. While he was recuperating, Chamberlain read his obituary in New York newspapers and, like Mark Twain, felt the notice somewhat premature.

Chamberlain, after a relatively short period in the Naval Academy Hospital at Annapolis, was back in action. In December he went north on sick leave—this time hospitalized in Philadelphia. A month later he was back in action and fought at White Oak Road. Here again his horse, Charlemagne, was shot down. Confederate General Eppa Hunter sometime latter spoke of Chamberlain's gallant action at the White Oak Road. At Five Forks, called by Southerners the Waterloo of the Confederacy, Chamberlain again played an active role. This is generally considered one of the most confused battles of the war. Thousands of pages have been written about this particular conflict, which virtually marked the end of the war.

Chamberlain saw both Lee and Grant as they left their conference at McLean's house in the village of Appomattox.

"Knightliest Soldier"

On Palm Sunday, April 9, 1865, General Griffin of the 24th Corps summoned Chamberlain to his headquarters and told him he was to have the honor of receiving the formal surrender of the Confederate arms and colors. The ceremony took place on a chill gray spring day, the anniversary of the attack of Fort Sumter in Charleston, S.C., Chamberlain was mounted on Charlemagne. There was no band, no drum. Chamberlain had told his regimental commander to salute General Gordon and his Confederate troops.

As Gordon and his men drew abreast of the Union officers, Chamberlain spoke a word to a man nearby and a bugle call sounded. The entire Division of the 5th Corps, regiment by regiment in succession, brought its muskets from "order arms" to "carry arms," the marching salute. Gordon gave the command to his men to "carry arms."

Chamberlain recorded that absolute silence prevailed, that the Confederates stacked their arms, unslung their cartridge boxes and hung them on the stacks, and then folded their tattered colors and laid them down. On a much later occasion Gordon referred to Chamberlain as "one of the knightliest soldiers of the Federal Army."

One of the most interesting accounts I have read dealing with Chamberlain is that given by Wallace of how quietly and efficiently Chamberlain broke the news of Lincoln's assassination to his men when he received the wire from Washington on April 15th.

In May Chamberlain with Charlemagne was in Washington for the grand review in which the Army of the Potomac paraded on Pennsylvania Avenue in the national capital. The Maine general found it a great emotional experience, with battle flags, bands, the prancing cavalry, the gaily bedecked windows and housetops and the cheering onlookers.

The 20th Maine broke up in June, and the men and General Chamberlain returned to their respective homes.

Governor of Maine

Not many months later, Chamberlain underwent surgery again for the wound he had received at Petersburg. Then he resumed teaching at Bowdoin. In the spring of 1866 he was put forward by the Republicans as a candidate for governor and on the first ballot at the June convention got 599 votes to 438 for [his opponent] Spring. At about this time he acted briefly as president of Bowdoin and also was awarded a Doctor of Laws degree by Pennsylvania College (later to become known as Gettysburg College).

In those days in Maine a man was elected as governor for a one-year term. In the election held in Sept., Chamberlain got 69,637 votes to 41,917 cast for Pillsbury. This was the largest plurality ever polled by a gubernatorial candidate in Maine up to that time. In his inaugural in Jan. 1867 Chamberlain asked the Legislature to ratify the 14th amendment.

He showed interest in the agricultural college at Orono, advocated more facilities for care of the insane, a reform school where the young and comparatively innocent might be separated from the incorrigibles.

He said that the state prison should be enlarged and capital punishment should be accepted or rejected. He showed concern at the departure of Maine's young people by the thousands every year for more promising opportunities in other states. He wanted steps to be taken to get Scandinavian immigrants to Maine. He wanted a hydrographic survey of the principal rivers and urged the extension of railroads.

Principles First

Chamberlain was renominated and reelected in 1867. He ran into some opposition in 1868 because he supported Senator William Pitt Fessenden, who had the courage to be among the minority who would not support the Radical Republicans Thadeus Stevens and Ben Butler who were working for the conviction of President Johnson. Here, as in other acts of his career, he showed independence of judgment and placed principle above party. Friends feared not only for his career, but also for his life. The Republican failure to get Johnson out of office caused the party to work harder to elect a Republican as governor. In Sept. 1868, Chamberlain got 72,523 votes to the 56,207 cast for Pillsbury.

Chamberlain was criticized for his attitude relative to prohibition and capital punishment. He was renominated by the Republicans in June 1869, and that same month was granted the Doctor of Laws degree by Bowdoin. He was reelected governor in Sept. over two opponents; his inaugural address in 1870 was again carefully prepared and dealt with much the same problems as had his previous addresses.

He was not mentioned as a candidate in 1870. As William DeWitt Hyde of Bowdoin subsequently said of him, he was a statesman in advance of his time. As President Hyde said, he showed patience and fairness. He had refused to be a mere party man. He was a man with moral principles. He had shown a wide range of interests and a true appreciation of the needs of his state.

President of Bowdoin College

When Samuel Harris, President of Bowdoin, accepted a position at Yale in 1871, the Board of Trustees, of which Chamberlain was a member, unanimously offered him the Presidency of Bowdoin College. The Overseers approved the choice and it was received enthusiastically by many of the alumni.

Chamberlain almost immediately made some innovations, doing away with some of the formal prayers such as those before breakfast and evening prayers except for Sunday. Saturday classes were abolished. Commencement was changed to June. Library hours were extended. Tuition was raised. Room rates were not to be uniform but would depend on the desirability of the room. He favored military drill, which would develop the boy physically.

Chamberlain left his mark on the college curriculum. There were more courses in science and modern languages, and the students had some freedom in the selection of their courses. He may be said to have been a little ahead of the times. Robert E. Peary was a product of the Engineering School that Chamberlain established, and so Bowdoin may, in some degree, credit Chamberlain with the renown that [Peary's discovery] of the North Pole and the later exploits that Donald MacMillan have brought to Bowdoin College, already known throughout the country as the alma mater of Longfellow and Hawthorne.

Throughout his presidency at Bowdoin, Chamberlain suffered from ill health from his Civil War wound. In addition to his college duties he made many addresses at town affairs, and at somewhat distant meetings of the Grand Army of the Republic. During these years he enjoyed the companionship of his family and friends in his Brunswick home and on a schooner yacht, the *Pinafore*, exploring the islands of Casco Bay.

In March 1883 he was suffering from his wound and asked for leave of absence for the rest of the college year. He underwent an operation. Chamberlain attended his last faculty meeting on Sept. 10, 1883. The Boards accepted his resignation but he agreed to lecture for a time in political economy and in constitutional law. He gave this up in 1885.

William DeWitt Hyde, his successor, said that at one time or another between 1855 and 1885 Chamberlain taught every subject in the curriculum except math and physical science.

Willard M. Wallace, Chamberlain's biographer, shows admiration for his versatility as professor and president and one must certainly agree that Chamberlain rendered a remarkable service to Bowdoin College, his own alma mater.

Non-Academic Honors

While President of Bowdoin, Chamberlain delivered an address on "Maine: Her place in History" at the Centennial Exposition at Philadelphia on Nov. 4, 1876. This he later gave at a meeting of the Maine Legislature on Feb. 6, 1877, after which it was published as a state document.

Because of his position as President of Bowdoin, his ability as a social mixer, and his knowledge of languages, he was appointed as a U.S. Commissioner to the Paris Exposition in 1878. He used his time profitably while in France to visit public libraries and museums to read about the French in Maine in our colonial period.

Using the educational exhibits at the Exposition he prepared a scholarly paper on education which he submitted to the U.S. Government. This covered 165 printed pages. Chamberlain thought the U.S. was ahead in the education of girls, but felt our colleges were behind in the study of social and political science. He wrote that more attention should be given in this country to adult education. The report represents much industry in the collection of facts and shows effective organization of the vast amount of material used.

After the Sept. 1874 election in Maine there was much fear by Republicans that Democrats and Greenbackers would fuse in the legislature. James G. Blaine, an ambitious Republican, then a U.S. Senator, fearing that Conkling, a bitter rival, might get Grant in for a third term in 1880, became involved in complicating the tensions in Augusta. There were cries of fraud and of corruption from some few candidates who had been "counted out." Some complained that Governor [Alonzo] Garcelon aimed to establish a dictatorship. Many armed men flocked to Augusta.

Keeps Peace in Maine

Governor Garcelon requested that Chamberlain, as Major General of Militia, report to Augusta to protect public property. Chamberlain operated from a little office in the Capitol, trying to be neutral. He wore no arms, but no doubt his military uniform gave some recognition to his authority. He insisted on civil authority and legal action.

Strong pressure was brought to bear upon him to recognize a governor. He insisted that the state legislature and Supreme Court were the legal authorities to settle the disputed election.

One plot to kill Chamberlain was discovered by the mayor. Then there were rumors of a plot to kidnap Chamberlain. This he is said to have foiled by changing his lodgings every night. A story is told that one day a man rushed into his office in the Capitol saying that there was a gang of men outside waiting to kill him.

Chamberlain, so the story goes, promptly walked outside and addressed the angry group. "Men, you wish to kill me, I hear . . . I am here to preserve the peace and honor of this State, until the rightful government is seated . . . It is for me to see that the laws of this State are put into effect, without force, but with calm thought and purpose . . . If anybody wants to kill me . . . here I am."

Then he silently stood there. Soon a Civil War veteran spoke up and said he would kill anyone who laid a hand on the general. The mob apparently gradually withdrew.

Chamberlain, by his good independent judgment, unusual composure in the crisis, forceful personality and tact saved Maine in 1880 from what might have been a bloody insurrection that would have cost many lives and given Maine a bad name. Those had been 12 very anxious days from January 5 to 17th, 1880. With the selection of Davis as Governor by the State Legislature and the decision of the Supreme Court that the election was legal, Chamberlain was free to return to his duties at Bowdoin. He had performed a difficult duty well. Though there had been many criticisms of him there were many commendatory remarks as well. He had been "Champion of Civil Liberty in Maine."

There was some mention of Chamberlain being selected by the State legislature as a U.S. Senator, but this never came about. Eugene Hale, a strong Blaine man, succeeded Hannibal Hamlin and when Blaine resigned from the Senate to become Secretary of State to Garfield in 1881, William P. Frye, another Blaine supporter, was elected to the U.S. Senate. Fortunately for Maine both Hale and Frye were worthy individuals though in the opinion of Willard Wallace the rejection of Chamberlain as a Senatorial candidate was a loss to Maine and to the United States.

In the winter of 1884 there was some mention of Chamberlain being sent as minister to

Russia. Nothing came of this as nothing had come of the perhaps more remote possibility of his appointment, in 1876, to the U.S. Embassy in London or, in 1877, to that in Paris.

Surveyor of Port of Portland

Friends finally secured for him the position of Surveyor of the Port of Portland and he was appointed by President McKinley on March 20, 1900, at an annual salary of $4,500. He was disappointed at not receiving the collectorship which would have required more "executive ability and experience of great affairs."

Chamberlain did not accept the job as a sinecure. He took a morning train from Brunswick to Portland returning home at the end of the day. Sometimes he stayed overnight at the Falmouth Hotel in Portland and, subsequently, he secured a house on Ocean Avenue in Portland so as to be nearer his work.

With renewal in 1900 of inflammation of his old wound, he secured a leave of absence from the Secretary of the Treasury and in Nov. 1890 went to the Mediterranean, where he visited Italy and Egypt.

Family Man

In 1905 he was saddened by the death of his wife, Fanny. He did enjoy his daughter, "Daise," and her daughters, his son Wyllys, his sister Sadie, and his niece, Alice. Chamberlain enjoyed many friends and welcomed them to his Brunswick home. He also kept up a large correspondence, and it seems evident that he had done many a person a kindness which was greatly appreciated and never would be forgotten.

On Lincoln's birthday, Feb. 12, 1909, at the Academy of Music in Philadelphia, he delivered the main address, entitled, "Abraham Lincoln Seen From the Field."

He wrote "My Story of Fredericksburg" for *Cosmopolitan* in 1913 and in the same year "Through Blood and Fire at Gettysburg" was published [by] *Hearst's* magazine. One of his later publications was a book covering the final campaign of the Army of the Potomac under the title *The Passing of the Armies*. This is dramatic, realistic, picturesque. Personalities are clearly drawn and actions are vividly portrayed.

Suffered Much

Chamberlain had suffered much—generally quietly—at various times in his life since Petersburg when his old wound became in-

flamed. Near the end of 1913 he was ill in his Ocean Avenue home in Portland. He died, quietly, on the morning of Feb. 24, 1914. Fully 3,000 people attended the services at City Hall in Portland on Feb. 27th. Then his flag draped casket was taken to Union Station and by train to Brunswick.

Another service was held in the First Parish Church in Brunswick. This was the church where he had led the choir towards the end of his undergraduate days at Bowdoin. Here he had been married; here he had presided at many a Bowdoin commencement. The service was conducted by Rev. Chauncey Goodrich and President William DeWitt Hyde delivered the eulogy. The faculty and students, many of the townfolk, the local G.A.R. post and Brunswick National Guard attended.

Chamberlain was buried in Pine Grove Cemetery near the Bowdoin College campus.

He is one of whom William DeWitt Hyde could say that he belonged to all men and all ages.

ALSO SEE

"At Home with Gen. Joshua L. Chamberlain in Old Longfellow House, Brunswick," *Lewiston Journal Illustrated Magazine,* 17 August 1907, pp. 8–10.

"Fighting Professor," *Down East* 9, July 1963, pp. 32–33.

"Gen. Chamberlain's 'Battle Bracelet' Is Work of Art," *Lewiston Journal Illustrated Magazine,* 1968, pp. 3, 4.

"The Governors of Maine: Third Series, No. 20—Joshua L. Chamberlain," *Lewiston Journal Illustrated Magazine*, 5 January 1907, pp. 4–5.

"The Happy Warrior—General Joshua Chamberlain," *Down East* 3, November 1956/January 1957, pp. 30–34.

"The Hero of Little Round Top as His Friends Knew Him," *Lewiston Journal Illustrated Magazine,* 25 May 1918, p. 1.

"Joshua Chamberlain," *Down East,* March 1987, pp. 46–49, 57–60.

"Joshua Chamberlain—Maine Writer Recalls Interview With 'Hero of Little Round Top,'" *Lewiston Journal Illustrated Magazine,* 6 October 1928, p. 1.

"Mighty Mite of Faculty Beat Bowdoin '62 Grads to Colors," *Portland Press Herald,* 28 August 1962, p. 11.

"Sterling Leader of the 20th Maine," *Morning Sentinel,* 1 August 1992, p. 6 M.

DOROTHEA LYNDE DIX—
CIVIL WAR NURSE AND PHILANTHROPIST

CHARLOTTE M. H. BEATH

Far up on the Penobscot River lies the little town of Hampden, with its farms and mills and the old academy which came into being more than a hundred years ago. Sweeping down to the bank of the river is a beautiful park used in summer by the people of Bangor for a place of rest and recreation. But away back at the beginning of the nineteenth century this park was only a farm and it was here, on an April morning, that a little girl first opened her eyes to the world. Who could then guess the great future that lay before her, or could even dimly foresee that on account of her noble work for suffering humanity her fame would ring through America, even to the Old World, and that thousands of afflicted persons whose sufferings she had relieved, would rise up and bless the name of Dorothea Lynde Dix.

Her childhood was not a happy one. Indeed, in after years she sometimes said sadly, "I never knew childhood." Her father, Joseph Dix, was of good old Puritan ancestry, but he had no settled business and does not seem to have been very strong-mined. On religious subjects, especially, he was almost unbalanced, and sometimes wrote and published tracts which little Dorothea was made to paste and sew together. Her mother, who was much older than her father, didn't understand her, so it may well be imagined that the sensitive, high-spirited child found her home life very unpleasant.

At the age of twelve Dorothea rebelled against making tracts any longer, left her father's roof, and went to her grandmother's home in Boston. Even at this early age she displayed traits which marked all her after-life—played traits which marked all her after-life—a strong will, faith in her own ability, and an imperative nature which would never endure opposition. Her grandmother was a wise, kind, dignified woman and her grandfather was a well-known doctor and chemist, much like Dorothea in character. The little girl was much happier here and spent two pleasant years, attending school and learning many valuable lessons from her wise grandmother. We can well believe that she studied hard and made good progress in learning, for, at the age of fifteen, still little more than a child, she decided to teach school herself!

So she went to Worcester and opened a school for small children. Just imagine this little girl of fifteen standing before her twenty pupils, instructing them in reading, writing and the multiplication table, with such side lines as manners and morals and the happily forgotten art of making samplers! The young teacher was very strict and had no intention of spoiling her pupils by sparing the rod. One of the little boys whom she punished every day grew up to be a brave soldier and a general. "I don't know that she had any grudge against me," he said, "but it was her nature to use the whip." But another says: "The future general was never still[,] and a whipping a day was necessary." The little girls were punished in other ways. One of them had to go through the streets for a week with a large card on her back, bearing the words: "A very bad girl indeed."

Dorothea's two brothers went to her school, as her father had now moved to

ORIGINALLY PUBLISHED IN *LEWISTON JOURNAL ILLUSTRATED MAGAZINE*, 8 MARCH 1924.

Worcester, but she did not allow the relationship to lessen her severity. Her brothers were obliged to "eat, drink, sleep and wink" at her direction. All the children had to learn and recite a chapter of the Bible on Monday morning, standing with their toes on a line, hands folded and eyes turned devoutly upward.

Although a faithful teacher, Dorothea's sternness caused her school to be rather unpopular, and after a while it was closed. She did not by any means wish to give up teaching so she went back to Boston and studied very hard until she was nineteen, when she considered that she was fitted to teach young ladies and opened a day school in Boston.

This school proved to be very successful and became so crowded that she moved it to her grandmother's house, called the "Dix Mansion." Soon pupils began to come from the first families, not only of Boston, but of New England. Dorothea's work was very hard, as she not only taught in the school, but managed the household, supported her two brothers, nursed her aged grandmother and, finally, through a growing sympathy for the poor, opened a charity school.

Her health was never very good, and this labor proved too much for her. At the end of six years her failing strength forced her to give up her duties. She then became a governess in the family of William Ellery Channing, D.D., and with them went to the West Indies.

Here the warm climate, combined with complete freedom from care, partly restored her health while her mind was refreshed by contact with the strange customs and the study of the flora and the fauna of the new land. When she came back to Boston she reopened her school, where her knowledge and experience made her an authority on education and her school a model. But after five years of work, her health again failed and she went abroad, where she remained for over a year. While she was abroad her grandmother died, leaving her a part of her estate, the income from which was enough for her own support and also allowed her to give much to the poor in whom she had a great and increasing interest.

She was now about thirty-nine years old, tall and slender and rather good-looking, although her face wore a very decided and at times stern expression. Her voice was low but very distinct and full of authority. In manner she was imperative almost to arrogance, and far more disposed to dictate then to receive

advice from others. She never married, perhaps preferring her independent life and possibly frightening away all would-be admirers by a manner exactly the reverse of coquettish.

About this time she began to take great interest in prisons and in the insane, and started upon the career which was to make her name world-famous.

DOROTHEA LYNDE DIX

A jail or an insane asylum can never be a desirable place in which to pass one's life, but in those days the innocent and the criminal, the sane and the insane, were herded together under conditions which made a prison the abiding place of horror. All over the world people shut their eyes to these conditions or calmly accepted them as right and natural. Miss Dix, with very little public support, but upheld by her strong will and sense of right, set out to correct some of these evils.

Her first step was to obtain an order from the judge in Worcester for the heating of bitterly cold rooms in which some insane people were kept. She then started out to inspect all such places in the State. Even she, strong-minded and prepared for brutality, was shocked by what she found. She had so far advanced from the days of her first school in Worcester, however, that she was able to conceal her wrath until the hour was ripe to strike. So with growing indignation she inspected every dark corner and loathsome cell and wrote down all the information she gathered in a notebook.

Then, when all was ready, she put together these facts in a stirring appeal to the Massachusetts Legislature. She spared no one, and she herself was not spared, for this was a new field for a woman, and for a time public opinion stormed against her. But the wisest men saw that she was right and came over to her side. As a result the Legislature passed a bill to enlarge the Worcester State Hospital and to provide better care for the insane.

Her success gave her a sense of her own power, and knowing that conditions in other states must be as bad as in Massachusetts, she resolved to give the rest of her life to the cause of the insane.

So for the next few years she worked in Rhode Island, New Jersey, and in some of the middle and southern states, meeting and overcoming opposition and handicapped by her own ill-health. "I am exhausted under this perpetual effort," she wrote to a friend. "You have no idea of the labor of conversing and convincing. Some evenings I have at once twenty gentlemen for three hours' steady conversation."

Her methods must have been convincing, however, for in every state wherever she went her efforts won steadily growing success, and she left behind her a trail of better conditions for the poor, unfortunate people, and a new attitude toward them in the mind of the public.

She introduced a bill into Congress asking for about 12,000,000 acres of the public land, which was to be sold and the proceeds used for the insane. This bill passed both branches of Congress but President Pierce would not sign it. This was such a disappointment to Miss Dix that her splendid courage was for a time completely paralyzed. Heartsick, she turned to Europe for consolation and in a peaceful corner of England rallied her strength anew.

Her restless spirit would not allow her to remain quiet long. With a royal commission from Queen Victoria she traveled over the country inspecting the madhouses and always arousing interest and help. Nearly all the countries of Europe were visited one after another. Filled with the true American spirit, which bends before no earthly king, she did not fear to approach the throne to present her case and ask for assistance for the afflicted. Pope Pius IX, especially, became much interested and warmly thanked her for her efforts.

At last, after two years, she came back to the United States, where the storm-cloud of the Rebellion was already commencing to dart its lightnings over a troubled land. On April 19, 1861, in the streets of hostile Baltimore was shed the first blood of one of the greatest wars in history. The next day saw Dorothea Dix in Washington offering her services to the United States Government. Her reputation was world-wide, and without hesitation the Secretary of War made her "Superintendent of Women Nurses."

This position gave her great power, and she used it with unerring wisdom and justice, as the following instance will show. One day while inspecting the wards of a hospital, she came upon three invalid soldiers being punished for some offense by being hung up by the thumbs. "Who ordered this?" she asked in her imperious way. "The surgeon in charge," was the answer. In a few moments Miss Dix stood before the unlucky officer and ordered the men to be immediately released. The surgeon was furious and would have no interference with his affairs, especially from a woman. Miss Dix went straight to General Butler, the Department Commander, and asked whether she or the surgeon outranked the other. "Miss Dix, of course," was the reply. That settled the matter; the men were freed and the surgeon disgraced.

Seeing that the hospital stores were lacking in many comforts and even necessities, she collected food, clothing and medicine from the Northern states to be given to the sick soldiers, thus winning the everlasting gratitude of thousands of suffering men.

Lossing's *History of the Civil War* says: "Like an angel of mercy she labored day and night for the relief of suffering soldiers. She went from battlefield to battlefield when the carnage was over, and from camp to camp, giving, with her own hand, comforts to the wounded and soothing the troubled spirits of the dying. The amount of happiness that resulted from the services of this woman can never be estimated."

She would never accept any pay for her work, and when the war was over a stand of arms of the United States colors was made and presented to her. After her death this was given, by her request, to Harvard College.

However great her work in the Rebellion might appear to others, Miss Dix herself regarded it as merely an episode in her career, and as soon as the four terrible years were over resumed her labors for the insane. For fifteen years she battled on, but while her gallant spirit was as eager as ever, the infirmities of age were fast gathering upon her. But as she became less active the great world force that she had set in motion, the desire to give sympathy and material help to the mentally distressed, grew ever stronger as the years went by.

It would be impossible to estimate all of her deeds of mercy or properly to estimate the value of her work. The fact that there are now standing thirty-two institutions for the insane which she either founded or greatly enlarged, showed that her life was not spent in vain. The great and learned of all nations honored her and she held a sacred place in the hearts of thousands of the poor and lowly.

Though never strong in body, yet she lived to a good old age. The last five years of her life were spent in Trenton, N.J., in the State Hospital, which she herself founded and for which she had always had a special and tender regard. Historians differ as to the exact number of her years, ranging all the way from 85 to 93, but all agreed that up to the very last her remarkable mind, her strong will, and the proud spirit which could not own defeat, never failed her.

After her death, a manuscript copy of Whittier's poem, "At Last," was found under her pillow and read at the burial in Mt. Auburn. The much worn copy shows how her mind loved to linger over the exquisite lines beginning,

> When on my day of life the night
> is falling,
> And, in the winds from unsunned spaces
> blown,
> I hear far voices out of darkness calling
> My feet to paths unknown.

In her will she bequeathed $5000 to the Massachusetts S.P.C.A. for the purpose of erecting a drinking fountain for animals, and in 1888 a granite fountain bearing her name was placed in Custom House Square in Boston, to be a perpetual reminder of her kindness and mercy.

Though only her earliest years were passed in Maine, we are proud to claim her and to feel that the rugged arms of our great State cradled her in infancy, perhaps thus imparting some of those sterling traits and characteristics which made Dorothea Lynde Dix the great and noble woman that she was.

ALSO SEE

"Adventures and Experience of a Civil War Nurse," *Lewiston Journal Illustrated Magazine*, 20 January 1923, p. 3; 27 January, p. 2; 4 February, pp. 2, 16; 11 February, p. 5; 18 February, p. 12; 25 February, p. 11; 3 March, pp. 10, 11; 10 March, p. 11; 17 March, p. 11; 24 March, p. 11.

"Dorothea Lynde Dix," *Sprague Journal of Maine History* 5, November 1917/January 1918. pp. 199–209.

"Institutional and Prison Reform Work of Dorothea Dix, Maine Native," *Lewiston Journal Illustrated Magazine*, 18 August 1945, pp. 1–2.

"Life's Labor Was in Worthy Cause," *Portland Sunday Telegram,* 4 May 1902, p. 1.

"Maine Home of Dorothea Dix," *Lewiston Journal Illustrated Magazine*, 9 February 1907, pp. 8–9.

"Melville C. Freeman Rates Dorothea Lynde Dix as 6th Among America's Great," *Portland Evening Express,* 19 April 1956, p. 2.

"Nurse Fought for Humanity and Died for Her Country," *Maine Sunday Telegram,* 29 May 1988, pp. 1A, 14A.

Lew Estes—
From Private to General by Twenty-One

GRANVILLE FERNALD

You are waiting to hear the name of my hero—the boy whose true history as a soldier is like a page from the romances of the brave knights whose deeds illustrate the history of the wonderful ages of chivalry. It is Estes.

I must investigate him. I go to my library and take Hodsdon's reports of Maine's contribution of men to the Union Army, and I quickly get on the track of the typical Maine soldier. I find the following in the roster of commissioned officers of Maine Volunteers in the War of 1861–1865:

- Estes, Llewellyn G., First Lieutenant A, 1 Cavalry.
- Same, Captain A, 1 Cavalry.
- Promoted A.A.G. Volunteers, 1 Cavalry.

From that it is easy and really exciting to trace the progress of our patriotic, ambitious, Downeast youth by rapid steps from a raw recruit to the dignity and consequence of shoulder straps; from the routine of organization and drill at Augusta in the winter of 1861–1862 to the subsequent experiences of the camp, the bivouac, the raiding and fighting in Virginia, Maryland, and Pennsylvania, and the romance of the march with—or really ahead of—Sherman, to the sea, and beyond that to the conquest of Johnston's army and the era of victory and peace.

In 1861 there resided in Old Town, Penobscot county, the family to which belonged the subject of this brief sketch. His father was absent in California. The recruiting officers for the volunteer army were abroad in the land, and it is no wonder that Lew Estes, in the enthusiasm of his eighteenth year of life, should burst the bonds of maternal restraint, and, against the pleadings and tears of his fond, anxious mother, enlist in Company A, First Maine Cavalry, on September 21, 1861. The date given in Hodsdon's book is October 19, but that is the date of muster-in to the United States service; and 21 is the age given in the same record of Maine's soldiers, but that is a fiction—a convenient dodge by which a great many Maine boys of tender age managed to mortgage themselves to Uncle Sam "for three years or the duration of the war." They were boys, and beardless, but with brave hearts beating under their blue jackets.

In nine days after the young recruit was enrolled, he was appointed to the position of orderly sergeant of his company, one of the most responsible stations in the company or regiment.

In May, 1862, only six months after his enlistment, he was promoted to be 1st lieutenant of his company, in which position he served with the regiment in Virginia, gaining much experience and attracting attention from superior officers for skill and daring in the execution of important movements, and in close action with the enemy's forces. It is stated to the writer, by an intimate army comrade of Estes, that Col. Judson Kilpatrick of the Harris Light Cavalry (2d N.Y.) also commanding a brigade of cavalry, had particularly noticed our Maine boy engaging the enemy at the head of a small body of men of the First Maine, and when the organization of the cavalry corps of the Army of the Potomac oc-

ORIGINALLY PUBLISHED IN *MAINE BUGLE*, APRIL 1898.

curred in 1863. Colonel Kilpatrick called on Colonel Douty of the Maine First to detail an officer for adjutant-general of his staff. Colonel Douty referred the matter to Lieutenant-Colonel Smith, who at once thought of the right man for Kilpatrick and responded: "Yes; there's Estes; he's smart and bright as a dollar, but he won't work in harness worth a cent."

Kilpatrick, being promoted to brigadier-general and appointed to the command of the First Brigade, Third Cavalry division, had Estes (who had recently been promoted to captain of his company) permanently detached from his company and appointed adjutant-general on his staff, dating from July 1, 1863. In that honorable position, in the most intimate relations with the commanding general of the brigade, Captain Estes might have avoided participation to a great extent in the dangers of a cavalry charge and close conflicts with the enemy, but the Maine youth was always ready and eager for the fray of battle.

The following instance of the gallant behavior of Lieutenant Estes under circumstances of peril is founded on the narrative of the War Records of Maine, and the official report of General Kilpatrick: "The celebrated Stoneman raid through the rebel lines and around Richmond occurred in May, 1863, while the battle of Chancellorsville was being fought. On this occasion Lieutenant Estes received special honorable mention in the report of Colonel Kilpatrick for volunteering to carry a dispatch to Major-General Hooker. He failed in the attempt, but with his escort of ten men he captured and paroled one major, two captains, a lieutenant, and fifteen men of the enemy. He was soon afterward captured with his escort, but managed to capture his captors in turn, and soon a force of Union cavalry swept down and took in the whole of both parties."

In the memorable cavalry assault upon the rebel lines at Gettysburg, led by that intrepid cavalry leader, Brigadier-General Elon J. Farnsworth, under the direction of Kilpatrick, Captain Estes, by permission of his commander, rode with Farnsworth as a volunteer aide.

After Captain Estes's detachment to the staff of Kilpatrick, he never returned to duty or was identified with the subsequent history of the First Maine Cavalry. He followed all the fortunes of his impetuous commander, and found congenial association with the gallant men of the staff, and the brave officers of the cavalry line who served under that distinguished leader till the close of the war. He participated in all the campaigns of the Army of the Potomac to the time Kilpatrick joined the Army of the Mississippi in April, 1864. At this time, Captain Estes was only past his twentieth birthday.

"Of all the officers intimately associated with Kilpatrick," says my informant, who was also on staff duty with him during the Atlanta campaign and those of the Savannah and the Carolinas, "not one was so closely related to him in every respect as Estes. Estes had the confidence and esteem of his commander in all things. Whatever Estes did was just right; even to putting a cowardly colonel under arrest and then taking command of his regiment and charging into an entrenched town, clearing it of rebel troops at the point of the saber, as was the case at Van Wert, Georgia. There was no man in the cavalry corps of Sherman's army more widely known and respected than the Maine boy, still under age, and only a captain. His twenty-first birthday occurred during the occupation of Savannah by Sherman, and on that day, the twenty-seventh of December, 1864, Kilpatrick's report to Sherman of the operations of the cavalry on the "March to the Sea," is dated, at the close of which he says: "Captain Estes, my assistant adjutant-general, deserves special notice, not only for the faithful discharge of his eminent duties, but for his reckless daring and invaluable assistance in every skirmish and engagement. This officer deserves and I earnestly hope that he may be promoted."

The official records of the Civil War show other instances of special mention of the Penobscot boy for remarkable gallantry and skill in handling troops, but one bit of daring was done under the eye of General Howard, commanding the Army of the Tennessee, and related in his report of the Atlanta Campaign of 1864. It was in August, when the Army of the Tennessee, as the right wing of Sherman's Army was flanking Hood's Army, while Atlanta was being evacuated by Hood, that a fierce fight occurred at Flint River Bridge, which was an object of contention between the Union forces under General Logan and a large body of rebel troops, "Which," says General Howard, "were reported to be from two brigades to a corps. I found," says General Howard, "that scarcely a drop of water could be obtained without retiring a mile, and that there was none ahead short of Flint River." A lodgement of the eastern side of that river would enable him to accomplish two desired objects: to break the railroad and secure an abundance of water for his army. "After a short rest," he continues, "the columns marched on, General Logan's, preceded by a squadron of cavalry under Captain Estes of Kilpatrick's staff, and the other columns preceded by Kilpatrick's main body, cutting their own roads for the most part of the way. Captain Estes pushed so fast that the rebel cavalry could make no other stand from Renfroe to the Flint. On reaching Flint it was discovered that the bridge was not destroyed, the enemy defending it from barricades on the opposite bank. I directed it to be carried. Captain Estes deployed his cavalry, now increased to parts of two regiments armed with Spencer rifles. He was followed by Hazen's skirmishers. The cavalry rushed for the river bank and fired so fast that the rebels could with difficulty reply. Under cover of this fire a charge was made across the bridge, and the first and second line of barricades seized."

A few days after the dashing charge and complete success with a small force just mentioned, we find Captain Estes again volunteering to drive back a large rebel force at the head of the Ninety-second Illinois Mounted Infantry, of which General Kilpatrick says: "Captain Estes and the officers of the Ninety-second Illinois are alone entitled to all the praise of this successful exploit."

His position as leader of the assault at Flint River was purely voluntary, and in response to a call from General Howard. The fact is, he often tired of the routine of the camp and the office, and craved the excitement of the raid, the charge and clash of arms in the front of the army.

The brilliant services of such a man could not fail to be rewarded by promotion. He was promoted to be major in September 1864, and lieutenant-colonel in 1865. In General Kilpatrick's report of the final campaign he again gives Adjutant-General Estes a meed of gratitude as follows: "To Major Estes, my adjutant-general, I am greatly indebted for my success in the raid around Atlanta and the campaigns of Georgia and the Carolinas. He deserves and should be made a brigadier-general." General

Sherman adds by endorsement: "This officer I recommend for gallantry and great skill in battle."

General John L. Hodsdon, adjutant-general of Maine during the war, says: "The career of General Estes was indeed remarkable. In the short space of less than three years, through his skill and bravery, without the aid of powerful political friends, be advanced from the position of private in the ranks to that of brigadier-general before he reached the twenty-fourth year of his age. He was once made prisoner, three times wounded, and participated in no less than one hundred and twenty-one engagements!"

It is said that no other officer of the volunteer army has to his credit a record of so many engagements as General Estes.

As to the age of General Estes above given, at which he was made a brigadier-general, thereby hangs an explanation. Private Estes at the time of his enlistment was only in his eighteenth year, having been born December 27th, 1843, but as at that time it was difficult for boys so young as he to enlist, he was enrolled as twenty-one years of age, as appears by the roster of his regiment (Adjutant-General's Report, Maine, 1863) so he was only a little past his majority when his commission as Brigadier-General of Volunteers was given him. It is dated September 30, 1865. In March, 1865, General Kilpatrick and Sherman had strongly recommended him to be promoted to the full rank of brigadier, which he would have received but for the discontinuance of the war. From March to September 30, 1865, General Estes was adjutant-general of western North Carolina, comprising forty-one counties, in which office he displayed the same qualities of heroism and patriotic zeal that marked all his previous army service. He resigned his commission September 30, 1865.

Since the retirement of General Estes from the public service, he has been cultivating the arts of peace in various spheres of civil life. He resided a number of years in North Carolina, but for a few years past has been a resident of Washington, where he is engaged in a quiet business enterprise. He is one of the most affable and kind-hearted of men; a churchman and a Republican.

Many instances of General Estes's wonderful bravery and his coolness during the most fearful hand-to-hand conflicts with the rebel cavalry, are related to the writer by his old army chum, as he fights over again the campaigns of the sixties while his cigar goes out amid the imaginary clash of sabers or the rattletybang of the carbines.

The captain had a large, powerful horse which was peculiarly marked in different parts of his body, or parti-colored. He bore the name of "Old Spot," and was better known through the whole cavalry corps than any other horse—as there was no other like him. Even the rebels knew Old Spot, as they had met him on many fields, bearing his intrepid rider always in advance of the Yankee squadron. When Estes started for the enemy, he was like a centaur of the fable, and Old Spot in full sympathy and of superior mettle and unequaled stride, immediately distanced the flying troopers following Estes's daring leadership, until he would be the most conspicuous object in the scene.

While fighting through the Carolinas, Old Spot was captured by a private in a North Carolina regiment, during a raid of Hampton's Cavalry on Kilpatrick's headquarters in the early morning, which is graphically described to the writer by General Estes: "Kilpatrick slept in a house; I slept in an ambulance with the books and fixtures of the office, in company with another officer of the staff. Kilpatrick discovered the raid first. I ran out and skedaddled into the swamp. We rallied immediately and retook everything except the horses. I had shown some courtesies to the colonel of the regiment while he was a prisoner of war in our hands, and as he knew Old Spot was my horse, he sent me a message under a flag of truce, that as much as he would like to return my horse to me he could not do so, as it was the property of the captor. I finally got possession of Old Spot at the final surrender, but it cost me two other horses and $100 in gold. Old Spot died on my plantation in Enfield, N.C., a veteran of seventeen years, bearing three wounds received in battle, and was like an old soldier, a relic of the battle-shocked wartime."

While commanding the Department of the East, at New York, General O. O. Howard, in memory of the great service of General Estes to the government, and in particular for the brilliant exploit already described, voluntarily addressed the war department as follows:

HEADQUARTERS DEPARTMENT
OF THE EAST,
Governor's Island, New York,
May 8, 1894.

To the Adjutant-General, United States Army, Washington. D. C.:

SIR:—I have the honor to recommend that Captain Llewellyn G. Estes, who served under my personal observation on the staff of General Kilpatrick, during the campaign against Atlanta in 1864, may be awarded a medal of honor, for conspicuous gallantry and bravery in action at the crossing of Flint river, Georgia, August 30, 1864.

The circumstances which brought Captain Estes under my observation were as follows:

The Army of the Tennessee was advancing upon Jonesboro; it was late in the afternoon (about 5 p.m.) when we found the enemy guarding the bridge over Flint river from barricades on the other side. I was anxious to secure a lodgement on the eastern bank of the river, that I might be able to break the railroad next morning, and at the same time to secure the waters of the Flint for my army. We had been skirmishing all day; about 5 p.m. I sent to find out who had command of the advance cavalry. Captain Estes reported to me; I told him I was ordered to encamp there that night, but I had no water for my army, and the enemy's troops were harassing me in front, and I wanted them cleared away, and asked him if he could drive them off. He replied that he could do so, and I ordered him to try and drive them away. Captain Estes immediately rode off; took the Ninety-second Illinois Cavalry and most gallantly charged at their head, drove the enemy from his barricades—charging to the river without stopping, giving no opportunity for the Confederates to reform. Captain Estes then reported to me, and asked if I wanted him to take the bridge; I asked him if he could do it, to which be replied that he could do it with his men dismounted. I ordered him to try; he immediately dismounted two troops armed with Spencer rifles, and putting himself at the head charged across the bridge which was partially destroyed, only the stringers being left for a footing. He drove the enemy away, and replaced the planking of the bridge.

This action at Flint river was phenomenal; and the promptitude and gallantry of Captain Estes and his men under a very sharp fire was unsurpassed. The "Rebellion Records," of which extracts were made, fully corroborate these statements.

Very respectfully, your obedient servant,

(Signed) O. O. Howard,
Major-general United States Army,
commanding Department of the East.

A supplementary communication was afterwards sent to the War Department as follows:

HEADQUARTERS DEPARTMENT
OF THE EAST,
Governor's Island, New York,
July 13, 1894

To the Adjutant-General, United States Army, Washington, D. C.:

SIR:—As I think it is my omission not having properly stated the case of Captain Llewellyn G. Estes, who served under my observation on General Kilpatrick's staff during the war, in my letter addressed to you, and dated May 8, 1894, recommending him for a medal of honor. I respectfully ask for a reconsideration of his case on the part of the assistant secretary of war.

Some things now have come to my knowledge. First: That at the time of the acts of special gallantry for which I recommended that he be given a medal of honor, Captain Estes was General Kilpatrick's adjutant-general. I called upon Kilpatrick for some one who would accomplish an extraordinary and unusual feat,—namely, with a squadron of cavalry surprise the enemy's rear guard, force an immediate retreat, drive it across the river, and secure the bridge. It now appears that Captain Estes volunteered for this duty; how gallantly he performed it is set forth in my letter of May 8.

The manner in which Captain Estes

performed this duty for which he volunteered, struck me at the time and remains in my mind as one of the most gallant acts of our war. The captain not only accomplished fully what he undertook, but did so under most trying circumstances. The bridge over which he charged was on fire at the time and partially destroyed; leading his men over the burning timbers, he drove the enemy from his position, extinguished the fire, and saved the bridge, which was repaired for our use.

All the circumstances surrounding this action made it striking and impressive; the necessity of securing water for my army, and a lodgement on the eastern bank, the burning bridge, and the barricades of the enemy, the charge across the burning timbers, and the relief given by its success, not only impressed me, but all others present at the time, as is shown by the mention of Captain Estes in the reports.

The action of Captain Estes at Flint River was purely voluntary, and beyond the mere call of duty; it was an extraordinary act, and not within the regular line of official duty; he was an adjutant-general at the time, yet volunteered for, and took command of troops in, a most difficult undertaking.

Trusting that the above statement may lead to a favorable consideration of my recommendation that Captain Estes be given a medal of honor,

I am very respectfully,
Your obedient servant,

(signed) Oliver O. Howard,
Major-general United States Army,
commanding Department of the East.

RECORD AND PENSION OFFICE,
WAR DEPARTMENT.
Washington City, Aug. 29, 1894.

General Llewellyn G. Estes,
Washington, D.C.:

GENERAL:—I have the honor to inform you that by direction of the president, and in accordance with the act of congress approved March 3, 1863, providing for the presentation of medals of honor to such officers, non-commissioned officers, and privates as have most distinguished themselves in action, the acting secretary of war has awarded you a medal of honor for most distinguished gallantry in action at Flint River, Georgia, August 30, 1864. The papers upon which this award was made have been returned to this office with the following remarks endorsed thereon by the acting secretary of war:

"This officer, while serving as assistant adjutant-general on the staff of General Kilpatrick, voluntarily took command of troops, and, making a gallant charge across a burning bridge upon the rear guard of the enemy, drove them from their barricades and extinguished the fire, thus securing water for the Union Army, and enabling it to take an advantageous position on the further bank."

The medal has been forwarded you by registered mail. Please acknowledge receipt.

(Signed) Very respectfully,
F. C. Ainsworth,
Colonel United States Army,
Chief, Record and Pension Office.

Also See

"Maine's Youngest Veteran," *Portland Transcript* 51, 1 February 1888, p. 346.

"The Youngest Veteran," *Portland Transcript* 51, 15 February 1888,, p. 362.

Hannibal Hamlin, of Maine, Lincoln's Right Hand During the War

L. C. BATEMAN

The entire literary world has recently been flooded with reminiscences of our martyr President, Abraham Lincoln. Magazines and newspapers alike have teemed with articles in which every phase of his character has been brought into the limelight, and a thousand familiar anecdotes have been retold. This is well. The life of a great character has a marvelous influence in molding the lives of those who may follow, and in this age of sordid commercialism we cannot too often impress upon the minds of those we love the great fact that noble deeds can never die.

The American people are prone to select some one person upon whom to lavish all their words of praise. The name of Lincoln has been selected as the one which best typifies the undying spirit of loyalty during the dark days of Civil War, and he alone stands out as the great personality of that struggle. We must not forget, however, that noble men stood by his side. With all his magnificent powers he would have been helpless before the demon of treason had not other brave souls cheered his heart, upheld his arm and counseled him in the hour of danger. In the adulation of one we are apt to forget the others. It does not detract from the merits or the fame of the noble Lincoln to do justice to the memory of others. Amidst this universal acclaim of admiration it may be well to pause a brief moment and twine a laurel wreath for the brow of the one man who stood between him and universal anarchy. That man was Hannibal Hamlin, upon whose broad shoulders would have fallen the burden and responsibility had the hand of the assassin been raised at an earlier date.

Had Hamlin been in a position to succeed Lincoln after he had fallen by the hand of Booth, a different chapter would have been written in our national history.

Hannibal Hamlin was a man of the most tender and humane feeling. He was ever tender, kindly and just in all his private relations, and however fiercely he might denounce an opponent on some matter of public policy, he never allowed this to disturb the serenity of his personal feelings. For the memory of Lincoln he had the greatest reverence, and one of his last public acts was to urge his countrymen to make Lincoln's birthday a public holiday.

Hamlin was a man of the people, and no official dignity stood between him and those of a lowly rank. The writer of this article has a vivid recollection of this from personal experience with Mr. Hamlin away back in the time of Civil War. The writer's first term of military service was in the Lewiston Light Infantry when it was called out to do guard duty in Fort McClary at Kittery Point. This company was consolidated with the Norway company ,and as ranking captain the command was under Sylvanus Cobb, Jr., the great romance writer. After serving at the fort for five months the company was relieved by the Bangor militia company, and of this the Vice-President had long been a member. Mr. Hamlin determined to go with his command and perform his whole military duty although he could easily have secured a substitute or a release.

When the Bangor company reached the

Originally published in Lewiston Journal Illustrated Magazine, 13 February 1909.

fort they immediately relieved the Lewiston and Norway men. It was the fortune of the writer to be on guard at Post number one at the time, this being the main entrance to the fortification. As this was the most important station, Private Hamlin was given the place. With all due solemnity, he was challenged on his approach to the gate and forced to give the password over the point of the bayonet placed against his portly stomach. It is safe to say that the next man who approached that spot was compelled to do exactly the same thing. After standing at his post for two hours he in his turn was relieved, and was marched back to the barracks by the corporal of the guard. He drew his rations of hard tack and coffee, and sat down, like a tailor, on the floor, to eat them. The boys all gathered around him, and for a full hour there was a hilarious time in that camp. Hamlin joked, told stories and entered heartily into the spirit of the occasion. In a short time came the order to fall in, and the Lewiston company marched away with the cheers and good wishes of the Vice-President of the United States ringing in their ears. Years afterward the writer met Mr. Hamlin in Bangor, and the two men sat down on a trunk at the railway station and had a long talk about the days of Auld Lang Syne. Hamlin assured him that he never enjoyed anything better than his military service at Fort McClary.

Hamlin was an able man, but it was not for his intellectual vigor that he was most beloved or for which he will be the longest remembered. After all it is not great intellectual ability that wins the love of mankind, but it is that touch of nature that makes the world akin. Hamlin possessed those homely virtues that are found in the common walks of life and which shine the brightest when surrounded with the charms of nature. He loved the country, and it was when on his farm that life to him seemed to be the sweetest and nature appeared in its loveliest garb. Nothing angered him more than to see anyone abuse either horse or dog, and he was never so happy as when listening to the warbling of birds, the lowing of cattle, and the bleating of lambs. His love of family and friends was almost equaled by his love of the animal creation.

The opening years of the nineteenth century were prolific in the birth of children who were destined to develop into great men, and head and shoulders above the majority stands the name of Hannibal Hamlin as one of the immortal few that were not born to die. It was strong stock from which he sprang. The Hamlin de Balon, who came over from Normandy with William the Conqueror in 1066 was a direct ancestor, and the English family of that name dates from the battle of Hastings.

It is unnecessary for the purpose of this article to trace this family down through a thousand years, but enough to know that the first Hamlin who came to America was among the second installment of the English Pilgrims. This was James Hamlin, who with his wife and children landed on Cape Cod in 1629 and became the founder of all the existing branches of that family tree in this country. Dying in 1690, he left a large family of children whose descendants spread out in different directions and over different states. Several grandsons came to Maine at the close of the Revolution, and among these were the twin brothers Cyrus and Hannibal. Cyrus Hamlin settled in Livermore, and being a medical graduate he at once commenced the practice of his profession. Dr. Hamlin married the daughter of old Deacon Livermore, patriarch of the town, and became intimately connected with the Washburn family of the same place. Here he remained until Paris Hill became the shire town of Oxford County, when with his wife and children he removed to that village.

The practice of Dr. Hamlin soon became very extensive, and his financial condition was such that he built a fine old-time colonial mansion, which still stands as one of the noted landmarks of Paris Hill. It was a place of culture and refinement, and the home of Hamlin soon became one of the social centers of the county. Not only was the doctor skilled in the medical art, but he was equally apt in the game of politics, and soon became sheriff of the county. Close by his residence was the old jail, while just in front was the noble common which still remains as the beauty spot of the town.

It was here on the 27th of August, 1809, that the son, Hannibal Hamlin was born, and here it was that he spent his boyhood days. As a child he was full of mischief and was an especial thorn in the side of good old Elder Hooper, the former parson of the Hill. It was manly mischief, however, for among all the legends of his early pranks, there are none of a malicious nature. The worst among them all was the joke, if such it can be called, that he played on a village skinflint: in company with several other boys, Hannibal went to the old man and told him that they knew where there was a tree filled with wild bees and honey. After much parleying, the hive was sold to the miser for the sum of three dollars, and the boys agreed to pilot him to the tree. This they did, and landed him directly under a huge nest of hornets that immediately proceeded to make things lively for the would-be purchaser. It is said that the people of the village freely forgave the boys even if the miser didn't.

Young Hannibal was a great lover of outdoor sports, and hunting, fishing, and boating became his chief amusements. As he grew older he developed into a powerful athlete, and in all sports requiring strength and endurance, he became

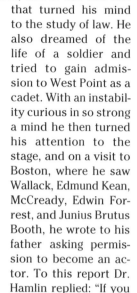
HANNIBAL HAMLIN

a recognized champion. At all the old-time musters he was a regular attendant, and wrestling was one of the favorite games on those occasions. In this sport he was an acknowledged master, and at one of these times was challenged by a burly blacksmith of giant strength. The trial commenced, and skill and speed won the day. In less time than it takes to tell the story, the bully was on his back while Hannibal was receiving the cheers and congratulations of the crowd. The stories of his physical prowess have become classics on Paris Hill, and round a score of firesides they are still recounted with an honest pride.

Dr. Cyrus Hamlin was a Federalist in politics when he first settled on Paris Hill, but later became an ardent Whig. Hannibal, on the other hand, had ideas of his own, and refusing to follow his father's footsteps, became equally devoted to Jefferson and the democracy. He was a born politician, and even before he had attained his majority became recognized as one of the most aggressive and able among the Democratic leaders.

The early education of young Hamlin was obtained in the schools of Paris Hill and Hebron Academy, while this was supplemented by the experience learned in the stern school of life. In the village of Paris Hill, Governor

Enoch Lincoln had his home, and from that stern patriot Hannibal Hamlin received those ideas of human liberty and that hatred of slavery which developed into a passion in later years. His mind was enlarged and broadened out by his free access to the great library owned by the governor, and it was this fact that turned his mind to the study of law. He also dreamed of the life of a soldier and tried to gain admission to West Point as a cadet. With an instability curious in so strong a mind he then turned his attention to the stage, and on a visit to Boston, where he saw Wallack, Edmund Kean, McCready, Edwin Forrest, and Junius Brutus Booth, he wrote to his father asking permission to become an actor. To this report Dr. Hamlin replied: "If you want to be a fool, and give up opportunities for a great career, you can go on the stage, but if you want to be sensible and make use of your talents in a sensible calling, come home!" And the boy came home!

The next few years were devoted to various callings. He picked up a smattering of civil engineering and also taught several terms of school. Then he commenced the study of law and was deeply engaged in Blackstone when his father was stricken with a fatal illness and in a few days was dead. This event changed many of his plans, and for a time he again settled down to a quiet life in Paris Hill.

In 1829 came the exciting election of Andrew Jackson. Although barely turning his majority, Hamlin at once took the stump for "Old Hickory," and became an effective and important factor in the campaign which followed. Shortly after this he and Horatio King bought a small weekly paper called *The Jeffersonian* that had been established at Paris Hill. This the partners continued to run for a few months and then Hamlin sold out and devoted his whole attention to his law studies.

The next move was to enter the law office of Fessenden & Deblois in Portland, as a student, and here he imbibed a still deeper hatred of slavery as well as more legal lore. On his return to Paris Hill in 1833 he was admitted to the bar, and shortly afterwards married the daughter of Judge Emory, one of the great legal lights of the State.

The next few years were more or less of a struggle. For a short time he practiced law in the town of Lincoln, and then went to Hampden. At that time this place was more of a town than it is today, and in a short time the young lawyer had built up a fine practice. Here he continued until his election to Congress in 1843, and the little office where he received his clients still remains as one of the landmarks of the old maritime town.

While the practice of law was congenial to his tastes, fate had marked out another and a higher course for him to follow. His election to Congress had brought out other and stronger qualities, and from that time his life became one that was devoted to the public.

The early political career of Hannibal Hamlin is chiefly interesting for its connection with the rise and formation of new political combinations and parties. From the first Jackson campaign in 1829, the Democratic party was in full swing in Maine the greater part of the time down to 1856. This party was the early love of Hamlin and by it he was first elected to the Legislature. There he remained for five successive terms and by his ability and aggressive nature became recognized as one of its greatest champions. This was the formative period of his character, and it was this service that gave him the parliamentary experience that was the foundation of his subsequent career. He was terrible in invective, and on one occasion, when a tippling member had ridiculed his swarthy complexion, Hamlin completely crushed him by saying:

"Almighty God gave me my complexion. The brandy bottle was the cause of yours! Which is the more honorable?"

The question of slavery was beginning to cast its dark shadows across the political horizon of the country long before Hamlin had acquired more than a local fame. For this institution he had an inborn hatred. The great Democratic leader, John C. Calhoun, was weaving a states rights web as a bulwark and last refuge for the perpetuation of slavery, and Hamlin, true to his convictions, clearly foresaw the coming storm and the realign-

ment of political parties. One of his first speeches in Congress was a bitter attack on the institution of slavery, and this was sufficient to place him out of harmony with all the great leaders of his party. The fatal victory of Polk in 1844 only widened the chasm, although it strengthened Hamlin in his own state. In 1848 he was elected to the United States Senate, and from that time on his star was in the ascendant. Serving in the golden period of American oratory, he was yet able to hold his own with such men as Webster, Calhoun, Clay, Benton, and Thomas Corwin. It was then that he became familiar with Abraham Lincoln, who was serving his only term in Congress, although he had no actual acquaintance with the man until associated with him on the presidential ticket in 1860.

Between 1850 and 1855, political events multiplied with great rapidity, and the relations between Senator Hamlin and his party became strained to the breaking point. State after state north of the Mason and Dixon line was swinging into the abolition column, while the temper of the Southern Democratic leaders was becoming more intolerant. The noble Sumner was stricken down by the ruffian Preston Brooks, and the heart of the entire North was being aroused. The end was near, and, shortly after the repeal of the Missouri Compromise, Hamlin arose in his seat in the Senate and formally withdrew from the Democratic party. It was the turning point of his political life and gave the entire abolitionist sentiment of the nation new life and new hope.

The desertion of Hamlin from its ranks sounded the death knell of the Democratic party in Maine, and from that blow it never recovered. The Republican party was formed, and he became one of its founders and cornerstones. He was a warm supporter of Fremont and Dayton in 1856, and, although the ticket was defeated, the Republican party made a tremendous stride in growth. Hamlin was elected governor of Maine as the first stepping-stone to power in the new party with which he was now affiliated, and very curiously he was re-elected to the Senate within a week from the time that he was chosen governor. Such unusual honors brought him into the limelight of the nation, and he at once became conspicuous as an available candidate for still higher promotions.

Then came the presidential campaign of 1860, and Mr. Hamlin was promptly discussed for the head of the ticket. Nothing but his own modesty prevented him from being brought forward as the candidate from New England, and had this been done his popularity throughout the North would have swept him into the chair that was won by the then almost unknown Lincoln. This he refused to even consider, but after the nomination of the latter the movement to place him on the ticket with Lincoln was too strong to resist. On the second ballot he received a great majority of the ballots and became the candidate for Vice-President.

The issue on the question of slavery was at last clear cut, and the campaign that followed was a stormy one. In order to break down his prestige the southern Democrats started the story that he had Negro blood in his veins, but this falsehood reacted upon its own authors. Poetry played no small part in the election, and one of the most popular songs sung at every rally ended with this chorus:

> Then give us Abe, and Hamlin, too,
> To guide our gallant ship;
> With stalwart boys to man the deck,
> We'll have a merry trip.

The remainder of the campaign and the events which followed need not be repeated here. They are a part of the history of our country and as such are familiar to every schoolboy in the land. Throughout the four long years of bloody war Hamlin was a tower of strength to the Union cause. In the hours of darkest danger he was ever by the side of Lincoln to cheer his heart and uphold his arm. On no other man did the martyr President lean with greater confidence, and no one was ever more ready to give aid and support. By a base conspiracy of political leaders he was defrauded of a renomination, and this act of injustice caused a terrible blow to the country. Hamlin was hurt neither in character nor reputation, but the nation alone suffered an irreparable injury. The ill-starred administration of Andrew Johnson brought the country almost to the verge of anarchy and delayed the work of reconstruction for many years. At a time when the helm of state needed the strong hand of a Lincoln or a Hamlin, it was destined to be guided by one who came perilously near figuring in history as a traitor. But that is history, and history need not be repeated here.

• • •

The public life of Mr. Hamlin did not close with the expiration of his term as Vice-President. He was again returned to the Senate, and there he became one of the staunchest supporters of Grant during his stormy administration. Later he was sent as minister to Spain, and by his diplomatic ability succeeded in smoothing out some of the tangled spots that disturbed the two countries at that time. In fact, he never lost his interest in public affairs and held several positions of minor note in his later years.

If Hannibal Hamlin's life had been grand, not less so was the final scene. On the 4th day of July, 1891, the end came swiftly and the great soul of Hannibal Hamlin passed beyond the Bar. Fitting indeed it was that he who had served his country so faithfully and well should receive the final summons on its natal day. The example that he set will not be forgotten, and his sterling virtues and rugged patriotism will remain as a standard for the generations yet to come.

A product of the intellectual and moral soil of Maine, the people of our State have a just pride in Hamlin's character and his achievements, and in this centennial year of his birth they can do no better than to recall his memory and the great services he rendered to his country in her hour of need.

ALSO SEE

"The Colored Troops," War Papers: Read Before the Commandery of the State of Maine 3, 1908, PortlandL Lefavor-Tower Company,

"The Governors of Maine: Second Series, No. 15 —Hannibal Hamlin," *Lewiston Journal Illustrated Magazine*, 14 July 1906, p. 4.

"Hannibal Hamlin Letters Revealed," *Portland Press Herald,* 22 August 1959, p. 14.

"Hannibal Hamlin of Maine, Vice Pres. of U.S. Under Lincoln and Born in the Same Year," *Portland Evening Express,* 11 February 1909 (Lincoln Centennial Supplement), pp. 5, 7.

"Hannibal Hamlin of Maine Vied with Abraham Lincoln in Prominence," *Lewiston Journal Illustrated Magazine*, 25 February 1928, p. 1.

"Hannibal Hamlin Served in Time of Crisis, Too," *Maine Sunday Telegram,* 1 September 1908, p. 7A.

"Hannibal Hamlin, the Forgotten Man as Millions Honor Lincoln," *Portland Press Herald,* 12 February 1948, pp. 1, 20.

"A Lark with Vice-President, Hannibal Hamlin and Military Service Under a Literary Captain," *Lewiston Journal Illustrated Magazine*, 2 December 1922, pp. 4–5.

"Men of Maine, No. 114: Hannibal Hamlin," *Portland Press Herald,* 10 April 1952, p. 10.

"100 Years Ago a Maine Man was Nominated as Lincoln's Running Mate by Republicans," *Portland Sunday Telegram,* 31 July 1960, p. 9A.

"Paris Hill Birthplace of Hannibal Hamlin, Lincoln's Vice President," *Portland Press Herald,* 7 January 1970, p. 6.

"Paris Hill Houses—Cross Roads Where Vice President Hannibal Hamlin Courted and Wed Both His Wives," *Lewiston Journal Illustrated Magazine*, 4 January 1941, p. 1.

"Was an Injustice Done Hannibal Hamlin in 1864?" *Lewiston Journal Illustrated Magazine*, 28 August 1909, p. 9.

"Woman Remembers as a Child Helping Entertain Vice-Pres. Hannibal Hamlin in Grandfather's Home in Alfred," *Lewiston Journal Illustrated Magazine*, 11 February 1939, p. 1.

AN ILLUSTRIOUS SON OF MAINE—
GENERAL O.O. HOWARD, CIVIL WAR HERO

EMILY HAM

Oliver Otis Howard was born in Leeds, Kennebec County (now Androscoggin County), November 8, 1830, on a portion of a vast section of land taken up by his great-grandfather, Roger Stinchfield, one of two pioneer brothers.

It was settled by his grandfather, Captain Seth Howard, and afterwards carried on by his parents, Roland Bailey and Eliza Howard.

His early boyhood days were spent on the farm, and his education actively begun in the district school, from which he attended Monmouth Academy, where he took a college preparatory course, and at the age of 16, he was enrolled at Bowdoin College. At the age of 19 he graduated. Unsolicited, he received an appointment from Maine as a cadet in the military academy at West Point, which he entered Sept., 1, 1850, and from which he graduated No. 4 in rank in June, 1854, and was appointed brevet second lieutenant of ordnance, and sent to Florida.

The same year he was made first lieutenant and was appointed instructor of mathematics at West Point, where he remained till the breaking out of the Civil War.

In June, 1861, he resigned his commission to take command of the Third Maine volunteers. The only company of this regiment which had had any military training was the Bath City Greys, a corps that had no superior in discipline and soldierly bearing of its members. The regiment was composed of hardy men, some of them lumbermen from the backwoods, and they felt a little timid at being commanded by a West Point Officer.

But they were quite astonished when, after making them an address, the young man took off his hat and led them in prayer. He, however, worked his way into their affections rapidly, for they soon found that he was a noble, conscientious and thorough officer. In the early morning of June 5th, the day after the regiment had been mustered into the United States service, they broke camp to leave for the seat of war.

On their passage through New York City an elegant regimental flag was presented them by Stewart L. Woodford, U.S. district attorney, in behalf of the sons of Maine, and received with appropriate acknowledgments by Col. Howard.

The first desperate battle in which the regiment participated took place at Bull Run. Col. Howard commanded a brigade, and he bore himself so gallantly that he was promoted to brigadier-general and assigned a brigade in the Army of the Potomac.

The Third Maine regiment was then turned over to Col. Staples. General Howard takes this occasion to say that he leaves his old regiment with many feelings of regret. When he left he carried with him the love of the whole regiment, which ever afterward felt inspired by the noble example of moral heroism he had given them.

In the Peninsular campaign General Howard lost his right arm at the battle of Fair Oaks, while in command of the Second brigade, which belonged to Richardson's division, that came across the flooded Chickahominy to the rescue of the hard-pressed army.

In the opening of the second day's fight,

ORIGINALLY PUBLISHED IN *LEWISTON JOURNAL ILLUSTRATED MAGAZINE*, 26 MAY 1917.

his brigade was put in front, and he held it steadily, only by great personal efforts and daring.

Riding backward and forward along the lines, he roused them by stirring appeals and reckless exposure of his own person. He was determined that the brigade should stand firm while he stood. His staff closed around him; but soon one, then another fell—his own brother was shot down beside him; yet he still kept riding through the fire. At last, a cannon ball carried away his right arm. It is said that he shook the mutilated stump in front of his brigade, and urged them to stand firm and behave like men.

As he was borne from the field, he passed General Kearny who had lost an arm, and jokingly said: "General, hereafter we will buy our gloves together."

This took him from the field during the rest of the Peninsular Campaign, but when McClellan organized his Maryland campaign, he was again in the saddle.

At the battle of Antietam he commanded Burns's brigade until General Sedgwick was wounded, when he took command of his division. At the battle of Fredericksburg he commanded a division in the Second corps, and at the battle of Chancellorsville he commanded the Eleventh corps.

At the battle of Gettysburg, after General Reynolds fell, mortally wounded, the command of the field fell on him, when he withdrew to Cemetery Hill, and here General Hancock, sent forward by Meade, found him, and the two agreed that there the great battle should be fought.

The battle of Gettysburg was the most important battle of the war, and the only one fought on Northern soil.

General Lee, with 90,000 men, was on the rapid march to overwhelm the diminished army of Hooker, capture Washington, and enrich the Confederacy by the plunder of the cities and the granaries of Pennsylvania. He concentrated his giant army at Gettysburg—Howard was sent forward to retard the advance of the rebels, while divisions of the Union army were hurrying, by forced marches, to the position where it was decided that the battle should take place.

With 8,000 men, General Howard met the brunt of battle and drove back the foe. His corps was posted on Cemetery Hill. Its capture was certain victory to the rebels. Lee, the ablest general of the rebel army, gathered all his men for that purpose. It was late in the afternoon; the enormous masses of Early's division advanced to the attack.

There stood General Howard, with his calm, manly face, an empty coat sleeve pinned to his shoulder, a reminder of a hard-fought battle. At the early dawn the batteries of General Howard thundered forth their renewal of the fight—and during all the time the rebel attack was pressed on the left; the summit of Cemetery Hill smoked and trembled with his artillery.

General Howard, who was guiding this tempest of war, was reclining on a green hillock close beside a tombstone, with his staff about him: he steadily watched the progress of the fight. "I have seen many men in action," said an eye-witness, "but I never saw one so cool as this general of the Eleventh corps."

The gloom of night spread over the awful scene, after the battle, and in the morning Lee commenced his retreat. With the fragments of his army he hastened back to Virginia, having lost 40,000 men. Gettysburg sealed the righteous act of Lincoln and decided the victory.

This incident was told by General Howard:

"After the battle of Chattanooga, my corps with Sherman had been in pursuit of the enemy for three days, and we had marched nearly 120 miles, and then marched back again. The result was, that our clothes and our shoes were worn out; the men had scarcely any blankets to cover them and

GENERAL O. O. HOWARD

they were toiling along on their journey home.

"Just as we had passed the mountain ridge, the division commander, thinking the men had marched far enough for one day, put them comfortably into camp, told them to make their coffee and then sent word to me to know if they had permission to remain there during the night. It was raining hard, but I knew the position was an improper one, and it was not the fulfillment of my orders, so that I sent back word, 'No; march forward to Tungston Station.' It was cold, dark and stormy, but the men had to be turned out again. How did they take it, do you ask? They went singing along the route (noble, patient fellows!) without a complaining word."

General Howard was a man whose religious convictions were intense, positive, entering into and coloring every event of his life.

When exposed to fire, there was no braver man than he. He went into action with a cool and quiet determination, inspired by a sense of a sacred duty to be performed. He was constantly censured for exposing himself to the fire of the enemy, but it is difficult to say whether the censure was just or not, for every commander of a corps of an army is the best judge of the necessities of the hour.

His personal appearance corresponded with his moral nature, and yet, with all the gentleness, kindness and patience he possessed, there was combined one of manly resolution and firmness of purpose that reveals the great leader.

It is difficult to conceive how a man so truly devotional as General Howard could love the profession of arms. It seems equally strange that one engrossed with military duties and associated with camp life should exhibit the Christian graces far more brightly than most men whose occupation kept them constantly under religious influences.

But whether on the march or the battlefield, he so maintained his Christian character that he was known throughout the army as the "Christian soldier," modest and retiring; his merits alone pushed him, despite himself, to eminence.

When in conversation with General Sumner, he said he did not aspire to the command of a corps, Sumner replied: "You surprise me, General Howard! I would command the whole world if I could."

Once, hearing a soldier swearing in the full blaze of the enemy's fire, General Howard approached him and said gently: "Don't swear so, my man. You may be killed at any moment. Surely you do not wish to go into the next world with dreadful oaths on your lips." On another occasion, while walking in the forest alone, he came upon two men quarreling with each other. He said to them: "Men, I am sorry you had such bad mothers."

They regarded him curiously, then looked at each other, when one of them, casting his eyes on the ground said: "I had not a bad mother! My mother was a good woman!" "But, replied General Howard, "she taught you to swear!" "No, indeed," protested the soldier, "she did not teach me to swear; she always punished me for swearing!" "And mine, also," cried the other, as if in doing some brave and meritorious deed, and the rough soldiers became like children, while vindicating the names and memories of their cherished mothers, the recollections or remembrances of whom may have been the only cases in their depraved hearts.

After this conversation they promised him they would try to live better lives. Noble, generous to a fault, he won all hearts by the power of love, yet in the tumult of a doubtful fight he was the impersonation of courage. To see him riding along the perilous edge of battle, all heedless of shot and shell, waving the empty sleeve aloft as a banner to his men, was enough to make heroes of cowards. It was a glory to any nation to have such a man at the head of its armies.

After the surrender of the rebel armies and the close of the war, General Howard was assigned to duty in the War Department on the 12th of May 1865, as commissioner of the Bureau of Refugees, Freedmen, and Abandoned Lands; he had charge of this bureau for the next seven years, and there never was a more striking instance of putting the right man in the right place than this appointment. It was much complained of at times, yet he was abundantly successful in its administration, particularly in its industrial and educational features, having founded many permanent institutions of learning, such as Howard University, Hampton Institute, Atlanta University, Lincoln, Fiske, Straight, and others. With the Negroes he was firm, yet just and kind, and [woprked to adjust] many difficulties [encountered by] this unfortunate race.

In 1872, he was chosen by General Grant, then President, and sent to make peace with the only Indian tribe then at war with the government, the Chrisicana Apaches; and also to settle numerous difficulties with other tribes in Arizona and New Mexico; all this General Howard accomplished without arms.

On complaints about his administration of the Freedmen's bureau there were two investigations; one in 1870 by a committee of Congress, which ended in a vote of thanks to him by the Representatives; the other was by a court of inquiry composed of seven general officers of the army. This ended in a complete acquittal of all the charges preferred against him and in unrestricted commendation.

He had hardly completed this bureau work when he was assigned to command the Department of the Columbia, August, 1874. During the next six years he, in command, passed through two Indian wars, one called the Nez Perce war, the other Piute and Bannock. He brought the wars, after many battles and long-fighting campaigns to a successful termination.

In the spring of 1879 he captured another Indian tribe called the "Sheepeaters," near the Salmon River, brought them in as prisoners, and put them at work at Vancouver and their children at school. From the Department of the Columbia, in the winter of 1880–1881, he was assigned to command the Department of the Platte, to which he gave successful administration until his promotion to major general in the regular army, 19th of May, 1886.

He then passed to the military division of the Pacific, which included the Department of Columbia, of California and Arizona. This division he administered to the satisfaction of the War Department and the President until November, 1888, when he was transferred to command the military division of the Atlantic. This division he held until the divisions were broken up; after that he commanded the Department of the East, which was substantially the same as the division of the Atlantic, until his retirement by law, Nov. 7, 1894. He then removed to Burlington, Vt., where he resided until his death.

From 1897 to 1901, he was managing director of Lincoln Memorial University, an industrial school for whites at Cumberland Gap, Tennessee.

General Howard was the author of the following books: *Donald's School Days, Nez Perce Joseph, or the Nez Perces in Peace and War, Agenor de Garparin* (a biographic sketch, and partly a translation), *General Taylor* (in the Great Commander series), *Fighting for Humanity, Personal Experiences Among the American Indians,* and numerous articles, a part of them of a military character, but the most on subjects of current interest, published by syndicates, monthlies and dailies, appearing at all times from 1865 to 1901.

General Howard prepared lectures upon the lives of Grant, Sherman, Thomas and Slocum, also upon war subjects and others of public interest, and delivered them with acceptance before large audiences; in fact, his lectures seemed to be in greater demand than his writings, although his books found ready publishers.

During the Spanish-American war, he served on the Y.M.C.A. commission, speaking in all the camps and visiting Santiago, Cuba. Few military men reach such an eminence as General Howard, and while the career of more brilliant men will lose luster with time, his name will shine among the honored sons of Maine who served the country so faithfully, and future history will accord him a high place in the temple of military fame. His whole life was a sermon preached to the government, the army and the people.

Also See

"'Christian Soldier' General Howard of Leeds," *Lewiston Journal Illustrated Magazine,* 3 February 1945, pp. 7–8.

"Howard University, 100 Years Old, Was Founded by General from Maine," *Portland Sunday Telegram,* 7 May 1967, p. 3D.

"Maine at Last to Erect Fitting Memorial to Her Famous Son, Gen. O. O. Howard, Hero of Gettysburg," *Lewiston Journal Illustrated Magazine,* 21 February 1931, pp. 1–2.

"Men of Maine: Oliver Otis Howard," *Portland Press Herald,* 11 April 1952, p. 16.

"Oliver Otis Howard, a Maine Hero," *Lewiston Journal Illustrated Magazine,* 8 September 1928, p. 2.

"Sketch of Major-General O. O. Howard," *Northern Monthly* 1, April 1864, pp. 102–105.

Two Generals in Rebel Grey, Danville Leadbetter and Zebulon York, Were State of Mainers

FRED HUMISTON

It is common knowledge, or at least it should be, that the State of Maine furnished the Union Army and Navy in the Civil War with more men, proportionately, than did any other state. In fact, the City of Portland alone, sent off 5,000 of its sons—and Portland was a much smaller city in those exciting days.

It is not so commonly known, however, that Maine gave the Union several of its generals; men who earned the right to wear the stars in battle. These brave officers led the untried Maine soldiers in actions that saved the self-same Union time and again: Howard, Ames, Chamberlain, Berry, to name a few.

These are names to conjure with, yet this is not their story. It is a concise and factual account of two other men who left the old Pine Tree State to achieve success in both civilian and military life, men who also became generals and fought bravely in battle, like other Mainers.

One of these officers became attached to the high command; at times he served as adviser to divisional chiefs in the field. The other was a fire-eating field officer. Both fought to the very end. There is only one seam in the bright pattern of their careers: they wore uniforms of the wrong color!

The writer found this research fact a hard one to swallow, and no doubt the reader, if he is a Mainer, is still in a state of shock. But many southerners fought on our side (Major Anderson of Sumter and Old "Pop" Thomas, for example).

No, we have no reason to feel mortified by the knowledge that two of Maine's sons fought on the wrong side. On the contrary, we should regard their records with pride, for they were brave and honorable men. Circumstances no doubt had a large part in forming their decision to join the Confederate cause, nor do we know the amount of soul-searching behind it. It was a war of father against son, of one brother against another.

The western cattlemen have a name for steers that stray from the herd. They call them mavericks.

Can we not, therefore, take the broad-minded view; that if these men, Danville Leadbetter and Zebulon York, strayed from the straight and narrow trails of orthodoxy, it was only that—and they still remained Mainers.

Danville Leadbetter

Danville Leadbetter was born August 26, 1811, at Leeds, Maine, also the birthplace of the famous Union general, O. O. Howard. . . .

Graduated from West Point in 1836, third in his class, he served in all parts of the country as an engineer officer in the construction of fortifications.

He resigned his commission Dec. 31, 1857, at Mobile, where he had been occupied the preceding four years in the construction and repair of the harbor forts. He was offered the appointment as chief engineer for the State of Alabama.

ORIGINALLY PUBLISHED IN *PORTLAND SUNDAY TELEGRAM*, 19 FEBRUARY 1961.

When Alabama left the Union, Leadbetter was commissioned as an engineer officer in the Confederate Army, and from Feb. 27, 1862, served with the rank of brigadier-general. (From Aug. 3, 1861, until Nov. 11, 1861, he served as acting chief of the Engineer Bureau, in Richmond.)

It was he who superintended the construction of the Mobile defenses, laid out

GENERAL DANVILLE LEADBETTER

Bragg's lines at Chattanooga and advised him respecting the disposition of the Confederate troops. He also accompanied General James "Old Pete" Longstreet to Knoxville, helping him plan the ill-fated campaign against that place. Later, he served as chief of engineers on the staff of General Joseph E. Johnston, in the great retrograde movement on Atlanta, and at the close of the war, was again at Mobile.

No record of General Leadbetter's capture has been found; or of his parole. The records do show that he first went to Mexico, and then to Canada, where he died at Clifton, Sept. 26, 1866. (Niagara Falls, Ontario, was called Clifton from 1856 to 1881.) Subsequently, he was interred in Magnolia Cemetery, Mobile.

It is difficult adequately to appraise General Leadbetter's services to the Confederacy. . . . Although apparently highly esteemed by the Confederate high command, from President Davis down, including Generals Bragg, Maury, Beauregard, Joe Johnston, "Old Pete" Longstreet, and other high officers, there was one standout.

This standout was General E. P. Alexander, the famous artilleryman and chief of Ordnance, Army of Northern Virginia, and one of the three artillery brigadier-generals in that army.

General Alexander took an exceedingly dim view of General Leadbetter, the Confederate from the damn Yankee Abolitionist State of Maine. Furthermore, he didn't hesitate to make plain his dislike for the "renegade Mainer," by word of mouth and in print.

"Everything Leadbetter touches goes wrong," Alexander said. "Why the adoption of his views by Longstreet at Knoxville robbed Old Pete of his few remaining chances of victory." Alexander then commented acidly, "that Leadbetter, being the oldest and most experienced engineer officer in the Confederate service, he was supposed to be the most efficient."

Zebulon York

Zebulon York was born Oct. 10, 1819, at Avon, Franklin County, Maine. Educated at Wesleyan Seminary, Kent's Hill, Maine, he later attended Transylvania University, Kentucky. From there he went to the University of Louisiana, from which he was graduated in law. Evidently York liked the South and the southern way of life. He decided to stay. He worked hard and became the leading attorney of Vidalia, Louisiana. Like everyone else, he dabbled in cotton; before long he had accumulated a large fortune in cotton planting.

GENERAL ZEBULON YORK

At the outbreak of the Civil War, this native Mainer and his partner owned six great plantations, with 1,700 Negro slaves. Together, the two men were about the largest slave owners in the entire South. The annual production of their plantations was 4,500 bales, and they paid the largest realty taxes in the state.

York organized a company of the 14th Louisiana Infantry, and was successively elected its major, lieutenant-colonel, and colonel. He fought with his regiment on the Peninsula and throughout the Seven Days Battles; also, at Second Manassas, in Maryland, and at Fredericksburg.

During Chancellorsville, York was on recruiting duty in Louisiana. However, he returned to his regiment in time to lead it at Gettysburg.

York was promoted to brigadier-general May 31, 1864, during the Virginia campaign and given the remnants of Hays' and Stafford's old Louisiana brigades.

Gallantly leading his troops in the Shenandoah Valley during the summer and autumn, his left arm was so badly shattered at the Battle of Winchester, Sept. 19, that amputation was required.

On his recovery, York then engaged in recruiting among the foreign-born Union prisoners of war confined in Confederate camps, and was on this duty when the war ended. He was paroled May 6, 1865.

York was financially ruined by the course of events following the surrender. The Carpet Baggers immediately pounced on his huge real estate holdings, his chattels were sold, and his bank accounts nonexistent. In later years he operated the York House at Natchez, Mississippi, becoming well-known throughout the South as a hotel man. Natchez is where this son of Maine died, Aug. 5, 1900, and it is where he is buried.

Hardly had the battle smoke blown away and the dust settled on the war-rutted roads of Virginia, when a new and united nation began slowly to emerge. Painfully, at first, the old hates dwindled with the fierce scream of the Rebel yell among the southern hills, but true men, both North and South finally brought to fruition Abraham Lincoln's dream of unity forever.

And now, 100 years after the opening of the great conflict, it is comforting knowledge to the generous-minded Mainers, that those two lonely graves in the Deep South are not so far away; that actually, they are in friendly soil. For we are all Americans together, both the living and the dead—as in fact, we always were!

Also See

"At Least Four Men Were Confederate Officers," *Portland Sunday Telegram,* 24 July 1966, p. 8A.

"Bowdoin Graduates in Confederate Army," *Lewiston Journal Illustrated Magazine,* 24 April 1915, pp. 10–11.

Battles, Campaigns, and Events

Of the Civil War's many battles, campaigns, and events, Maine people were involved in a surprising number. When the Warrington Navy Yard near Pensacola, Florida, was treacherously surrendered to the Confederacy on January 12, 1861, old salt William Conway (from Camden) was chained for refusing to haul down the American flag. But he never received an official medal for his conduct, and died an obscure figure in November 1865, while still in service.

The first of many thousand Civil War casualties, Sumner H. Needham was born in Norway, Maine, and moved to Essex County, Massachusetts, as a young man. In spring 1861, Needham joined the Sixth Massachusetts Regiment. On April 19, a mob attacked the regiment as they marched through Baltimore on their way to Washington, and Needham fell mortally wounded from a bullet.

President Lincoln demonstrated his commitment to limit (and untimately end) slavery by executing Portland-born Nat Gordon on February 7, 1862. Nat, the captain of the *Erie,* had been captured at sea with a cargo of slaves in 1860. It is something of a surprise to learn that the only man to be convicted and executed in the United States for piracy and slave trading was a Mainer.

On March 9, 1862, young Williston Jennings, a North Wayne native, witnessed the battle between the *Monitor* and *Merrimac.* He apparently observed the entire four-hour battle firsthand from his vantage point aboard the nearby *Cambridge.* His letter home describes the battle and also gives an excellent account of the events that took place for six days afterward.

George Stone's article on the siege of Charleston (March 13, 1863 to February 18, 1865) is interesting on several levels. It provides an overview of Civil War signal codes, details information about the siege's progress, and vividly recreates the recapture of

Fort Sumter. Stone himself was born in New York. After the war he earned his baccalaureate and master's degrees from Wesleyan University. Professor Stone taught for seven years at Kent's Hill School in Readfield, Maine. While there, he married his second wife, Mary H. Hill, of Richmond, and also wrote a monograph in the glacial geology of Maine.

On the home front, strange though it may seem, Confederates invaded Maine by land and sea.

On the evening of April 27, 1863, the *Caleb Cushing*, a Revenue Service cutter headquartered in Portland, was captured by Confederate raiders, who set their chained prisoners adrift in small boats and set their prize afire about five miles off Peaks Island. (Ironically, when the *Caleb Cushing*'s crew were rescued, they were initially treated as traitors, rather than unfortunate patriots, for it was believed they had deserted and stolen the ship themselves.)

The keystone to Union victory in the Civil War was the 20th Maine Regiment's defense of Little Round Top during the battle of Gettysburg in July, 1863. In this section's exciting account of the action, Joshua Chamberlain reveals that he survived only because of a Confederate sharpshooter's whim.

The biggest Medal of Honor fiasco ever to occur was centered on a Maine regiment. Eight hundred and sixty-four members of the 27th Maine, including approximately five hundred and sixty who didn't even stay, were awarded the medals for remaining in Washington four extra days beyond their term of enlistment in order to protect Congress and the President. (At the time it was thought that Lee might double back from Pennsylvania; instead, he stood and fought at Gettysburg.) In 1917, all the erroneously awarded medals were revoked by a review board.

Hebron, Maine, native, Caroline S. Tripp was an eyewitness to the New York City draft riots of July 12–17, 1863. They were in response to Lincoln's May 8 proclamation that a draft would begin that month. A bakery and confectioner's clerk, Ms. Tripp was trapped in her workplace for three days. From her description of lynchings, it is clear that many Northerners resented Blacks for having dragged them into war.

F. E. Stanley, the eyewitness author of the Kingfield Rebellion article, is one of the famous brothers who developed the Stanley Steamer. On July 23, 1863, state troops were dispatched to heavily Democratic Kingfield to put down draft disturbances. But expected resistance did not materialize, and the rebellion ended on a rather festive note.

The Spring 1864 Red River campaign of General Banks (March 16 to May 13) involved many Maine troops (including

one woman disguised as a man). It was a military fiasco for several reasons. About the only good thing that occurred was that Maine lumbermen from the 29th and 30th regiments saved the Union fleet by building dams to raise the river's water level and provide clearance enough for the Union boats to escape downriver.

The Confederates had a few coastal raiders in addition to their many blockade runners. The most notorious was the *Alabama*. It aroused bitter resentment not only because of its success (it sank at least two Maine vessels, The *Dorcus Prince* in May 1863 and the *Anna F. Schmidt* in June 1863), but because, in reality, it was an English ship, "armed with British guns to war with a country with which she professed to be at peace." On June 15, 1864, the *Alabama* was finally tracked down and challenged by the *Kearsarge*, a vessel built in Kittery, Maine. The *Kearsarge* crew's calculated and accurate shooting won the day.

Within thirty days during the spring of 1864 (May 19 to June 18), the 1st Maine Artillery, a unit of some 1,600 men, suffered almost 1,200 casualties. It was the heaviest loss of any Union regiment in the war. Should you wonder how this could happen to an artillery unit, the answer is they fought as infantry in some of the bloodiest civil war battles, including Spotsylvania, Cold Harbor, and Petersburg.

On July 18, 1864, a Confederate raiding party invaded Calais, Maine. Their leader, Captain William Collins and his two comrades were captured without fight. Later, Collins escaped from the Maine State Prison and fought again for the Confederates.

On April 9, 1865, Lieutenant Wilmer McClean must have felt like fainting. After Bull Run, the first great battle of the Civil War, was fought on his property, he had fled to obscure Appomattox for relief. Now, four years later, the war had followed him, and Grant and Lee were signing articles of unconditional surrender in his living room. This occasion marked the nation's second birth, and as Joshua L. Chamberlain's memoir indicates, he was at the forefront of the ceremony. Chamberlain commanded the parade of surrender in which Lee's army formally handed in their arms and colors on April 12, 1865. The war was finally over, and Chamberlain and his Maine men could at last return to the state and homes they left so long before

WILLIAM CONWAY,
A FORGOTTEN CAMDEN HERO

JOHN O. JOHNSON

This is the story, long forgotten, of the first patriot of the War of the Rebellion, and of the first surrender of the forces of the United States Navy to the rebels. I have reference to the disgraceful surrender of the United States Navy Yard, at Warrington, near Pensacola, Fla., January 12, 1861, which was wholly brought about by the traitorous acts of officers holding commissions in and wearing the uniform of the United States Navy. It is a long and interesting story of which very little is known. I do not intend, however, to give it in detail—simply enough to establish the record of a patriot. As often happens, he was a man from Maine, and he was but a bluejacket.

The officers of the yard at that time were as follows: Commandant Captain James Armstrong, an old man who had served in the navy for more than fifty years; he was a midshipman in the War of 1812, and had recently been invalided home from the command of the squadron in India with chronic diarrhea, from which he was a great sufferer. When he was ordered to that station from his home in Boston, he protested against it, saying that he was too old, and too feeble to be ordered to that climate. But his protest was without avail. He went, leaving his family at home, with the hope that within a few months at most he would again be ordered North. His only associates were the officers of the yard. The two officers who were nearest to him in rank and position, and the ones looked to for advice and counsel, were traitors to their country, though officers in the United States Navy, and both of them were from the North.

A few days before the surrender of the yard, the gunboat *Wyandotte*, Lieutenant-Commander O. N. Berryman, arrived at the yard from Key West, and the store-ship *Supply*, Commander Henry Walke, also arrived with stores from New York. Neither of these vessels amounted to much for offensive purposes, but they could have defended the yard against all offenders had they been ordered to do so. The *Supply* was on her way to Vera Cruz, but had called at Pensacola to land supplies. These were the only vessels there, and they had not been in port twenty-four hours before Commanders Walke and Berryman, as well as their officers, began to distrust the loyalty of the officers of the yard, especially Farrand, and his aide and brother-in-law Renshaw. They saw but too plainly how completely the venerable and perplexed commandant was in the hands of the traitors by whom he was surrounded, and among whom the northerners were the vilest of all.

There were three forts in the vicinity of the navy yard, namely Forts McRee, Barrancas and Pickens, which that rebel sympathizer, Secretary of War Floyd, had prevented being reinforced. But on January 3, 1861, the headquarters of the army at Washington had awakened from the lethargy that Secretary Floyd had purposely put upon it long enough to send an order to Lieutenant A. J. Slemmer of the army, who was commander of the three forts, to take measures to prevent either of the forts in Pensacola harbor from seizure by

ORIGINALLY PUBLISHED IN: MILITARY ORDER OF THE LOYAL LEGION OF THE UNITED STATES, EDS., *WAR PAPERS: READ BEFORE THE COMMANDERY OF THE STATE OF MAINE,* PORTLAND, 1908, VOL. 3.

surprise or assault, consulting first the commandant of the navy yard, who would probably have instructions to cooperate with him. This order reached Lieutenant Slemmer January 9, but he knew very well that he would be unable to hold the three forts with but forty-six men, all the force he had. He decided to abandon Forts McKee and Barrancas, which were on the main land, and occupy Fort Pickens, which was on Santa Rosa Island, at the mouth of Pensacola harbor, if it was possible for him to do so. What could be thought of the loyalty and intelligence of the headquarters at Washington which at the eleventh hour could dictate such an order!

Calling on the commandant of the navy yard immediately, Lieutenant Slemmer found that that officer was in receipt of orders from the Navy Department to cooperate with him in his measures of defense, and he received from him (Armstrong) the assurance of assistance in every way, including the services of the *Supply* and the *Wyandotte.* The commandant said that he did not think that he could hold the navy yard if attacked, but promised to have Slemmer and his command, together with supplies and ammunition, taken over to Fort Pickens at one-thirty P.M. on that day, January 9.

But no sooner had Lieutenant Slemmer left the office than the treacherous Farrand slipped in, and so worked upon the mind of the old man that he failed to keep faith with Slemmer. Farrand made Armstrong believe that it would be an outrage, a crime, to cooperate with this young army lieutenant, and so provoke a bloody conflict with the Florida state troops that would hand down his name in perpetual execration everywhere throughout the country. In this strait, Lieutenant Slemmer again visited the commandant and remonstrated with him for his failure to keep his promise. Finally, in the presence of Farrand, Berryman and Renshaw, Captain Armstrong gave orders for the *Wyandotte* to be at the wharf at Barrancas at four o'clock P.M., on that day in readiness to transport the garrison to Fort Pickens.

Nevertheless the *Wyandotte* did not move that day. Farrand had evidently gotten in his dastardly work again. His game was delay. He was in constant communication with the rebels at Pensacola, but nine miles away. He knew that within forty-eight hours they would demand the surrender of the navy yard, and he hoped the way to occupy Fort Pickens would be opened also. At eight o'clock the next morning, which was the tenth, Lieutenant John Irwin of the *Wyandotte* went to Fort Barrancas with a big scow, which the army folks at once loaded with provisions and ammunition, brought together all the other boats they could collect, without orders from the commandant, and towed them all across the harbor to Fort Pickens; Lieutenant-Commander Berryman also transferred from his ship to the fort thirty ordinary seamen and thirty stand of arms. At this time the old captain, under the malign influence that he could not escape, and distracted by the complications surrounding him, began to give such erratic and contradictory orders that Commander Walke of the *Supply* and Lieutenant-Commander Berryman of the *Wyandotte* made up their minds that their principal business was to cooperate with Lieutenant Slemmer of the army in making Fort Pickens secure from the attack of the rebels.

On the day of the occupation of Fort Pickens, Lieutenant Erben, of the *Supply*—now Rear-Admiral Erben (retired)—went down to Fort McRee with a boat's crew from the *Supply* and threw into the sea all the powder stored there, to prevent its falling into the hands of the rebels. Twenty-two thousand pounds were thus destroyed. When he returned from that duty, Lieutenant Erben went on shore in the evening, called at the commandant's house and reported what he had done, and as the navy yard was being threatened by the rebel troops at Pensacola, volunteered to destroy the ammunition in the naval magazine located a short distance outside the navy yard.

Captain Armstrong sent for Farrand, to advise with him in relation to the matter. That officer immediately advised the arrest of Erben and sending him on board ship, asserting that he (Erben) was drunk. But this the commandant refused to do. At this Farrand rose up in great rage, and throwing a chair at Erben's head, left the room in great abruptness. Erben remained for a short time, talking with the commandant, and, bidding him good night, departed. The moment he got outside the front door Farrand, who had been lying in wait for him on the piazza, stepped up to him and, shaking his fist in his face, exclaimed:

"Damn you, I will teach you how to treat your superior officers."

He was so violent that Erben caught him by the throat, saying: "Damn you, I will have you hanged as a traitor, as you are."

They rolled off the piazza in their struggle, and Erben landing uppermost, Farrand began to shout for assistance. At this, Renshaw, who had been in hiding in the shrubbery, came to Farrand's assistance. But Assistant Surgeon W. A. King, of the *Supply,* who had come on shore with Erben, came up on

Erben's side, and the two traitors, seeing a row very imminent in which they were likely to come out second, ran off to the other quarters, telling the officers' wives that Erben intended to blow them all up.

Farrand's whole conduct had been so unmistakably disloyal, that Erben anti the other loyal officers of the navy hall determined to seize him at the first opportunity and carry him on board ship. Lieutenant Berryman said that he would receive him on board the *Wyandotte,* and if necessary put him in the coal bunkers for safe keeping. But Farrand was too wary. He felt that he was suspected and obnoxious to the officers and men on board the ships, and that the best measure of personal safety for him was to keep away from the waterfront. He could not be induced to approach the wharf on any matter of duty whatsoever. Had he ventured there, he was sure to have been seized, and he seemed to have had such a presentiment. He carried things with a high hand at the upper end of the yard with the distracted old commandant;

but when he looked in the direction of the wharf, and saw the old flag under which he had been educated, his conscience made him a coward.

"He made a narrow escape," says Erben; "for had he been captured he would never have got on shore again." And Lieutenant Erben goes on to say that whatever orders Captain Armstrong gave for the protection of the yard, Farrand without his knowledge would countermand. Farrand knew the very hour that Victor M. Randolph would present his rebel forces at the gate of the navy yard, and was there to receive and welcome him, dressed in the full uniform of a United States naval officer; while Captain Armstrong was kept in entire ignorance of the whole affair and did not know that the rebels were approaching till they were reported at the gate, and the two commissioners selected by the governor of Florida were conducted to him by Farrand. All the details of the surrender were conducted by Farrand, even to the punishing of the faithful old quartermaster for refusing to haul down the flag in surrender when ordered to do so by the traitor Renshaw.

This faithful old seaman was William Conway, of Camden, Me. He had obeyed the order to stand by the halyards, but when ordered to haul down the flag in capitulation he said: "I will not do it, sir! That is the flag of my country under which I have sailed many years. I love it; and will not dishonor it by hauling it down now."

Renshaw had to do the traitorous work with his own hands, and then he and Farrand set about punishing the old quartermaster by putting him in irons for his fidelity to the old flag, which they had dishonored while holding the commission of an officer in the United States Navy; for Farrand resigned on the sixteenth and Renshaw on the twenty-first, after they had surrendered the yard on the twelfth. Their resignations were accepted by the Secretary of the Navy, when they should have been dismissed with dishonor and hung when caught. Erben says that the yard easily could have been defended, had the *Supply* and *Wyandotte* been ordered up to protect the approach to the yard, which was a road that ran for a half mile along the beach. As it was, the feeble old commandant was so hoodwinked and muddled by his traitorous officers, that he surrendered to a rabble of about four hundred Florida and Alabama troops. The two ships in the offing hoisted all the flags they had in defiance of the disgraceful surrender.

In the surrendering of this navy yard, we have the very singular and striking circumstance of a captain in the United States Navy acting as a commissioner, appointed by the governor of Florida, to receive the surrender of the property of the United States in the name of the State of Florida, a territory the United States had purchased from Spain but forty-two years before, and had spent millions for the protection of its people in the war with the Indians, known as the Florida War. The two commissioners appointed by the governor of Florida to receive the surrender of the navy yard were Colonel W. H. Chase, of the Florida state militia, and Captain Victor M. Randolph, of the United States Navy. Florida passed the ordinance of secession January 10, 1861. On that day Randolph sent in his resignation as a captain in the United States Navy, and on the same day was appointed a commissioner by the governor of the seceded State. But his resignation papers did not reach Washington till after the surrender of the yard.

A court martial was held at Washington on the conduct of Captain Armstrong in relation to his surrender of the Warrington Navy Yard, near Pensacola, Fla., on the following charges:

1st. Failing to take the ordinary and proper measures for the defense of said yard and property.

2d. Disobedience of orders and conduct unbecoming an officer.

This court convened at Washington, February 8, 1861, and consisted of the following officers: Captain George W. Storer, president; Captain Elie A. F. Lavallette and Captain Levin M. Powell. After a long session, Captain Armstrong was found guilty on both charges and was suspended for five years, half that time without pay.

It was during this trial that the noble conduct of the old quartermaster was brought to the front, and the following report in relation thereto was sent to the Secretary of the Navy:

Washington, D. C., April 3, 1861

The president and members and judge advocate of the court lately held in the City of Washington, D. C., for the trial of Commodore* Armstrong, beg leave respectfully to submit to the Honorable Secretary of the Navy, the propriety, justice and good policy of bestowing some appropriate mark of its approbation of the loyalty, spirit and good conduct of William Conway, quartermaster of the navy on duty at the navy yard at Warrington, Fla., when the same was surrendered on the twelfth of January, 1861; who with manly pride and in a spirit of patriotic devotion refused to obey the order to haul down the national flag on the occasion of that surrender. The evidence of this honorable devotion to the dignity and credit of the flag of his country is found in the record of the testimony in Commodore Armstrong's case. Respectfully submitted by order of court.

A. B. Magruder, Judge Advocate

To this report Secretary Welles added these words:

It appears from the testimony taken in Captain Armstrong's case that William Conway, an aged seaman, doing duty as quartermaster in the Warrington (Pensacola) Navy Yard at the time of its surrender, when ordered by Lieutenant Renshaw to haul down the national flag, promptly and indignantly refused to obey the order. The love and reverence thus impulsively exhibited for his country's flag in the hour of its peril is not the less worthy of being called noble and chivalric because displayed by one in an humble station. It is the more deserving of commendation, for subordinates in the service are not usually expected to set examples of patriotism and fidelity to their trusts, but to follow them. The department deems it no more than strict justice to William Conway that this testimonial from the court in his behalf should be made known throughout the service. It therefore directs that this general order be publicly read, as early as practicable after its receipt, by the commander of all naval stations and all vessels in the navy in commission in the presence of the officers and men under their command.

*He is elsewhere in the papers referred to as "Captain Armstrong," and January 12, 1861, he signed the letter to the Secretary of the Navy announcing the surrender, "James Armstrong, Captain United States Navy."

The following is the order of Secretary Welles to Flag Officer McKeen, United States Navy, commanding Gulf Blockading Squadron, for the transmission of a gold medal to Quartermaster Conway, and other communications relative thereto are added:

Navy Department, November 11, 1861

SIR:—I herewith transmit a letter from the department to William Conway, who is on board one of the vessels of your squadron, together with a gold medal presented to him by his countrymen in California, as a testimonial of their appreciation of his conduct in refusing to haul down the flag of his country at the surrender, at Pensacola, to the rebels, on January 12, 1861.

A copy of the letter addressed to William Conway by the citizens who presented the medal, and of the letter of Major-General Halleck, the bearer of it to the department, is also submitted.

You will please to have the medal handed to William Conway on the quarter-deck of the vessel to which he belongs, in the presence of the officers and crew thereof, and the correspondence read at the same time. I am, respectfully, your obedient servant,

Gideon Welles

Navy Department, November 11, 1861
William Conway
United States Gulf
Blockading Squadron

SIR:—It gives me great pleasure to cause to be delivered to you the accompanying letter and gold medal from your countrymen in California, presented to you as a testimonial of their high appreciation of your noble and patriotic conduct in refusing to haul down the flag of your country while others (your superiors in position) were wanting in fidelity to it. I also forward a copy of the letter of Major-General Halleck, who was selected as the bearer of these testimonials, and by his request I have directed them to be transmitted to you—which you will please to accept with the assurance of my regard. Very respectfully,

Gideon Welles
Secretary of the Navy
Washington, D.C.

November 6, 1861
Hon. Gideon Welles,
Secretary of the Navy

SIR:—I have received from certain citizens of California the accompanying letter and medal, to be delivered to William Conway, quartermaster United States Navy, as a mark of their appreciation of his noble conduct in refusing to haul down the flag of his country; but as I am unable to see Mr. Conway personally, I respectfully request they may be transmitted to him by the Navy Department. Very respectfully, your obedient servant,

H. W. Halleck, Major-General
United States Army

San Francisco, September 20, 1861
William Conway, Quartermaster
United States Navy

DEAR SIR:—The undersigned citizens of California from New England have read with pride and gratification the story of your brave and patriotic refusal to haul down the flag of your country. As a mark of our appreciation of your conduct, we request you to accept the accompanying medal of California gold, together with our best wishes for your prosperity and happiness.

F. W. Brooks, Henry L. Dodge,
F. A. Fabent, H. F. Cutter,
W. T. Reynolds,
Henry F. Teschemascher,
Geo. J. Brooks, Geo. H. Faulkner
(and 140 others)

With such testimonials as these, one would little think the person receiving them would be almost entirely forgotten in the lapse of forty-four years, but such indeed is the case. I well remember Conway, though I had not seen him since before the war. In 1858, when but a lad, I was first mate of the brig *Tocoa,* of Rockport, Me. Captain Thomas Fitzgerald was master, and the present Captain Ed. Harkness (if living) was second mate. William Conway, then termed an old man-o'-war's-man, was home on furlough, and having a sister living at Rockport (I have forgotten her name), he was staying with her. During the three weeks that we were getting the vessel ready for sea we saw much of Conway, as he spent a large portion of his time on board with us. We had to take the vessel to Rockland to haul out on the ways, and as we had no crew shipped, he volunteered with others to help work the vessel round to that port. In this manner I came to know him very well, so that when two and one-half years later, he refused to haul down the flag by order of the traitor Renshaw, I felt that I had more than a passing interest in the Camden sailor, and was proud that I knew him. During the time between the surrender of the navy yard at Pensacola and the reading on board every ship in the service of the general orders relative to his noble conduct, I had entered the navy as a volunteer officer and was attached to the U.S. bark *Midnight,* stationed as by fate's decree off Fort Pickens, in sight of the Pensacola Navy Yard, when this order reached us. At the reading of the same, with all hands at muster, and being the only officer from Maine, and in fact the only man on board ship with the exception of one ordinary seaman, from this state, I stretched to my utmost height and drank in patriotism and courage from the reading that lasted me through the four years that I served in the navy, helping me to make such a record as did not, I hope, disgrace my country, my state or my people.

Many years ago I learned through some source that Conway was dead. How, when and where he died I did not learn, but presumed that he died with his people at Camden and was buried with his ancestors. Of late I have had a desire to visit his last resting-place and to stand with bowed head beside his grave. While on my way to the Waymouth celebration, held at Thomaston, in July, 1905, I stopped off at Camden for that purpose. Judge of my disappointment, when I made inquiry for Conway in his native town, to find that no one knew of or had ever heard of him.

At last I inquired of an old friend, . . . Henry Payson, of Rockport, who had lived in the town for fifteen years and was a member of the G.A.R. Post. He had never heard of William Conway, but he made inquiry of an old gentleman named Ogier, who remembered something in relation to Conway and his history. Mr. Payson informed me that there was a lady named Conway living in Camden and kindly took me to her place. She proved to be a niece, who told me that she and a cousin of hers, Mrs. Louise E. Robbins, of Thomaston, were the only living relatives of William Conway; that she thought he died in Brooklyn, N.Y., in 1865 and that he was

buried in the naval cemetery there, but she was not certain. She also informed me that the gold medal was in the possession of the other niece, Mrs. Robbins.

As I stood by the beautiful monument erected in a Camden public square in honor of the country's defenders from that town, I was chagrined to learn that Conway's name, though perhaps "the noblest Roman among them all," was not written there. The thought occurred to me, why is this? If this same William Conway had been the commander of a ship in our navy, and had been commanded by an enemy of superior force to haul down the flag of his country as a token of surrender, and he had used the self-same words that he used at Pensacola, viz: "I will not do it, sir; it is the flag of my country, under which I have sailed for many years and I will not dishonor it now!" his name would have been sung in song and told in story down to the end of all time and a monument erected to perpetuate his memory. But being only a common sailor he died "unwept, unhonored and unsung," his name not even a memory in his native town.

This should not be. The tide of oblivion should not be permitted to set in that direction. In the language of Secretary Welles: "The love and reverence thus impulsively exhibited for his country's flag in the hour of its peril is not the less worthy of being called noble and chivalric because displayed by one in an humble station," and the following words from Kipling's "Recessional" would seem to be fitting here:

> God of our fathers, known of old,—
> Lord of our far-flung battle line—
> Beneath whose awful hand we hold
> Dominion over palm and pine—
> Lord, God of Hosts, be with us yet,
> Lest we forget—lest we forget.
>
> Far called our navies melt away,
> On dune and headland sinks the fire—
> Lo, all our pomp of yesterday
> Is one with Nineveh and Tyre!
> Judge of our Nation, spare us yet,
> Lest we forget—lest we forget.

I have said I was disappointed in learning that the name of William Conway had been forgotten in his native town. But on second thought it is not so surprising, for during the lapse of forty-four years or more the population of the thriving town of Camden has greatly changed, and it would be simply an impossibility for those born since the Civil War to have any personal remembrance of him; while with the older residents time has naturally dimmed the memory. Moreover, all the official documents relating to Conway were deposited in the Navy Department at Washington, where no outsider had access to them till within the past ten years.

Happily, in this time Congress had enacted a law for the publication of the records of the doings of the United States Navy in the War of the Rebellion, and for their distribution throughout the land in order to show to those, who care to know, what the navy did. From one of these books, *The Official Records of the Union and Confederate Navies in the War of the Rebellion* (series I, volume 4), I obtained my information relative to the Court of Enquiry before which Captain Armstrong was brought, and also the copies of the papers in relation to Quartermaster Conway which I have already read. Otherwise Conway has been allowed to sink out of sight; for up to the time I dug his name out from under the avalanche of forgetfulness, not one word had been said or written in relation to him, as far as I can learn, except in a very short and inaccurate sketch of the affair at Pensacola covering about one half-page in Abbott's *History of the War*, and a few words in *The Battles and Leaders of the Civil War* (volume 1, page 26), in connection with a pencil sketch of Conway by William Waud. From Rear-Admiral Joseph B. Coghlan, U.S.N., commandant at the Navy Yard at Brooklyn, N.Y., I learned that William Conway died at the naval hospital there November 30, 1865, while still in the service, and was buried in the naval cemetery at that place in a grave which cannot now be located.

When I read Admiral Coghlan's letter I should not have been more astounded had I been hit on the head with a hammer. For that record shows that in less than five years after Conway uttered those memorable words at Pensacola, refusing to dishonor the flag of his country by lowering it at the demand of traitors, and having died while still in the service of his country, at a home port and in a time of peace, his body was dumped into an unknown grave. For this almost criminal neglect I know not whom to censure. But someone blundered.

Surely the name of this loyal American sailor should be rescued from oblivion. I believe his name is fully as worthy of honor as is that of John Paul Jones, for while Conway was distinctively an American, Paul Jones claimed to be a citizen of the world. In Conway we have a brave old American tar, who shifted his quid of tobacco, gave the waistbands of his trousers a hitch, and stood as firm as the rock of Gibraltar for one country and one flag. For this I think his name should be placed on a pinnacle of fame, and what could be more fitting than to have this honored organization, which bears the proud title of the "Loyal Legion of the United States," take the first steps toward the erection of a suitable memorial in his honor! For who is there among us who would not have been thrilled to his fingers' ends could he have listened to the loyal words of that loyal old American sailor, "I will not do it, sir! It is the flag of my country under which I have sailed for many years, and I will not dishonor it by hauling it down now."

ALSO SEE

"The Conway Memorial," *Camden Herald*, 2 June 1960, p. 4.

A Norway Man, Sumner H. Needham, Was First Killed in Civil War

ANONYMOUS

Norway is proud of the distinction of being the birthplace of the first man [mortally wounded] in the war of the Rebellion. Sumner H. Needham was born at Norway, Me., Mar. 2, 1828, and lived in town for some years, going from Maine to Massachusetts, where he finally located in Lawrence.

[Needham was] killed in the Baltimore riots, [his] career . . . thus being cut off at the very beginning of the war. He was a brave man and had already proved his bravery by heroic conduct that had greatly endeared him to his friends. His portrait hangs in the G.A.R. hall of Norway and is one of the treasured possessions of Harry Rust Post. . . . [It shows a broad-faced, dark-haired man with a bushy beard and wide-set, somewhat wild-looking eyes.]

Sumner Henry Needham was the son of Evi and Maria (Latham) Needham, and was grandson of John Needham, the Revolutionary patriot and one of the earliest settlers of Norway. He was born at Norway March 2, 1828, and moved from here to Greenwood and then to Bethel. He was one of a large family of children, having four brothers and two sisters. Only two of the family are left, Mrs. Melinda Needham Bean of Bethel, and Mrs. Emma C. Newell of Saco, Maine. His brother, Charles M. Needham, was chief bugler in a Rhode Island cavalry, and died at Tampa, Florida, 1907.

When he lived in Bethel, Sumner Needham worked at first with his father on the farm, but when he was 21 he went to Law-rence, Massachusetts, and learned to do mechanical work. He married Miss Hannah Johnson, a Maine girl from Sanford, soon after he went to Lawrence. Their son, Sumner Henry Needham, was born in November, 1861. The last known of him, he lived in Lawrence. Mrs. Needham died a few years ago.

Sumner Needham joined the Lawrence Light Infantry and early in the spring of 1861, enlisted in the Sixth Massachusetts Regiment. The stormy passage of that regiment through Baltimore at the time the mob attacked the men of the regiment has been vividly described in history.

The men mustered on Boston common, and on April 17, 1861, started for Washington. On the 19th, in passing through Baltimore, from the Philadelphia to the Washington railroad station, the regiment was attacked by a mob. Four soldiers were killed, and the first shot was fired at Sumner H. Needham. The other soldiers whose names are known are Addison O. Whitney, and Luther C. Ladd, both of Lowell, Massachusetts.

The regiment finally reached the train on the Baltimore and Washington railroad, and soon afterward, arrived at the Capital. This riot, where Needham was killed, was the shedding of the first blood in the great Rebellion.

After Needham was shot he was taken to the Lombard street hospital and died on the

ORIGINALLY PUBLISHED IN *LEWISTON JOURNAL ILLUSTRATED MAGAZINE*, 28 MARCH 1908.

27th of April. He was a member of the Universalist church of Lawrence, and the day after his death, the church passed resolutions of sympathy for his afflicted family.

Mr. Needham had served a number of years in the Lawrence Light Infantry and had been First Lieutenant, but he had resigned and reenlisted in 1860, and was serving as corporal at the time of his death. He was taken to Lawrence, and his funeral was attended with special services as are seldom accorded to any but dignitaries high in office. Both state and city governments were present. He was buried in Bellevue cemetery, Lawrence. The city of Lawrence erected a thousand-dollar monument to his memory, and gave a deed of it to his widow.

ALSO SEE

"Echo of the Drum: Maine Rushed to Enlist," *Portland City Telegram,* 27 November 1960, p. 13D.

"Legislature in Emergency Session Rallied State at Civil War Outreak," *Kennebec Journal,* 16 November 1961, p. 13.

"Passage of the 6th Mass. Regiment Through Baltimore, April 19, 1861." *Maryland Historical Magazine* 14, March 1919, pp. 60–76.

THE FIRST AMERICAN SLAVER CONVICTED AS A PIRATE

C. NEWHALL FOGG

The blackest period of the country's history was that of the American slave trade, and the dreadful fate of Captain Nathaniel Gordon, born and raised in Portland, Maine, marked the beginning of the end of the infamous traffic.

When Nat Gordon was a young fellow at the York Street sea front home his father had built in 1740, he heard much of the slave trade, of the adventurous life of the slaver, the mystery of barracoon, and it is probable that these attractive romances affected his youthful imagination long before he understood slaving's commercial value.

Actual horrors of the slave ship, and the tragedy of the middle passage were not then known to the boy from the square-roofed house, and he and other lads of the neighborhood haunted the wharves when the big ships came in.

A companionable boy of likable ways and much charm of personality, young Gordon was even then a leader. Quick to learn, he was a keen observer, and as he grew older he realized no trade paid larger investment returns than that of slaver.

From the time the unnamed Dutch trader of 1619 sailed up the river to Jamestown with a cargo of slaves, to the days of Abraham Lincoln's suppression of this nefarious traffic, the slave trade was a national disgrace. But men older and wiser than Nat Gordon hesitated not to share the profits of the business, and he just followed the example of even better born men.

Captain Nat, the Slaver

Just how Nat Gordon became a slaver is not known. But no doubt, while pursuing legiti-

mate business as commander of a ship, he fell in with men who had amassed wealth from this unlawful trade. Young and ambitious, he grew more covetous. During his third voyage as commander of the *Erie*, he was captured as a slaver, tried and convicted under the law of 1823, as a pirate; the first slave trader convicted of piracy in America.

Yet even before this, strange tales about the popular captain had circulated, brought back from the Indies by ships' crews homeward bound: of picturesque isles far out in mid-ocean, where pirates landed now and again to divide their treasure; where slavers sometimes splashed their oars through the shallow waters to the shore.

No absolute proof of Captain Nat's involvement in such circumstances has come down through the years, but there are stories of rich silks and jewels, or gold cups and vases later found in his York Street house.

However, we do know that in the summer of 1860 Captain Nat took his ship *Erie*—that he had bought in New York—to Havana to complete an outfit for the slave trade. His two previous slave voyages had proved remarkably profitable and he was anxious for another.

He sailed 45 miles up the Congo into the interior. After discharging his cargo of liquor, he made ready for his return voyage, on the seventh day of August, by taking on board a cargo of slaves near the mouth of the river. With slaves packed 'tween decks, Captain Nat sailed for Cuba. Of the eight hundred and

ORIGINALLY PUBLISHED IN *LEWISTON JOURNAL ILLUSTRATED MAGAZINE*, 11 MAY 1910.

ninety slaves he took, only 172 were men. One hundred and six were women and the rest were boys and girls. It was easier and safer to carry children.

But the *Erie* was spotted and captured by the United States warship *Mohican*. After the slaves were freed in Liberia, Gordon, on his ill-fated vessel, was brought to New York for trial.

Since the ship had been seized with her dreadful cargo on board, the evidence was plain and she was condemned and sold at auction in October of that same year. Although but 500 tons, she was a staunch-built ship, and brought in $7,823.25.

Then came Gordon's punishment. He was condemned as a pirate under the law of 1820. During the early years of the 19th century, privateers made frequent attacks on unarmed merchant vessels. West India waters swarmed with pirates and slavers, and when it suited them, it was an easy matter for slavers to turn pirates, and pirates, slavers. The Piracy Act of 1820 was an attempt to stamp out such a state of affairs.

Death Penalty Act

The bill became an act on May 5th, 1820, and on May 12th, a resolution passed the House "That the President of the United States be requested to negotiate with all the Governments where Ministers of the United States are or shall be accredited, on the means of effecting an entire and immediate abolition of the slave trade."

Although initially limited to a period of two years, on the 30th of January, 1823, the law was made perpetual.

It was in accordance to these sections relating to the slave trade (given below) that Captain Nat Gordon was tried as a pirate.

And be it further enacted, that if any citizen of the United States being of the crew or ship's company of any foreign ship or vessel engaged in the slave trade, or any person whatever being of the crew or ship's company of any ship or vessel owned in whole or in part, or navigated for, or in behalf of, any citizen or citizens of the United States, shall land from any ship or vessel, and, on any foreign shore, seize any negro or mulatto, not held to service or labor by the laws of either the states or territories of the United States, with intent to make such negro or mulatto a slave, or

shall decoy, or forcibly bring or carry, or shall receive, such negro or mulatto on board any such ship or vessel, with intent as aforesaid, such citizen or person shall be adjudged a pirate, and on conviction thereof, before the Circuit Court of the United States, for the district therein he may be brought or found, shall suffer death.

And be it further enacted. That if any citizen of the United States, being of the crew or ship's company of any foreign ship or vessel engaged in the slave trade, or any person whatever, being of the crew or ship's company of any ship or vessel owned wholly or in part, or navigated for, or in behalf of any citizen or citizens of the United States, shall forcibly confine, or detain, or aid or abet in forcibly confining, or detaining, on board such ship or vessel any negro or mulatto not held to service by the laws of either the States or Territories of the United States, with intent to make such negro or mulatto a slave, or shall on board any such ship or vessel, offer or attempt to sell, as a slave, any negro or mulatto, not held to service as aforesaid, or shall on the high seas, or anywhere on tide water transfer or deliver over, to any other ship or vessel, any negro or mulatto not held to service as aforesaid, with intent to make such negro or mulatto a slave, or shall land or deliver on shore, from on board any such ship or vessel, any such negro or mulatto, with intent to make sale of, or, having previously sold, such negro or mulatto as a slave, such citizen or person shall be adjudged a pirate, and, on conviction thereof before the Circuit Court of the United States for the district wherein he shall be brought or found, shall suffer death.

Trial of Captain Nat

Gordon was condemned; but he had powerful friends who worked strenuously in his behalf and the first case ended with a mistrial. Then a new administration came to power and the new district attorney, E. Delafield Smith, was a man who never juggled the law for sake of compromise.

Gordon's second trial began November 6, 1961. Ex-judge Dean and P. J. Joachimson, both men experienced in cases of this nature, defended him. Judge Nelson presided. A jury was obtained in two hours. As was customary at that time when the captain of a slaver was arrested, the plea was that Gordon was a passenger. The slave captains, ever in danger of arrest, always took with them on their voyages some foreigner, and when their vessels were boarded by alien ships, they turned the command over to this man.

At first people failed to take much interest in this trail. The Civil War was on, and at the first trial, Gordon had secured a disagreement of the jury. According to all the laws of precedent, he was almost certain to go free again. So the people read the war news and took little heed of the trial. The court room saw few spectators.

On Friday evening November 8, or black Friday as it proved to be to the captain of the slaver, Judge Nelson delivered his charge and the jury retired at seven o'clock. After only 20 minutes they returned with the verdict, "Guilty!"

Captain Nat was apparently unmoved. There was no scene in the courtroom and the few people present accepted the verdict matter-of-factly. It apparently did not dawn on them that they had assisted in the making of history.

But the next day after the verdict appeared in the papers, New York redeemed her attitude of indifference. Motions for a new trial were denied, and when on Saturday morning, November 20th, Nat Gordon stood up and heard his sentence, the courtroom thronged with people wanting to hear the sentence of the first American slaver convicted as a pirate.

Gordon took his sentence calmly. And when the usual question was put, he stated that he had nothing whatever to say.

Judge Nelson reviewed the facts connected with the trial, then ordered that the slaver be executed between the hours of noon and three in the afternoon of February 7, 1862, by being hanged by the neck until dead.

Nat Gordon did not lack friends or sympathizers and great efforts were made to save him. On February 7, news came of a two-week Presidential respite, and it was thought Lincoln had commuted the sentence. But Marshal Murray undeceived Jordan as to this, telling him there was no hope whatever. On the last day of Jordan's life one of his lawyers sent word that the governor of the State had sent an appeal to the President and requested that the execution be deferred until the answer came. But Marshal Murray told Jordan it had been arranged with the President that no telegram from any source should interfere with the demands of Justice.

Execution of the Slaver.

The morning of the execution dawned, a clear, cold February day, the 21st of the month. What must have been the feelings of Gordon knowing that this was his last day on earth? It was a stormy time in the nation's history, and, in the past, Negroes had been hanged to the lamp posts by New York mobs. So perhaps there was hope, for there had been whispers of a mob that had vowed to break into the jail and rescue him.

But the Government was prepared. Gordon must die; no mob should free him. Early that morning, just after the midnight hour rang out, the navy yard dispatched a guard of 20 marines to the city prison. They loaded their muskets with ball cartridges and fixed their bayonets upon marching into the yard. Groups of men lingering in the prison's neighborhood slunk away; there would be no attempt at rescue by mobs.

On that February morning Captain Nat apparently gave up all hope of pardon. Friends had secretly conveyed to him a dose of strychnine, and this he managed to swallow unobserved. He cried triumphantly, as it began to work, "I've cheated you! I've cheated you!"

But Gordon was not to escape the shame of the gallows. The doctors saved him. He wrote a number of notes after recovering from the poison and was conscious when led from his cell. The Marshal came just before the noon hour and read the death warrant, asking the prisoner if he had anything to say.

In a firm voice Gordon made this remarkable speech:

My conscience is clear. I have no fault to find with the treatment I have received from the marshal and his deputy, Mr. Thompson; but any public man who will get up in open court and say to the jury, "if you convict this prisoner I will be the first man to sign a petition for his pardon," and will then go to the Executive to prevent his commuting the sentence, is a man who will do anything to promote his own ends, I do not care what people may say.

Made in the shadow of the gallows though it was, this last speech of the Portland slaver was untrue, as the charge against district attorney Smith had no foundation whatever. The stenographic report of the trial was carefully read and it was found that Smith's speech to the jury contained nothing to confirm Gordon's statement.

On that February noontime of 1862, Gordon went to the gallows pale with terror, his head hanging over his shoulders, and so weak he could hardly walk. He had to be supported as he tottered under the fatal beam; and he went into eternity, with a black lie the last words from his lips.

At a given signal the cord was snapped asunder by the executioner's axe and Nathaniel Gordon was hoisted aloft into mid-air. A few convulsive twitches of the body followed. The veins of his neck and hands swelled and stood out hard; then the limbs lost their rigidity, the flesh assumed a livid hue, and the slave trader, now a lump of dishonored clay, swung slowly to and fro in the frosty air.

Thus died Captain Nat Gordon of Portland. A convicted pirate.

Also See

"Ambition Nagged Nat to Be First, and by Gorry He Was," *Portland Sunday Telegram,* 8 January 1961, p. 10B.

"Forgotten Mainers: Local Slaver's Travels End on Noose," *Maine Sunday Telegram,* 15 February 1987, pp. 19A, 36A.

"Infamous Slave Captain Died on the Gallows," *Lewiston Journal Illustrated Magazine,* 28 March 1970, p. 8.

"Make Him an Example,"*American History Illustrated Magazine,* January 1983, pp. 40–45.

"Misadventures of a Maine Slaver," *American Neptune* 19, 1959, pp. 114–119.

"Portland, Century Ago, Sought to Improve Relations with Embittered Southern States," *Portland Evening Express,* 3 January 1961, p. 24.

"Portland Reflections," *Portland Evening Express,* 5 June 1975, p. 9.

"Slavery in Maine," *Collections of the Maine Historical Society,* 1st Series, 7, 1876, pp. 209–216.

"Slave Trade Flourished in Kittery, Wells Area," *Portland Press Herald*, 4 November 1963, p. 17.

THE BATTLE OF *MERRIMAC* AND *MONITOR* AS SEEN FROM THE FORECAS'LE

WILLISTON JENNINGS

The great battle between the *Merrimac* and the *Monitor* at Hampton Roads in 1862 has always been regarded as the most important in its results of any naval conflict since the days when a king sat on the mountain brow and looked over sea-born Salamis. It appeared to be one of the most unequal of contests, as the *Monitor* was but a tiny speck by the side of the mighty monster she had engaged. The one was supposed to be invulnerable and had already put out of commission several of the strongest warships of the North. The work of destruction was still going on, and another day would see the annihilation of the Union navy. It was a critical moment in the history of the world, and the result seemed to be foregone. Suddenly the *Monitor* appeared. It was but a tiny speck on the ocean and no naval officer had ever seen its like before. No one in that great fleet believed that it could for a moment cope with the rebel ram or even thought that it was a serious attempt to turn the tide of battle, but there was one old man hundreds of miles away who had supreme confidence that the hour of destiny had arrived and that the navies of the world were about to be revolutionized. That man was Ericsson, the mechanical genius who had invented the *Monitor* and who believed that no vessel afloat could compass its defeat.

The world knows the result of that naval duel. The little craft that had aptly been called a cheese box on a raft in a few hours destroyed the great ironclad, and the whole civilized world heard the news with amazement. England was fairly paralyzed as she clearly saw her mighty navy was now but a useless toy. A new idea had upset all her ships of the line and rendered them absolutely worthless. But one thing remained for her to do. Her wooden ships must be discarded and a new navy constructed at an expense of hundreds of millions of dollars. France, Italy, and all the other nations clearly saw the same result, and their statesmen stood paralyzed in the face of this great fact. Lieutenant Worthern had made his name immortal but the name of Ericsson was on every lip.

The history of that world-famous and epoch-making battle has been written many times but in every instance those reports have come from the quarterdeck. The *Lewiston Journal* has the honor of presenting for the first time the story from the forecastle. After 47 years have passed, an old letter has been unearthed that was written by a man who was in the conflict, and who wrote while the whole bloody incident was fresh in his mind. This letter was written by a mere boy, who little dreamed at the time that it would ever see the light of day. It was written to his mother while the roar of the battle was still ringing in his ears.

The writer of that letter was Williston Jennings, who is now agent and head manager of the North Wayne Tool Manufacturing Company, and who is well-known all over this part of Maine. In the opening days of the Rebellion he left his country home in North Wayne and enlisted in the navy. Assigned to the United States warship *Cambridge,* he was soon on the field of action and it was his fate to be at Hampton Roads when the terrible *Merrimac*

ORIGINALLY PUBLISHED IN *LEWISTON JOURNAL ILLUSTRATED MAGAZINE*, 3 JULY 1909.

began her work of destruction among the Union fleet. The *Cambridge* had been marked as one of the victims of the very day when the *Monitor* appeared and the rebel ram met its fate. All of the Union vessels had been mixed up in the fight and some sunken while others were crippled. This work of destruction was still going on when the *Monitor* appeared. The *Cambridge* had been injured and crippled more or less and was only too glad to pull out of the fight and give the *Monitor* the right of way. This example was followed by all the other warships, and the *Merrimac* and *Monitor* were allowed to fight the duel to a finish while the men on the other vessels looked on as spectators of the strange scene.

Among those who saw the entire conflict was young Jennings of North Wayne. From the deck of the *Cambridge* he watched the battle from beginning to the end. He then immediately commenced to write the details of the fight to his mother, Mrs. Mary Lobdell, North Wayne. This letter was written at intervals during the next few days. Whenever he could spare any time from his sea duties he would go to his bunk and write. The post-office facilities were by no means good, and as no mail could be sent until some vessel started North, the boy continued to write until such opportunity came.

It must be apparent that a young boy could not grasp the full meaning of the battle as could the great statesmen of the world. They saw that their navies were worthless. Young Jennings only saw a battle and he wrote as any boy would naturally write to his mother. The letter was received and has been treasured all these years. Mr. Jennings has been very reluctant to give it to the press as he feared that the literary style would not be up to the mark. The *Journal* assures him that in that very fact lies its greatest value. It was written to describe a great battle instead of trying to make it a prize essay. It was written at the time of the battle when every detail and incident were fresh in his mind. To change its phraseology in the slightest degree would only be to modernize it and lessen its historic interest and feel ashamed of either grammar or rhetoric. He was not posing as a graduating student from some literary institution, but was representing the patriotism and valor of the boys in 1862 in the forecastle of a fighting ship. That letter, with all its grammatical imperfections, should be his proudest possession today. It was an immortal glory to be in that world-famous battle, and that he lived to tell the tale is a matter of congratulation. Mr. Jennings is still with us and one of the most honored citizens of Maine. He could produce a letter of finer literary excellence today, but he can never again write one of the thrilling and dramatic interest, of the great historic value of the one written down in Newport News in 1862. It is a letter that will live in history as being the only description of the most momentous naval battle of all time written from the forecastle. We herewith give the letter in full exactly as it was written:

U.S.S. *Cambridge,* at sea
March 10th, 1862

Dear Mother,

You will hear about the fight between the *Merrimac* and others of the Rebel fleet, and our Naval Fleet at Hampton Roads, long before this reaches you and will be worried about me when you see that the *Cambridge* was in it. I should have written you at once, but we went to sea at a moment's notice, but will write you now and sent it by the first ship that goes North, and if I have time will give you all the details, as you always want me to. On the 8th of March we lay inside of Cape Henry, and run up to Fort Monroe for our mail, we sent a boat ashore after it and returned for the boat about noon.

Just as we took in our boat we saw a fleet coming around Sewall's Point, and the *Merrimac* was leading. She looked like a flat boat with a house roof with gables cut on an angle, something like a hopper roof. A signal gun was fired and our fleet was underway very quick. The *Minnesota, Roanoke* and *St. Lawrence* slipped their cables and were taken in tow, the *Cambridge* taking the *St. Lawrence.* We soon passed the *Roanoke,* her shaft being broken. As we passed Sewall's Point the Rebs opened fire on our fleet. We replied, but all of our shots fell short. Our rifle pivot guns reached them after the first shot, and as long as we were in range every shot struck inside their works. The *St. Lawrence* fired a second full broadside, but could not reach them, neither could we with our 8-inch guns. The *Congress,* of 40 guns, and the *Cumberland,* of 30, lay off Newport News and the *Merrimac* made direct for the *Cumberland,* opening fire on her with her forward pivot guns and on the *Congress* at the same time with her port batteries. She then rammed the *Cumberland,* striking her starboard side near her fore-rigging, and still kept up a constant fire on both the *Congress* and *Cumberland.* The *Congress* slipped her cable and went aground. Both ships kept up a continual firing, also the shore battery at Newport News. We were not in range and could render no assistance, as the *Merrimac* lay between us and our two ships. The *Cumberland* was soon flooded, but she still kept up the fight, until she sank, her top-masts above water and her flag still flying.

The *Merrimac* then took her position off the *Congress*'s starboard bow, firing broadside after broadside until she struck her colors and run up the white flag. Several small Rebel steamers assisted in taking off the men, but the shore batteries kept up a fire on them until they were driven off. Our officers say that many of our men were killed by the shore batteries. The enemy in the meantime had been reinforced by three steamers from up the James River, the officers say they are the *Jamestown, Yorktown,* and *Teaser.* They opened fire on both the shore batteries and our fleet. The *Minnesota* had grounded, but in a position to use her batteries, the others of our fleet were not in position to use their guns to advantage, except those of us that were light craft, of which there were several, who fought our own ships and kept the others in the best possible position. The *Merrimac* took her position off the *Minnesota*'s starboard bow, and the others of the fleet off our port beam. Our hawser was cut by a shot and we went to the assistance of the *Minnesota,* opening fire with broadside and pivot guns, and for a long time both our 8-inch and two pivot rifle guns were used, until signaled by the *St. Lawrence* to come to her assistance. A line was given her and we got her in position where she could use her guns.

(March 11: We are off Beaufort, N.C. today. The fort opened fire on us but did not strike us.)

It took the third line before we were successful. The last time we made fast to her, as shot struck our stern-post and she would not answer her helm, we were headed directly for the *Merrimac,* and I thought for a time that Captain Parker was agoing to ram the *Merrimac,* but she finally answered her helm. The *St. Lawrence* opened fire with her port battery and two pivots, and a constant rain of shot and shell was kept up. At one time it seemed as if every gun in our fleet was fired at the same time, and when the smoke lifted, a small steamer was sinking alongside of the *Merrimac.* Our hawser was cut again, and the *St. Lawrence* was once more adrift. About that time the *Merrimac* hauled out of the fight and was apparently uninjured, except her flag staff and smokestack and such other damage as would not seriously injure her to any extent. It was then about 6 o'clock and she was of deep draft, and had grounded once during the engagement. We kept up a continual fire so long as any of their fleet was in range. After dark we again made fast to the *St. Lawrence* and towed her to her anchorage off Fort Monroe. Captain Parker reported to Captain Marston of the Flag Ship *Roanoke* and asked permission to go to the assistance of the *Minnesota* and stayed by her during the night, but received orders to come to anchor.

Quite a number of our men are wounded. Midshipman Cushing, J. H. Woods and Frank A. Kelly of our guns crew. About 9 o'clock that night a funny-looking little craft came in and lay-to off our starboard bow, she looked like a raft with a big tank on her deck. The officers say it is Ericsson's *Monitor* and is iron clad, her deck was almost awash, certainly not over two feet above water. She reported to the flag ship and then steamed up to where the *Minnesota* lay aground. The *Congress* was on fire and lighted up the Roads, the fire extended from her hull to her main truck, her standing rigging was all of a blaze, and about 1 o'clock the fire reached her magazine, and she blew up.

(Mar. 12—Off Beaufort, and have made ready for action at a moment's call. Our guns are all shotted. The *Nashville* is inside the harbor and has dropped down near its mouth, apparently intends to make her escape.)

All hands was called at daylight and ordered to stow our hammocks and cloth bags around the engine and boiler. The Rebel fleet hove in sight off Sewall's Point, we hove up anchor and stood for the *Minnesota,* but was signaled by the Flag Ship to lay-to. The *Merrimac* and two other steamers bear down on the *Minnesota* and opened fire, a shot apparently struck her and must have done serious damage. The *Minnesota* replied, but just then that little flat boat with a tub on her deck hove in sight and made straight for the *Merrimac,* the other two steamers put about and lay-to under the batteries off Sewall's Point. The *Merrimac* opened fire on the little craft, but she did not reply until she was close-haul, then she slowed up and opened fire, and it was a constant roar of guns for at least about 2½ hours, and with no apparent damage to either of them. About that time the little Ironclad hauled off and I was not the only one that felt anxious, for there was thousands watching the engagement, but very soon time was called, and the battle was on. The *Merrimac* made several attempts to ram her as she did the *Cumberland,* but she was so slow that before she could get at her the little craft was somewhere else.

(March 13 — Off Beaufort. There is a heavy cannonading up the sound. *Nashville* still inside the harbor.)

At one time she did strike her, but she was not fairly bow on and she got a shot in return that must have injured her, but still the fight went on. The *Merrimac* would apparently try for position, but she was slow at best, and must have been more than 25 feet draft, and could not be handled much better than a raft of logs. After the fight was on they were at no time more than a third of a mile apart, and for nearly four hours almost alongside of each other. The *Merrimac* gradually fell back towards the mouth of the Elizabeth river.

(March 14—On Beaufort. We cruised outside nearly all day, weather growing rough.)

Just at this time we were ordered to sea, but as we left the Roads the *Merrimac* was out of sight behind Sewall's Point, and the little craft steaming for the *Minnesota,* so conclude we are victorious, but may not know for sure for a long time all of the details. At one time during the engagement the *Minnesota,* the big Union gun on the beach, the Battery on the Rip Raps, and the *Cambridge* (we lay above the Rip Raps, towards Sewall's Point) all took part in the action, but after a few shots were signaled to cease firing, for we were as liable to strike one as the other.

March 15—Off Beaufort and it is blowing a gale, have kept underway all day so far. The *Nashville* is getting up steam and has dropped down nearer the mouth of the harbor and come to anchor. We hope we can capture her, but there are three channels leading out of the harbor which makes it much against us. I don't think she will come out in daylight, if she does she will have a warm time of it. Well, mother, the fight is over and I have had time to give you all the little details. I hope you and father will not be worried about me before you get this letter (that is if I ever get a chance to send it). Of course you will want to know (as you have before) how I felt during the battle. I must say that I enjoyed the last day's fight after I felt sure that the little Ironclad would whip the *Merrimac,* much better than I did the first day's fight. When I saw the *Cumberland* go down and the *Congress* riddled with shot and shell and compelled to strike her colors I felt a bit weak in the knees, was almost afraid they would tremble, but they didn't. After I got to work I was all right. I don't believe I was anymore scared than a messmate of mine who squat down behind a ¾-inch hose box made of pine, while our gun was not in action to protect himself from a 100-pound shot; it made me laugh. I presume I was as scared as he, but I would not have done it if I had known I should have been shot. Tell Will Taylor that I got his letter the 8th, just as we were going into the fight, and finished reading it just before we opened fire. Please give my regards to all the boys and girls. With love to you and father and the children. The weather is very rough and the ship rolls and pitches so that it is hard to write, and shall have to close. Will you please send me some papers. I have not seen one except those you sent me since I shipped.

March 16—I will write you just a line. We are off Beaufort, and the gale has somewhat abated. The *State of George* sails north today and I shall have a chance to send this letter by her this afternoon. I think we shall have to go north soon to have the *Cambridge* repaired. She is cut up badly, in both her top-hamper and hull, with her timbers stove-in on her port side, her bow-spirit gone close to her figure-head, her after pivot gun split at the muzzle, davits and stern-post bent, in fact, she is a hard looking craft. I should like to go ashore once more, I have not been for about seven months. I shall have to close, to get this off on this ship.

Yours Affectionately,
Will

Also See

"Cyrus Cobb, Mechanic Falls Veteran Soldier and Traveler," *Lewiston Journal Illustrated Magazine,* 29 February, 1908, p. 10.

"Mr. F. W. Willey's Recollections of the Sinking of the *Cumberland*," *Portland Sunday Telegram,* 2 June 1901, p. 1.

"Sole Maine Survivor of Uncle Sam's Old Wooden Navy," *Lewiston Journal Illustrated Magazine,* 14 June 1913, p. 2.

"The Loss of the *Monitor*,"*War Papers: Read Before the Commandery of the State of Maine* 2, 1902, pp. 77–90.

THE CAPTURE OF THE CALEB CUSHING

WILLIAM B. KENNISTON

Several years ago Mr. Samuel Prince, of Yarmouth, Me., and I were discussing the beauties of Casco Bay and Portland harbor and the advantages of those waters as a place for sailing.

"What a curious little back entrance to the harbor that passage between Cow and Diamond islands is," I remarked. "You've been through it, haven't you?"

"Been through the passage between Cow and Diamond islands," exclaimed Mr. Prince. "well I should say I had! Why, dear man, I've rowed through it as a boy, and sailed through it as a young man and one night in June, years ago, I was towed through it a prisoner in irons and under guard. And here," he said getting up from his rocking chair and taking something rusty and jingling from a hook in the wall below the mantel, "here are the hand-cuffs I wore that night."

Few men have carried into old age a face more peaceful or one giving less evidence of fights and brawls and those things usually associated with the wearers of hand-cuffs than has Mr. Samuel Prince. I knew him as a man of eminent respectability and that he had ever been "in irons and under guard" seemed hardly possible. My astonishment, not to say incredulity, must have been apparent for the old man laughed heartily as he watched me examine the rusty irons and in reply to my questioning look, told the following story:

"In April, 1863," he began, "I shipped as seaman on the U.S. Revenue Cutter *Caleb Cushing*, stationed off the Maine coast with headquarters at Portland. The *Cushing* was a brigantine of about two hundred tons, and carried between twenty and thirty men. She had not been built for the Revenue service, but had been a merchant vessel, and was fitted out as a cutter after the beginning of the war, to take the place of the regular cutter that had been turned over to the navy and sent South.

"A revenue cutter, as you know, is not intended for a fighter. Her duties correspond more nearly to those of a policeman than of a soldier. She patrols the coast, renders aid to vessels in distress, helps shipwrecked mariners, sees to it that the buoys and other markings of the channels and ledges are all right, and looks after things on her beat generally. Ordinarily a cutter carries no cannon, but as there was always the possibility of an attack on our ports and shipping by the southerners, the *Cushing* was mounted with two guns, a 32-pounder amidships and a brass 15-pounder on the gallant fo'castle. "When she had been fitted out as a cutter, some eight to ten compartments had been made in the floor of the berth deck. In one of the compartments there was stored from 600 to 800 pounds of powder. In the others were provisions, and pork in another, and so on. I have been told that there was a regular magazine in the after part of the vessel, opening out of the captain's stateroom, the door concealed by a mirror, but whether this was true or not, I don't know. I do know there was powder in the compartment I have told you of, for I helped to store it there myself.

"Shortly after I shipped on the *Cushing* the captain became ill, and was put ashore at Portland. The command then fell to the first lieutenant. This lieutenant was a native of Savannah, Ga., and for some reason, perhaps solely because of his southern birth, he was unpopular both with his brother officers and the crew. It was sometimes whispered about

ORIGINALLY PUBLISHED IN *LEWISTON JOURNAL ILLUSTRATED MAGAZINE*, 30 MAY 1908.

that he was at heart in sympathy with the South, and would bear watching.

"The weather was fine all the spring, and we had an easy time. We cruised back and forth along the coast, but were never more than a few days from Portland. There were constant rumors of a southern fleet, always 'just a few miles out,' but they invariably proved to be false. The southern cruiser *Tacony*, that had done a deal of mischief to our shipping in Cuban waters the winter before, was reported to be coming North, and we kept a sharp lookout for her. But we saw neither the *Tacony* nor any other hostile craft.

"Late in June the captain died, and on the evening of the 27th we lay at anchor in Portland harbor, just off Custom House wharf, awaiting the appointment of a new commander. Nearly all the officers of the Cushing belonged in Portland, and that night all of them but the first lieutenant, the quartermaster and one or two petty officers went ashore on leave.

"The weather was fine, and there was not the usual number of vessels in the harbor. Late in the afternoon a fishing schooner, the *Archer*, had come in through Hussey's Sound, just before the light southerly breeze died away, and dropped anchor nearby. She was our only neighbor. Her battered, poorly painted hull and patched and weather-beaten sails contrasted sadly with our trim and rakish appearance.

"It was Saturday night, very warm and pleasant. The harbor was full of small craft all the evening. There was a party at Peaks Island, and it was nearly midnight when the last of the young people who had attended it had returned and the harbor was quiet.

"I stood watch from 10 o'clock to 12, and then turned in. When I had been in my hammock about a half hour, and was just dropping off to sleep, I heard men climbing over the side and then the sound of many footsteps on deck.

"'It's the new captain,' I thought, 'come to take command.' The next instant I learned my mistake. A voice close to my ear cried: 'Surrender, in the name of the Southern Confederacy!' For an instant I lay as one paralyzed, then jumped up to find the berth deck swarming with men armed with pistols and cutlasses, and everything in confusion.

"There was hardly the semblance of a struggle; not that there were not brave men in the crew of the *Cushing* but when men who

have gone to sleep unarmed, with a sense of perfect security, are awakened to find pistols held to their heads by enemies, armed and desperate, their bravery has hardly a chance. It took but a few minutes to have the whole crew of the *Cushing* prisoners. We were handcuffed in pairs, and my companion in misery happened to be a Dutchman. When we were all in irons, and had been huddled together in the forward part of the berth deck, the lieutenant, quartermaster and one or two petty officers, half-dressed, and also in irons, were brought from their staterooms and placed with us.

"'Now, boys,' said [Lieutenant Charles Reed,] the man who seemed to be in command of the invaders, addressing us not unkindly, 'what we want is the *Cushing*, not you Yanks. If you behave yourselves, we'll put you off on some island as we go out of the harbor. If you make trouble, you'll be shot and thrown overboard.' With that he left two stalwart Rebels, with a cocked pistol in each hand, to guard us, and with the rest hurried on deck.

"Presently we heard the rattle of the anchor chain. They tried to slip it, but for some reason couldn't undo the end from its fastening, and had to weigh the anchor. There was very little wind. The southerly breeze of the afternoon had died out at sunset, and it was too early for the usual off-shore breeze of the morning. They set sail, however, and in a few minutes we were moving slowly down the harbor.

"As soon as we were under way, a half dozen of the Rebels came down to the berth deck and began to search for powder. They pulled open the compartments in the floor, that I have told you of, one after the other, but, in their hurry and excitement, by chance they failed to open the one containing it, and in a short time they gave up the search.

"Before long the slight breeze died out entirely, and our captors manned two boats and took the vessel in tow. It was slow work, but there never was a gang of men more anxious to get to sea than they were, and they kept at it till long after daylight. Then the wind came up again, not strong, but enough for steerage way, and, pretty well exhausted, they came aboard for breakfast.

"Among the prisoners there was a boy about fifteen years of age, who had been assistant to the cook. This boy was freed from his irons, and told to build a fire and make some coffee. After our captors had been served, we were given breakfast of coffee and hardtack. I am afraid some of our number had little appetite even for that much.

"The morning wore away slowly. When they had breakfast and rested awhile, the Rebels again took their boats and continued the towing. We had been expecting to be called on deck at any moment to be sent ashore, as we had been promised: for certainly we had 'behaved' ourselves. We were beginning to think we must be well outside the islands, and were wondering what would be done with us. We were anything but a happy crowd. Glum and sullen we sat in the dim light of the berth deck, and reviewed the situation. Who our captors were, except they were Rebels, we had not the least idea. Where they had come from we could not guess. We had no hope for being pursued and retaken, for we knew there was no armed craft in the harbor, while, as I have said, the *Cushing* carried two cannon. There seemed nothing for us, but that we would be taken South, and held as prisoners of war in some Rebel prison. But in thinking this, we had not, as you shall see, relied sufficiently on Yankee energy, ingenuity, and bravery.

"Shortly after noon we heard the Rebels who had been towing scramble on deck in a great hurry, and we wondered what was up. We were not kept long in doubt. The booming of a cannon some distance away, and then in an instant after, the almost deafening report of our 32-pounder as she replied, showing us we were being pursued, and by an armed craft too. In a few minutes the distant cannon spoke again, and this time was replied to by our 15-pounder.

"A few minutes after this second shot, a voice shouted down the companion way, 'bring those prisoners on deck!' We hurried up the steps, and almost before we had a chance to look about to see what manner of craft was bold enough to give us chase, we were ordered to get into our boats, and were hustled over the side. When we were in the boats, and about to shove off, I shouted to the Rebels on deck to throw us down some keys, for we were still in irons. Someone threw down a handful that fell in a shower into the boat. We didn't stop to unloose the irons then, however, but pushed off and manned the oars as we were.

"Then we looked about to get our bearings. We were about five miles outside of Peak's Island. Hardly a mile away were our pursuers, the New York steamer *Chesapeake*, and the Boston packet *Forest City*, while somewhat farther off was a fleet of smaller steamers and sailing craft that had come out to see the chase. Fearing that our friends on the steamer might mistake us for the enemy, the only white shirt in the crowd, that of the lieu-

Lieutenant Charles Reed, who captured the Caleb Cushing

tenant, was hung upon an oar and raised in the bow of the boat. Then we pulled away for the nearest steamer, the *Chesapeake*.

"We had rowed but a short distance from the *Cushing* when smoke began to rise from her hatches. The Rebels, as I have told you, could not find our powder, and seeing they must certainly be taken, spilled a barrel of oil on the berth deck, and set it afire. Then they took to their boats, and pulled away in an opposite direction to the one we had taken. The cutter took fire quickly and in a few minutes was a mass of flames. She burned for an hour or so, and then blew up with a tremendous explosion.

"In the meantime, we had been picked up by the steamer *Chesapeake*. We had been through a hard trying time, and we expected to get from the men on the steamer sympathy and condolence. In this we were bitterly disappointed. To be surprised and captured by a gang of men springing from we knew not where; to be manacled, and carried to sea; to be under the fire of the steamer pursuing; all this was hard and not without danger, but to be hissed and hooted at, and called traitors, and every degrading epithet in the language

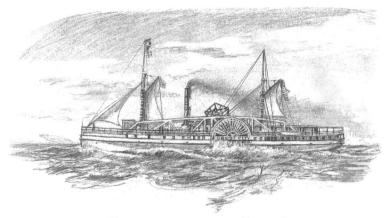

THE COASTWISE SIDEWHEELER FOREST CITY

by those from whom we had looked for friendliness, and kindness was harder yet, and we could not understand it. In the midst of derisive shouts and cries, we were ordered to be taken below, and kept under a strong guard.

"We soon leaned the reason for this apparently harsh treatment. When the *Cushing* had been missed from her anchorage that morning by the officers returning from their shore leave, with one accord they had concluded that the Lieutenant, who, as I have told you, was a Southerner by birth, had stolen the vessel. They thought he must have taken the opportunity, when so many of the officers were ashore, to bribe a part of the crew by promise of large rewards, overcome the rest, and away to the South with his prize. That a gang of Rebels could have entered the harbor under the very shadow of the forts, and have captured the *Cushing*, crew and all, did not seem reasonable nor possible. Believing this to be true, it was little wonder that they had no sympathy for us.

"The Rebels were picked up by the *Forest City*, and then the true situation was found out, which was more than we ourselves knew. The Rebels were the officers and crew of the *Tacony*, which we in the *Cushing* had looked for all the spring, and it was our innocent looking little neighbor, the *Archer*, that had brought them into Portland harbor. They had captured the *Archer* two days before, off Damariscove Island, had set her crew ashore, all but one man, whom they held to act as pilot, sunk their own vessel, and came to Portland. Their plan was to capture the *Cushing*, get her all ready to start, and then set fire to some of the wharves, and warehouses, and especially to destroy two wooden war vessels, then on the stocks in the city. In the confusion and excitement that would follow, they expected to get to sea, unnoticed. The almost dead calm prevented their carrying out this plan.

"About a mile from the *Cushing*, her sails flapping, and useless in the calm, the *Archer* was captured. There were three men upon her. One of them was the Maine fisherman, whom they had expected to use as a pilot. He was in irons for refusing to act in that capacity. The guns of the *Tacony*, and several nautical instruments were found on the *Archer*, and a great quantity of oakum, rolled into balls and soaked in oil, ready for use in setting the fires they had planned. She was captured without resistance, and taken in tow by a tug.

"When we arrived at the city, a mob met us at the wharf, and gave us a reception very similar to what we had received when the steamer picked us up. The people had, of course, not learned the true state of affairs, and believed the crew, or a part of them, at least, had been disloyal. We were marched under a strong guard to the jail, where we were left till the next day, when an investigation was held and we were given our liberty.

"The Rebels were held as prisoners of war, at Fort Preble for a time, then sent to Fort Warren, and were afterwards, I believe, exchanged."

ALSO SEE

"Account of the Capture of Two Escaped Confederate Prisoners from Fort Warren," *Eastern Argus,* 21 August 1863, p. 3.

"Account of the Efforts of a Confederate Officer to Steal a U.S. Revenue Cutter, *Caleb Cushing,*" *Portland Press Herald,* 29 May 1982, p. 84.

"Account of the Theft of the U.S. Revenue Cutter *Caleb Cushing*," *Maine Sunday Telegram,* 26 June 1988, pp. 31A, 34A.

"Capture by Rebels of Revenue Cutter *Caleb Cushing* in Portland Harbor," *Eastern Argus,* 29 June 1863, p. 2.

"Citizens Rushed to Fend 'Invasion' 100 Years Ago," *Portland Press Herald,* 27 June 1963, p. 48.

"Civil War Came to Maine, 80 Years Ago Today," *Lewiston Journal Illustrated Magazine,* 26 June 1943, p. 1.

"Confederate Cruiser Played Havoc with Friendship Vessels During Bay Visit," *Midcoast Progress Review,* 26 February 1972, p. 4B.

"A Confederate Raid," Winfield Martin Thompson, *The Rudder* 16, 1905, pp. 130–136, 243–250.

"Confederate Raid on Portland Harbor," Arthur Menzies Johnson, *Down East* 7, July 1961, pp. 52–54 , 62–64.

"An Incident on the Coast of Maine in 1861," *Magazine of History* 15, 1912, pp. 38–41.

"Little Sidewheeler Manned by Crew of Soldiers Pursues, Helps Capture Rebel Raiders in Cutter," *Portland Press Herald,* 20 October 1962, p. 16B.

"Maine's Only Civil War Battle Comic Opera Affair," *Portland Evening Express,* 27 June 1963, p. 17.

"Rebel Cutters Made Exciting Times Along Maine Coast in Civil War," *Lewiston Journal Illustrated Magazine,* 29 May 1942, p. 7.

"Rebel Officer Fails at Ship Stealing," *Portland Evening Express,* 29 May 1982, p. 84.

"The Rebs Invade Portland Harbor," Francis Whiting Hatch, *Yankee* 18, July 1954, pp. 38–39.

"The Story of the Blowing up of the Revenue Cutter *Caleb Cushing* in Portland Harbor June 27, 1863," *Portland Sunday Telegram,* 18 May 1958, p. 1D.

"The *Tacony* Affair," 1863 Report of the Adjutant General of Maine, pp. 15–23.

"Two Confederate Prisoners Captured Near the Isles of Shoals," *Eastern Argus*, 22 August 1863, p. 3.

"Unsung Battleground of the Civil War," *Down East,* May 1983, pp. 62–66.

THROUGH BLOOD AND FIRE
AT GETTYSBURG

JOSHUA L. CHAMBERLAIN

Nightfall brought us to Hanover, Pennsylvania, and to a halt. And it was the evening of the first day of July, 1863. All day we had been marching north from Maryland, searching and pushing out on all roads for the hoped-for collision with Lee—eagerly, hurriedly, yet cautiously, with skirmishers and flankers out to sound the first challenge, and our main body ready for the call. Fanwise our divisions had been spread out to cover Washington, but more was at stake than the capitol city of the Union: there was that important political and international question, the recognition of the Southern Confederacy as independent by France and England. This recognition, denying the very contentions of the North from the beginning, would have been almost fatal to it. And Lee need not win a decided victory in the field to bring about the recognition; his capture and occupation on an important and strategic point in the North would have been enough.

All day, ever and again, we had seen detachments of Lee's cavalry; even as we passed an outlying field to our encampment the red slanting sunlight fell softly across the grim relics of a cavalry fight of the afternoon, the survivors of which had swept on, flying and pursuing.

Worn and famished we stacked arms in camping order, hoping to bivouac beside them, and scampered like madcaps for those two prime factors of a desultory supper—water and fence-rails; for the finding of which the Yankee volunteer has an aptitude which should be ranked among the spiritual intuitions, though in their old-school theology most farmers of our acquaintance were inclined to reckon the aptitude among the carnal appetites of the totally depraved. Some of the forage wagons had now got up, and there was a brief rally at their tail-ends for quick justice to be dispensed. But the unregenerate fires had hardly blackened the coffee-dippers, and the hardtack hardly been hammered into working order by the bayonet-shanks, when everything was stopped short by whispers of disaster away on the left: the enemy had struck our column at Gettysburg, and driven it back with terrible loss; Reynolds, the commander, had been killed, and the remnant scarcely able to hold on to the hillsides unless rescue came before morning. These were only rumors hitting owl-like in the gathering shadows. We could not quite believe them, but they deepened our mood.

Suddenly the startling bugle-call from unseen headquarters. "The General!" it rang! "To the march! No moment of delay!" Word was coming, too. Staff officers dashed from corps, to division, to brigade, to regiment, to battery —until the order flew like the hawk, and not the owl. "To Gettysburg!" it said, a forced march of sixteen miles. But what forced it? And what opposed? Not supper, nor sleep, nor sore feet and aching limbs.

In a moment, the whole corps was in marching order; rest, rations, earth itself forgotten; one thought,—to be first on that Gettysburg road. The iron-faced veterans were transformed to boys. They insisted on starting out with colors living, so that even the night might know what manner of men were coming to redeem the day.

ORIGINALLY PUBLISHED IN
HEARST'S MAGAZINE 23, JUNE 1913.

All things, even the most common, were magnified and made mysterious by the strange spell of night. At a turn of the road a staff-officer, with an air of authority, told each colonel as he came up, that McClellan was in command again, and riding ahead of us on the road. Then wild cheers rolled from the crowding column into the brooding sky, and the earth shook under the quickened tread. Now from a dark angle of the roadside came a whisper, whether from earthly or unearthly voice one cannot feel quite sure, that the august form of Washington had been seen that afternoon at sunset riding over the Gettysburg hills. Let no one smile at me! I half believed it myself,—so did the powers of the other world draw nigh!

But there were wayside greetings such as we had never met before. We were in a free state, and among friendly people. All along the road, citizens came out to contemplate this martial array with a certain awe, and greet us with hearty welcome. But, most of all, our dark way was illumined by groups of girls in sweet attire gathered on the embowered lawns of modest homes, with lights and banners and flowers, and stirring songs whose import and effect were quite other than impersonal. Those who were not sisters of the muse of song waved their welcome in the ripple of white handkerchiefs—which token the gallant young gentlemen of the staff were prompt to take as summons to parley, and boldly rode up to meet with soft, half-tone scenes under the summer night; those meetings looked much like proposals for exchange of prisoners, or unconditional surrender. And others still, not daring; quite so much, but unable to repress the gracious impulse of giving, offered their silent benediction in a cup of water. And we remembered then with what sanction it was that water had been turned to wine in Cana of Galilee!

Snatching an hour's sleep by the roadside just before dawn, we reached at about seven o'clock in the morning the heights east of Gettysburg, confronting the ground over which the lost battle of the first day had ebbed. After a little, we were moved to the left, across Rock Creek and up the Baltimore Pike to an open field more nearly overlooking the town. On our front and left were the troops of the Eleventh and First Corps; on a commanding height to our right was strongly established the Twelfth Corps of our army. Told to rest awhile, we first resumed the

homely repast so sharply interrupted the evening before. Next we stretched ourselves on the ground to make up lost sleep, and rest our feet after a twenty-four hours' scarcely broken march, and get our heads level for the coming test.

We knew that a great battle was soon to be fought, a desperate and momentous one. But what much more impressed my mind was the great calm, the uncertainty of overture, and seeming lack of tactical plan for the tremendous issue. We were aware that other troops were coming up, on one side and the other; but we had no means of knowing or judging which side would take the offensive and which the defensive, or where the battle would begin. All the forenoon we had no other intimation as to this, than the order given in an impressive tone to hold ourselves ready to take part in an attack on our right; but whether to be begun by us or the enemy, we neither knew, nor could guess.

We were on Cemetery Hill, the apex of the angle made by an extended ridge, on the right bending sharply back for a mile to end in a lofty wooded crest known as Culp's Hill, and on the left running southerly from the Cemetery, declining somewhat in its course till at the distance of two miles or more it makes an abrupt and rugged rise in a rocky spur 500 feet high, named Little Round Top.; This was as now the outpost of a steep and craggy peak southward, one hundred and fifty feet higher, terminating the range, named Great Round Top. These landmarks for the whole region near and far, to the west and north especially, in a military point of view commanded the entire ground available for a great battle.

Within the wings of this sharp-beaked ridge there entered and met in the town two great thoroughfares, the Baltimore Pike and Taneytown Road, perfectly commanded by the Little Round Top. The latter road opened the direct way to Washington, and in the aspect of affairs was our only practicable line of retreat in case of disaster. Our Second Corps, Hancock's, had taken position on the ridge, from the Cemetery, southerly: and on the extension on this line our Third Corps, Sickles's, was forming—its left, we were told, resting on the northern slope of Little Round Top. This formation indicated a defensive attitude for us, and deepened our confidence in Meade.

Opposite Cemetery Ridge occupied by

us, westerly, something like a mile away, is another ridge, extending from behind the upper limits of the town to nearly opposite the Great Round top. This is known as Seminary Ridge, so named from the Lutheran Seminary on its northern slope. Between these two ridges comes another great thoroughfare, the Emmitsburg Road, entering the town close past the base of Cemetery Hill—thus all three thoroughfares mentioned converged. Along this ridge Hill's Confederate Corps had established itself, and up this Emmitsburg Road from Chambersburg, Longstreet's Corps were advancing. Ewell's Confederate Corp's held the town, and Early's Division extended northerly and easterly around to the front of Culp's Hill. Their attack, it is curious to observe, was from the north and east—from the direction of York and Hanover—so quickly and completely had Lee turned from his first, and so far successful, attempt to occupy the northern cities, to face the army of the Potomac now threatening their rear.

Our orders and expectations still kept us looking anxiously to the right, where yesterday's battle had left off, and the new one was to begin. But all was as yet uncertain. We were told that General Meade was now conferring with his Corps commanders as to the best point and part for the battle to open. But this symposium was cut short, and a plan of opening announced by a thundering burst of artillery from the rocks and woods away in front of the Round Tops, where we least of all expected it. A crash of musketry followed.

So the awakening bugle, sounded "To the left! At utmost speed!" Down to the left we pushed—the whole Fifth Corps—our brigade nearest and leading; at the double-quick, straight for the strife; not seeking roads, nor minding roughness of ground, thorn-hedges, stone-fences, or miry swamps mid-way, earth quaking, sky ablaze, and a deepening uproar as we drew near. We soon saw that our Third Corps was not where we thought between the Second Corps and the Round Tops—but had been moved forward a mile, it seemed, almost to the Emmitsburg Road.

The fight was desperate already. We passed along its rear, first getting a glimpse of the Peach Orchard on the right, where our troops were caught between Hill's Corps on Seminary Ridge and Longstreet's Corps fast arriving on the Emmitsburg Road;—and the havoc was terrible. We passed on to the

Wheat-field where heroic men standing bright as golden grain were ravaged by Death's wild reapers from the woods. Here we halted to be shown our places. We had a momentary glimpse of the Third Corps left in front of Round Top, and the fearful struggle at the Devil's Den, and Hood's out-flanking troops swarming beyond. Our halt was brief, but our senses alert. I saw our First and Second Brigades go on to the roaring woods, between the Peach Orchard and the Wheat-field.

In another instant, a staff officer from General Warren rushed up, to find Sykes, our Corps Commander, to beg him to send a brigade at least, to seize Little Round Top before the enemy's surging waves should overwhelm it. Other supplications were in the air; calling for aid everywhere. Our Vincent, soldierly and self-reliant, hearing this entreaty for Round Top, waited word from no superior, but taking the responsibility ordered us to turn and push for Round Top at all possible speed, and dashed ahead to study how best to place us. We broke to the right and rear, found a rude log bridge over Plum Run, and a rough farm-road leading to the base of the mountain. Here, as we could, we took the double-quick.

Now we learned that Warren, chief engineer of our army, sent by Meade to see how things were going on the left, drawn to Little Round Top by its evident importance, found to his astonishment that it was unoccupied except by a little group of signal-men, earnestly observing the movements over in the region of the Emmitsburg Road beyond the Devil's Den. Warren, to test a surmise, sent word to a battery of ours in position below, to throw a solid shot into a mass of woods in that vicinity. The whir of the shot overhead brought out the glitter of many musket-barrels and bayonets in the slanting sunlight—the revelation of fact, the end of dreams! In a moment more, the fierce attack fell on our Third Corps' left, lashed the Devil's Den into a seething cauldron, leaving free a large Confederate force to sweep past for the base of the Round Tops. They would make short work in taking the height, and Warren did likewise in his call for the race.

Earnestly we scanned that rugged Peak which was to be the touchstone of that day's battle. It bore a rough forbidding face, wrinkled with jagged ledges, bearded with mighty boulders; even the smooth spots were strewn with fragments of rock like the play-ground or battle-ground of giants in the elemental storms of old. Straggling trees wrestled with the rocks for a foot-hold; some were in a rich vein of mold and shot up stark and grim. Altogether it was a strange and solemn place, looking forlorn and barren now, but to be made rich enough soon with precious blood, and far-wept tears.

As we mounted its lower gradient, Longstreet's batteries across Plum Run had us in full view, and turned their whole force upon our path, to sweep the heights free of us till their gray line, now straining towards them, could take them by foot or hand. Shells burst overhead and brought down tree-tops as the hissing fragments fell; or glanced along the shelving ledges and launched splinters of rock to multiply their terrors; solid shot swept close above our heads, their compressed, burning breath driving the men's breath like lead to the bottom of their breasts.

At that fiery moment three brothers of us were riding abreast, and a solid shot driving close past our faces disturbed me. "Boys," I said, "I don't like this. Another such shot might made it hard for mother. Tom, go to the rear of the regiment, and see that it is well closed up! John, pass up ahead and look out a place for our wounded." Tom, the youngest lieutenant of Company G. was serving as adjutant of the regiment; John, a little older, was sent out by the Christian Commission for this battle, and I had applied for him. We had no surgeon; the old ones were gone, and the new ones not come. So I pressed him into field hospital service, with Chaplain French and the ambulance men, under charge of Hospital Steward Baker.

As we neared the summit of the mountain, the shot so raked the crest that we had to keep our men below it to save their heads, although this did not wholly avert the visits of treetops and splinters of rock and iron, while the boulders and clefts and pitfalls in our path made it seem like the replica of the evil "den" across the sweetly named Plum Run.

Reaching the southern face of Little Round Top, I found Vincent there, with intense poise and look. He said with a voice of awe, as if translating the tables of the eternal law, "I place you here! This is the left of the Union line. You understand. You are to hold this ground at all costs!" I did understand—full well; but had more to learn about costs.

The regiment coming up "right in front" was put in position by a quite uncommon or-der, "on the right by file into line"; both that we should thus be facing the enemy when we came to a front, and also be ready to commence firing as fast as each man arrived. This is a rather slow style of formation, but this time it was needful. Knowing that we had no supports on the left, I dispatched a stalwart company under the level-headed Captain Morrill in that direction, with orders to move along up the valley to our front and left, between us and the eastern base of the Great Round Top, to keep within supporting distance of us, and to act as the exigencies of the battle should require.

The Twentieth Maine Regiment had 358 men equipped for duty in the ranks, with twenty-eight officers. They were all well-seasoned soldiers, and what is more, well-rounded men, body and brain. One somewhat important side-note must have place here, in order properly to appreciate the mental and moral attitude of the men before us. One hundred and twenty of these men from the Second Maine were recruits, whom some recruiting officer had led into the belief that they should be discharged with their regiment at the end of its term of service. In their enthusiasm they had not noticed that they were signing enlistment papers for "three years of the war"; and when they had been held in the field after the discharge of the regiment they had refused to do military duty, and had been sequestrated in a prisoners camp as mutineers, waiting court-martial. The exigency of our movement the last of May had not permitted this semi-civil: and orders from the Secretary of War had directed me to take these men up on my rolls and put them to duty. This made it still harder for them to accept, as they had never enlisted in this regiment. However, they had been soon brought over to me under guard of the One Hundred and Eighteenth Pennsylvania, with fixed bayonets; with orders to me to take them into my regiment and "make them do duty, or shoot them down the moment they refused"; these had been the very words of the Corps Commander in person. The responsibility, I had thought, gave me some discretionary power. So I had placed their names on our rolls, distributed them by groups, to equalize companies, and particularly to break up the "esprit de corps" of banded mutineers. Then I had called them together and pointed out to them the situation; that they could not be entertained as civilian guests by me; that they were by authority of the United States on my rolls as soldiers, and I should treat them as soldiers should be treated; that they should lose no rights by obeying orders, and I would see what could be done for their claim. It is pleasant to record that all but one or two had gone back manfully to duty, to become some of the best soldiers in the regiment, as I was to prove this very day.

The exigency was great. I released the pioneers and provost guard altogether, and set them to their companies. All but the drummer boys and hospital attendants went into the ranks. Even the cooks and servants, not liable to such service, asked to go in. Others whom I knew to be sick or footsore, and had given a pass to "fall out" on the forced marches of the day and night before, came up, now that the battle was on; dragging themselves along on lame and bleeding feet, finding their regiment with the sagacity of the brave, and their places where need is greatest and hearts truest. "Places?" Did any of these heroic men ever leave them?—although for all too many we passed their names at evening roll-call thereafter, with only the heart's answer, "Here forever!"

Our line looked towards the Great Round Top, frowning above us not a gunshot away, and raising grave thoughts of what might happen if the enemy should gain foothold there, even if impracticable for artillery. We had enough of that, as it was. For the tremendous cannonade from across the Plum Run gorge was still pounding the Little Round Top crests: happily, not as yet striking my line, which it would have enfiladed if it got the range.

The other regiments of the brigade were forming on our right; the Eighty-third Pennsylvania, the Forty-fourth New York, and the Sixteenth Michigan. I was observing and meditating as to the impending and the possible, when something of the real was substituted by a visit from Colonel Rice. He thought it would be profitable for us to utilize these few minutes by going to the clearer space on the right of his regiment to take a look at the aspect of things in the Plum Run valley—the direction of the advance on our front. It was a forewarning indeed. The enemy had already turned the Third Corps left, the Devil's Den was a smoking crater, the Plum Run gorge was a whirling maelstrom; one force was charging our advanced batteries near the Wheat-field; the flanking force was pressing past the base

of the Round Tops; all rolling towards us in tumultuous waves.

It was a stirring, not to say appalling, sight: here a whole battery of shot and shell cutting a ragged chasm through a serried mass, flinging men and horses like drift aside; there, a rifle volley at close range, with reeling shock, hands tossed in air, muskets dropped with death's quick relax, or clutched with last, convulsive energy, men falling like grass before the scythe—others with manhood's proud calm and rally; there, a little group kneeling above some favorite officer slain,—his intense spirit still animating the fiery steed pressing headlong with empty saddle to the van; here, a defiant regiment of ours, broken, slaughtered, captured; or survivors, of both sides crouching among the rocks for shelter from the terrible crossfire where there is no rear! But all advancing—all the frenzied force, victors and vanquished, each scarcely knowing which—surging and foaming towards us; death around, behind, before, and madness everywhere!

Yes, brave Rice! it was well for us to see this; the better to see it through. A look into each other's eyes; without a word, we resumed our respective places.

Ten minutes had not passed. Suddenly the thunder of artillery and crash of iron that had all the while been roaring over the Round Top crests stopped short.

We understood this, too. The storming lines, that had swept past the Third Corps' flank, had got up the base of Little Round Top, and under the range and reach of their guns. They were close upon us among the rocks, we knew, unseen, because so near.

In a minute more came the role of musketry. It struck the exposed right center of our brigade.

Promptly answered, repulsed, and renewed again and again, it soon reached us, still extending. Two brigades of Hood's Division had attacked—Texas and Alabama. The Fourth Alabama reached our right, the Forty-seventh Alabama joined and crowded in, but gradually, owing to their echelon advance. Soon seen companies of this regiment were in our front. We had all we could stand. My attention was sharply called, now here, now there. In the thick of the fight and smoke, Lieutenant Nichols, a bright officer near our center, ran up to tell me something queer was going on in his front, behind those engaging us.

I sprang forward, mounted a great rock in

the midst of his company line, and was soon able to resolve the "queer" impression into positive knowledge. Thick groups in gray were pushing up along the smooth dale between the Round Tops in a direction to gain our left flank. There was no mistaking this. If they could hold our attention by a hot fight in front while they got in force on that flank, it would be bad for us and our whole defense. How many were coming we could not know. We were rather too busy to send out a reconnaissance. If a strong force should gain our rear, our brigade would be caught as by a mighty shears-blade, and be cut and crushed. What would follow it was easy to foresee. This must not be. Our orders to hold that ground had to be liberally interpreted. That front had to be held, and that rear covered.

GENERAL JOSHUA L. CHAMBERLAIN

Something must be done,—quickly and coolly. I called the captains and told them my tactics: to keep the front fire at the hottest, without special regard to its need or immediate effect, and at the same time, as they found opportunity, to take side steps to the left, coming gradually into one rank, file-closers and all. Then I took the colors with their guard and placed them at our extreme left, where a great boulder gave token and support; thence bending back at a right angle the whole body gained ground leftward and made twice our original front. And were not so long doing it. This was a difficult movement to execute under such a fire, requiring coolness as well as heat. Of rare quality were my officers and men. I shall never cease to admire and honor them for what they did in this desperate crisis.

Now as an important element of the situation, let our thought turn to what was going on meanwhile to the right of us. When Warren saw us started for Little Round Top, looking still intently down, he saw Hood's two brigades breaking past the Third Corps' left and sweeping straight for Little Round Top. Then he flew down to bring reinforcement for this vital place and moment. He came upon the One Hundred and Fortieth New York, of Weed's Brigade of our Second Division, just going in to Sickles' relief, and dispatched it headlong for Round Top. Weed was to follow, and Ayres' whole division—but not yet. Warren also laid hold of Hazlett, with his battery, D of the Fifth Regulars, and sent him to scale those heights—if in the power of man so to master nature. Meantime the tremendous blow of the Fourth and Fifth Texas struck the right of our brigade, and our Sixteenth Michigan reeled and staggered back under the shock. Confusion followed. Vincent felt that all was lost unless the very gods should intervene. Sword aloft and face aflame, he rushed in among the broken companies in desperate effort to rally them, man by man. By sheer force of his superb personality he restored a portion of his line, and was urging up the rest. "Don't yield an inch now, men, or all is lost!" he cried, when an answering volley scorched the very faces of the men, and Vincent's soul went up in a chariot of fire. In that agonizing moment, came tearing up the One Hundred and Fortieth New York, gallant O'Rorke at the head. Not waiting to load a musket or form a line, they sprang forward into that turmoil. Met by a withering volley that killed its fine young colonel and laid low many of his intrepid officers and a hundred of his men, this splendid regiment, by a providence we may well call divine, saved us all in that moment of threatened doom.

To add a tragic splendor to this dark scene, in the midst of it all, the indomitable Hazlett was trying to get his guns—tenpounder rifled parrotts—up to a working place on the summit close beyond. Finally he was obliged to take his horses entirely off, and lift his guns by hand and handspike up the craggy steep, whence he launched death and defiance wide and far around.

The roar of all this tumult reached us on the left, and heightened the intensity of our resolve. Meanwhile the flanking column worked around to our left and joined with those before us in a fierce assault, which lasted with increasing fury for an intense hour. The two lines met and broke and mingled in the shock. The crush of musketry gave way to cuts and thrusts, grapplings and wrestlings. The edge of conflict swayed to and fro, with wild whirlpools and eddies. At times I saw around me more of the enemy than of my own men; gaps opening, swallowing, closing again with sharp convulsive energy; squads of stalwart men who had cut their way through us, disappearing as if translated. All around, strange, mingled roar—shouts of defiance, rally, and desperation; and underneath, murmured entreaty and stilted moans; gasping prayers, snatches of Sabbath song, whispers of loved names; everywhere men torn and broken, staggering, creeping, quivering on the earth, and dead faces with strangely fixed eyes staring stark into the sky. Things which cannot be told—nor dreamed.

How men [held] on, each one knows—not I. But manhood commands admiration. There was one fine young fellow, who had been cut down early in the fight with a ghastly wound across his forehead, and who I had thought might possibly be saved with prompt attention. So I had sent him back to our little field hospital, at least to die in peace. Within a half-hour, in a desperate rally I saw that noble youth amidst the rolling smoke as an apparition from the dead, with bloody bandage for the only covering of his head, in the thick of the fight, high-borne and pressing on as they that shall see death no more. I shall know him when I see him again, on whatever shore!

So, too, another. In the very deepest of the struggle while our shattered line had pressed the enemy well below their first point of contact, and the struggle to regain it was fierce, I saw through a sudden rift in the thick smoke our colors standing alone. I first thought some optical illusion imposed upon me. But as forms emerged through the drifting smoke, the truth came to view. The cross-fire had cut keenly; the center had been almost shot away; only two of the color-guard had been left, and they fighting to fill the whole space; and in the center, wreathed in battle smoke, stood the Color-Sergeant, Andrew Tozier. His color-staff planted in the ground at his side, the upper part clasped in his elbow, so holding the flag upright, with musket and cartridges seized from the fallen

comrade at his side he was defending his sacred trust in the manner of the songs of chivalry. It was a stirring picture—its import still more stirring. That color must be saved, and that center too. I sent first to the regiment on our right for a dozen men to help us here, but they could not spare a man. I then called my young brother, Tom, the adjutant, and sent him forward to close that gap somehow; if no men could be drawn from neighboring companies, to draw back the salient angle and contract our center. The fire down there at this moment was so hot I thought it impossible for him to get there alive; and I dispatched immediately after him Sergeant Thomas, whom I had made a special orderly, with the same instructions. It needed them both; and both came back with personal proofs of the perilous undertaking. It was strange that the enemy did not seize that moment and point of weakness. Perhaps they saw no weakness. Perhaps it was awe or admiration that held them back from breaking in upon that sublime scene.

When that mad carnival lulled,—from some strange instinct in human nature and without any reason in the situation that can be seen—when the battling edges drew asunder, there stood our little line, groups and gaps, notched like saw-teeth, but sharp as steel, tempered in infernal heats like a magic sword of the Goths. We were on the appointed and entrusted line. We had held ground—"at all costs!"

But sad surprise! It had seemed to us we were all the while holding our own, and had never left it. But now that the smoke dissolved, we saw our dead and wounded all out in front of us, mingled with more of the enemy. They were scattered all the way down to the very feet of the baffled hostile line now rallying in the low shrubbery for a new onset. We could not wait for this. They knew our weakness now. And they were gathering force. No place for tactics now! The appeal must be to primal instincts of human nature!

"Shall they die there, under the enemy's feet, and under your eyes?" Words like those brokenly uttered, from heart to heart, struck the stalwart groups holding together for a stand, and roused them to the front quicker than any voice or bugle of command. These true-hearted men but a little before buffeted back and forth by superior force, and now bracing for a dubious test, dashed down the death-strewn slope into the face of the rallied and recovering foe, and hurled them, tore them from above our fallen as the tiger avenges its young. Nor did they stop till they had cleared the farthest verge of the field, redeemed by the loving for the lost—the brave for the brave.

Now came a longer lull. But this meant, not rest, but thought and action. First, it was to gather our wounded, and bear them to the sheltered lawn for saving life, or peace in dying; the dead, too, that not even our feet should do them dishonor in the coming encounter. Then—such is heavenly human pity—the wounded of our Country's foes; brothers in blood for us now, so far from other caring; borne to like refuge and succor by the drummer-boys who had become angels of the field.

In this lull I took a turn over the dismal field to see what could be done for the living, in ranks or recumbent; and came upon a manly form and face I well remembered. He was a sergeant earlier in the field of Antietam and Fredericksburg; and for refusing to perform some menial personal service for a bullying quartermaster in winter camp, was reduced to the ranks by a commander who had not carefully investigated the case. It was a degradation, and the injustice of it rankled in his high-born spirit. But his well-bred pride would not allow him to ask for justice as a favor. I had kept this in mind, for early action. Now he was lying there, stretched on an open front where a brave stand had been made, face to the sky, a great bullet-hole in the middle of his breast, from which he had loosened the clothing, to ease his breathing, and the rich blood was pouring in a stream. I bent down over him. His face lightened; his lips moved. But I spoke first, "My dear boy, it has gone hard with you. You shall be cared for!" He whispered. "Tell my mother I did not die a coward!" It was the prayer of home-bred manhood poured out with his life-blood. I knew and answered him, "You did a sergeant. I promote you for faithful service and noble courage on the field of Gettysburg!" This was all he wanted. No word more. I had him borne from the field, but his high spirit had passed to its place. It is needless to add that as soon as a piece of parchment could be found after that battle, a warrant was made out promoting George Washington Buck to sergeant in the terms told him; and this evidence placed the sad, proud mother's name on the rolls of the Country's benefactors.

As for myself, so far I had escaped. How close an escape I had had I did not know till afterwards. I think I may mention here, as a psychological incident, that some years after the war, I received a letter written in a comely but manly style by one subscribing himself "a member of the Fifteenth Alabama," in these words:

Dear Sir:
   I want to tell you of a little passage in the battle of Round Top, Gettysburg, concerning you and me, which I am now glad of. Twice in that fight I had your life in my hands. I got a safe place between two big rocks, and drew bead fair and square on you. You were standing in the open behind your line, full exposed. I knew your rank by your uniform and your actions, and I thought it a mighty good thing to put you out of the way. I rested my gun on the rock and took steady aim. I started to pull the trigger, but some queer notion stopped me. Then I got ashamed of my weakness and went through the same motions again. I had you, perfectly certain. But that same queer something shut right down on me. I couldn't pull the trigger, and gave it up,—that is, your life. I am glad of it now, and hope you are.
                    Yours truly.

I thought he was that, and answered him accordingly, asking him to come up North and see whether I was worth what he missed. But my answer never found him, nor could I afterwards.

The silence and the doubt of the momentary lull were quickly dispelled. The formidable Fifteenth Alabama, repulsed and as we hoped dispersed, now in solid and orderly array—still more than twice our numbers—came rolling through the fringe of chaparral on our left. No dash: no yells; no demonstrations for effect; but settled purpose and determination! We opened on them as best we could. The fire was returned, cutting us to the quick.

The Forty-Seventh Alabama had rallied on our right. We were enveloped in fire, and sure to be overwhelmed in fact when the great surge struck us. Whatever might be other where, what was here before us was evident; these far-outnumbering, confident eyes, yet watching for a sign of weakness. Already I could see the bold flankers on their right darting out and creeping catlike under the smoke to gain our left, thrown back as it was. It was for us, then, once for all. Our thin line was broken, and the enemy were in rear of the whole Round Top defense—infantry, artillery, humanity itself—with the Round Top and the day theirs.

Now, too, our fire was slackening; our last rounds of shot had been fired; what I had sent for could not get to us. I saw the faces of my men one after another, when they had fired their last cartridge, turn anxiously towards mine for a moment: then square to the front again. To the front for them lay death; to the rear what they would die to save. My thought was running deep. I was combining the elements of a "forlorn hope," and had just communicated this to Captain Spear of the wheeling flank, on which the initiative was to fall. Just then—so will a little incident fleck a brooding cloud of doom with a tint of human tenderness—brave, warm-hearted Lieutenant Melcher, of the Color Company, whose Captain and nearly half his men were down, came up and asked if he might take his company and go forward and pick up one or two of his men left wounded on the field, and bring them in before the enemy got too near. This would be a most hazardous move in itself, and in this desperate moment, we could not break our line. But I admired him. With a glance, he understood, I answered, "Yes, sir, in a moment! I am about to order a charge!"

Not a moment was to be lost! Five minutes more of such a defensive, and the last roll-call would sound for us! Desperate as the chances were, there was nothing for it, but to take the offensive. I stepped to the colors. The men turned towards me. One word was enough,—"BAYONET!"—It caught like fire, and swept along the ranks. The men took it up with a shout,—one could not say, whether from the pit, or the song of the morning star! It were vain to order "Forward." No mortal could have heard it in the mighty hosanna that was winging the sky. Nor would he wait to hear. There are things still as of the first creation, "whose seed is in itself." The grating clash of steel in fixing bayonets told its own story; the color rose in front; the whole line quivered for the start; the edge of the left-wing rippled, swung, tossed among the rocks, straightened, charged curve from scimitar to sickle-shape; and the bristling archers swooped down upon the serried host—down

into the face of half a thousand! Two hundred men!

It was a great right wheel. Our left swung first. The advancing foe stopped, tried to make a stand amidst the trees and boulders, but the frenzied bayonets pressing through every space forced a constant settling to the rear. Morrill, with his detached company and the remnants of our valorous sharpshooters who had held the enemy so long in check on the slopes the Great Round Top, now fell upon the flank of the retiring crowd, and it turned to full retreat—some up amidst the crags of Great Round Top, but most down the smooth vale towards their own main line on Plum Run. This tended to mass them before our center. Here their stand was more stubborn. At the first dash the commanding officer I happened to confront, coming on fiercely, sword in one hand and big navy revolver in the other, fires one barrel almost in my face; but seeing the quick saber-point at his throat, reverses arms, gives sword and pistol into my hands and yields himself prisoner. I took him at his word, but could not give him further attention. I passed him over into the custody of a brave sergeant at my side, to whom I gave the sword as emblem of his authority, but kept the pistol with its loaded barrels, which I thought might come handy soon, as indeed it did.

Ranks were broken; many retired before us somewhat hastily; some threw their muskets to the ground—even loaded; sunk on their knees, threw up their hands, calling out, "We surrender. Don't kill us!" As if we wanted to do that! We kill only to resist killing. And these were manly men, whom we would befriend, and by no means kill, if they came our way in peace and good will. Charging right through and over these, we struck the second line of the Forty-seventh Alabama doing their best to stand, but offering little resistance. Their Lieutenant-Colonel as I passed—and a fine gentleman was Colonel Bulger—introduced himself as my prisoner, and as he was wounded, I had him cared for as best we could. Still swinging to the right as a great gate on its hinges, we swept the front clean of assailants. We were taking in prisoners by scores—more than we could hold, or send to the rear, so that many made final escape up Great Round Top. Halfway down to the throat of the vale I came upon Colonel Powell of the Fourth Alabama, a man of courtly bearing, who was badly wounded. I sent him to the

Eighty-third Pennsylvania, nearest to us and better able to care of him than we were.

When we reached the front of the Forty-fourth New York, I thought it far enough. Beyond on the right the Texas Brigade had rallied or rendezvoused. I took thought of that. Most of the fugitives before us, rather than run the gauntlet of our whole brigade, had taken the shelter of the rocks of Great Round Top, on our left, as we now faced. It was hazardous to be so far out, in the very presence of so many baffled but far from beaten veterans of Hood's renowned division. A sudden rush on either flank might not only cut us off, but cut in behind us and seize that vital point which it was our orders and our trust to hold. But it was no light task to get our men to stop. They were under the momentum of their deed. They thought they were "on the road to Richmond." They had to be reasoned with, persuaded, but at last faced about and marched back to that dedicated crest with swelling hearts.

Not without sad interest and service was the return. For many of the wounded had to be gathered up. There was a burden, too, of the living. Nearly four hundred prisoners remained in our hands—two for every man of ours.

Shortly the twilight deepened, and we disposed ourselves to meet any new assault that might come from the courage of exasperation. But the attack was not renewed. Whether that cold steel had chilled the ardor, which flaming muzzles seem to enliven and sustain, or the revulsion of the retiring mood was not yet over, a wide silence brooded over the hostile line. Our worn-out men, bid at last to rest, fitted themselves to their environment or followed their souls' behest. Some bent as if senseless to the earth, some gazed up at the stars and sent wireless messages through them to dear ones far-away; some wandered dreamily away in a search for water to wash from their throats the nitrous fumes of battle; others too manly to seek a surgeon, looked even for a shred of cartridge paper to staunch a too-free wound, or yet more deeply drawn sought the sheltered nook where our wounded had been borne to render such aid as they could, and take the farewell message home from lips of brave men to hearts that had to be more brave.

At nine o'clock the next morning we were withdrawn, being relieved by our First Brigade. But we were sent to anything but a place of rest. Our new position was in support of Hancock's troops near the left center of the Union line, which proved to be the point aimed at by Pickett's charge that afternoon.

This is the story of my participation in the action and the passion of the second day at Gettyburg.

It was certainly a narrow chance for us, and for the Round Tops. Had we not used up our ammunition, and had we continued to meet the enemy musket to musket, this "give and take" would soon have finished us by reason of the enemy's superior numbers. Or had the Fifteenth Alabama continued their onset not regarding our preposterous demonstrations, they would have walked over our bodies to their victory. Or, still again, if one more Confederate regiment had come upon our flank, we must have been rolled into a zero figure and swallowed up in the envelopment. It was a psychological success,—a miracle in the scheme of military science. Those brave Alabama fellows—none braver or better in either army—were victims of a surprise, of their quick and mobile imagination.

Return we now to our field and our parting. On the Fourth of July we took part in a reconnaissance over the wreck-strewn field amidst scenes of insupportable horror. Pushing out as far as Willoughby's Run, finding no enemy, we returned to our ground. We were now told to rest and be ready to move from the field the next day.

But there was neither removal nor rest for us, till we had gone up the Round Top slopes to bid farewell to our dead. We found them there on the sheltered lawn where we had laid them, on the velvet moss fringed by the low cedars that veiled the place with peace and beauty. I rode up near, and flinging the rein upon my horse's neck, dismounted to bend over them for a soldier's farewell. There they lay, side by side, with touch of elbow still; brave bronzed faces where the last thought was written: manly resolution, heroic self-giving, divine reconciliation; or where on some fair young face the sweet mother-look had come out under death's soft whisper.

We buried them there, in a grave, alas, too wide, on the sunny side of a great rock, eternal witnesses of their worth—the rock and the sun. Rude head-boards made of ammunition boxes, rudely carved under tear-dimmed eyes, marked and named each grave, and told each home.

I went—it is not long ago—to stand again upon that crest whose one day's crown of fire has passed into the blazoned coronet of fame; to look again upon the rocks whereon were laid as on the altar the lives of Vincent and O'Rorke, of Weed and Hazlett—all the chief commanders. And farther on, where my own young heroes mounted to fall no more—Billings, the valor of whose onward-looking eyes not death itself could quench; Kendall, almost maiden-sweet and fair, yet heeding not the bolts that dashed his life-blood on the rocks; Estes and Steele, and Noyes and Buck, lifted high above self, pure in heart as they that shall see God; and far up the rugged sides of Great Round Top, swept in darkness and silence like its own, where the impetuous Linscott halted at last before the morning star.

I thought of those other noble men of every type, commanders all, who bore their wounds so bravely—many to meet their end on later fields—and those on whose true hearts further high trusts were to be laid. Nor did I forget those others, whether their names are written on the scrolls of honor and fame, or their dust left on some far field and nameless here—nameless never to me, nor nameless, I trust in God, where they are tonight.

I sat there alone, on the storied crest, till the sun went down as it did before over the misty hills, and the darkness crept up the slopes, till from all earthly sight I was buried as with those before. But oh, what radiant companionship rose around, what steadfast ranks of power, what bearing of heroic souls. Oh, the glory that beamed through those nights and days. Nobody will ever know it here!—I am sorry most of all for that. The proud young valor that rose above the mortal, and then at last was mortal after all; the chivalry of hand and heart that in other days and other hands would have sent their names ringing down in song and story!

They did not know it themselves—those boys of ours whose remembered faces in every home should be cherished symbols of the true, for life or death—what were their lofty deeds of body, mind, heart, soul, on that tremendous day.

Unknown—but kept! The earth itself shall be its treasurer. It holds something of ours besides graves. These strange influences of material nature, its mountains and seas, its sunset skies and nights of stars, its colors and tones and odors, carry something of the mutual, reciprocal. It is a sympathy. On that other side it is represented to us as suffering. The whole creation travailing in pain together, in earnest expectation, waiting for the adoption—having right, then, to something which is to be its own.

And so these Gettysburg hills which lifted up such splendid valor, and drank in such high heart's blood, shall hold the mighty secret in their bosom till the great day of revelation and recompense, when these heights shall flame again with transfigured light—they, too, have part in that adoption, which is the manifestation of the sons of God!

Also See

"Account of Gen. Joshua L. Chamberlain's Tactics in Defending Little Round Top," *Portland Press Herald*, 25 May 1987, pp. 1, 10.

"Account of 20th Maine Regiment's Heroic Stand at Little Roundtop During the Civil War," *Portland Press Herald*, 4 July 1975, p. 13.

"Beside Gen. Chamberlain at Little Round Top," *Lewiston Journal Illustrated Magazine*, 31 May 1924, p. 5.

"Durham's Hero of the Hilltop," *Lewiston Journal Illustrated Magazine*, 24 May 1930, p. 2.

"Hero of Battles of Five Oaks and Little Round Top in Civil War," *Lewiston Journal Illustrated Magazine*, 21 June 1913, pp. 8–9.

"'The Hero of Little Round Top' Recalled That Day in Interview," *Lewiston Journal Illustrated Magazine*, 26 May 1962, p. 3.

"How General Chamberlain with the 20th Maine Held Little Round Top," *Lewiston Journal Illustrated Magazine*, 25 May 1912, pp. 1–3.

"Little Round Top: a Battle Saved by Mainers," *Bangor Daily News*, 12–13 July 1983, pp. 1WE, 8WE.

"A Maine Private in the Civil War—the Twentieth Maine Volunteers at Little Round Top," *Down East* 3, May 1957, pp. 24–29.

"The Nineteenth Maine Regiment at Gettysburg," *War Papers: Read Before the Commandery of the State of Maine* 4, 1915, Portland: Lefavor-Tower Company, p. 250–63.

"The Sixteenth Maine Regiment at Gettysburg," *War Papers: Read Before the Commandery of the State of Maine* 4, 1915, Portland: Lefavor-Tower Company, p. 150–70.

"20th Maine Regiment Beats Confederate's Force to Hill," *Portland Evening Express*, 2 July 1963, p. 19.

THE GREAT MEDAL OF HONOR CAPER

CHRISTOPHER HYDE

The Congressional Medal of Honor, a bronze medallion depicting Minerva, goddess of wisdom, repulsing the imp Discord, is our nation's most prestigious military award. Those who have received it are few—only 3,551 since the medal's establishment, in 1861—and their acts of bravery have been investigated almost as carefully as the Catholic church's candidates for sainthood. The requirements are strict and well-defined: the Medal of Honor is reserved for the individual who "while an officer or enlisted man . . . shall . . . in action involving actual conflict with an enemy, distinguish himself conspicuously by gallantry and intrepidity at the risk of his life above and beyond the call of duty." So high is the honor that it has been said that one must practically be dead to have earned it. In World War II, for example, sixty medals were awarded posthumously for falling on live grenades; in the Korean War, of 131 awarded, only thirty-seven went to living men.

Like most marks of human esteem, however, the Medal of Honor has had its ups and downs. In fact, shortly after it was established, in the midst of the Civil War, it was won by—or handed out to—an entire Maine regiment, from cook to quartermaster. But only about a third of the regiment ever actually received the medals, and even these were recalled some fifty years later, in a sort of posthumous dishonorable discharge intended to set the record straight.

The hapless regiment was the Maine Twenty-seventh. Had it not been for the great medal snafu, the Twenty-seventh's service during the Civil War, from September, 1862, to June, 1863, would have gone unhonored, unsung, and unrecalled. To be sure, there were casualties among its troops, but rather than being caused by valiant service in the field, they resulted from diseases contracted in the pestilential atmosphere of Washington, D.C. The regiment, in effect, won the Medal of Honor for sentry duty.

No one has ever completely straightened out the mess. A Maine historian and Philadelphia advertising man named John Pullen tried his hand at it in a book, *Shower of Stars,* published in 1966, but even his exhaustive research left some loose ends, and they continue to flap in the wind. Somewhere in Kittery today there may well be a kid with a shoebox full of bronze portraits of Minerva repulsing Discord. Local youngsters in years past, it is said, used the stars for sheriff's badges when playing cops and robbers.

The story begins with a Kittery family doctor named Mark F. Wentworth. Wentworth was a bearded bear of a man, so big he couldn't fit into a ready-made shirt, with the kind of chiseled-in-granite features you often see in nineteenth-century portraits. A Maine farm boy, he had worked his way through medical school, from Dartmouth to the University of Pennsylvania.

At the beginning of the Civil War, Wentworth was forty-one. He held important posts at the Kittery Navy Yard, was active in Republican Party politics, and was a good friend of Lincoln's first vice-president, Hannibal Hamlin, whom he had served as chief of staff during Hamlin's term as Maine's governor.

In Kittery, Wentworth was quite definitely a power. Yet in the *History of York County,* a kind of chamber-of-commerce puff piece written in 1880, the only mention Wentworth merits is in the list of those who fought in the "Slaveholders' Rebellion." (Southerners like

FROM *DOWN EAST,* NOVEMBER 1981.

to call it the "War of Northern Aggression.") Every other prominent man in every village of York County is given his eulogy. But not Wentworth. If the old histories worked like some modern-day *Who's Whos*, one might guess he was given short shrift for refusing to pay his subscription. But the good doctor's modesty

COLONEL MARK WENTWORTH

is a more likely explanation, for among the acknowledgments at the front of the book appears the name Mark F. Wentworth (not [Colonel], not M.D.). It seems he helpfully supplied the book's author with information about everyone but himself.

Like many Mainers at the time the Slaveholders' Rebellion broke out in 1861, Wentworth was anxious to do his part to preserve the Union. He used his own money to refurbish Fort McClary, near Kittery, and equip it with guns discarded from the navy yard. He drilled the men, but what he really wanted was to go where the action was. So he decided to raise the Twenty-seventh Maine. In those days, one of the ways to become a colonel was to set up one's own regiment.

The Twenty-seventh's members were nine-month volunteers because by signing up for a minimum of nine months a man could do his duty, avoid the draft, and earn a substantial incentive payment put up by the town and those citizens who had more important things to do than go to war. (One regiment was greeted upon its arrival at the front by a cheer from the ranks alluding to its bonus: "Two hundred dollahs and a *cow!*")

The colonel was Rufus Tapley, another self-made man, lawyer, legislator, and as it turned out, summer soldier. Wentworth was lieutenant colonel. The regiment was officially organized on September 30, 1862, and left Portland for Washington on October 20.

For Wentworth's collection of farm boys, most of whom had never been out of York County, the three-day journey must have seemed the adventure of a lifetime. There were tearful farewells at Portland Depot and another round of them at South Berwick Junction. The trip to Boston was followed by an overnight steamship ride from Fall River to Jersey City. Then came openhanded hospitality in Philadelphia at the Cooper Shop Refreshment Saloon, and more cheers as the troops boarded the cattle cars for Baltimore.

After this buildup, the nation's capital, steaming in the rain, must have been a vast disappointment. The symbol of the Union was little more than a miserable village with grandiose expectations. Wild razorback hogs rooted in the muddy streets, the climate and the water were decidedly unhealthy, and the population was accounted to be about half "Secesh." Camp Chase, on Arlington Heights, where the Twenty-seventh was first stationed, was a tent city on a hill, its trees chopped down for firewood, its soil scarred and eroded by streaming wagon roads. One York County soldier wrote in a letter home that they were camped on the grounds of Robert E. Lee's mansion. "He is not here now," he added.

But General Lee was coming back, or so it seemed to most of the citizens of Washington, who viewed the event with alarm or anticipation, depending on their politics. Lee's army had stampeded Congress itself at the First Battle of Bull Run. The lawmakers set out that morning in high spirits for the battlefield, with fried chicken in hampers, tablecloths, wives, children, and dogs, intending to picnic on the high ground and watch the fight. That evening one of the few things that slowed down the rout of the Union troops was a carriage jam of panic-stricken congressmen, blocking the only bridge back to the capital.

Congress never got that close to a battle again, but Washington became very nervous over the Union reverses at the Second Battle of Bull Run, at Antietam, at Chambersburg, and at the victories of the Confederate ironclad ship, the *Merrimac*, before the *Monitor* fought it to a draw. Perhaps they remembered how easily the British had burned the White House fifty years before. The Confederate raider Colonel John Singleton Mosby played on their fears, dancing around the city like a will-o'-the-wisp, goading the defenders into a perpetual state of alarm. As a result, almost a hundred companies, and batteries that could better have been employed elsewhere, were kept guarding the capital. And that was the fate of the Twenty-seventh Maine.

The capture of Washington might possibly have brought England into the war on the side of the Confederacy. The defense of Major L'Enfant's swamp on the Potomac, however, used up so many troops that it undoubtedly prolonged the war. From October 28 to December 12, the patient Twenty-seventh mounted guard at Camp Seward near Arlington. They moved further out, in December, to an eight-mile line running from the Potomac near Mount Vernon to the tracks of the Orange and Alexandria Railroad, and finally, from March 24 to June 25, they served as pickets on the outermost line of defense, near Chantilly, Virginia.

Colonel Tapley got bored with soldiering, resigned, and went home to Saco in February, leaving Wentworth as acting colonel. Nothing much bothered the Mainers, except the weather, typhoid, and pneumonia. Mosby's Raiders attended to other parts of the line, or perhaps they went home for Christmas.

In late June, destiny brushed the Twenty-seventh with the hem of her robe—and then stalked on. In front of their lines the Mainers could see whole armies raising storms of dust: Hooker's troops trying to stay between Lee's northward advance and the capital. A few days later, the armies were to meet at a Pennsylvania farm town called Gettysburg.

The Twenty-seventh almost marched to reinforce Meade at Gettysburg. Almost, but not quite. At the last minute, the War Department discovered that the regiment's term of enlistment was up—crisis or no crisis—and sent the Maine volunteers back up to Arlington Heights on June 25.

They arrived to find Washington in an even greater panic than usual. The girls in the brothels had already begun sewing Confederate flags on their garters, it was reported. There was nothing between Lee and the capital, if he should win at Gettysburg, except a few government clerks who had been issued rifles . . . and the Twenty-seventh Maine.

Wentworth's Twenty-seventh by now was a disciplined but completely untried force, just the thing Washington needed for a last-ditch defense against Lee. Secretary of War Stanton immediately appealed to a Maine congressman, the Honorable Daniel E. Somes, to ask the regiment to extend its term of service until the danger to Gettysburg was past.

Stanton also talked to Colonel Wentworth and promised him that all the men who stayed would receive, as an added inducement, the new Medal of Honor.

The history of the medal is a book in itself. Until the Civil War, Americans had never paid much attention to such "foreign fripperies," but something was needed to replace the confusing practice of creating brevet, or honorary, officers as a reward for distinguished conduct in the field. Congress authorized the Medal of Honor for the navy in 1861 and for the army in 1862. A Philadelphia jeweler created the original design in bronze, with the Union, symbolized by Minerva, repulsing Discord, a Confederate demon.

It wasn't much of an inducement. In fact, there is no record of a medal even being mentioned to the men during the stormy meeting on June 30 when the extension of service was proposed. They would have most probably preferred a cow.

After a morning of speeches, roll calls, harassment, and man-to-man talks, the Arlington "town meeting" concluded, with somewhere between 299 and 312 men out of a total of 864 agreeing to stay. The rest took the train home to make hay. The conduct of the war probably had little to do with their reasoning. A bargain was a bargain. They had served their time, Washington had cried wolf too often, and making hay was an important job that couldn't be done by women and children.

By July 4 the danger was over. A brother regiment, the Twentieth Maine, had saved the day with a bayonet charge at Little Round Top, the Army of Northern Virginia was in retreat, and Meade's troops had collapsed, exhausted, on their guns. Vice President Hannibal Hamlin returned from Chicago to Gettysburg shortly after the battle, and with civilian exuberance, exhorted Meade to pursue Lee, a dangerous thing to do under any circumstances but foolhardy to attempt with an army that had barely hung onto the high ground by the skin of its teeth.

The remaining members of the Twenty-seventh left Washington that day, the explosions of Independence Day firecrackers the closest they had come in their entire stay to the sounds of battle. They arrived in Portland on the sixth and were mustered out on the seventeenth.

Colonel Wentworth, who by a quirk of the calendar had just missed seeing action in the decisive battle of the war, pestered anyone who would listen to give him another command. In 1864 he was given the Maine Thirty-second, one of the last regiments mustered in the state, over-officered and manned mostly by boys who had lied about their ages.

Grant threw it into the Wilderness. In seven months the Thirty-second fought seven battles; at Petersburg, it practically disappeared. Wentworth himself was shot through the hip and was carried out in an action under fire that well deserved the sort of recognition now associated with the Medal of Honor.

While recuperating in Kittery, Wentworth received a puzzled message from Governor Cony in Augusta. The governor had just been sent a barrel of medals, 864 in all, each inscribed with the name of a man in the Twenty-seventh, and what should he do with them? Wentworth said he would take care of it.

The War Department never forgets—and never learns. Instead of awarding the medal only to the men who had stayed on in Washington, Stanton had given it to the whole regiment.

Maybe he reasoned that since a part of the regiment had stayed, all of it had stayed—on paper. Maybe it was too hard to decide who was entitled and who was not. What about officers who had volunteered to stay but were ordered to shepherd the first load of troops back to Portland? Maybe Stanton didn't care.

Colonel Wentworth didn't feel that way. He had been severely wounded, and he looked at soldierlike qualities from a different angle. He knew better than anyone else who had stayed, who had gone, and who had volunteered. He awarded the medal, accordingly, to only 299 men. One can imagine him driving his team along sandy York County lanes, delivering each medal personally with his thanks. It is the kind of thing a man like Wentworth might feel obliged to do.

The rest of the medals he sent back to Augusta. The bureaucrats there still didn't know what to do with them, and apparently—things get hazier from here on—returned them to Wentworth, who seems to have put the box of extras in his carriage barn and forgotten about them. A descendant remembered seeing them there, but what happened to them after the Colonel's death remains a mystery.

No one ever questioned Wentworth's right to decide who should receive the Medal of Honor. Few ever questioned Wentworth's right to do anything. He did send a list of his selections to Augusta, where it was lost in the rat's nest of government records (it turned up only recently), and that was that.

The mass award of medals, since few people knew that Wentworth had reduced the number by 565, generated some controversy occasionally among those interested in such matters, but it was not until 1917 that anything was done about it. In that year a board of review, determining that it was impossible to verify officially the names of those who had volunteered, stripped the Twenty-seventh of *all* its medals. But by that time most of the Twenty-seventh had gone on to a greater reward and their descendants were not inclined to relinquish a family heirloom.

Here, apparently, the matter rests—and will continue to do so—until someone rummaging in a Maine attic one day happens upon a box full of medals depicting Minerva vanquishing Discord.

ALSO SEE

"Account of the Experiences of the 27th Maine Regiment in the Civil War," *Down East*, November 1981, pp. 54–57.

"Army Forgets Heroic Maine Civil War Unit," *Portland Press Herald*, 25 July 1959, p. 1.

"The Case of the 27th Maine," from Joseph L. Schott, *Above and Beyond: A History of the Medal of Honor from the Civil War to Vietnam*, Boston: Boston Publishing Company, 1985.

"864 Maine Heroes Who Never Were," *Portland Sunday Telegram*, 18 September 1966, p. 2D.

"Few Remember 27th Maine Volunteers," *Kennebec Journal*, 30 May 1958, p. 5.

"Maine Men Awarded medal of Honot During Civil War," *Lewiston Journal Illustrated Magazine*, 30 May 1925, p. 9.

"Maine Men Fighting for Union Performed Fine Deeds of Valor," *Lewiston Journal Illustrated Magazine, 26 December 1959*, pp. 5–7.

"Wears a medal of Honor," *Lewiston Journal Illustrated Magazine*, 3 September 1904, p. 4.

TERRORS OF NEW YORK
DRAFT RIOTS RECALLED

ERNEST C. MARRINER

During the past four years many interesting comparisons have been drawn between activities of the World War and happenings of the Civil War of 1861 to 1865. These parallels have appeared in all sorts of writing from personal letters by the doughboys to critical analyses by profound experts like Frank A. Simonds.

It was such a comparison that came recently to the little town of Hebron in the form of a letter from a former teacher at Hebron Academy. The writer said he had had the good fortune to be in New York City on the occasion of both peace celebrations: the false jubilee of November 8 and the real jollification of November 11. He went on to make this very interesting statement: "An old New Yorker told me that the riotous merry-making reminded him of nothing so much as of the great draft riots of 1863, except that on the present occasion the crowds were good natured."

Now it happens that in this same little hamlet of Hebron there lives one who has vivid personal recollections of those terrible days in the metropolis—days which, according to one historian, surpassed the Reign of Terror of the French Revolution in their unlicensed barbarity.

Half a mile north of Hebron Academy, on the road to Buckfield, lives Miss Caroline S. Tripp, a genial cultured lady, 76 years young. In a little cottage nestled among the bold Oxford hills she lives alone with her two cats and her three Wyandotte hens. But yet not alone either—for her friends are legion, and they make a beaten path to her door. It is a rare day that does not see at least one caller at the little white cottage.

Her correspondence is voluminous. Though in these latter years it tires her to write, she keeps in touch with her many friends in distant parts. To all quarters of New England, to Texas, to California go her interesting epistles, and eagerly she watches the rural delivery box at the top of the hill for the no less interesting replies.

Her recollections of Hebron in general and of historic Hebron Academy in particular would fill the pages of a closely printed book. She remembers seeing a chubby little boy trudging past her house on his way to school in the long, long ago. She asked her mother who he was and received the reply, "That's little Johnny Long." In later years the great governor of Massachusetts and Secretary of the Navy paid her more than one friendly call.

She has vivid recollections of Hannibal Hamlin and of other illustrious men of bygone days. She has seen three generations of academy students, including no less than 65 classes, pass out into the world, some of them to attain places of marked distinction. More recently she has housed several of the students under her own roof, and they are today numbered among her staunchest friends.

But not all of Miss Tripp's life has been spent in Hebron. For nine years she worked in New York City, and those were eventful years for the nation, for they included the period of the Civil War from 1861 to 1865, as well as the trying days of reconstruction until 1870.

Miss Tripp's employment in New York was as a clerk in the store of John White,

ORIGINALLY PUBLISHED IN LEWISTON JOURNAL ILLUSTRATED MAGAZINE, 4 JANUARY 1919.

baker and confectioner at 15 Catherine Street, at that time a part of the fashionable shopping district of the city. In the sixties Mr. White was the most famous caterer in New York, and his party dinners, served on his beautiful Havilland china, were much in demand. He supplied with bread and pastry some twenty of the Sound steamers, as well as ocean-going vessels.

While Miss Tripp was in his employ, she helped put up the large order of bread and crackers for the *Quaker City,* when that well-known liner took Mark Twain on the famous voyage about which he wrote his *Innocents Abroad.* It is interesting to know that Franklin White, grandson of John, still conducts the business at the old stand.

Around the experiences of Miss Tripp, the country girl in the great metropolis, a Dickens would weave a novel to place beside *David Copperfield* and *Great Expectations.* For want of Dickens, or even of a realistic Boswell, most of her adventures must go untold; but for this once let the little old lady tell in her own charming way her recollections of those terrible days when the draft rioters held New York in their anarchistic sway.

Perhaps, before recording Miss Tripp's narrative, it would be well to refresh our minds with the recorded history of those days, especially since many of the younger generation have only a vague idea of what a reign of Bolshevik madness swept the city when the draft call came.

According to *Harper's Encyclopedia of United States History*, President Lincoln issued on May 8, 1863, a proclamation for a draft to begin in July, and caused the appointment in every Congressional district of an enrolling board. Organized resistance to the measure instantly appeared, chiefly centering in a society known as the Knights of the Golden Circle. This was a secret organization founded for the overthrow of the government, and had been persistently, though clandestinely, at work since 1840. They seized upon the draft as a pretext for revolution. It was planned to start trouble in New York, and thence spread rebellion into other states. Morgan's raid in Indiana and Ohio was a part of the scheme. The plot failed because the peace faction refused to join it, in all probability because the great victories at Gettysburg and Vicksburg had subdued much of the pacifist feeling in the North. In New York City, however, mob

rule did prevail for three terrible days. When, on Monday, July 13, the draft began in a building on Third Avenue at 46th Street, a large crowd, who had already cut the telegraph wires into the city, suddenly appeared, attacked the building, drove out the clerks, tore up the papers, poured a can of kerosene over the floor, and set fire to the building. Disorders broke out simultaneously at several other points, there evidently being somewhere a central controlling head. Under the influence of liquor, the rioters made a business of arson and plunder. They laid in ashes the Negro orphan asylum, and the terrified inmates, who fled in every direction, were pursued and cruelly beaten. Finally the police, aided by the military, suppressed the insurrection in the city, but not until over a thousand persons had been killed or wounded, and property to the amount of $2,000,000 had been destroyed.

"Since the draft had first been announced, there had been threats of all sorts of trouble," said Miss Tripp. "Mr. White was a strong Republican and an ardent Lincoln man. He had more than once been threatened with personal violence by the trouble makers.

"The first we knew of any organized disturbance was on the morning of July 13, when Mr. Woodward, Mr. White's nephew, came into the store, bearing the information that a mob was running wild, tearing up streetcar tracks, cutting telegraph wires, and spreading terror among the Negroes. Mr. Woodward told us to look out for trouble, as the mob had sworn vengeance on all loyal Republicans.

"During the forenoon a boy came into the store and purchased a double amount of bread. He gave as his reason for the extra purchase, 'You won't have any tomorrow.'

"As the day progressed, we got additional news of the evil temper of the mob and the lawless violence they were perpetrating in other parts of the city. The police seemed powerless to deal with the situation.

"The famous Seventh Regiment of National Guard, made up of gentlemen's sons from New York, had been partially mobilized. About half of the regiment had been taken to Washington; the rest were awaiting call. Mr. White's twin sons were both members of this regiment. One of them was at the store when the riots broke out. Immediately he went to the Armory, organized the remnant of the regiment, and had it ready for business when the order came from Washington to put the city under martial law.

"Knowing what depredations the mob was committing in daylight, we were naturally anxious about the coming hours of darkness. We barricaded the heavy doors with tables and chairs, removed to the second floor every instrument that could possibly be used as a

Lieutenant Oliver G. White led the Federal troops who quelled the riot.

weapon, and there awaited developments. The kitchen girls filled all sorts of receptacles with boiling water, ready to pour it on the heads of approaching trouble-makers.

"About midnight a crowd of a thousand men and boys, most of them infuriated by liquor, gathered at the corner of Chatham Square and Catherine Street. Their avowed purpose was to burn the store of John White and do personal violence to the owner.

"Had the mob actually attacked the store," continued Miss Tripp, "our poor weapons and barricades would have been of slight avail. Our mere show of resistance would probably have so infuriated the drunken crowd that we should have been murdered on the spot.

"It is almost certain, then," avowed the little old lady, "that our very lives were saved by the influence of a friendly Irishman. Most of the trouble, by the way, was caused by the Irish; but in this case it was a cool-headed Irishman who saved us. Patrick O'Donnell, a seller of ready-made clothing in a store next door to Mr. White, had more than once proved a good friend to the baker. In this crit-

ical hour he remonstrated with the crowd to such good purpose that he finally persuaded them to wait until the next night. By that time their wrath against Mr. White had either cooled or been directed elsewhere, for during the remaining days of the disorder there were no more attempts against the store.

"While we were not actually attacked, that was a terrible night," said Miss Tripp with a noticeable shudder. "When dawn broke we could see the body of a Negro dangling from a rude gallows in Chatham Square. Early in the morning a terror-stricken boy, covered with blood, ran into the store to elude his pursuers. Another boy, a colored fellow, said he had hidden in a coal bin for three days.

"Even before he knew of any personal danger, Mr. White realized there would surely be trouble if the Negro stewards of the steamers came to his store to leave their usual orders. It was necessary that someone go to the wharves and warn the stewards not to come ashore. But the temper of the mob was such as to permit few people to traverse the downtown streets. In fact, only Irishmen were reasonably safe.

"Fortunately, Mr. White had in his employ a loyal Irish boy named Henry Sadler. He was sent to meet the incoming boats, warn the stewards, and take their orders. This saved those colored men from injury, but for several days it was impossible to deliver goods on the waterfront.

"When we knew that the Seventh Regiment was at work," continued Miss Tripp, "we felt easier. One boy in that regiment told me that he had personally disposed of three rioters. By the morning of the 17th the military were in full control and the worst was over. But they were awful days while they lasted."

While her experience with the draft riots was perhaps Miss Tripp's most thrilling adventure in the big city, she has other experiences well worth recollecting. She remembers the astounding sight of the office of the New York Tribune barricaded with huge piles of print papers to protect it against the fury of the mob. She recalls with patriotic pride how a regiment of New England infantry arrived in New York without quarters. Through some oversight or departmental error no place had been provided for them. At once the greathearted resourceful Henry Ward Beecher opened his magnificent church in Brooklyn as quarter for the troops. "When they left in the morning," declared Miss Tripp, "one would never have known that anyone had been there. Wasn't that wonderful?" She recalls distinctly the announcement of Lee's surrender at Appomatox. "Mr. Woodward told me," she said, "that he was in front of the Tribune office when the news came. All the men in the crowd at once doffed their hats and sang 'Praise God from Whom All Blessings Flow.' Where but in our own America would you witness a sight like that?"

These recollections of a historic past may be as interesting to the reader as they were to the writer. But one portion of the interview the writer cannot share with you. It was a generous slice of Miss Tripp's famous apple pie. And such pie! It is justly famous beyond the borders of the little town of Hebron. Two generations of Academy students have hoarded their quarters to taste its luscious sweetness. Let Charlie Lamb revel in the thoughts of his roast crackling pig; let Dickens shout the praise of the Christmas plum pudding; let ancient Homer sing of the nectar of the gods. None of these delicacies present to the writer the *summa cum laude* of the culinary art. He prefers Miss Tripp's apple pie.

THE KINGFIELD REBELLION AS I RECALL IT

F. E. STANLEY

You ask me to write the story of the "Kingfield Riot." I assume that you mean the one which occurred in 1863 and which we sometimes call the Kingfield Rebellion. More than a half century has passed since that episode in the history of Kingfield, and though I have few records of the events other than those which memory furnishes, yet the account which I give I am certain is correct in all its important features.

First let me say the term *riot* does not adequately express the significance of the affair, for, although not of large proportions, nor accompanied by any serious injury to persons or property, yet, since it was the outcome of sentiments which were widespread, it was considered of national importance as the account will show. The story is about the attempt that was made in Kingfield in 1863 to resist the draft.

In order to understand the motives that actuated the men in Kingfield to conduct themselves as they did at that time, it will be necessary to consider briefly the history of this nation previous to the Civil War and to understand the causes that resulted in that bloody conflict.

The United Sates is a constitutional democracy. The states which united to form the nation were formerly British colonies, and when separating themselves from the mother country, they announced to the world the reasons for the separation. Those reasons were all based on the principle that all men are created with an equal right to life, liberty and freedom and the pursuit of happiness. But in the so-called Southern states there was an institution which was a complete denial of the principle of equal freedom, an institution of absolute slavery; to buy and sell human beings; to compel them to perform any service which their masters required; and to treat them in all respects as though they were domestic animals, was a custom upheld by the laws of the Southern states. The slave owners even regarded the institution of slavery of greater importance than their membership in the Union. But in the Northern states slavery was prohibited and a majority of the people in the free states looked upon slavery as a relic of barbarism.

So the questions—"Is slavery a just and legitimate institution?" "Should it extend into the territories?" and "Shall the new states coming into the Union be slave or free states?" became the dominant political issue which separated the two sections of the Union and arrayed the South against the North.

Then, growing out of the slavery issue, was the question of state rights, or the relations of state sovereignty to the sovereignty of the Federal Union. The slave-owners of the South and the pro-slavery element of the North advocated the theory that state sovereignty was supreme; that there was practically no limit to the political rights of a state except those that were self-imposed. The slave-owners even maintained that membership in the Union was a voluntary arrangement, which could be terminated at any time whenever a majority of the people of a state decided that their interests demanded it.

Now all this clamoring for "State rights," was simply for the right or the privilege to extend and perpetuate the institution of slavery. The Constitution of the United States did not prevent a state from doing anything that was morally right and in harmony with the princi-

ORIGINALLY PUBLISHED IN *LEWISTON JOURNAL ILLUSTRATED MAGAZINE*, 27 APRIL 1918.

ples of justice. But the slave-owners wanted the privilege of doing what was condemned by all the principles of Christian civilization, and they and their representatives in Congress were intolerant, over-bearing and aggressive and any opposition to the slave interests was always met by the threat of secession. And even in the North, where a majority of the people were opposed to the extension of slavery, there were few who thought it should be interfered with where it existed and the abolitionist was extremely unpopular.

In 1835, William Lloyd Garrison was assaulted and dragged through the streets of Boston by a mob which threatened to hang him, simply because he had been speaking and publishing a paper advocating the abolition

Francis Edgar Stanley

of slavery. So there were in Massachusetts, the home of Daniel Webster, Charles Sumner and Wendell Phillips, many who upheld slavery, and the most cruel persecution of those who advocated its abolition. The brutal intolerance of the slave interests became more apparent and the threat of secession more alarming as the years went by, and finally the climax was reached in 1860.

A few years before that date, two men had appeared on the political scene, who were destined to play a very important part in the history of this nation. They were political opponents and residents of the state of Illinois. One was the most able and popular Democrat of the North and the other, a conspicuous leader in the new Republican party, which was organized in 1856. Stephen A. Douglas was the Democrat and Abraham Lincoln, the Republican.

In the political contests in Illinois, they had been opposing candidates for the same office and had many times met in joint debate. In those debates they had stated the principles of their respective parties so plainly that there could be no uncertainty as to their political faith.

Douglas was an advocate of state rights though not quite to the extent that a state had a right to secede, as that, he said, would be to deny to the government the power for its own preservation. But he did advocate the doctrine that the inhabitants of a territory should be allowed to decide by popular vote whether they would allow slavery in their domain. So Douglas was not opposed to slavery where it existed, or to its extension into the territories or new states. But Lincoln, in the joint debate with Douglas, had shown himself an uncompromising foe to slavery and an advocate of the supremacy of national sovereignty, and the constitutional rights of the Federal Government to prohibit slavery in the territories.

With this slavery issue and with these two great leaders prominently before the people, there came the presidential election of 1860, an event which will always remain one of the most important in American history. The Democratic party, having its strength largely in the South, was the party that upheld slavery, and, when aided by the Democrats of the North, were in the majority and had enjoyed a long lease of power. But when they met in convention in 1860 to nominate a candidate for the Presidency, they disagreed on some of the principles of the platform and adjourned without making a nomination. Later they held separate conventions. The Southern Democrats nominated John C. Breckenridge, who was then Democratic Vice-President, and the Democrats of the North named as their candidate, Stephen A. Douglas of Illinois. The difference in the principles of the two parties related principally to the question of the extension of slavery. Either of the candidates could have been elected if he could have had the entire Democratic vote, but their failure to co-operate gave the Republicans their great opportunity.

The Republican National Convention met at Chicago, May 16, 1860, and nominated for

President, Abraham Lincoln of Illinois; and for Vice-President, Hannibal Hamlin of Maine. The principles set forth in the platform were those which Lincoln had stated in the debates referred to, and he had stated them so plainly and with such sincerity, that he was the personification of Republicanism.

Stephen A. Douglas, the candidate of the Northern Democrats, was closely identified with the principles of his party, as he had been the leader in the state rights and popular sovereignty movements. Douglas was responsible, more than anyone else, for the split in the Democratic party which resulted in the election of Lincoln, and for that reason must always be held in grateful remembrance. Never were presidential candidates more intimately associated with their parties than were Lincoln and Douglas, and never were the issues more clearly understood than in the presidential campaign of 1860.

Then the fact that Hannibal Hamlin, the candidate for Vice-President, was a native of Maine, added to the interest and importance of the campaign in the minds of the people of our state. Hamlin was well and favorably known in Maine. He had served several terms in the State Legislature and had been several times Speaker of the House. He had been Governor of the State and at the time of his nomination, was United States Senator from Maine, a position which he resigned to accept the nomination for the Vice-Presidency.

In order to understand the peculiar situation in Kingfield, it is necessary to know that Eben F. Pillsbury of Farmington, one of the most, if not the most, able and influential of the Democrats in Maine, was a native of Kingfield. He was several times candidate for Governor, but always the candidate of the minority party. In private life, Pillsbury was a man of unblemished character and reputation; a polished gentleman, genial and extremely popular. He was a lawyer of exceptional ability, an eloquent speaker and a born political leader. So it is not unreasonable to assume that it was due to his influence, to some extent, that there was in Kingfield, during the period of the Civil War, a large Democratic majority. We use the term *large* relatively, of course, as the population of the town up to 1870 had never exceeded six hundred.

In Kingfield, as throughout the whole country, the campaign, as carried on by the Democrats, was for the most part a personal attack upon Abraham Lincoln, of the most bitter and abusive kind, and of all the Democratic campaign speakers who came to Kingfield during that contest none could equal Pillsbury in abusive denunciation of "Abe Lincoln —the black Republican" as he was called by his opponents.

As we look back to those times we can see that the contest was a very unequal one. The principles for which the Democrats were contending were not such as to inspire the people of the North with patriotism and political enthusiasm, and so the leaders were forced to appeal to prejudice.

But the Republicans knew that their cause was a just and noble one. It required no tampering with conscience to enjoy the faith that the extension of slavery ought to be repressed, and certainly the preservation of the Union was a cause worth fighting for. But think of fighting for slavery and secession! So the result of the election was what might have been anticipated. The South went solid for Breckenridge, while every Northern state but one, gave a majority for Lincoln and Hamlin, giving them 180 electoral votes to 123 for all the other candidates.

Never shall I forget when my father came home and brought the news of the election. "Lincoln," he said, "is elected and we shall have civil war." And his prediction proved true. In six weeks from the time of the election a State Convention met at Charleston, South Carolina, and passed an ordinance declaring "That the Union now existing between South Carolina and other states under the name of the United States, is hereby dissolved." This example was followed by ten other Southern states, and on February 4, 1861, or one month before Lincoln was inaugurated, a congress of the states that had seceded met and adopted a constitution and named the organization "The Confederate States of America," with Jefferson Davis for President.

Then the Democrats of Kingfield, as throughout the North, had little to say and there was nothing they could do. Many of them, when they expressed an opinion, said the South had acted too hastily—that the Southern states ought to have waited until after Lincoln was inaugurated and had shown his policy before seceding. Throughout the whole country there was a calm, which was only a premonition of the tempest which was about to burst forth and drench the nation in blood.

When Lincoln was inaugurated and assumed the duties of his office he found himself robbed of the means for defending the Capitol against an attack from a hostile army.

During the administration of Buchanan, Lincoln's immediate predecessor, about everything had been done which could be done to favor the South and handicap the North. Under the directions of General Floyd, Buchanan's Secretary of War, the regular army had been dispersed to different parts of the country. Also he had transferred large quantities of arms and ammunition from the arsenals of the North to those of the South. Then the United States Navy, by orders of Secretary Toucey, was, for the most part, absent in foreign ports. So the new administration was placed at a great disadvantage.

With all this evidence before them the Democrats of Kingfield did not believe that the South would make war on the North, but that the seceding states had peacefully taken themselves out of the Union and that it would be wisdom on the part of the administration to recognize their independence and not attempt to force them to return. But all those false notions were banished when the news came that Fort Sumter had been attacked by the Rebels and that Major Anderson, with a garrison of 128 men, had been defeated after a two days' battle and had surrendered on April 14, 1861.

This news of the beginning of hostilities brought a tremendous wave of patriotic enthusiasm, which swept over the Northern states from the Atlantic to the Pacific and banished for the time all party differences. In Kingfield even, there were no Republicans or Democrats, but all men were Union men and ready to do their part to put down the rebellion and preserve the Union.

Simon Packard, a Democrat, got out his fife; Sam Norton, also a Democrat, tuned up his "tenor drum," and Sewel Vase, a Republican had a new calf-skin head fitted to his bass drum and the Kingfield Fife and Drum Band was ready for business.

Kingfield was the first town in Franklin County to organize an independent company and commence a system of military training and in that way to give the young men their first lessons in military tactics. Several other towns in that section followed the example. Later representatives of several of the companies met and decided to hold a muster somewhere in the county during the fall of 1861 and selected Kingfield as the place for the meet-

ing. Kingfield was still further honored when they selected for colonel of the regiment which assembled at that muster, William Dolbier, the captain of the Kingfield Company.

So that, during the first year of the war, there was nothing to indicate that Kingfield was lacking in loyalty or patriotic enthusiasm. Eben F. Pillsbury, of whom we have spoken, came out in support of the administration and by his eloquent speeches and persuasive influence, did much to induce the young men of Kingfield and other towns to enlist when there came the call for volunteers.

At each call of the President, Kingfield responded as promptly as other towns in Maine, and during 1861 and 1862 her quota was quickly filled. But during those two years the Rebel army was generally victorious, and it became evident that we were in for a long and bloody conflict, and that the outcome was doubtful. Then, in Kingfield, as throughout the North, those who were opposed to the election of Lincoln began to criticize the administration and to predict that the South would win the war and gain its independence. Those grumblings and criticisms became more pronounced as the news was received of each battle where the Southern army was victorious, and when those who were opposed to the prosecution of the war began to show their sympathy for the South and their disloyalty, we called them Secessionists and Copperheads.

Well can I remember how pleased and even jubilant some of them appeared when we received the news of the second battle of Bull Run, which occurred August 19 and 30, 1862. The Union forces in that battle were commanded by General Pape and the Confederates were under General Lee. Pape was utterly defeated and his broken and dispirited columns were driven back upon Washington. The Capitol of the nation was actually in danger, and there were men in Kingfield and in many other towns in Maine, who were glad! It seems incredible.

But the climax of disloyalty and Copperheadism was not yet reached. Up to that time all that the opponents of the Administration could really complain of was the inefficient management in the prosecution of the war, for they had to admit that it was, on the part of the North, a war of defense, and that there was no alternative for the President but to do everything in his power to put down the rebellion and preserve the Union.

But on September 22, 1862, there occurred an event which marks an epoch in American history no less important than the Declaration of Independence, and it may be regarded as the crowning achievement in the life of Abraham Lincoln. On that date Lincoln issued a proclamation, declaring that on January 1, 1863, the slaves of all the states that were in the rebellion, would be free.

The immediate effect was to win from the anti-slavery element a more hearty support, while on the other hand, it furnished the Copperheads something tangible to kick about. "Now," they said, "we understand what Lincoln and his army are fighting for, they are fighting to free the 'niggers.' We never will lend our support to accomplish that."

From that time the Copperheads expressed their opposition to the prosecution of the war and their sympathy with the South openly, and their influence was so widespread that volunteers were not forthcoming to replenish the army and the government had to resort to conscription. The conscription law went into effect in the spring of 1863 and all able-bodied men between the ages of 20 and 45 were liable to be drafted. Those that were drafted could either go into the army or pay an exemption free of $300. The first draft called for 12 men from Kingfield, and several in excess of that number were drafted to provide for rejections on account of unfitness. Nathan Saunders was the enrolling officer at Kingfield who had sent in the names of those liable to be drafted. He was a Republican and not over popular in that Democratic town.

When the result of the first draft was announced a singular thing was discovered. The number of Democrats drafted was proportionately much greater than seemed fair. In the town there were about one-half more Democrats than Republicans, but the Democrats drafted, outnumbered the Republicans four to one. That, the Copperheads said, could not be the result of chance. Either Saunders had not sent in the names of all the Republicans, or he had indicated who were Republicans and who Democrats and the list had been tampered with at headquarters.

The drafted men and their sympathizers got together and talked the matter over, and the more they talked the madder they got. Then, to give the affair the finishing touch, two of the Republicans who had been drafted both apparently in perfect health, reported for examination and were exempted. Then the anger of the Copperheads knew no bounds. They decided to vent their spite on Saunders. Accordingly they got together one evening and decided to mob him. Just what punishment to inflict they could hardly decide, so they concluded to go to his home and call him out, and with threats of tar and feathers and possibly hanging, to compel him to own up to the fraud about the list of names.

But when they reached the house, after repeated knockings, they were informed that Saunders had left town that afternoon and would not be back for several weeks. So they decided to vent their spite on the building. Some said, "Burn it down;" others, "Smash the windows," but they finally decided to decorate it in a manner appropriate for the residence of a "Black Republican." As the building was white, they striped it with black paint. The effect was very striking, and for several months Saunders' store, as the house was called, attracted more attention than any other building in Franklin County.

So Kingfield became the leading secession town, as it had formerly been the leading town to begin military training.

Shortly after this there was a Democratic "mass-meeting" at Kingfield and Eben F. Pillsbury was the principal speaker. Pillsbury had made a complete turnabout since Lincoln's Emancipation Proclamation and become one of the bitterest opponents of the administration and the prosecution of the war. He declared the proclamation of Lincoln freeing the "niggers" the height of absurdity as the South could never be conquered, and he pronounced the conscription law unconstitutional, and that, in his opinion, it could not be enforced.

At this point in his speech he stopped to take a drink of water, when someone asked, "Can we resist the draft?" He turned toward the questioner and with his characteristic smile replied: "I am asked if you can resist the draft." And holding up the glass of water, he continued—"My answer it this: The United States Government is just as weak as this water. You can draw your own conclusions."

That reply was the match which fired the train. There was no longer any doubt in the minds of the Copperheads of their ability to resist the draft and they acted accordingly. Up to that time the drafted men had not been officially notified, so they decided that the first thing to do was to prevent the officer who was coming to Kingfield to summons drafted men, from serving the notices.

Accordingly they kept a man on guard at the village ready to give notice when the officer arrived. They had not long to wait before the marshal, whose name was Lambert, drove over from Phillips, a town some fifteen miles away, and having his team cared for at the stable, went to the hotel for dinner. The drafted men and their sympathizers, having been notified, quickly arrived in goodly numbers and as Lambert came from the dining room, they met him and demanded his surrender. He saw that resistance was useless and so asked them what they wanted. They said they wanted the papers which he was intending to serve in summonsing the drafted men, and that if he cared for his personal safety he had better hand them over and be quick about it.

Lambert complied, and the papers were taken and destroyed. Then he was escorted to the street, where he found his team in readiness, that matter having been attended to, and he was told that he had just five minutes to get outside of the town limits. As the town line was only a mile away, he made the distance, according to all accounts, and had more than a minute to spare.

That was the second aggressive act and the Copperheads were victorious. They had resisted the draft, as they thought, and they were jubilant. "It was just as easy as Pillsbury told us it would be," they said.

That evening many came to the village to hear the news and the Rebel sympathizers were happy. But one of the Union men of the village, who disapproved of their conduct, said they would find that driving the marshal away and burning the papers was not all there was to resisting the draft.

But he was told to "shut up, we are running this town, and no nigger worshiper can make any talk like that in Kingfield unless he is looking for trouble."

There was no one in Kingfield that evening who was looking for trouble. But the next day a thing happened that gave the Rebels something to think about. Several of the Secessionists were at the post-office when a team drove up, and in the carriage with the driver was a man wearing the army uniform. He was a captain, home on a furlough, and his left arm was in a sling, the bone having been shattered by a Rebel bullet.

The team stopped in front of the post-office and the captain, who was well known in the town, asked for the news. He was told that the best news they knew of was what happened yesterday in Kingfield, and then the man who was acting as the informer commenced to give an account of the affair, but before he had finished the captain interrupted him. "*Stop,*" he said, "*right where you are.* Are you Copperheads such fools as to think you can resist the draft? Every one of you drafted men will have to report for examination or you will be regarded as deserters, and you know what that means."

At that one of the drafted men stepped out and took hold of the bridle and commenced to turn the team around at the same time saying, "You had better mind your own business. You can't make such talk as *that* here, we are running this town."

"Let go of that bridle," commanded the Captain, and leveling a revolver at the man's head he continued. "You say, I better mind my own business. Do you know what my business is? Just now it is shooting Rebels and I will shoot one in Kingfield as quickly as I would down in Virginia." The man obeyed and quickly placed himself at a safe distance as he evidently did not enjoy looking into the muzzle of a revolver. Then the Captain continued to express his opinion of the conduct of the drafted men and their sympathies in language that was plain but not complimentary, and none of the secessionists dared to reply.

That little episode did not convince the Rebels that their attempt to resist the draft was a failure, but it did make them more cautious. They were foolish enough to think they could prevent a knowledge of the affair from reaching the government headquarters at Augusta, so they had guards stationed at each road leading out of Kingfield, and they tried to exact a promise from everyone leaving town not to give information that would interfere with their success. Then came the encouraging news of the draft riots in other places and their confidence was restored. And when they heard that the draft riot in New York City had reached proportions entirely beyond the control of the police, they were jubilant. "As goes Kingfield, so goes New York and our government," was the slogan, and the Copperheads were happy.

But their happiness was of short duration. Already plans had been made to enforce the draft at Kingfield and the adjoining towns

(Freeman and Salem had followed the example of Kingfield and resisted the serving of the notifications). Provost Marshall Baker had detailed the Lewiston Light Infantry, numbering 66 members including the officers, to proceed to Kingfield and put down the rebellion. They were reinforced by 21 enlisted men, (mainly soldiers from the Second Regiment) who came over from Augusta making a Company of 87 men.

They were commanded by Captain J. T. Stevens of the Lewiston Light Infantry. Private E. Sands was detailed as Quartermaster and Captains Knowlton and Nye and Private W. W. Ayer, A. O. Morgan and Dr. Martin were detailed to serve the notifications where the former officers had been molested.

This Company, fully uniformed and equipped, and provided with 10 rounds of ammunition and rations for four days, took the cars of the Androscoggin R. R. for Farmington. The camp equipage and commissary stores, together with the horses for the officers who were to serve the notifications, were also put aboard.

The train left Lewiston at 3 P.M., July 23, 1863, and reached Farmington at six the same afternoon. There they camped for the night, and at 5:30 the next morning they started on their march for Kingfield, a distance of 22 miles. They passed through New Vineyard and New Portland, and wherever they stopped they received a generous welcome. They reached West New Portland at 1 o'clock, where they rested for two and a half hours. There they were given a great feast and were shown every kindness and assistance that the people could render.

Several of the soldiers had become so footsore that walking was extremely painful, and the men of the village furnished teams to carry them the last six miles of the journey. They did not go quite to Kingfield Village, as the soldiers (about 12 or 15 in number) did not think it prudent to meet the enemy until the whole company were together.

No news of the coming of the soldiers had reached Kingfield up to the morning of July 24th, the morning that the Company left Farmington on their 22-mile tramp, so there was quite a surprise in store for the inhabitants. Captains Knowlton and Nye and the others who had been detailed to serve the notifications and who were provided with horses left Farmington at about the time the infantry started, and rode to Kingfield, reaching there at 10 o'clock. So the first intimation that the people of Kingfield had that a military Company was on the way was when those officers came cantering into the Village. One of the men who was prominent among the rioters was just riding into the Village on horseback, and as he reined up in front of the Hotel he looked up the street and saw the officers coming at a smart canter down the hill, headed directly toward him. He just took one glance, long enough to see the blue uniforms and sparkling brass buttons, and then wheeling his horse, he went tearing along over the bridge and down the road towards his home, shouting at the top of his voice, *"There's a Regiment of Cavalry coming into town."* His hat blew off [and] he did not stop to pick it up but urged his horse to the utmost speed until he reached his home. Then, as the story goes, he hid himself in the woods and did not dare appear until he had been found by his friends and told that the danger was passed.

Of course, the news of the arrival of the Officers quickly spread through Kingfield and the adjoining towns, and several more of the male residents took to the woods for safety.

Also it was reported, on what was considered good authority, that one of the most influential democrats of Kingfield was so frightened at the sight of the mounted Officers that he fled to the outskirts of the town and, seeing the door of a farm house open, rushed in and in his frenzy crawled under a bed. But the fear and excitement quickly subsided when it was learned that the business of the officers was to serve the notification papers and not to make arrests.

Then word came from Farmington, brought by special messenger who reached Kingfield shortly after the arrival of the officers, giving the rebels their cue. "Make no resistance, and treat the soldiers kindly," was the word passed around, and it had the desired effect. Those who were in hiding were found by their friends, and, when informed of the situation, came forward and received their notifications. That simplified the work of the officers, and by noon of the next day after their arrival every drafted man had been notified and the work of the expedition was accomplished.

When the people of Kingfield were informed by the officers that a company of soldiers were on the way, preparations were made to receive them, and they were by no means hostile preparations. Again, as when the news was received that Fort Sumter had fallen, every man in Kingfield was a union man. Democrats and Republicans vied with each other to see who could do most for the comfort and convenience of the visitors.

The "fife and drum band" was summoned and arrangements were made to meet the soldiers at the town line and escort them to their camping ground near the village. Shortly after five o'clock the band, followed by some fifty men and boys, started down the road on this errand. No word had been received by the soldiers that an escort was coming to meet them, and, when those that had ridden up from New Portland heard the sound of the drums they thought the Kingfield rebels were coming, and there was quite a flurry of excitement. One of the soldiers assumed command and ordered the men to prepare for action. *"See that your guns are in order, but don't fire until I give the command."* They formed in line and were ready for battle. The main division was not more than a mile or two away, but this advance section showed no signs of falling back to meet them. Whether they stood their ground because they were courageous, or too footsore to retreat will probably never be known, for I doubt if any of those dozen or fifteen men are living to tell the story.

But when the band and the rest of the procession appeared above the crest of the hill a quarter of a mile away, it could be seen that it was no hostile army coming to attack them, but, instead probably a group of citizens coming to greet them and tender to them "the freedom of town." And such proved to be the fact. When the citizens arrived at the place of meeting the man in charge gave the command to halt.

The band stopped playing and then came forward and saluted the soldiers and informed them that they had come to welcome them to Kingfield and escort them to their camping ground. Then there were mutual introductions and hand shakings, and everybody was happy. After a wait of half an hour or more the rest of the company arrived, and Captain Stevens was introduced to the man in charge of the Kingfield party and informed that there was nothing for the soldiers to do, but to enjoy themselves, and that everybody in Kingfield would help them. So after a rest of a few minutes, Captain Stevens gave the command, "Fall in!" and the Company headed by the band, playing "The Girl I Left Behind Me," marched gaily into Kingfield. At six o'clock they arrived at their camping grounds, pitched their tents and after rations were served, turned in and slept soundly.

The next day the soldiers were given permission to go about the town and enjoy themselves as they chose. Some went fishing, but most of them stayed on the grounds, and the veterans brought forward some games to amuse the visitors.

At three P.M. a collation was provided by the citizens and a table was arranged long enough to seat the entire company and the "distinguished" visitors. The table was loaded with baked beans and brown bread steaming hot, gingerbread, doughnuts, custard pie and other good things which the country wives and daughters know so well how to prepare.

After they had finished the repast, there was a call for a speech. Captain Stevens responded and in a few words thanked the citizens of Kingfield for their hospitality, but said he could not make a speech. "But," he continued, "one of the men in my company is well able to perform that function, and I take pleasure in introducing private Nelson Dingley, Jr. Mr. Dingley, who was afterwards to take such a prominent place in the affairs of the State and Nation, was then but thirty-one years old and not very widely known. He arose and commenced to speak, but was interrupted by someone calling out, "Stand up on the table so that we can all see you."

He mounted the table and made a speech that was both instructive and amusing. He said their reception was vastly different from what they anticipated. "We expected a volley of bullets and cannon balls, but instead we have been met by a volley of baked beans, doughnuts and custard pie. We can hardly believe that there is any disloyalty in this town, judging from our reception, or that there were ever any riotous proceedings." He then gave a brief account of the war situation. "Up to the beginning of this present month," he said, "the outlook for the Union was dark, but now the light is breaking." "What I believe will be the decisive battle of the war, the battle of Gettysburg, has been fought and won, and Lee has been driven back over the Potomac. General Grant has captured Vicksburg and Port Hudson has surrendered to General Banks, so we have control of the Mississippi River and Rebeldom is cut in two. He closed by thanking the people for their hospitality, and congratulated the drafted men for the good sense they had shown in coming forward and receiving their notifications without making the officers any trouble, and, finally, expressed the hope that Kingfield would always remain, in fact, what it appears to be at the present time, one of the most loyal towns in Maine. His hope was a true prophesy for ever since that time Kingfield has been a patriotic town.

That afternoon the soldiers folded their tents and marched away and the Kingfield rebellion passed into history.

ALSO SEE

"Another Version of the Kingfield Rebellion," *Lewiston Journal Illustrated Magazine,* 8 June, 1918, p. 7.

"I Remember: the Kingfield Rebellion," *Down East* 9, June 1963, p. 77.

"Streaked Mountain in the Civil War," *Lewiston Journal Illustrated Magazine,* 1 June 1918, pp. 1–2.

MAINE MEN TO THE RESCUE. THEY SAVED A UNION FLEET IN 1864 IN LOUISIANA

GEORGE A. BILLIAS

One of the most dramatic episodes in the Civil War concerns the improbable but true story of how Maine lumbermen helped to rescue the Union fleet stranded in the upper rapids of the Red River in the spring of 1864.

The incident was revealing from many different viewpoints: it gave some insight into the ingenuity of army engineers, showed how the peacetime skill of Maine woodsmen were used for wartime purposes, and demonstrated anew the truth of the old platitude that where there's a will there's a way.

Ill-conceived, poorly planned, and ineptly executed, the Red River expedition turned out to be a military fiasco. Proposed by General-in-Chief Henry Halleck, known throughout the army as "Old Brains," the campaign was anything but well-reasoned, because it called for operations west of the Mississippi, an area of doubtful military value.

The objectives of the expedition, were threefold: to capture cotton stores; to give aid to the "free state" cause in Louisiana; and to seize Shreveport, Confederate capital of the sugar state and the key to the control of the Red River.

One of the reasons why the campaign failed was the man who was placed in charge, General Nathaniel Banks. A military amateur who owed his high rank to political pull rather than to his ability as a combat commander, Banks found himself involved in an expedition that was far beyond the scope of his limited talent.

For one thing, this was to be a combined operation in which naval as well as land forces were to be employed. For another, there was a time limit during which the mission had to be carried out. The waters of the Red River remained high enough to permit the use of naval craft only during a short time in the summer, and part of Banks's land forces were on loan from another command for just one month. Banks did not possess the military competence to cope with such complexities.

The campaign got under way when a joint expedition composed of 10,000 men under Major General A. J. Smith, and a flotilla of gunboats and transports, under Rear-Admiral David Porter, ascended the river to Alexandria on March 16, 1864. Eventually they were joined by Banks's army, and together they worked their way northward to Shreveport.

At the same time, another force under General F. Steele began to march southward from Arkansas toward the same objective. Between them, Banks and Steele were to crush the Confederate forces in the area under General Kirby Smith and General Richard Taylor and to link up at Shreveport.

Disaster was not long in coming. On April 8, "Prince Dick" Taylor crashed into Banks's badly organized columns at Mansfield and administered a bloody defeat. The very next day Taylor lashed out again at the Union forces who had taken up a strong position at Pleasant Hill. This time it was Taylor who tasted defeat, as he was repulsed with heavy losses.

Although Banks was of the opinion that the advance on Shreveport should be contin-

ORIGINALLY PUBLISHED IN *THE NEW ENGLAND SOCIAL STUDIES BULLETIN*, 1958, AND *PORTLAND EVENING EXPRESS*, 15 JANUARY 1959.

ued, his generals advised a retreat and he acted accordingly. It was relatively easy for the army to retreat overland; it was quite another matter for the Union navy to return down a river whose water level was falling rapidly. . . .

As the fleet approached the falls above Alexandria it was clear that the river was very low. Gunboats and transports repeatedly struck bottom, and one vessel which ran aground, the *Eastport,* had to be deliberately destroyed by her crew. The ten gunboats and two tugs in Porter's force appeared to be trapped. Unless the vessels could be freed, the fleet was doomed to destruction, for the army was scheduled to move out soon.

Fortunately, one man came forward with an idea to save the fleet. Lt. Col. Joseph Bailey, a former Wisconsin lumberman turned army engineer, proposed that a series of wing dams be built to raise the water level and to help float the vessels over the falls. Bailey knew what he was talking about because he had salvaged some mired vessels in a similar manner during the Port Hudson campaign. Porter had been "damning" the river ever since the navy had undertaken its retreat. Bailey proposed to dam the Red in a more constructive way.

To carry out this ingenious engineering feat, Bailey turned to lumbermen from Maine regiments for assistance. Elements from both the 29th and 30th Maine regiments were engaged on this project. To be sure, many others besides Maine men were employed, but the lumbermen from Down East were particularly well qualified for the task at hand. As one Maine colonel testified before Congress, such dams were in common use in the Pine Tree State.

The wing dams constructed were composed of a variety of materials. On the lower falls, one tree-dam was built from huge logs, brush, brick and stone, and cross-tied with heavy timbers and other devices. Extending 300 feet into the river from the left bank, this dam had four large coal barges weighted with bricks at its outermost edge. From the right bank, the dam was met by large log cribs filled with stones. Lumber torn from fences and buildings, machinery ripped out from nearby sugar mills, and stones drawn from an old quarry close at hand were all used to complete the project.

For eight days and nights, Maine men labored on this gigantic enterprise that absorbed the energies of 3,000 men and 200 to 300 mule teams. Cutting trees, wheeling bricks, and often working up to their necks in water, the soldiers remained, surprisingly enough, in good humor despite the difficult conditions. Their spirits and the waters of the Red River rose simultaneously. By the afternoon of the eighth day, May 3, the dam was nearly complete and almost ready for its first test.

The waters on the upper falls had risen sufficiently for three of the lighter vessels to float down to the lower rapids preparatory to passing the dam. Within another day, the waters would have been high enough for all the vessels to negotiate the upper falls. At this point catastrophe struck.

The morning of May 9, the pressure of the rising waters became so great that it swept away two of the stone barges, opening a breach in the lower dam. With sinking hearts, the Maine men watched as the barges swung in below the dam on one side. It looked as though all their efforts had been in vain.

But such was not to be the case. Porter was determined to try and pass the dam while there was still a glimmer of hope and to save what vessels he could. He ordered the *Lexington,* one of his heavier craft on the upper falls, to proceed downstream at full speed. The test was to be made, but under the most trying of conditions.

The *Lexington* succeeded in getting over the upper falls just in the nick of time, for the water level was falling rapidly as she passed over. She then steered directly for the opening in the lower dam. Porter graphically described what happened to her: "She entered the gap with a full head of steam on, pitched down the roaring torrent, made two or three spasmodic rolls, hung for a moment on the rocks below, was swept into deep water by the current and rounded to, safely into the bank."

The *Neosho* followed next. Her hatches were all battened down and every precaution was taken against any accident. However, she did not fare as well because her pilot disobeyed orders. Instead of carrying a full head of steam, he ordered her engines to be stopped. The result was that her hull disappeared from sight under water as she passed through the dam. Everyone thought she was lost. She rose, however, swept along over the rocks by the current, and escaped with only one hole in her bottom. The *Fort Hindman* and

Osage came through beautifully and were unscathed.

The accident to the dam, instead of disheartening Bailey, only induced him to renew his exertions, especially after he had seen the success of the four vessels. Maine soldiers, after seeing the labor of eight days swept away in a moment, now returned to work cheerfully as they grew confident that the remaining gunboats could be saved.

Even the accident that had plunged them into gloom had its bright side. The two barges that had been carried away were anchored against some rocks below the dam and acted as a fine cushion which prevented vessels running the gauntlet from crashing into certain destruction.

The force of the water was too great and the current too swift to allow for the construction of a continuous dam, 600 feet across the river, in the little time that remained, Bailey decided to leave the gap [of] 55 feet in the dam and to build a series of wing dams on the upper falls.

This was accomplished within three days, and on May 11, the *Mound City, Carondelet,* and *Pittsburgh* succeeded in passing down to the dam. The next day the *Ozark, Louisville, Chillicothe* and the two tugs managed to do likewise.

During May 12 and 13, all of these vessels negotiated the tricky passage through the dam and floated to safety with only minor accidents. By the afternoon of May 13, the craft, all coaled and re-ammunitioned, steamed down the river with a convoy of transports. The waters of the lower Red River were navigated without incident and the fleet was able to return to the mouth of the stream safely.

General Banks termed the operation one of the most remarkable achievements of the war, and Admiral Porter called it "the best engineering feat ever performed." Bailey's idea had saved a valuable fleet, whose economic worth alone was $2,000,000. Militarily his accomplishment was even more important because it deprived the Confederates of a significant triumph in the western theater of operations.

In his report of the expedition, Porter concluded with this remark: "I trust some future historian will treat this matter as it deserves to be treated, because it is a subject in which the whole country should feel an interest, and the noble men who succeeded so admirably in this arduous task should not lose one atom of credit so justly due them." Ranked among the "noble men who succeeded so admirably" should be listed the names of the soldiers of the 29th and 30th Maine regiments.

See Also

"Hitherto Unpublished Records of the Red River Campaign, from the diary of Thomas Pratt of the 30th Maine," *Lewiston Journal Illustrated Magazine,* 29 May 1915, pp. 5, 11; and 5 June 1915, pps. 11, 16.

"Notes of the Red River Campaign of 1864," Military Order of the Loyal Legion of the United States, *War Papers: Read Before the Commandery of the State of Maine* 4, 1915, pp. 264–81.

"The Red River Expedition of 1864," Military Order of the Loyal Legion of the United States, *War Papers: Read Before the Commandery of the State of Maine* 1, 1898, pp. 181–90.

"When the Maine Boys Campaigned with Banks,"*Lewiston Journal Illustrated Magazine,* 8 August 1908, pp. 5, 11.

THE *ALABAMA* VERSUS THE *KEARSARGE*: A NAVAL BATTLE THAT WILL NEVER BE FORGOTTEN

L.C. BATEMAN

Memorial Day is once more at hand, and it is fitting that some tale of the Civil War should be told that will remind our people of the terrible strife when a million brave men went down to the dark river in order that our country might live.

Stories of war are always thrilling. The blood flows faster and the eye grows brighter as we recall and recount the scenes that tried men's souls in the long ago. Memory may fail in all the smaller details; the long and weary marches, the sleepless nights beneath the pitying stars and the vigils around the mighty bivouac fire are now but dim recollections of the past. The long line in blue has now grown thin and the tales of war must soon be told by other lips and written by other hands.

This is but the fate of each passing generation. History only records events long after they have happened, and even then only in perspective. The men who take part in any great event are least able to tell the story with absolute impartiality. Long after they have passed to pleasant dreams the facts that they have left behind are carefully sifted and arranged for the benefit of mankind. Exaggerations and misstatements are then illuminated and only the great headlights are left in bold perspective.

The history of every great war leaves but few great events and men for future generations to recall. The closing days of the 18th century leaves only the name of Napoleon as the outstanding figure, while the brave Ney is forgotten. The great naval conflict between the fleet of Xerxes and the allied Greeks is practically only known by the immortal lines of Byron:

A king sat on the rocky brow
That looks o'er sea born Satimis,
And ships by thousands lay below,
And men in nations—all were his!
He counted them at break of day,
And when the sun set where were they?

The battle of the Nile tells the story of Lord Nelson but all other names are forgotten.

The future student will know but two great names in connection with our Civil War. Lincoln and Grant will remain immortal and grow the brighter with the flight of time. Among the land battles, Gettysburg will alone remain, but even the name of Mead is already forgotten because of his failure to follow up his advantage.

Two great events on the restless sea alone will live. These are the battle between the *Merrimac* and the *Monitor*, and the destruction of the *Alabama* off the coast of France. The first of these changed the navies of the world; the last spelled the fate of the Confederacy. And it is of this conflict that we now write.

It was in the early summer of 1864, and the darkest hour in the war of the Rebellion. A

ORIGINALLY PUBLISHED IN *LEWISTON JOURNAL ILLUSTRATED MAGAZINE*, 27 MAY 1922.

shadow sat on every northern face when it was known that the *Alabama* was making a fearful havoc with our merchant ships. (It had sunk at least two Maine vessels: the *Dorcas Prince* in May, 1863, and the *Anna F. Schmidt* in June, 1863.) The indignation had risen to a high point when it was known that this was an English ship and armed with British guns to war with a country with which she professed to be at peace.

She did not even claim to be a Confederate ship, but simply performed her acts of piracy under the Confederate flag. It was a short-lived triumph in which our enemy and her sympathizers indulged, and bitterly did England rue the day that she furnished this modern corsair to the South.

The *Alabama* was a very swift warship and seemed to be endowed with magic life. She easily escaped all our fastest cruisers and pursued her work of devastation to the great delight of the champions of rebellion. To all appearances she bore a charmed life, and rarely did she enter a foreign harbor as all her supplies were obtained from her commercial victims on the sea. A Nemesis at last appeared. As early as 1862 Captain John A. Winslow was placed in command of the Kittery-built sloop *Kearsarge*, with instructions to hunt down this pirate of the seas. This was anything but easy to do as the ocean was wide and the *Alabama* never remained long in one place. At last the *Kearsarge* crossed to the European shores where it was reported that the corsair had last been seen. It was a long and weary hunt but persistence was at last rewarded. Word came that the *Alabama* had been seen to enter the harbor of Cherbourg, on the French coast, and immediately Winslow ordered all steam put on and started for that port. Of course he could not enter that harbor to fight the confederate but contented himself to remain the legal limit away.

The *Alabama* was commanded by Captain Raphael Semmes, a brave and skilled officer of the Confederacy. He was now in an embarrassing position. To remain in a French port where the eyes of the world were watching him would appear like an act of cowardice, and this could not be endorsed by the commander. But one choice was left to Semmes. He realized that the strength of the *Kearsarge* was about the same as the *Alabama*. Up to this time he had been engaged in sinking unarmed merchantmen, but now he was faced by a foe that was worthy of his steel. In order to retain the respect of his English friends and French hosts he was compelled to meet the *Kearsarge*. It was the supreme moment of his life. To submit to being blockaded by a ship no stronger than his own was out of the question. To win in such a contest would be of immeasurable benefit to the South. Putting on a bold face he sent a challenge to Winslow for an open battle on the sea.

This challenge was at once accepted. Captain Winslow knew only too well what it meant. The *Alabama* was a slightly larger ship and carried one more gun. Trained English gunners were at their posts. Winslow was burning with indignation to think that he was not only fighting the best ship of the South but also the best trained men of the English navy. He understood that defeat meant death to himself and crew, but also a mortal blow to his country. To be taken a captive into a French port was more than his brave soul could bear, and he at once prepared to win or die. The *Kearsarge* was stripped to the gunwales of all unnecessary articles and every man was at his post.

It was Sunday morning, June 19th, when the Alabama steamed out of the harbor of Cherbourg to meet the Kearsarge. The day was beautiful, with scarcely a breath of wind to ruffle the ocean or anything to indicate the bloody tragedy about to be enacted. The telegraph had been busy notifying Paris and the surrounding country of what was coming, and men and women were soon steaming into the city and lining the shores of the harbor to witness the great duel. A French frigate accompanied the Alabama out of the harbor to make sure that their guest would not be attacked until beyond the legal limit of three miles from the shore.

It was at 10:30 o'clock when Captain Winslow saw the *Alabama* coming toward him and he immediately veered his ship and stood out to sea. At first it was thought by those on the shore that this was an act of cowardice and that the *Kearsarge* was running away. As a matter of fact, it was the shrewdest move made by the commander. He wished to get far enough away to avoid all question of harbor jurisdiction and to prevent the *Alabama* from escaping in case of defeat. This movement was a success, as the battle was fought at six miles from the shore.

In another moment the *Kearsarge* turned and bore straight down upon her enemy. The

Alabama at once fired a full broadside from her starboard battery, while slowing down her speed. This did no damage, and then came the turn of the *Kearsarge*. In rapid succession the *Alabama* fired two more broadsides but not a shot struck her adversary.

Winslow cleared for action and made no reply until within 700 yards, when he belched forth a full broadside. The two ships were brought broadside to broadside, but it was soon evident that Semmes did not propose firing at close quarters.

Fearing that his enemy might start for the shore, Winslow kept his vessel at full speed, with the intention of reaching the stern of the *Alabama*, where the most effective work could be done. In order to escape this move, the *Alabama* sheered so as to keep broadside to the *Kearsarge*, and thus both vessels kept up full speed in circular movement around a common center. All this time Winslow was watching to prevent the *Alabama* from running toward the shore. The firing of the British ship was both rapid and wild, and little or no damage was done. For the first half hour not a man on the *Kearsarge* was injured, and then a seventy-pound shell tore through her bulwarks and exploded on the quarter-deck, wounding several men, one of whom soon died. This was the only severe damage received by the Union.

Winslow now saw his advantage. He ordered his gunners to work slowly and aim deliberately. Especial attention was given by the men at the two eleven-inch guns, and it was soon seen that their work was terribly effective. One shot alone struck down eighteen men on the deck of the *Alabama*. Other shots tore through the rigging and swept away the quarter deck. The coal bunker came next and the engines were put of commission. It soon became a veritable hell on the *Alabama*. Great holes were torn through the sides of the ship, letting in a deluge of water.

For a full hour this terrible carnage went on. The crew of the Alabama became discouraged and their shots went wilder than ever. Every shot from the Kearsarge found its mark: and in one hour the Alabama was a helpless wreck on the water. Still, Semmes refused to strike his flag and Winslow was relentless. The English gunners failed to get the range and no damage was done.

On the contrary, the decks of the *Alabama* were but shambles and a slaughter house. Half her crew were soon dead and the greater part of the remainder were weltering in their blood. Still, Semmes held on, while Winslow with grim determination continued to pour shot and shell into the helpless wreck. Once again the commander of the *Alabama* tried to reach the shore but it was useless. The end had come. After another shot, her flag vanished. Winslow thought it might have been carried away by the shot, but the next moment a white flag fluttered in the breeze and the firing ceased.

The *Kearsarge* now steamed ahead and laid across the bow of the sinking ship. The white flag was still in place and in a moment a boat containing an officer of the *Alabama* came alongside to inform Captain Winslow that Semmes had surrendered, as his ship was sinking. Winslow at once ordered his own boats lowered in order to save the remnant of the *Alabama*'s crew. Most of these were now struggling in the water and one by one they were picked up.

Then came one of the most despicable tricks connected with the warfare. An English steam yacht was hailed and asked to come and help rescue the drowning men. As soon as this was done the yacht started for the English shore, and it was learned that Semmes had thrown away his sword and was aboard! The tradition of all nations and all navies is that a conquered foe must deliver his sword to the conqueror. Winslow was expecting this and intended to receive Semmes as one gentleman should receive a fallen foe. He would have been treated with all courtesy although a prisoner.

To say that Winslow was astounded by such cowardly conduct expresses it but mildly. His first impulse was to send a broadside into the escaping yacht and sink her but the thought came that the skipper was confused by the scenes through which he had passed and the *Kearsarge* withheld the shot. The commander of the yacht was a man named Lancaster, and instead of being ashamed of his contemptible conduct, he was actually proud. Even that was not the worst of the matter. All England seemed to glory in the act and both Semmes and Lancaster were made popular heroes by the civilian authorities. To the credit of the English navy, many of the officers condemned the act and declined to associate or even speak with Semmes.

In his report to Secretary Welles of the American navy, Captain Winslow recounted all the facts, and in his reply Secretary Welles says:

> The *Alabama* represented the best maritime effort of the best English workshops. Her battery was composed of the well-tried 32-pounders. . . , of the famous 68-pounder of the British navy, and of the only successful rifled 100-pounder yet produced in England. The crew were recruited in Great Britain and many of them received superior training on board her majesty's gunnery ship—the *Excellent.* The *Kearsarge* is one of the first gunboats built at our navy yards at the commencement of the Rebellion and lacks the improvements of the vessels now under construction.

> The President has signified his intention to recommend that you receive a vote of thanks from Congress in order that you may be advanced to the rank of commodore. Lieutenant Commander James S. Thornton, the executive officer of the *Kearsarge,* will be recommended to the Senate for advancement ten numbers in his grade.

Continuing, Secretary Welles says:

> That the wretched commander of the *Alabama* should have resorted to any dishonorable means to escape after his surrender; that he should have thrown overboard the sword that was no longer his; that before encountering an armed antagonist the mercenary rover of the sea should have removed the chronometers and other plunder stolen from peaceful commerce are not matters of surprise, for each act is characteristic of one who has been false to his country and flag. You could not, however, have expected that gentlemen, or those claiming to be gentlemen, would on such an occasion, act in bad faith, and that, having been called upon or permitted to assist in rescuing persons and property which had been surrendered to you, they would run away with either.

These scathing words of Secretary Welles thoroughly cover the lack of honor in Semmes, and the discreditable conduct of England. It is well to know that in 1873 an international board of arbitration recognized the disgraceful position into which England had placed herself, and awarded fifteen million dollars in damages to the United States for sinkings done by the *Alabama* and the other two British-built raiders, the *Florida* and *Shenandoah.* And England, in an apparent admission of culpability, readily paid the bill.

ALSO SEE

"The Burning of the *Anna F. Schmidt,*" *Down East,* April 1969, pp. 30–31, 62, 67–68.

"Down-East Ships of the Union Navy," David C. Switzer, *United States Naval Institute Proceedings,* 90, November 1964, pp. 82–88.

"How a Damariscotta Man Came to Wear Handcuffs," *Lewiston Journal Illustrated Magazine,* 3 February 1923, p. 12.

SIGNALS AT THE SIEGE OF CHARLESTON

GEORGE H. STONE

Napoleon declared that the art of war is the art of concentration. To this end cooperation between different forces is necessary, but cannot be secured without means of prompt communication. In the crisis of battle the saving of a few minutes in sending an order may mean all the difference between victory and defeat, hence the inestimable value of efficient military signals.

Those who wish to study in detail the system of signals used during the Civil War, should consult *The Manual of Signals*, by General Albert J. Myer, N.Y., 1868. For an account of the field operations of the signal corps during that period, the reader is referred to *The Signal Corps in the War of the Rebellion,* by Lieut. J. Willard Brown of East Boston, Mass. This large book is a monument of industry in collecting description of the signals and a chapter on the Confederate signal corps.

Briefly stated, the signals most used by both armies during the Civil War were what is commonly known as the wigwag system of signals. Flags by day and torches by night are attached to poles held vertically in the hands of the operator, who makes motions with the flags and torches by waving them in various ways. The most visible of these motions are the wavings to the right and left, answering to the dots and dashes of the Morse telegraphic code. Thirty combinations of the right and left motions can be made, using no more than four motions in each combination. Twenty-six of these combinations can be used to represent the letters of the alphabet, leaving four to represent the syllables "and," "ing," and "tion," and one to mark the end of a word, two at the end of a sentence, and three at the end of a message.

The system of wigwag signals is insepara-

bly connected with the name of General Albert J. Myer. In 1856 he was a surgeon in the U.S. Army, and while in New Mexico he saw the Indians signaling to each other by waving their spears. Very soon he had worked out a scheme of wigwag signals. This he reported to his superiors and was assigned to special duty as signal officer, and thus it happened that his system received its first trial in the field. Among the officers who were instructed by Major Myer in the use of the new signals was Captain E. P. Alexander, who, when the Civil War broke out, became for a time the chief signal officer of the Confederate army. He organized a signal corps to use Myers' signals so promptly that it took an important part in the first battle of Bull Run. Major Myer was appointed chief signal officer of the Union army, but such was the indifference and opposition he encountered that he was not able to bring a signal service into the field till two months or more after the Confederate signal service was in successful operation.

During the Civil War both of the opposing signal services used the same flag and torch motions. Both used a standard or common code. This was at first supposed to be sufficiently secret, but as time went on both sides were able to read more or less of the enemy's signals, and by degrees both adopted the practice of sending all important messages in cipher.

Since our Civil War the system of wigwag signals has come into use by every progressive army in the world, and it still holds a prominent place in signaling in spite of the larger use of the telegraph and the invention of the telephone and wireless telegraph. The

ORIGINALLY PUBLISHED IN *LEWISTON JOURNAL ILLUSTRATED MAGAZINE*, 30 OCTOBER & 6 NOVEMBER 1909.

apparatus for the latter is as yet too bulky for rapid field transportation, and the flag can wave a message right over an enemy in a way not possible to the telephone and telegraph through wires. Each new war shows more clearly the advantage of instant communication between all parts of the field of war. Other things equal, if an Oyama has more perfect means of communication with all points of his battle front of fifty miles or more, he will be able to beat a Kuropatkin, having a less efficient system of signals.

The story of the military operations near Charleston fills a large page of history and need here be referred to only in the briefest way. A combined naval and land force entered Port Royal, the deepest harbor on the South Carolina coast on November 17, 1861. They captured the fortifications at Hilton Head, and that place became the headquarters of the Federal forces till the end of the war. In the summer of 1862 an expedition from Hilton Head attacked the fort at Secessionville on James Island, the island bordering Charleston harbor on the south. This assault was repulsed with great loss. In the summer of 1863 a larger expedition advanced and speedily occupied all the islands along the coast until Morris Island was reached. This island forms the outer barrier of Charleston harbor on the southeast and had been strongly fortified by the Confederates. Though General Gilmore, the Union commander, was a brilliant engineer, it was not until after a long, bloody and famous stage that Battery Wagner, the principal defense of the island, was captured. With the occupation of Morris Island our advance in that direction ended. During 1864 and the early part of 1865 a force of three or four thousand men held the islands that had been captured near Charleston and these made a few demonstrations along the coast, but the only practical result was to compel the Confederates to keep a considerable force in that region.

The general facts as to the use of signals by both of the opposing armies in the vicinity of Charleston are well stated in Lieut. Brown's history. Signals were of especial value in a region dotted with islands which are separated by tide-water bayous and broad swamps. In both armies the signal men helped maintain prompt cooperation between the different forces, and the commanders on both sides have testified their high appreciation of the value of these services.

In preparing his history of the field operations of the Signal Corps Mr. Brown has necessarily depended on the official reports as they are published in the *Rebellion Record*, or are otherwise accessible. These reports are those of commissioned officers exclusively. It thus appears that if enlisted men (sergeants and privates) are sent out to do something and write reports of the results, it is not history. Only that portion of the report of the enlisted man will enter the published record which filters through the report of his superior. The truth will thus be colored to suit the views of that official, or it may be misunderstood or suppressed. Officialdom has had its say for forty years, it is now time for the enlisted men to supply some of the missing and hitherto unpublished episodes of the history. (I was at that time a private in the U.S. Signal Corps, and served at or near Charleston from January 4, 1864, until July 4, 1865.) As compared with the general operations they are of course of minor importance.

Each of the above signal services were sooner or later able to read the other's signals. In this the Confederates led off in South Carolina. On the night of March 13, 1863, the signal party on duty at Spanish Wells near Beaufort, S.C., were taken prisoners. They included a lieutenant and three privates. Two of these privates declared, after their return from prison, that the third private had deserted to the Confederates and betrayed the United States common code. Be this as it may, it is known that the Confederates began to read our signals soon after this time, the most noted among them being Lieut. Markoe, who for a long time was stationed at Battery Beauregard on Sullivan's Island, the island forming the outer barrier of Charleston harbor on the northeast. When the Confederates evacuated Charleston there was left at the city signal station a large book containing a record of all the messages that had come to that station for several years. Among them were a large number of our messages which had been intercepted by Lieut. Markoe or others, and it was surprising how valuable to the Confederate commanders must have been the information thus obtained. Quite a number of the messages intercepted by the Confederate operators are printed in Mr. Brown's book. The message of all others which makes one's blood boil is the one noticed by Brown but not printed, sent by Gen. Gilmore to Admiral Dahlgren on July 13, 1863, to cease firing at a certain hour, as he was about to charge Fort Wagner. Of course, in any case that would have been a bloody charge, but doubtless the Confederates were helped by the fact that they had several hours' notice of the coming assault. I copied this and many other of our messages which had been read by the Confederates and from which they gained important information, but the copies have mostly been lost.

Early in February, 1864, our forces made a raid onto the southeast part of Johns Island. They advanced so rapidly that they surprised a Confederate signal station and the officer was compelled to retreat before he could carry away with him his record of messages. This book was found to contain all the U.S. messages which had been sent by the Botany Bay station, one of a line of stations which then extended from Hilton Head to Morris Island. Strict orders were at once issued to send all official messages in cipher, and it is believed that from that date the opposing signal corps never gained any important information by reading our signals.

Immediately after the discovery on Johns Island that the enemy were reading our signals, two officers went to Morris Island and tried to decipher the Confederate signals, but after several weeks of failure they abandoned the effort. Soon after, in May, 1864, Sergeant (afterward Lieutenant) John D. Colvin of the Signal Corps, was detailed at his own request to go to Fort Strong (the Confederate Battery Wagner) for the purpose of reading the enemy's signals if possible. From this fort the first (or last) fourteen Confederate signal stations were visible, two or three of them being occupied only temporarily. The most important station was at the city. It was on a building constructed on piles, just off "The Battery," an open plaza at the south end of Charleston. The next most important station was at Battery Bee, at the western end of Sullivans Island. On Sullivans Island there were also stations at the north end of the island and at Battery Beauregard and Fort Moultrie. There were stations at Forts Sumter and Johnson and Castle Pinckney, Secessionville, and other minor points.

Within a short time Sergeant Colvin succeeded in reading the Confederate common code. Thereafter his career was brilliant. He was able to gain very important information of the enemy's movements and for this he was thanked and complimented in a general order issued by Major General Foster, and later he was promoted to be a lieutenant. Many of his exploits are related in Mr. Brown's book. Repeatedly the Confederate operators sent messages in cipher and changed their cipher, but all of these he was for several months able to read. The Confederate Lieut. Markoe inadvertently aided Colvin in working out these ciphers. After reading one of our messages sent in common code (at this period they were either unimportant or fakes sent to deceive) he would signal the message to Battery Bee, from whence it went to the city. He usually changed the wording of the intercepted messages, but sadly for him he did not change it sufficiently, for it was generally possible to recognize enough of our message to give to Colvin the needed clue to the Confederate cipher. It was also a great help to know the past messages and hence be able to guess the subject of a given message.

The Confederate Signal Code

A 2111	K 2212	U 111	1 22222
B 211	L 2112	V 1211	2 12222
C 212	M 2122	W 1112	3 11222
D 222	N 221	X 1121	4 11122
E 2222	O 112	Y 1212	5 11112
F 21	P 122	Z 1111	6 21111
G 2211	Q 1222	and 1122	7 22111
H 2221	R 121	ing 2121	8 22211
I 11	S 12		9 22221
J 22	T 1		0 11111

Explanation: The numeral "1" in this code signifies a flag motion to the left, "2," a motion to the right. This was known to us as the "Confederate Common Code," it being the only code in use on that side, their so-called cipher codes of numbers being really substituted alphabets.

During the summer of 1864 the Confederate signal corps discovered that we were reading their signals. At that time it was the common story current among the enlisted men of our corps that immediately after General Polk was killed in Georgia (during the Atlanta campaign) a message was signaled from his headquarters announcing his death to General Johnston. This was read by a Union signal officer, and the news of Gen. Polk's death quickly spread throughout Sherman's army. A correspondent of a New York newspaper mentioned this news in his correspondence and stated that it came from an intercepted signal message. That paper was in Richmond within 48 hours. Be this story true or not, it is certain that in October or early November, 1864, a new cipher came into use among the Confederate signal operators at Charleston, and henceforth they were careful to send all important messages in cipher.

Some explanations are at this point necessary in order that the reader may understand what follows. In signal language a code consists of the letters of the alphabet, together with the numbers which describe the flag motions representing the several letters. In what is known as a "straight code," each letter is represented by the same flag motion or combination of motions in the course of the whole message. All the Confederate cipher codes that were in use at Charleston up to this time, including all that Sergeant Colvin ever deciphered, were "straight codes."

On Jan. 4, 1865, Sergeant Colvin was left as senior sergeant in charge of the signal detachment near Charleston. Within ten minutes he ordered me from the John Adams, the flagship of the blockading squadron off Charleston, to Fort Strong to assist him in reading the Confederate signals. On my reporting for duty at the fort that afternoon, he gave me the Confederate common code to learn. He also showed me several of their cipher codes, and within a few minutes I had constructed what we called the Confederate "disc." It was made in imitation of the U.S. cipher apparatus, and consisted of two circular plates or wheels, each having twenty-six teeth. On the teeth of one of the wheels were marked the letters of the alphabet in their usual order; on the teeth of the other wheel were the numbers representing the common Confederate code, also in their proper order. By rotating one of these wheels twenty-six different codes could be obtained, including both the Confederate common code and all the cipher codes which Sergeant Colvin had discovered. He was much interested in this disc but said: "This will not help us; they are now using something much harder, and I have not been able to decipher it." He had, however, preserved a record of the numbers or flag-motions of numerous messages which had been sent in the new cipher during the two months or so preceding.

For several days we then worked jointly on this cipher, but up to noon of Sunday, January 8, 1865, we had made no progress. We had tried all the schemes we could think of

and all failed to give us the remotest clue as to the law of the cipher. At the time mentioned, Sergeant Colvin left Fort Strong while I continued work on the cipher.

It has been stated that the Confederate Lieut. Markoe had given aid to the working out of his own cipher by signaling our messages. But he had now grown more cautious; at least, for some reason he had so changed the wording of our messages before forwarding that from them alone only a faint clue could have been discovered as to the law of the cipher. Among the messages sent in the common Confederate code and read by us was an order from General Hardee calling for a statement of the arms, equipments and stores on Sullivans Island. Soon after, a very long message was sent to General Hardee by the officer in command on that island, and at a venture I assumed this to be an answer to the first message. We were familiar with the names of the Confederate cannon, etc., and I wrote out a provisional translation of the cipher. This proved to be sufficiently correct, so that when it was compared with what points could be gained from Lieut. Markoe, of a sudden there flashed on my mind the idea that this cipher consisted of a series of codes to be used in succession in the same message.

Neither Colvin nor I had then heard of such a cipher. The discovery of the law of that cipher was chiefly the work of the imagination, for we had not sufficient data to work out by cold reason. Nobody can account for the vagaries of the imagination, and I have never been able to give any very definite description of the mental processes which finally worked out the details of the cipher. Even after the idea that this was a series of codes came to me, it was not easy to determine how many codes were in the series and what was their proper order. Suffice it to say that before night and several hours before Sergeant Colvin's return to the fort, I had been able to construct a table or chart showing all fifteen of the codes, and had written out directions for reading messages sent in this cipher that were so full and definite that no changes were ever necessary thereafter.

The real method of the Confederates was unknown to us, and I approached the subject from the standpoint of our own cipher. In our four-wheel "disc" there were changes in the order both of the letters and the numbers representing the flag motions. In studying the Confederate cipher it was therefore necessary to determine the laws of both the alphabet and the numbers. The fact that in all the straight Confederate cipher codes thus far discovered the letters remained in true alphabetic order indicated that this might be the law of the new cipher and was provisionally assumed as the starting point. The assumption proved to be correct, and but for this orderly arrangement I do not believe the law of the cipher could have been discovered. I then supposed that the new cipher consisted of a series of numeral codes taken from the assumed Confederate disc. According to this conception the letters of a message were divided into successive series of fifteen letters each. The first letter of the message was taken from the first code, the second from the second code and so on to the fifteenth letter which was taken from the fifteenth code. Then the series was repeated, the sixteenth letter was taken from the first code, and so on through the message. This became known to us as the "Confederate Series-Cipher."

In finding the law of the series, I described each of the successive codes by its position relative to the common code on the supposed Confederate disc. Thus the first code of the series was marked 1 R, signifying that it began one number to the right of the common code. The second code was marked X, meaning that it began across or opposite on the disc to the common code.

The third code was marked C, meaning correct, that is, this was the common code. The fourth code was marked 1 L, meaning it began one to the left of the common code. The other codes were marked as follows: 5th, C; 6th, X; 7th, 4 R; 8th, 6 R; 9th, 4 L; 10th, 3 L; 11th, X; 12th, C; 13th 9 R; 14th, C; 15th, X.

Expressed in terms of the common code, the first letters of these fifteen codes were actually chosen, and what they represented will be explained presently.

That the 15-series cipher was the most secret, confidential and difficult cipher used by the Confederate signal corps is shown by the following verbatim extract from a letter addressed to me by Mr. Augustine T. Smythe of the law firm of Smythe, Lee and Frost, of Charleston. Mr. Smythe writes that he served in the Confederate signal corps and took an active part in all the proceedings connected with the siege of Charleston. His letter is in answer to a letter of inquiry which I had shortly before written to him and is dated June 1, 1906:

The 15-series cipher of which you speak was a very ingenious contrivance, the key word was "Frederika Bremer," and it was a very difficult one to study, learn, and an exceedingly difficult one to decipher. If you accomplished this last feat you certainly deserve credit, for it was the best one we ever saw.

We did not then know what the Confederate cipher apparatus was like, though in one of the messages intercepted at Charleston it was called a reel. It consisted mainly of a rotating cylinder around which was wrapped a paper on which was printed an alphabetic square consisting of twenty-six horizontal alphabets and an equal number of vertical alphabets each one beginning with the letter succeeding the preceding alphabet. Among the messages sent in the series cipher and read by us was the following sent to the signal men at the various stations a few days before the fall of Charleston: "Signal operators will receive from the commanders of their posts orders to retire when Gen. Hardee's division is formed." This message well shows the value of the information we gained from the intercepted signals, for of course it meant that Charleston was soon to be evacuated. In sending this message the Confederate operators would write the letters of the message under those of the key words, and underneath them in turn the letters of the signal message as follows:

SIGNAL OPERATORS WILL RECEIVE FROM
—the message

FREDER IKABREMER FRED ERIKABR EMER
—key word

TVGMAY SVAONTVRF XVEK RRGKABR FZOZ
—cipher as signaled

It will be noted that the letters of the key word "Frederika Bremer" are contained in all the alphabets both horizontal and vertical. In order, then, to use the cipher we must know which code to apply the key word to. My recollection is very strong (my copies of the Confederate series cipher have been accidentally lost and I can only depend on my memory in this matter) that there was no substitution in the case of the third letter of the series, in other words the letter E was the same in the cipher as in the message to be sent. This means that the key word is applied to the fifth vertical alphabet under the letter E. We then look in the uppermost horizontal alphabet for the successive letters of the message. Below this letter we pass vertically till we come to the horizontal alphabet in which is found the corresponding letter of the key word in the fifth vertical alphabet. This letter we substitute for the letter of the message. In deciphering a message the process is reversed.

That the letters of this cipher were applied to the fifth vertical column instead of the first (the first letters of these codes are quoted above) or the sixth under the letter F was a shrewd arrangement well designed to throw off anyone trying to find the law of the cipher by applying chance key words to an alphabetic square. So, too, the choice of the key word was admirable, for in the hurly burly of war time nobody would think of going across the ocean and selecting that charming novelist. I did not and could not find the law of the cipher by guessing the key word. The method of using a key word and an alphabetic square is given in Mr. Brown's book, but he uses a key of 12 and not 15 letters. The key word used at Charleston was not known by any of us until Mr. Smythe's letter stated it. Comparing this use of a key word and an alphabetic square, it is seen that the flag motions are the same in the two cases. In other words, the Confederates had but one signal code and they got their cipher by shuffling alphabets, while in finding the law of the cipher and reading messages I held on to the alphabet and shuffled the codes, and it is a matter of indifference which we do.

The critical reader will have noticed that in a table showing the series cipher only the codes or alphabets in use are given, while in the case of the alphabetic square on the Confederate reel the operators must pick out certain of the alphabets from the midst of others not used. This explains why we could read their cipher quicker than they could. When the alphabets represented by the letters of a key word are thus aggregated, it is seen that such a cipher is not so difficult as it seems to be while all the alphabets are spread out before us.

In the issue of the *Scientific American* for May 26, 1866, is published a letter from a correspondent at Norfolk, Va., under the caption, "Cipher Writing." Enclosed was a copy of a Confederate cipher telegraphic message which was printed for translation. Space does not permit quoting this letter or all of the letters called out by it. In the issue for June 16, 1866, the same periodical publishes a letter dated Wesleyan University, Middletown, Conn., and signed by George C. Round, late lieutenant and signal officer, U.S.A. Mr. Round (now for many years a resident of Manassas, Va.), sent to the editor both a translation of the message already printed and in turn a cipher message to be translated, which, by the way, no one ever claimed to read. Regarding the subject of cipher writing and this letter the editor remarks:

This subject seems to have awakened considerable interest and we were about to prepare a brief article in relation to it when we received the communication published below.

Mr. Round is the only correspondent who has succeeded in translating the cipher message of our Norfolk correspondent published in our issue of May 26th. His translation is *verbatim et literatim*. Probably our readers will find the task he sets for them a most onerous one, as he seems to be a master in the occult art of cryptography.

One paragraph of Mr. Round's letter is as follows:

I have never met this particular cipher before, but the general principles upon which the rebel ciphers were founded have been long known at the Signal Bureau at Washington, having first been discovered by George H. Stone, now a student at this university, then belonging to the signal detachment of the Department of the South.

My name having been brought into this case, it is only fair to add that all I did in connection with the deciphering of the message deciphered by Lieut. Round was first to attack it with the signal cipher in use at Charleston. Finding this would not decipher the message and having no time for study of it, I called the matter to Mr. Round's attention, telling him the message was probably written in a series cipher much like that used at Charleston. With this hint he was able to translate the cipher within a few hours; in fact, his letter is dated only two days after the publication of the original. I have recently compared the cipher with the translation and find the key word to be "complete victory," the key being applied to the first vertical alphabet of the alphabetic square under the letter A. There are several changes from the strict rule, which may be mistakes, but more probably there was provision for alternative letters. In their books both Gen. Myer and Lieut. Brown refer to this "complete victory" cipher as having been discovered at Vicksburg in 1863. If this was so, although this was wholly a telegraphic and not a signal cipher, it was a great mistake not to send it out to all the signal departments as a hint concerning the probable nature of the Confederate ciphers. It would have saved Sergeant Colvin and me many a headache could we have had the hint that we were attacking a 15-series cipher. As it was, we had not the slightest clue to the mystery of the new cipher.

These messages covered a wide range of subjects, most of them being official orders and reports. By degrees the names of a large number of officers in command on the other side became known to us, and sometimes a number of troops at certain posts were reported. None of these reports were considered above suspicion of being fakes unless they were sent in cipher. In his history, Mr. Brown has printed quite a number of messages intercepted by Lieut. Colvin. To these I will add a few of the later ones. Thus during January and early February, 1865, orders were repeatedly sent for laborers (slaves) to be sent to work on the fortification at Hatcher's Run, a few miles south of Charleston, showing that if General Sherman had advanced from Savannah directly on Charleston he would have met a very stubborn resistance. One day a raw recruit at Battery Bee was signaling with the operator at Sumter. In reply to some question of the man at Sumter (we could not see that station), the man at Bee replies: Sherman yesterday reached the rail at——. (He named a station on the railway from Charleston to Augusta, Ga., which I now forget.) As time went on, many messages showed that Charleston would soon be evacuated, and if our general had a sufficient force he could have caused Gen. Hardee considerable trouble at this time. Finally the time came when a cipher was sent to Sullivans Island notifying all posts that the last steamer would leave the Mount Pleasant wharf near midnight of February 17. Then Gen. Schimmelfennig acted instantly. He ordered two thousand men with cooked rations for four days to advance on the south end of James Island, where they stormed a small outwork, but carefully avoided the main fortifications. These troops advanced about midnight of the 17th and as expected they found the forts abandoned. In the darkness they groped their way northward and morning found them on the north side of the island looking across the harbor at the city. After some delay a boat was found and several officers and men crossed to the city. The commander than took charge at Charleston, he sent back boats from the city to James Island and our troops crossed the harbor as rapidly as they could. Charleston was then on fire in many places. The citizens were promptly organized and they efficiently aided our men to put out the fires. But for the information gained from the intercepted signals, our men would not have been on James Island prepared to go into the city as soon as the Confederates were fairly out. Without such previous notice they could not have reached Charleston from Morris Island till late in the day, in which case a large part of the city would have been burned.

In brief, all of the Confederate signal messages that had any military significance were at this time sent in cipher. If the law of the series cipher had not been discovered, no information of military value would have been gained by us from intercepted signals after the introduction of the new cipher in October or November, 1864. But the operators on the other side had unbounded confidence that the series cipher could not be read, hence they did not fear to send orders in that cipher. As a fact we knew all their plans and movements up to the time of the evacuation, for it should be remembered that Charleston was not captured by our forces but was evacuated by Gen. Hardee.

In order to read the enemy's signals, especially when the flagman was faced at right angles to our line of sight, we were furnished with telescopes having most excellent powers of definition. Much of the time, only by the motions of the hands could we tell whether the flag was moving to the right or left. Being able to see all the operators at the nearby stations so clearly, we soon knew them by sight and most of them by name.

A few days before the evacuation a new signal station was opened at a point on the coast several miles north of Sullivan's Island. One night the operator at the new station began to send a cipher message to the north end of Sullivan. The latter operator soon stopped him and signaled in common code: "I am alone, signal in the usual way; don't think the Yanks can see you." The mention of the fact that the operator was alone was caused by the practical necessity in both services to have someone write down the numbers of cipher messages while the man at the glass reads them and calls them out.

In order to prevent the Confederates from taking away military stores, General Schimmelfennig gave orders that during all of the night of the 17th of February every available army gun on Morris Island (the navy had a battery there) should every ten minutes fire on the bridge extending from the west end of Sullivan's Island over onto the mainland near Mount Pleasant. Lieut. T. M. S. Rhett, who commanded the last squad that left Sullivan's Island, tells me that they got safely over the bridge owing to the fact that the Federal gunners got to firing in volleys and they rushed across between the volleys.

Soon the powder smoke made it impossible to see from our observation station in the water battery of the fort, and Sergeant Colvin and I went up onto the bomb-proof where the smoke was less dense. During the evening several messages were sent from Battery Bee to the city, only part of which we were able to read (and those with great difficulty) owing to the fact that the operator there was under fire and partially protected himself by standing behind a parapet that hid some of his torch motions. As the evening wore on, the torch of the signal man at the city began to pitch and wobble in a way that in the case of anybody else would have suggested whiskey. His motions meant little or nothing and he was constantly ordering "Repeat." Then the operator of Battery Bee, who was under fire during all this delay got mad (we profoundly sympathized with him) and ordered "Send up a sober man." How he jerked that torch when the city man still continued to order "Repeat." I have never known spirits of turpentine [to] burn with so blue a flame as it did then for a few moments while Bee told that city man what he thought of him. Finally there came up a man who appeared to be able to read signals, although his torch made motions that were far from orthodox. At last he acknowledged the receipt of the message and he almost instantly answered, so that apparently the message had not been delivered but was answered by the signal operator on his own responsibility. This was the last message sent

from the city and was as follows: "Open every 76 on the Yankee ——," using an unprintable epithet, which I have always attributed to the hypothetical whiskey or the operator and not to a Confederate commander. Soon firing began from Fort Moultrie, partly from mortars. Whether the gunners were drunk or did not care what they did is not known, but for some reason all the shells from Moultrie burst over the swamp west of Fort Strong.

That was to us a glorious morning. The Confederates were burning their abandoned stores, and all night long looking off to the south, west and north, we had seen a multitude of fires reflected from the clouds. About four o'clock the burning ironclads, which were north and east of the city, began to blow up. It was a grand spectacle, as also had been the all-night bombardment by our guns on Morris Island. As a magazine exploded, a great column of fire shot up a thousand feet or so in the air. Soon the smoke took the form of a tall column spreading out at the top into a large vortex ring, so that the general shape was that of a tree. A moderate wind blew from the west, hence the columns of smoke from the successive explosions drifted east over the harbor and out to sea. It was our understanding that the state flag of South Carolina bore the palmetto and the rattlesnake. As the smoke clouds passed us somebody discovered the resemblance and shouted, "There goes the palmetto!" Soon the tall trunk of the tree had been dissipated and there was left only the remains of the vortex ring high in the air. It was composed of a series of small angular cloudlets. Then somebody shouted "There goes the rattlesnake!" The resemblance to the diamond-back was very striking. We accepted the omen as meaning that the emblems of South Carolina had drifted out to sea and had forever ceased to be a threat against the Union.

About sunrise two boats left Morris Island, one bound for Fort Moultrie, the other for Fort Sumter. Soon the navy, which had been passive all night during the bombardment by the land forces, suddenly woke up and also sent a boat toward Moultrie.

Then ensued an exciting race between the army and navy boats. Sergeant Colvin and I had the only telescopes there, so all the troops in the fort gathered around our station in the water battery. The commander of the fort ordered Colvin to keep watch on Sumter while I was to look after the boats that were racing toward Fort Moultrie. The boat for Fort Sumter was not visible from where we were, hence for a time all the interest centered in the race for Moultrie. Every little while the impatient commander asked again this question: "How is it now?" Each step of the subsequent proceedings I was required to call out as I watched through my glass. How now? Army still ahead! Army boat is nearing the shore! Navy man is gaining! Army has jumped into the water and is running up the slope! Now navy is ashore and gaining! Army man disappears near the fort, perhaps has got down into the ditch! Now the navy man disappears! Next we breathlessly wait for a minute or two, for nothing can be seen. Then the halyards are loosened and the Confederate flag comes down, while everybody shouts. Soon an American flag begins to rise and the questions come faster. Is it the army or the navy flag? There was not wind enough to spread the flag immediately, but soon I am able to announce that it is a large garrison flag. That settles it; the army has won. Then the clear voice of the fort commander rings out: "Three times three for the old flag on Moultrie!" and everybody shouts till he is hoarse. That was a queer looking crowd—we were all so black with powder smoke that from our complexions no one could have told whether his neighbor was African or Caucasian.

But while we are rejoicing over the old flag on that historic Revolutionary fort, the men who manned the boat for Fort Sumter have not been idle. A moving speck is seen on the top of the pile of brick and stone which is all that is left of Fort Sumter on the southeast, and the questions are hurled at Colvin from every side. Our glasses plainly show that it is a man, but he is so crazy with excitement that it is impossible to tell what it is which he is carrying. Colvin never minds the questions but keeps silence and watches. After what seems an age that lunatic over there on the fort, who has been waving something so frantically that it is impossible to recognize it, stumbles or for some reason holds still long enough so that we can see what it is. Then state pride asserts itself as Colvin, who is from the old Keystone State, drops his glass and springs up, swinging his hat and shouting, "It is the battle flag of the 52nd Pennsylvania!" Instantly the commander: "Three times three for the old flag on Sumter!" Did we shout? Well, not one of us could speak in a natural

tone of voice for a week. Not one of us has ever seen the time when he felt so ecstatic over any public event. All realized what the fall of Sumter without a blow meant. The end of the war was in sight. Columbia was burned the same day that Charleston was evacuated, and it was a military necessity for Hardee to get to Cheraw before Sherman. In itself Fort Sumter was of small account, but both sides prized it most highly because its sentimental value, as the place where the war started, was incalculable.

In summary, at Charleston the Confederates led off in intercepting signals, and probably the military value of the information they gained thereby was greater than what we afterward gained from them, owing to the fact that we began to read their signals after the hardest of the fighting was past. But it is an undoubted fact that they were never able to read our cipher. This is proved, first, by the fact that during all the time we were reading their signals, Lieut. MarKoe, the operator at Battery Beauregard never once signaled one of our cipher messages. Time and again we sent messages from Morris Island to the blockading fleet or elsewhere on purpose to test him. Right in the midst of common code messages would be placed a cipher message (of course in our genuine cipher) but while he would forward in his cipher all that was sent in common code he never sent one of the ciphers. Third, soon after the war General Myer offered a prize of fifty dollars to anyone not a member of the U.S. Signal Corps who would decipher a message in our cipher which he had printed, and no one ever claimed the reward. As stated above Lieut. Round also published a message and challenged translation, and with the same result.

On the other hand, before the end of the war the U.S. operators were able to read the most confidential cipher the Confederates had. The reader will be able to draw his own conclusions as to which of the opposing signal services came out ahead in the contest of wits.

ALSO SEE

"[Joseph Raynes] Is Last Maine Survivor of Famous Naval Battle," *Portland Sunday Telegram,* 15 February 1931, p. 1D.

How the First Maine Heavy Artillery Lost 1,179 Men in 30 Days

MAJOR CHARLES J. HOUSE

The organizations of heavy artillery constituted a peculiar and distinct branch of service in the late war. Practically speaking, during the first three years of the war, they were neither artillery nor infantry, though allied to both. Their uniform was of the infantry pattern though trimmed with the red of the artillery, and though they were well drilled in the tactics of all the heavy guns from the six-inch mortar to the hundred-pounder Parrott, yet they were fully armed and equipped as infantry and could show a better line and execute all the intricate movements of that branch of service with more precision than any infantry regiment in the field.

This was their Standing, when to the number of twenty-five thousand, in the month of May, 1864, this force was ordered from the defenses of Washington to join the forces of General Grant near Spotsylvania court house. From this time until the surrender of General Lee at Appomattox, they were to all intents and purposes so many regiments of infantry, working in the same brigades, making the same marches, enduring the same hardships and fighting the same battles with the infantry regiments, and, in short, after being incorporated into the infantry brigades their only distinction was the red trimming upon their uniforms and the crossed cannons upon their caps. As a general thing these regiments had been recruited and organized as infantry, then by special orders from the war department they were transferred to the heavy artillery branch of the service and recruited up to eighteen hundred men by filling the ten old companies to one hundred and fifty men each and by adding two new companies of equal numbers.

When the First Maine Heavy Artillery marched down Pennsylvania avenue in Washington, on the morning of May 15, 1864, it was a regiment of nominally eighteen hundred men, but of course all were not present for duty. Some had permanent details away from the command, others were scattered in northern hospitals, while a large contingent—including the large number of sick in our post hospital and many others who had been on light duty about camp, but were unable to bear the fatigues of the march—were left behind. Besides this, quite a number were detailed as cooks, orderlies, and hostlers. The exact number of men which the regiment took into battle the 19th of May, I have been unable to determine, but the knowledge I have of my own company and the written statements of several company commanders noted down at the time and from all the information I can gather, I am satisfied that not over sixteen hundred were with us that day.

The regiment embarked on a transport at the foot of 7th Street during the forenoon of May 15, and landed at Belle Plain the same evening, where it remained until the morning of the 17th, when it took up the line of march, passed through Fredericksburg and arrived at Spotsylvania at 11 o'clock that evening. We had now literally arrived at the seat of war and were liable to be called into action at any time. Made up from good material, perhaps no better and certainly no worse than the average regiment from the old Pine Tree State, the schooling we had received while in the defenses of Washington had made us thorough

Originally published in *Maine Bugle*, 1895.

soldiers so far as drill and discipline were concerned but we lacked the practical knowledge of fighting the enemy or how best to protect ourselves when in range of the enemy's bullets. This we learned later on in the hard school of experience, that is, what few of us there were left after thirty days of such schooling. Early on the morning of the 18th, we were awakened by the booming of cannon. We had heard the artillery firing at the second Bull Run battle in 1862, and at Aldie in 1863. and in each case were at a safe distance with no likelihood of being called into action, but now the case was different. The firing was only a mile or two away, and in less than ten minutes we were moving on double quick time towards the point of attack, going into line behind well built breastworks in support of what proved a feeble attack by our forces on the bloody angle, the scene of General Hancock's brilliant charge on the morning of the 12th. Here we prepared breakfast, accustomed ourselves to our new surroundings, and enjoyed as best we could our first day under fire. We were well out of the range of bullets but many shells burst along the line yet we moved out late in the afternoon with ranks unbroken, and at roll call the next morning, for the last time, every comrade answered, "Here."

All day the 19th, the troops from the right of our army were moving away to the left, and the Fredericksburg Pike, over which our supply trains were moving, became uncovered and the enemy, always feeling for an opportunity, had advanced a force under General Ewell, which had cautiously moved along until late in the afternoon. They then struck the wagon train protected only by a light guard—which was immediately swept away—and our supplies were in their hands. Our regiment chanced to be nearest the point of attack and it was started at once on the double quick. About the time we started a heavy shower came on, but on we rushed through rain and mud, and as we neared the train, we filed off to the right to bring ourselves into line, then made a dash for the wagons. The force of the enemy at that point was not a heavy one and they were brushed away without a halt on our part, some being captured but the larger part falling back to their main line. Advancing for half a mile through the thicket without meeting the enemy, we emerged into a clearing, a field of perhaps ten acres, divided nearly equally by a small sluggish brook fringed by

low trees and running from right to left. The ground sloped gently on our side of the brook but was steeper beyond up to the edge of the woods where the enemy were posted. The force driven from the wagon train were rushing up this hill as we came out of the woods, but were soon out of sight. The regiment moved two-thirds the way down the slope, where they were brought to a halt, and firing commenced, lasting two hours and twenty minutes. During all this time the men stood, fought just as you see them in pictures, and were the coolest lot of men I ever saw under any circumstances. They loaded, took aim and fired; then would deliberately clear the smoke from their guns by half cocking, throwing off the old cap and blowing into the muzzle, always giving the gun time to cool a little before reloading. Men were falling, to be sure, but those who were able got away to the rear while those who were not lay quietly along the line, and the survivors were too much engaged with their work to notice much about them until the enemy retired and the firing ceased.

I spoke of our being in an open field; so we were, but not all. We made so long a line that one or two companies on either flank extended into the woods and were more or less protected; in fact the loss in Company D amounted only to one killed, and he on the color guard out in the field, and three slightly wounded, while on the other hand, Company E, which was in the field and fully exposed, had twenty-three killed or mortally wounded and forty-seven others wounded, a total of seventy out of one hundred and thirty-five who went into action. The loss in the regiment was one hundred and fifty-five killed or mortally wounded and three hundred and sixty-nine wounded, a total of five hundred and twenty-four. This was an enormous loss, amounting to nearly one third of the number engaged.

In fact, up to this time since the war began, no regiment had suffered such a numerical loss in any one battle, but the end was not yet. There were two things which largely contributed to our loss. The first and most important was the position in which we were halted on the field. Had we remained at the edge of the woods on the hill, or even advanced across the brook, we should have been partially covered from the enemy's fire. Then had we thrown ourselves flat on the ground a less number of men would have been hit. After this the regiment never fought the enemy while standing except in making an advance. As soon as the firing slackened, Company E, of which I was a member, was deployed as skirmishers and advanced against the enemy so close that two of our men in the woods on the left of the company were taken prisoners, one of whom went to Andersonville, but the other not liking to take the chances of prison life tried his hand at making his escape. He was a wily fellow, fertile in resources and as cool as he was brave. He not only succeeded in making his escape back to our lines, but brought in a prisoner with him. It was not all smooth sailing for him, for he was obliged to shoot down two of the enemy who stood in the way of his escape. Near midnight the company was relieved and ordered in to a point on the hill in rear of where we had fought in the afternoon. The men came in through the darkness singly or by twos, and I venture the assertion that no more cordial greetings were ever accorded than were extended to each newcomer by those who had preceded him. We had been in service twenty-one months and had learned to trust and love each other as brothers. Is it any wonder that tears came unbidden: tears of sorrow that so many had fallen and of joy that so many had escaped?

Later on I accompanied a squad of men who were going on to the field to bring off the body of Lieutenant John F. Knowles of our company, who had been killed. As we neared the point where we had stood in line I noticed eight or ten of our men laid out side-by-side, the beams of the moon struggling through the fleecy clouds, lighting upturned faces smeared with the smoke of battle, some showing gaping wounds and all ghastly and lifeless. Looking to the right where the color guard and Company M had stood, was a similar lot of dead carefully laid out, beyond this another and another until the woods were reached, and the same thing away to the left. It was a solemn moment as I gazed on the scene at that midnight hour, my first look upon a deserted battle field, and how forcibly those rows of dead men reminded me of the gavels of reaped grain among which I had worked on my native hills, but here the reaper was the angel of death. I picked up a canteen to replace my own which had been pierced by two bullets and hurried from the field. One look was enough.

Ervin Chamberlain went into action on my left. This was his only battle and the impressions made on his mind were lasting. He told me a few weeks ago that the man on my right and the one on his left as well as the two who covered us in the rear rank were all killed or mortally wounded, and that he was hit seven times before being disabled, and I could count the marks of nine bullets which had made a close call on me. At eleven o'clock the night of the twentieth, the regiment began a rapid pace march for seventeen hours, with less than five minutes' rest during the time. Passing through Bowling Green we were halted near Milford station, where the regiment went into line and threw up breast works while Company D, under Lieutenant Henry E. Sellers, was advanced as a line of pickets, but were attacked by the enemy, losing one man killed, one wounded, and one prisoner.

On the twenty-third of May, we reached a point near the North Anna River and near night were subjected to severe shell fire, losing two or three men. We were kept in reserve until the afternoon of the twenty-fourth, when we crossed over the river on a bridge upon the run under one of the liveliest shell fires we ever got into. Probably twenty-five shells exploded over our heads while making the run, but one man only was hit, getting a slight scalp wound by a small sliver of iron. We labored most of the night building breastworks and remained here until the night of the twenty-sixth, when the army was withdrawn to begin another flanking movement on the north side of the river. Regimental losses were two killed or mortally wounded and five wounded. The twenty-eighth and twenty-ninth, we were near Hanovertown, where we had one man killed. The thirtieth we moved out near the Totopotomy Creek, and the morning of the thirty-first moved across the creek to help drive the enemy from their outer line of works. Getting into position we lay under a broiling sun and exposed to shell fire the rest of the day. Three men were killed and ten wounded, mostly by exploding shells, in this action. One shell exploded immediately over the left of Company K, which lay on the right of Company E. One K man was killed and two others wounded, but the E men were all unhurt, though several pieces of iron struck among us, one piece going through the gunstock of Corporal Fenlason, and another demolishing Sargent Chapin's canteen. In a few minutes some enterprising man who was short of cooking tools had melted the solder around the canteen's edges and, using a split stick handle, was busy frying meat and preparing his supper on the good half.

The next day, June first, commenced the battle, or rather series of battles of Cold Harbor. In this action our regiment was not directly engaged with the enemy, but were held in reserve while other regiments and brigades were being hurled under a terrible fire against a line of earth works so strong and well protected—by abatis, and almost impenetrable slashes—that no force of men, however brave, could hope to break so long as the works were well manned. Our work was to rush from point to point along the line, now to the right, then to the left in quick succession, always exposed more or less to the scattering fire from the not far away front. The heavy fighting was on the first and third of June, and the loss to the army amounted to some thirteen thousand men. Our regiment was continually under the scattering fire of the enemy, and scarcely a day passed from the first to the twelfth of June without one or more of our men being wounded. And reconnaissance by Company A, on the evening of the twelfth, resulted in the loss of five prisoners. Regimental losses in those twelve days, amounted to one killed, twenty-seven wounded, and seven prisoners.

At ten-thirty on the night of June twelfth, we moved out of the works, marched a few miles, then slept by the roadside the rest of the night. The thirteenth we crossed the Chickahominy and marched to the James River, which we crossed on transports on the fourteenth, and eleven o'clock on the night of the fifteenth, found us facing the enemy's lines in front of Petersburg. Late in the afternoon of the sixteenth, we advanced against the works in our front, but being in the second line and not directly engaged, we lost only a few men. After throwing up breastworks all night, we were given a day of comparative rest on the seventeenth, but occasionally lost a man, being kept well up to the front. That evening we were put into the front line on the right of the Prince George Courthouse road, and soon became engaged with the enemy. During a brisk fire of some twenty minutes, Major George W. Sabine was struck by a Minié ball (which passed through one thigh and lodged in the other) from the effects of which he died the following May. At four o'clock on the morning of the eighteenth, we advanced from this position, driving in the enemy's

pickets and discovering the fact that they had withdrawn the night before to another inner and stronger line. We took position along the road in front of the Hare field and buildings and soon built a strong line of earth works we felt capable of defending in case of an attack. Different corps had made several attempts to break through the enemy's line at various points during the course of the day but without success, when, well along in the afternoon General Birney, commander of the Second Corps, received from General Meade the following orders:

I have sent positive orders to Generals Burnside and Warren to attack at all hazards with their whole force. I find it useless to appoint an hour to effect co-operation, and am therefore compelled to give you the same order. You have a large corps, powerful and numerous, and I beg that you will at once, as soon as possible, assault in strong column. The day is fast going and I wish the practicability of carrying the enemy's line settled before dark.

Mott's division was selected as the assaulting column, and when the order was transmitted to him, he protested vigorously against so rash and hopeless an undertaking, but protests under such circumstances avail nothing. The order had to be obeyed. Our Third brigade was designated to make the direct assault with the other brigades well in hand to follow up any advantage we might possibly gain. The different regiments composing the brigade were withdrawn from the line and brought together under cover of the woods in the rear and then marched back into position in column in an open pine growth back from the road, so we should just clear the Hare house on the right as we advanced. As we came into position we were broken up into three battalions of four companies each, and, according to our instructions, found that the First battalion was to lead off, with each succeeding battalion following at a distance of twenty paces. The First Maine Heavy Artillery not only headed the column, but was, in fact, the only column with which the assault was made, for no other regiment advanced beyond the road. But it was just as well, for no ten thousand men in column could have pierced the enemy's line, manned as it was with infantry and artillery. The more to advance the more to be killed, that was all.

There was lead and canister enough and to spare.

From our position among the pines we could see the whole field over which we must pass and the earthworks beyond. We could see the men behind those works, no doubt elated at the prospect of the harvest of death they were about to reap, but the two batteries which were to be served with double shotted canister on either flank were under cover. It was perfectly safe to stand up now both for Union and Confederate troops, for on our part of the line, at least, the noise of battle was hushed, it was the lull before the storm. And now came the final preliminaries before starting. We were ordered to load and the guns were loaded and capped, then to fix bayonets which was done. Instructions were given not to fire a shot until we got into the enemy's works. "Pile up your knapsacks and leave two men from each company to guard them," ordered the colonel. The guards were detailed, and the men stripped to light marching order. For the next few minutes the guards were busy with pencil and notebook taking down addresses of wife, mother, sister, or loved one far away in Maine. When attention was called the men fell readily into place. There were nervous tightening of belts and a fiddling with musket grasps as they were brought to ready.

Teeth may have been set a little harder to prevent trembling from taking possession of us. The order was given and we dashed off at double quick time. A shower of lead struck us, but the men involuntarily pulled their cap visors down over their eyes and with bowed heads advanced against the storm. The shells crashed over our heads for a minute and then the deadly canister got in its work. The ranks melted and the lines grew thin but on we pressed, hoping against hope, a few getting nearly up to the abatis, when the order to retreat was given, and such as could, got off the field.

One verse of a little Poem written on this affair so graphically describes the slaughter that I give it as follows:

A short, sharp word
The sudden stillness stirred—
A blinding flash—
A thunderous crash—
A deaf'ning and incessant roar
While on us pour
in front—in flank
From rank to rank

Such blasts as never fell before—
One minute more
And all is o'er;
Six hundred daring men and four
Lie dead, or weltering in their gore.

Thus ended the Battle of Petersburg, and "the practicability of carrying the enemy's line" was settled in the negative. I wish to say a word here in regard to the time we were on the field. I have heard it estimated all the way from eight to twenty minutes by those present. But let us figure a little. The distance from our starting point to the enemy's line was three hundred and fifty yards. Now three hundred and fifty-two yards is one fifth of a mile, so the distance out and back is two fifths of a mile over which a man can easily walk in eight minutes going at the rate of a mile in twenty minutes. The average speed we attained in the advance and retreat must have shortened the time from a walk by half, so that it is altogether probable that in four minutes after starting every man except those disabled was off the field. in this battle our regiment lost a total of six hundred and four—two hundred and forty killed and died of wounds, and three hundred and sixty-four wounded—nearly all of which occurred in this assault of June the 18th.

The Eighth New York Heavy Artillery had suffered a loss at Cold Harbor which exceeded ours at Spotsylvania, but the First Maine Heavy Artillery loss at Petersburg stands out as being the heaviest that occurred in any regiment in any one battle during the whole war, while that at Spotsylvania stands third in the list, being exceeded only by the previously mentioned Eighth New York loss. During a period of thirty days, from May 19 to June 18, our losses had been as follows:

	KILLED	WOUNDED	TOTAL
Spotsylvania	155	369	524
Milford Station	1	1	2
North Anna	2	5	7
Hanover Town	1	0	1
Totopotomy	3	10	13
Cold Harbor	1	27	28
Petersburg	240	364	604
TOTAL	403	776	1,179

In addition, we had lost fourteen prisoners, twelve of whom died in Southern prisons. To the casual reader, the regiment suffered, as a result of this thirty days of fighting, four hundred and fifteen men dead, and seven hundred and seventy-six others more or less disabled for life, but to us of the regiment and to our families it means more. It means not only death, but individual suffering. Comparatively few of the killed die instantly, and those who linger from a few hours to many months have their cup of suffering filled to the brim.

And, what of the loved ones at home? It means sorrow without measure; it means an aged father or mother going down in poverty and grief to the grave for want of a staff to lean upon; it means a widowed wife and orphan children; it means other than literal wounds which are never healed on earth. The same thing holds true, though in a less degree, in all the ordinary losses in battle, but this aggrega-

tion of death, of suffering and of anguish, becomes terrible to contemplate on account of its magnitude. Considering the number of men engaged and the brief time in which this loss occurred, it is without a parallel in the history of modern warfare.

Also See

"The Charge of the Heavy Artillery," *The Maine Bugle,* January 1894, pp. 4–8.

"First Maine Heavy Artillery in Fall of 1864," The Maine Bugle, April 1897, pp. 133–40.

"1st Maine—Too Brave for Own Good," *Portland Sunday Telegram,* 25 December 1960, p. 12D.

THE CONFEDERATE RAID ON CALAIS

MASON PHILIP SMITH

Early in 1864, as General Grant's armies pushed south and began to tighten the vise on the Confederacy, the Rebel government sought to exploit dissatisfaction in the north over the conduct of the war by fomenting trouble in the Union states so that combat troops would be diverted from the war front. Operating from bases in Canada, the raiders planned to free and arm Confederate prisoners of war held captive in northern prisons and to use them in conjunction with members of pro-Southern secret societies to destroy property and terrorize northern cities. One such plot was aimed at the coast of Maine.

On the 14th of July, 1864, Maine Governor Samuel Cony in Augusta received a wire from J. Q. Howard, U.S. Consul at St. John, New Brunswick, warning of a Confederate raiding party which had set out the day before to "commit depredations on the Maine frontier." Howard also sent a report to his superiors in Washington stating, "Satisfactory evidence has been furnished me that one Major William Collins, late of the Rebel army, is now organizing in this vicinity a force to commit depredations on the Maine frontier. There is reason to believe that the somewhat notorious James McDonald and a precious scoundrel by the name of Jones are concerned in this new military movement."

Howard's report went on to say, "Collins is well known here and although a man of energy, is such an eminent fool as to suppose that he can march a small force through the northern states to Kentucky. He affirms that he is authorized by the 'Confederate Authorities' to burn and destroy and to show no quarter."

Governor Cony immediately telegraphed the mayors and authorities of Maine's principal cities and towns to be alert with their available forces to resist attacks in their areas and to be ready to render aid to repel attacks elsewhere.

On July 18th another wire from Consul Howard, this time to J. S. Lee, Cashier of the Calais Bank, pinpointed the raider's target. "Fourteen men left here in lead-colored sail and row boat for Calais. Would touch at Robbinston. Intention was to rob your bank in daytime. If they have not been alarmed, you can apprehend them quietly in the bank. William Collins is leader."

A message from the War Department in Washington authorized Major J.W.T. Gardiner, Acting Assistant Provost-Marshal-General in Augusta, to use troops of the Veterans Reserve Corps to man the forts at Portland and elsewhere in the emergency. In Calais a portion of Captain B. M. Flint's company of State Guards were detached for service, and pickets were stationed at different points around the town to give the alarm when the raiders appeared.

Three strangers strode into the Calais Bank at noon on July 18th. One man, William Collins, leader of the group, said he wanted to exchange some gold for greenbacks. As he talked his hand glided toward a revolver in his side pocket. Cashier Lee immediately gave the alarm, the guards rushed in, seized the three men and took them to the Municipal Court.

The prisoners were searched and a Confederate flag was found in Collins's pocket. He explained he had planned to raise it over the heights of the town. The prisoners boasted that if their companions had joined them they would have burned the town and committed other depredations.

A large crowd collected around the courthouse and there was talk of dealing summar-

ORIGINALLY PUBLISHED IN *DOWN EAST*, OCTOBER 1966.

ily with the prisoners on the grounds they had been ready to plunder the town and murder the inhabitants.

Judge Corthell questioned Collins and the other two raiders, Francis X. Jones and William Phillips, and set bail at $20,000. Collins, described by the *St. Croix Herald* as a "tall, keen-eyed man with a countenance indicative of treachery and baseness," told the judge the group had been planning to accomplish their raid "peaceably if they could, but forcibly if they must." When asked for it, Collins was unable to produce his Confederate commission. A note found in one of the raider's pockets said, "Thank your stars that other men did not come up, or your town would have been burned."

Rumors circulating around Calais claimed the rest of the raiders were enroute to free the captured Confederates, so the three prisoners were sent to the county jail at Machias under heavy guard. The State Guard continued to patrol Calais for another three weeks, but the rest of the Rebels failed to materialize.

G. H. Foster, of the firm of Foster & Nelson, was the only person wounded in the raid. In his excitement he accidentally fired his revolver, shooting himself in the foot.

Feeling against the raiders ran high in Washington County. In Eastport, where 100 muskets were handed out to citizens who were willing to stand in readiness to repel any further raids, the *Sentinel* cried, "We are sorry that punishment was not dealt out to them summarily. There was no doubt of their criminal intentions for their confessed purposes. Their immediate execution would have done much to put a stop to such fiendish projects, and that is what we especially need at the present time."

The *Machias Union* suggested residents of Washington County should "unite in respectfully asking of the Federal Government that no more men be taken for the general army from this county." It went on to ask, "Are not all able bodied men needed for domestic defense and protection?"

The prisoners arrived in Machias at 3 A.M. on the day following their raid at Calais and by nightfall Washington County Sheriff Benjamin W. Farrar had received a dispatch from Calais warning of an attempt to free them. As a precaution, two sentries were placed outside the cells. A six-pound field gun was brought up and placed in front of the jail and

every man with a gun was requested to be prepared to act at a minute's warning.

Collins confessed to the Sheriff that he was a captain in the Rebel service. He was an Irishman, but was born near Loch Lomond, Scotland. His parents brought him to New Brunswick as a boy and later he went to New York to obtain an education. The outbreak of the Civil War found him in the South, and he enlisted in the Confederate Army, serving in the 15th Mississippi Regiment under Bishop-General Leonidas Polk as a scout. However, his greatest service to the South was as a spy, for he obtained plans of the defenses of nearly all the large Northern cities.

Collins visited his old home in New Brunswick while formulating his plans against Maine. His sister wrote their brother, the Reverend John Collins, a Methodist minister in York, Maine: "William is home on business for the Confederate Army." This aroused suspicion in the mind of the good reverend, who rushed to New Brunswick to see William.

"I don't know what your plans are," he told the Confederate raider, "but I shall do all in my power to block them. Knowing that you are a spy, I should be a traitor to my country if I did not deliver you over to the hands of the authorities."

The Maine pastor went to Consul Howard and told him what he knew of his brother's plans. Detectives were assigned to follow William Collins, and when he left St. John with his group to raid the Calais Bank, Howard alerted the Maine authorities.

Little is known of the background of William Phillips other than that he was also Irish and a sailor. He told the authorities he had been "promised a chance to go on a piratical craft."

Francis X. Jones lived in Missouri at the beginning of the war, and when the hostilities began he joined the 1st Missouri Volunteers (Rebel) and fought at the Battle of Shiloh. When he was arrested in Calais he told the authorities his wife and child had been murdered by Federal troops under the command of Jim Lane, who earlier had led atrocious attacks on pro-slavery strongholds. Consul Howard reported to Washington that Jones was a Missouri guerrilla, the murderer of a Union officer on the staff of General James G. Blunt, and a perjurer who had lied so that two Union men were hanged for the crime he had committed.

Jones was discharged from his regiment

in July of 1863 and he entered the Confederate service, rising to the rank of captain in Company D of the 1st Corps Secret Service in the Department of Mississippi and East Louisiana. On 32 missions through the lines he carried dispatches from Confederate generals to agents in Union territory and in addition made two trips to Canada. After his first Canadian mission he returned to the South by ship, running the Union blockade at Wilmington, North Carolina. His second trip to Canada ended with his arrest at Calais.

It was Jones who confided to Sheriff Farrar the Confederates' plan to put Maine to the torch as a diversionary movement. The sheriff wrote Secretary of State William H. Seward in Washington about the Rebel plot and enclosed the letters Jones had written in the jail. Seward wrote back to Farrar, saying: "The information given therein is deemed important and you will please accept the thanks of the Department for your promptness in communicating it. Your suggestion, as to the method by which additional facts may be obtained, will be duly considered."

One of Jones's letters was to his mother in St. Louis. In a plea for her understanding he wrote: "Doubtlessly you will be greatly surprised and grieved to hear from me in such a place. We were captured (myself and companions) on the 18th instant. We are accused of attempting the robbery of the Bank in Calais in this state. We were acting under special orders from President Davis. We were also under the command of a regularly commissioned officer of the Confederate States Army. Had it been otherwise I would have flatly refused to have joined Capt. Wm. Collins's command when ordered to do so by the Confederate authorities." He closed by asking his mother for $5 to "enable me to purchase tobacco, needles, thread, etc. and other little necessities of prison life."

As a result of Sheriff Farrar's letter to the Secretary of State, Major Levi C. Turner, Assistant Judge Advocate, hurried to Machias from Washington to interview Jones and to obtain his confession. Both Collins and Phillips flatly refused to talk to Turner. Jones, however, did more than talk. He outlined the entire Confederate plot against Maine in a confession which filled fifteen pages.

Turner reported back to Secretary of State Stanton that Jones was a well educated man of about twenty-five, "familiar with the French & German languages." He wrote that Jones ". . . voluntarily, and without apparent reservation made a specific statement, or confession."

Jones also told the government investigator the raid on Maine was to consist of 5,000 to 6,000 men led by experienced officers of the Rebel army. The force would be made up of five columns, landed at different points on the Maine coast, but spaced to support each other. The troops would all be experienced raiders and would be joined by members of the various pro-Southern secret societies until the entire group numbered 12,000 to 15,000 men.

Acting in conjunction with this force was to be another from New Brunswick, comprised of 1,200 to 1,500 men. These men were to board sailing vessels and proceed to Maine convoyed by two Rebel steamers, *Tallahassee* and *Florida*. Jones told Turner that landing points on the coast had already been surveyed and mapped by engineers and said he himself had seen some of the maps.

The proposed raid on Maine was timed to occur simultaneously with a raid to be made into Iowa and Illinois by guerrillas from Missouri and Kansas, who were to seize prison camps and free the prisoners. Jones also mentioned a planned raid on the Union prison camp at Johnson's Island near Sandusky, Ohio. The approach of all these raiding forces was to be the signal for a general uprising at the time of the election on the part of secret organizations of Confederate sympathizers in the North and in the West.

The confessed Rebel agent gave Turner detailed descriptions of Rebel agents within Union lines and in many cases gave their aliases. He named Major Dudley Harris, alias Spencer, alias Barbour as the Rebel agent in Portland.

Turner reported back to Stanton in Washington on September 16, 1864, "The Rebel agents in Canada and the Provinces, named by him, are known to be such by officials hereabouts." Stopping in Portland on his way back to Washington, Turner talked with the marshal there about Major Dudley Harris, the Portland Rebel agent named by Jones. He was told "a person has frequently, within the last two months, called for letters at the Post Office addressed to Dudley Harris."

He also learned that several persons had been discovered surveying and mapping the most unfrequented bays and harbors along the Maine coast, which tended to corroborate

Jones's statements about Confederate activity on the coast.

In addition, though Jones could not have known it while he was in jail, the *Tallahassee* had been sighted along the coast. The *Machias Republican* reported on September 1st:

THE REBEL PIRATE TALLAHASEE. This villainous pirate is reported as making havoc among our fishermen on the eastern coast, and we fear there is much truth in it. The fishermen are as plentiful as blackberries and she would have nothing to do but run in among them and burn them. If Uncle Sam would let the job of catching this pirate, as well as others, to the lowest bidder, with the promise of the vessel to boot, she would be taken in three days.

The *Florida*, also named by Jones as one of the vessels to be used in the Maine expedition, left Brest, France on February 10th and stopped in Bermuda several months latter, where her captain received instructions to proceed to the New England coast to raid there. Enroute, the *Florida* tangled with a Union steam tug *America*, which eluded her and steamed for New York to warn the Secretary of the Navy, Gideon Wells, that the *Florida* was close enough to shore to chase and capture. Fleeing for the safety of the Canary Islands, the *Florida* abandoned the profitable New England raiding grounds. The Confederate vessel was later seized by the U.S.S. *Wachusett* in the harbor at Bahia, Brazil on October 7th, thus ended her threat to Maine.

The cases of Collins, Jones and Phillips were presented to the October, 1864, term of the Supreme Judicial Court meeting in the Washington County Court House at Machias. The three were charged with conspiracy to rob the Calais Bank. At first their case was taken under advisement, and it appeared at one time during the session that they would be treated as prisoners of war and not as common criminals. However, in the end, the trio were convicted of the civil crime of conspiracy and sentenced to three years in the State Prison at Thomaston.

During the time that the three Maine raiders were being tried in Machias, a group or Rebel raiders swept across the Vermont border and held-up three banks in St. Albans, Vermont, escaping with $200,000. From his cell Collins boasted the St. Albans raid was the work of his men.

The convicted men cheered Jefferson Davis as they left Machias for the prison in Thomaston. They boasted that they would be released as soon as Davis made a demand for them. The predictions of an early release were wrong. Jones served time in the State Prison until January 15, 1866, when he was pardoned. Phillips was pardoned on May 7, 1866.

The boastful Collins served exactly 36 days and then decided he had had enough of his new home. On November 26, 1864, just after the first ringing-up bell, Collins, along with four other men, left the prison carriage shop and ran to one of the guard posts, where they began to throw stones at the guard. Hitting him hard with their first stones and following these up with more volleys, they ripped a pair of steps away from the shoe shop, flung them against the wall and climbed over the top.

The guard fired three shots at the escaping prisoners, and other guards, who went to his assistance, succeeded in capturing one of the escapees, who had been wounded in the head. Another, who had broken his leg going over the wall, was found hiding in a nearby lime kiln. Collins, and the other two men commenced to swim the St. George River, which ran near the prison. One man drowned, but Collins and William Devine made it to the far shore. Devine, exhausted and chilled, stopped at a house to warm himself. There, he was detained by the lady of the house until officers arrived to arrest him.

Collins, plunging on, finally stopped at a house where he was harbored for the night. The next day from the top of a tall pine overlooking Broad Cove on the St. George River, he watched prison officers as they searched the countryside for him.

The warden at the State Prison offered $50 for his apprehension, which led the *Portland Transcript* to comment, "That won't fetch the rascal." The *Machias Republican*, reporting that Collins had been seen in Cushing said, "He ought to have been shot on sight."

Following Collins's escape the prison guards were armed with new rifles that would fire fifteen times in rapid succession. In addition, they were given an extra fifteen rounds to carry in their pockets, which gave them the ability to fire thirty rounds in a minute.

On the evening of January 2, 1865, a stranger walked into St. Stephens, New Brunswick, across the St. Croix River from Calais. He was recognized and, in answer to a question, freely admitted that he was Captain William Collins, the Calais bank raider and an escapee from the Maine State Prison. The next morning he left on foot for St. John, where he took a ship for the south. Rejoining the Confederate forces, he fought until the end of the war.

The flight of the *Florida* from the New England coast and Jones's confession both aided in the collapse of the Confederate plot against Maine. Acting on the information Jones gave Assistant Judge Advocate Turner, Federal agents on November 24, 1864 arrested Rebel agents in New York, Cincinnati, St. Louis, Baltimore, Indianapolis, Boston and Portland.

Ten years after the war, William Collins met his brother, the Reverend John Collins. Anxious to know whether his brother knew who had put the authorities on his track, the Reverend John asked him. "Do you know who betrayed you to the United States authorities?"

"No," the ex-raider replied as he drew a revolver from his pocket. "If I did I should loan him what lead there is in this gun. And I should do it so quickly that he wouldn't have time to say his prayers."

Relating the episode to a congregation years later, [the] Reverend Jones finished his talk by saying. "I didn't care to tell him all I knew about it."

Also See

"Betrayed Brother for his Country," *Lewiston Journal Illustrated Magazine,* 7 May 1910, pp. 1–2.

"1864 Confederate Raiders Strike Calais Bank" *Maine Sunday Telegram,* 13 August 1978, p. 31A.

"Way It Was: President Lincoln Sent Federal Aid to Help When a Rebel Raiding Party Attempted to Rob a Calais Bank," *Maine Sunday Telegram,* 13 August 1978, p. 31A.

"When Damariscotta was Threatened by Confederate Invasion," *Lewiston Journal Illustated Magazine,* 27 May 1922, pp. 3, 10.

APPOMATTOX

JOSHUA L. CHAMBERLAIN

The darkest hours before the dawn of April 9, 1865, shrouded the Fifth Corps sunk in feverish sleep by the roadside six miles away from Appomattox Station on the Southside Road. Scarcely is the first broken dream begun when a cavalryman comes splashing down the road and vigorously dismounts, pulling from his jacket-front a crumpled note. The sentinel standing watch by his commander, worn in body but alert in every sense, touches your shoulder. "Orders, sir, I think. "You rise on elbow, strike a match, and with smarting, streaming eyes read the brief, thrilling note, sent back by Sheridan to us infantry commanders. Like this, as I remember: "I have cut across the enemy at Appomattox Station, and captured three of his trains. If you can possibly push your infantry up here tonight, we will have great results in the morning." Ah, sleep no more. The startling bugle notes ring out "The General"—"To the march." Word is sent for the men to take a bite of such as they have for food: the promised rations will not be up till noon, and by that time we shall be perhaps too far away for such greeting. A few try to eat, no matter what. Meanwhile, almost with one foot in the stirrup, you take from the hands of the black boy a tin plate of nondescript food and a dipper of miscalled coffee;—all equally black, like the night around. You eat and drink at a swallow; mount, and away to get to the head of the column before you sound the "Forward." They are there—the men: shivering to their senses as if risen out of the earth, but something in them not of it. Now sounds the "Forward," for the last time in our long-drawn strife. And they move—these men—sleepless, supperless, breakfastless, sore-footed, stiff-jointed, sense-benumbed, but with flushed faces pressing for the front.

By sunrise we have reached Appomattox Station, where Sheridan has left the captured trains. A staff officer is here to turn us square to the right, to the Appomattox River, cutting across Lee's retreat. Already we hear the sharp ring of the horse-artillery, answered ever and anon by heavier field guns; and drawing nearer, the crack of cavalry carbines; and unmistakably, too, the graver roll of musketry of opposing infantry. There is no mistake. Sheridan is square across the enemy's front, and with that glorious cavalry alone is holding at bay all that is left of the proudest army of the Confederacy. It has come at last, —the supreme hour. No thought of human wants or weakness now: all for the front; all for the flag, for the final stroke to make its meaning real—these men of the Potomac and the James, side by side, at the double in time and column, now one and now the other in the road or the fields beside. One striking feature I can never forget,—Birney's black men abreast with us, pressing forward to save the white man's country.

We did not know exactly what was going on. We did know that our cavalry had been doing splendid work all night, and in fact now was holding at bay Lee's whole remaining army. I was proud to learn that Smith's Brigade—our First Maine Cavalry in the van— had waged the most critical part of the glorious fight.

Ord's troops were in lead, pushing for the roar of the guns to bring relief to our cavalry before Lee's anxious infantry should break through. The storm-center was now on the Lynchburg Pike, a mile or so beyond Appomattox Court House. The Fifth Corps fol-

FROM *THE PASSING OF THE ARMIES*,
NEW YORK: G.P. PUTNAM'S SONS, 1915.

lowed, Ayres' Division ahead; then our old Third Brigade of the First Division,—once mine, since Bartlett's; next, my command, my own brigade and Gregory's; at the rear of the column Crawford's fine division, but somehow unaccountably slow in its movements and march.

I was therefore in about the middle of our Fifth Corps column. The boom of the battle thickened ahead of us. We were intent for the front. Suddenly I am accosted by a cavalry staff officer dashing out of a rough wood road leading off to our right. "General, you command this column?"—"Two brigades of it, sir; about half the First Division, Fifth Corps."—"Sir, General Sheridan wishes you to break off from this column and come to his support. The rebel infantry is pressing him hard. Our men are falling back. Don't wait for orders through the regular channels, but act on this at once."

Of course I obey, without question. Sending word forward to Griffin, in command of our Fifth Corps, that he may understand and instruct Crawford to follow the main column and not me, I turn off my brigade and Gregory's and, guided by the staff officer, push out to see if we can do as well on a cavalry front as we had at their heels. My guide informed me of the situation. Ord's troops were holding Gordon's hard on the Lynchburg Pike; this latter command was now a formidable force, having taken in the heart of Stonewall Jackson's and A. P. Hill's corps, and what was left of Anderson's. But the rear of this column pressing on had made a demonstration indicating that they were now about to try a final forlorn hope to cut through near the Court House while the head of their column was engaging Ord. General Sheridan, to thwart this attempt, had taken Devins's Cavalry division back to meet them, at least until our infantry could be brought up. The barrier of cavalry alone could not withstand the desperate Confederate veterans essaying their last hope, and in fact was slowly receding. This explained the reason of our summons.

Sharp work now. Pushing through the woods at cavalry speed, we come out right upon Sheridan's battle flag gleaming amidst the smoke of his batteries in the edge of the open field. Weird-looking flag it is: fork-tailed, red and white, the two bands that composed it each charged with a star of the contrasting color; two eyes sternly glaring through the cannon-cloud. Beneath it, that storm-center

spirit, that form of condensed energies, mounted on the grim charger, Rienzi, that turned the battle of the Shenandoah,—both, rider and steed, of an unearthly shade of darkness, terrible to look upon, as if masking some unknown powers.

Right before us, our cavalry, Devins's division, gallantly stemming the surges of the old Stonewall brigade, desperate to beat its way through. I ride straight to Sheridan. A dark smile and impetuous gesture are my only orders. Forward into double lines of battle, past Sheridan, his guns, his cavalry, and on for the quivering crest. For a moment it is a glorious sight: every arm of the service in full play,—cavalry, artillery, infantry; then a sudden shifting scene as the cavalry, disengaged by successive squadrons, rally under their bugle-calls with beautiful precision and promptitude, and sweep like a storm-cloud beyond our right to close in on the enemy's left and complete the fateful envelopment.

Ord's troops are now square across the Lynchburg Pike. Ayres and Bartlett have joined them on their right, and all are in for it sharp. In this new front we take up the battle. Gregory follows in on my left. It is a formidable front we make. The scene darkens. In a few minutes the tide is turned; the incoming wave is at flood; the barrier recedes. In truth, the Stonewall men hardly show their well-proved mettle. They seem astonished to see before them these familiar flags of their old antagonists, not having thought it possible that we could match our cavalry and march around and across their pressing columns.

Their last hope is gone,—to break through our cavalry before our infantry can get up. Neither to Danville nor to Lynchburg can they cut their way; and close upon their rear, five miles away, are pressing the Second and Sixth Corps of the Army of the Potomac. It is the end! They are now giving way, but keep good front, by force of old habit. Halfway up the slope they make a stand, with what perhaps they think a good omen,—behind a stone wall. I try a little artillery on them, which directs their thoughts towards the crest behind them, and stiffen my lines for a rush, anxious for that crest myself. My intensity may have seemed like excitement. For Griffin comes up, quizzing me in his queer way of hitting off our weak points when we get a little too serious; accusing me of mistaking a blooming peach tree for a rebel flag, where I was dropping a few shells into a rallying crowd. I apologize—I was a little nearsighted, and hadn't been experienced in long-range fighting. But as for peaches, I was going to get some if the pits didn't sit too hard on our stomachs.

In a few minutes Griffin rides up again, in quite a different mood. "General," he says, "I want you to go back and bring up Crawford's Division. He is acting in the same old fashion that got Warren into trouble at Five Forks. He should have been up here long ago. We need him desperately. He deserves to be relieved of his command."—"General, do you mean to relieve me of mine, and make me a staff officer? It can't come to that."—"I mean to put YOU in command of that division," he answers; "I will publish an order to that effect."—"General, pardon me, but you must not do that. It would make trouble for everybody, and I do not desire the position. It would make great disturbance among Crawford's friends, and if you will pardon the suggestion, they may have influence enough at Washington to block your confirmation as Major-General. Besides, I think General Baxter of the Third Division is my senior; that must settle it."

This is a singular episode for such a moment. But it may be cited as showing the variety of commotions that occupied our minds.

But now comes up Ord with a positive order: "Don't expose your lines on that crest. The enemy have massed their guns to give it a raking fire the moment you set foot there." I thought I saw a qualifying look as he turned away. But left alone, youth struggled with prudence. My troops were in a bad position down here. I did not like to be "the under dog." It was much better to be on top and at least know what there was beyond. So I thought of Grant and his permission to "Push things" when we got them going; and of Sheridan and his last words as he rode away with his cavalry, smiting his hands together—"Now Smash 'em, I tell you; smash 'em!" So we took this for orders, and on the crest we stood. One booming cannon-shot passed close along our front, and in the next moment all was still.

We had done it,—had "exposed ourselves to the view of the enemy." But it was an exposure that worked two ways. For there burst upon our vision a mighty scene, fit cadence of the story of tumultuous years. Encompassed by the cordon of steel that crowned the heights about the Court House, on the slopes of the valley formed by the sources of the Appomattox, lay the remnants of that far-famed counterpart and companion of our own in momentous history,—the Army of Northern Virginia—Lee's army!

In the meantime Crawford's troops have begun to arrive, and form in between Gregory and Bartlett on our left.

It was hilly, broken ground, in effect a vast amphitheater, stretching a mile perhaps from crest to crest. On the several confronting slopes before us dusky masses of infantry suddenly resting in place; blocks of artillery, standing fast in column or mechanically swung into park; clouds of cavalry small and great, slowly moving, in simple restlessness; —all without apparent attempt; at offense or defense, or even military order.

In the hollow is the Appomattox,—which we had made the dead-line for our baffled foe, for its whole length, a hundred miles; here but a rivulet; that might almost be stepped over dry-shod, and at the road crossing not thought worth while to bridge.

Around its edges, now trodden to mire, swarms an indescribable crowd: worn-out soldier struggling to the front; demoralized citizen and denizen, white, black, and all shades between,—following Lee's army, or flying before these suddenly confronted terrible Yankees pictured to them as demon-shaped and bent; animals, too, of all forms and grades; vehicles of every description and non-description,—public and domestic, four-wheeled, or two, or one,—heading and moving in every direction, a swarming mass of chaotic confusion.

All this within sight of every eye on our bristling crest. Had one the heart to strike at beings so helpless, the Appomattox would quickly become a surpassing Red Sea horror. But the very spectacle brings every foot to an instinctive halt. We seem the possession of a dream. We are lost in a vision of human tragedy. But our light-twelve Napoleon guns come rattling up behind us to go into battery; we catch the glitter of the cavalry blades and brasses beneath the oak groves away to our right, and the ominous closing in on the fated foe.

So with a fervor of devout joy,—as when, perhaps, the old crusaders first caught sight of the holy city of their quest,—with an upgoing of the heart that was half paean, half prayer, we dash forward to the consummation. A Solitary field-piece in the edge of the town gives an angry but expiring defiance. We press down a little slope, through a swamp, over a bright swift stream. Our advance is already in the town,—only the narrow street between the opposing lines, and hardly that. There is wild work, that looks like fighting; but not much killing, nor even hurting. The disheartened enemy take it easy; our men take them easier. It is a wild, mild fusing,—earnest, but not deadly earnest.

A young orderly of mine, unable to contain himself, begs permission to go forward, and dashes in, sword-flourishing as if he were a terrible fellow,—and soon comes back, hugging four sabers to his breast, speechless at his achievement.

We were advancing, tactically fighting, and I was somewhat uncertain as to how much more of the strenuous should be required or expected. But I could not give over to this weak mood.

My right was "in the air," advanced, unsupported, towards the enemy's general line, exposed to flank attack by troops I could see in the distance across the stream. I held myself on that extreme flank, where I could see the cavalry which we had relieved, now forming in column of squadrons ready for a dash to the front, and I was anxiously hoping it would save us from the flank attack. Watching intently, my eye was caught by the figure of a horseman riding out between those lines, soon joined by another, and taking a direction across the cavalry front towards our position. They were nearly a mile away, and I curiously watched them till lost from sight; in the nearer broken ground and copses between.

Suddenly rose to sight another form, close in our own front,—a soldierly young figure, a Confederate staff officer undoubtedly. Now I see the white flag earnestly borne, and its possible purport sweeps before my inner vision like a wraith of morning mist. He comes steadily on, the mysterious form in gray, my mood so whimsically sensitive that I could even smile at the material of the flag,—wondering where in either army was found a towel, and one so white. But it bore a mighty message,—that simple emblem of homely service, wafted hitherward above the dark and crimsoned streams that never can wash themselves away.

The messenger draws near, dismounts; with graceful salutation and hardly suppressed emotion delivers his message: "Sir, I am from General Gordon. General Lee desires a cessation of hostilities until he can hear from General Grant as to the proposed surrender."

What word is this! so long so dearly fought for, so feverishly dreamed, but ever snatched away, held hidden and aloof; now smiting the senses with a dizzy flash! "Surrender"? We had no rumor of this from the messages that had been passing between Grant and Lee, for now these two days, behind us. "Surrender"! It takes a moment to gather one's speech. "Sir," I answer, "that matter exceeds my authority. I will send to my superior." General Lee is right. He can do no more. All this with a forced calmness, covering a tumult of heart and brain. I bid him wait a while, and the message goes up to my corps commander, General Griffin, leaving me amazed at the boding change.

Now from the right come foaming up in cavalry fashion the two forms I had watched from away beyond. A white flag again, held strong aloft, making straight for the little group beneath our battle-flag, high borne also,—the red Maltese cross on a field of white, that had thrilled hearts long ago. I see now that it is one of our cavalry staff in lead,—indeed I recognize him, Colonel Whitaker of Custer's staff; and, hardly keeping pace with him, a Confederate staff officer. Without dismounting, without salutation, the cavalryman shouts: "This is unconditional surrender! This is the end!" Then he hastily introduces his companion, and adds: "I am just from Gordon and Longstreet. Gordon says 'For God's sake, stop this infantry, or hell will be to pay!' I'll go to Sheridan," he adds, and dashes away with the white flag, leaving Longstreet's aide with me.*

I was doubtful of my duty. The flag of truce was in, but I had no right to act upon it without orders. There was still some firing from various quarters, lulling a little where the white flag passed near. But I did not press things quite so hard. Just then a last cannon-

*The various accounts that have been since given of the reception of the flag of truce on this occasion might lead to the impression upon readers of history that we were all under great agitation of mind and that our memories were somewhat confused or possibly our habit of truth telling. But those who were acquainted with the facts will not be disturbed in their inferences or judgments. In accordance with Lee's instructions several flags were sent out at important points along his own line, and several came in on our Appomattox front. The flag-bearers I refer to were Capt. P. M. Jones, now U. S. District Judge in Alabama, and Capt. Brown of Georgia.

shot from the edge of the town plunges through the breast of a gallant and dear young officer in my front line,—Lieutenant Clark, of the 185th New York,—the last man killed in the Army of the Potomac, if not the last in the Appomattox lines.** Not a strange thing for war,—this swift stroke of the mortal; but coming after the truce was in, it seemed a cruel fate for one so deserving to share his country's joy, and a sad peace-offering for us all.

Shortly comes the order, in due form, to cease firing and to halt. There was not much firing to cease from; but "halt," then and there? It is beyond human power to stop the men, whose one word and thought and action through crimsoned years had been but forward. They had seen the flag of truce, and could divine its outcome. But the habit was too strong; they cared not for points of direction, it was forward still,—forward to the end; forward to the new beginning; forward to the Nation's second birth!

But it struck them also in a quite human way. The more the captains cry, "Halt! the Rebels want to surrender," the more the men want to be there and see it. Still to the front, where the real fun is! And the forward movement takes an upward turn. For when we do succeed in stopping their advance we cannot keep their arms and legs from flying. To the top of fences, and haystacks, and chimneys they clamber, to toss their old caps higher in the air, and leave the earth as far below them as they can.

Dear old General Gregory gallops up to inquire the meaning of this strange departure from accustomed discipline. "Only that Lee wants time to surrender," I answer with stage solemnity. "Glory to God!" roars the grave and brave old General, dashing upon me with an impetuosity that nearly unhorsed us both, to grasp and wring my hand, which had not yet had time to lower the sword. "Yes, and on earth peace, good will towards men," I answered, bringing the thanksgiving from heavenward, manward.

"Your legs have done it, my men," shouts the gallant, gray-haired Ord, galloping up cap

in hand, generously forgiving our disobedience of orders, and rash "exposure" on the dubious crest. True enough, their legs had done it,—had "matched the cavalry" as Grant admitted, had cut around Lee's best doings, and commanded the grand halt. But other things too had "done it"; the blood was still fresh upon the Quaker Road, the White Oak Ridge, Five Forks, Farmville, High Bridge, and Sailor's Creek; and we take somewhat gravely this compliment of our new commander, of the Army of the James. At last, after "pardoning something to the spirit of liberty," we get things "quiet along the lines."

A truce is agreed upon until one o'clock—it is now ten. A conference is to be held, or rather colloquy, for no one here is authorized to say anything about the terms of surrender. Six or eight officers from each side meet between the lines, near the Court House, waiting Lee's answer to Grant's summons to surrender. There is lively chat here on this unaccustomed opportunity for exchange of notes and queries.

The first greetings are not all so dramatic as might be thought, for so grave an occasion. "Billy, old boy, how goes it?" asks one loyal West Pointer of a classmate he had been fighting for four years. "Bad, bad, Charlie, bad I tell you; but have you got any whisky?" was the response,—not poetic, not idealistic, but historic; founded on fact as to the strength of the demand, but without evidence of the questionable maxim that the demand creates the supply. More of the economic truth was manifest that scarcity enhances value.

Everybody seems acquiescent and for the moment cheerful,— except Sheridan. He does not like the cessation of hostilities, and does not conceal his opinion. His natural disposition was not sweetened by the circumstance that he was fired on by some of the Confederates as he was coming up to the meeting under the truce. He is for unconditional surrender, and thinks we should have banged right on and settled all questions without asking them. He strongly intimates that some of the free-thinking Rebel cavalry might take advantage of the truce to get away from us. But the Confederate officers, one and all, Gordon, Wilcox, Heth, "Rooney" Lee, and all the rest, assure him of their good faith, and that the game is up for them.

But suddenly a sharp firing cuts the air about our ears—musketry and artillery—out

**It has been claimed that the last man killed in the Appomattox lines belonged to the Army of the James. That may possibly be so, as the reception of flags began on our right, and probably did not reach the extreme left where the Army of the James was until some time after. So there may have been some firing and casualties after the truce had been received on our right. The honor of this last death is not a proper subject of quarrel.

beyond us on the Lynchburg pike, where it seems Sheridan had sent Gregg's command to stop any free-riding pranks that might be played. Gordon springs up from his pile of rails with an air of astonishment and vexation, declaring that for his part he had sent out in good faith orders to hold things as they are. And he glances more than inquiringly at Sheridan. "Oh, never mind!" says Sheridan, "I know about it. Let 'em fight!" with two simple words added, which, literally taken, are supposed to express a condemnatory judgment, but in Sheridan's rhetoric convey his appreciation of highly satisfactory qualities of his men,—especially just now.

One o'clock comes; no answer from Lee. Nothing for us but to shake hands and take arms to resume hostilities. As I turned to go, General Griffin said to me in a low voice, "Prepare to make, or receive, an attack in ten minutes!" It was a sudden change of tone in our relations, and brought a queer sensation. Where my troops had halted, the opposing lines were in close proximity. The men had stacked arms and were resting in place. It did not seem like war we were to recommence, but willful murder. But the order was only to "prepare," and that we did. Our troops were in good position, my advanced line across the road, and we stood fast intensely waiting. I had mounted, and sat looking at the scene before me, thinking of all that was impending and depending, when I felt coming in upon me a strange sense of some presence invisible but powerful—like those unearthly visitants told of in ancient story, charged with supernal message. Disquieted, I turned about, and there behind me, riding in between my two lines, appeared a commanding form, superbly mounted, richly accoutered, of imposing bearing, noble countenance, with expression of deep sadness over-mastered by deeper strength. It is no other than Robert E. Lee! And seen by me for the first time within my own lines. I sat immovable, with a certain awe and admiration. He was coming, with a single staff officer [Colonel Marshall, Chief of Staff], for the great appointed meeting which was to determine momentous issues.

Not long after, by another inleading road, appeared another form, plain, unassuming, simple, and familiar to our eyes, but to the thought as much inspiring awe as Lee in his splendor and his sadness. It is Grant! He, too, comes with a single aide [Colonel Newhall], a staff officer of Sheridan's who had come out to meet him. Slouched hat without cord; common soldier's blouse, unbuttoned, on which, however, the four stars; high boots, mud-splashed to the top; trousers tucked inside; no sword, but the sword-hand deep in the pocket; sitting his saddle with the ease of a born master, taking no notice of anything, all his faculties gathered into intense thought and mighty calm. He seemed greater than I had ever seen him,—a look as of another world about him. No wonder I forgot altogether to salute him. Anything like that would have been too little.

He rode on to meet Lee at the Court House. What momentous issues had these two souls to declare! Neither of them, in truth, free, nor held in individual bounds alone; no longer testing each other's powers and resources, no longer weighing the chances of daring or desperate conflict. Instruments of God's hands, they were now to record His decree!

But the final word is not long coming now. Staff officers are flying, crying "Lee surrenders!" Ah, there was some kind of strength left among those worn and famished men belting the hills around the springs of the Appomattox, who rent the air with shouting and uproar, as if earth and sea had joined the song! Our men did what they thought their share, and then went to sleep, as they had need to do; but in the opposite camp they acted as if they had got hold of something too good to keep, and gave it to the stars.

Besides, they had a supper that night, which was something of a novelty. For we had divided rations with our old antagonists now that they were by our side as suffering brothers. In truth, Longstreet had come over to our camp that evening with an unwonted moisture on his martial cheek and compressed words on his lips: "Gentlemen, I must speak plainly; we are starving over there. For God's sake! Can you send us something?" We were men; and we acted like men, knowing we should suffer for it ourselves. We were too short-rationed also, and had been for days, and must be for days to come. But we forgot Andersonville and Belle Isle that night, and sent over to that starving camp share and share alike for all there; nor thinking the merits of the case diminished by the circumstance that part of these provisions was what Sheridan had captured from their trains the night before.

Generals Gibbon, Griffin, and Merritt

were appointed commissioners to arrange the details of the surrender, and orders were issued in both armies that all officers and men should remain within the limits of their encampment.

Late that night I was summoned to headquarters, where General Griffin informed me that I was to command the parade on the occasion of the formal surrender of the arms and colors of Lee's army. He said the Confederates had begged hard to be allowed to stack their arms on the ground where they were, and let us go and pick them up after they had gone; but that Grant did not think this quite respectful enough to anybody, including the United States of America; and while he would have all private property respected, and would permit officers to retain their side-arms, he insisted that the surrendering army as such should march out in due order, and lay down all tokens of Confederate authority and organized hostility to the United States, in immediate presence of some representative portion of the Union Army. Griffin added in a significant tone that Grant wished the ceremony to be as simple as possible, and that nothing should be done to humiliate the manhood of the Southern soldiers.

I appreciated the honor of this appointment, although I did not take it much to myself. There were other things to think of. I only asked General Griffin to give me again my old Third Brigade, which I had commanded after Gettysburg, and with which I had been closely associated in the great battles of the first two years. Not for private reasons, however, was this request made, but because this was to be a crowning incident of history, and I thought these veterans deserved this recognition. I was therefore transferred from the First Brigade, of which I had been so proud, to the Third, representing the veterans of the Fifth Corps. The soul-drawing bugle-call "Lights Out!" did not mean darkness and silence that momentous evening; far into the night gleamed some irrepressible camp fire and echoed the irrepressible cheer in which men voiced their deepest thought—how different for each, no other knows!

At last we sleep—those who can. And so ended that 9th of April, 1865—Palm Sunday,—in that obscure little Virginia village now blazoned for immortal fame. Graver destinies were determined on that humble field than on many of classic and poetic fame. And though the issue brought bitterness to some, yet the heart of humanity the world over thrilled at the tidings. To us, I know, who there fell asleep that; night, amidst memories of things that never can be told, it came like that Palm Sunday of old, when the rejoicing multitude met the meekly riding King, and cried: "Peace in Heaven; glory in the highest."

Morning dawned; and then, in spite of all attempts to restrain it, came the visiting and sightseeing. Our camp was full of callers before we were up. They stood over our very heads now,—the men whose movements we used to study through field-glasses, or see close at hand framed in fire. We woke, and by force of habit started at the vision. But our resolute and much-enduring old antagonists were quick to change their mood when touched by appealing sentiment; they used their first vacation to come over and see what we were really made of, and what we had left for trade. Food was what was most needed; but was precisely what we also most lacked. Such as we parted with was not for sale, or barter; this went for "old times"—old comradeship across the lines. But tobacco, pipes, knives, money—or symbols of it,—shoes,—more precious still; and among the staff, even saddles, now and then, and other more trivial things that might serve as souvenirs, made an exchange about as brisk as the bullets had done a few days ago. The inundation of visitors grew so that it looked like a country fair, including the cattle-show. This exhibit broke up the order of the camp; and the authorities in charge had to interpose and forbid all visiting. All this day and part of the next our commissioners were busy arranging for the reception and transportation of surrendered property and the preparation of parole lists for the surrendering men. It was agreed that officers should sign paroles for their commands. But it took work and time to get the muster rolls in shape, not for "red tape" reasons, but for clear and explicit personal and public record. On our part, most of us had time to think,—looking backward, and also forward.

Most of all, we missed our companions of the Second and Sixth Corps. They were only three miles away and were under orders to move back at once to Burkeville. It seemed strange to us that these two corps should not be allowed that little three-mile march more, to be participants of this consummation to which they perhaps more than any had contributed. Many a longer detour had they made for less cause and less good.

But whatever of honor or privilege came to us of the Fifth Corps was accepted not as for any preeminent work or worth of ours, but in the name of the whole noble Army of the Potomac; with loving remembrance of every man, whether on horse or foot or cannon-caisson, whether with shoulder-strap of office or with knapsack,—of every man, whether his heart beat high with the joy of this hour, or was long since stilled in the shallow trenches that furrow the red earth from the Antietam to the Appomattox!

It may help to a connected understanding of these closing scenes, if we glance at the movements of that close-pressing column for a day or two before. On the evening of the 7th, General Grant had written General Lee a letter from Fannville, and sent it through General Humphreys' lines, asking Lee to surrender his army. Lee answered at once declining to surrender, but asking the terms Grant would offer. The pursuit being resumed on the morning of the 8th, Grant wrote to Lee a second letter, delivered through Humphreys' skirmish line and Fitzhugh Lee's rear-guard, proposing to meet him for the purpose of arranging terms of surrender. To this Lee replied that he had not intended to propose actual surrender, but to negotiate for peace, and to ask General Grant what terms he would offer on that basis; proposing a meeting at 10 o'clock on the morning of the 9th between the picket lines, for discussion of this question. Grant answered declining the appointment for this purpose, saying in effect that the only way to secure peace is for the South to lay down their arms.

General Grant must have felt that the end was fast coming, even without negotiations; and he seems quite earnest to impress this upon General Lee. For, after all the solicitude about sparing further bloodshed, he in no wise permits his pursuing columns to remit their activity. The natural result of this must be a battle, a destructive and decisive one. Indeed, in the present situation of our Second and Sixth Corps, this battle is imminent. Still, at this very juncture,—Lee being now in his immediate presence, so to speak, close upon Humphreys' skirmish line,—for reasons which he has not made fully apparent but which we of the White Oak Road could without difficulty surmise, General Grant deems it proper to

transfer his own personal presence, as he says, "to the head of the column," or, as Badeau puts it, "to join Sheridan's column." This was now fighting Gordon's command and Lee's cavalry at Appomattox Court House. Accordingly, General Grant, having sent this suggestive answer to General Lee, took a road leading south from a point a mile west of New Store, for a good twenty-mile ride over to Sheridan, leaving great responsibility on Humphreys and Wright. Lee was repeatedly sending word to Humphreys asking for a truce pending consideration of proposals for surrender. Humphreys answered that he had no authority to consent to this, but, on the contrary, must press him to the utmost; and at last, in answer to Lee's urgency, he even had to warn General Lee that he must retire from a position he was occupying somewhat too trustingly on the road not a hundred yards from the head of the Second Corps column. Lee's reason undoubtedly was that he was expecting the meeting with Grant which he had asked for between the skirmish lines at ten o'clock. Half an hour after the incident, and half a mile beyond this place, the Second Corps came up to Longstreet's entrenched lines three miles northeast of Appomattox Court House; and the Sixth Corps closely following, dispositions were made for instant attack. At this moment General Meade arrives on the ground, and the attack is suspended. For Lee in the meantime has sent a further letter through Humphreys to Grant, asking an interview on the basis of Grant's last letter, and Meade reading this, at once grants a truce of an hour on his own lines, awaiting the response from Grant. But Grant had already left that front. Had he been here, matters could have been quickly settled. A staff officer is sent to overtake General Grant, and at noon, half-way on his journey, the General sends back answer to Lee that he is pushing forward "to the front" for the purpose of meeting him, with the very queer advice that word may be sent to him on the road he is now on, at what point General Lee wishes the meeting to be— that is, by a messenger out-galloping Grant. There is not much choice for Lee now. Grant being on so long a road and at such distance from both of the two "columns," communication with him is for a time impracticable. In consequence of this necessary delay, Lee sent a flag of truce both to Meade in his rear and to Sheridan in his front, to ask for a suspension of hostilities until he could somewhere meet

General Grant, and himself took the shortest road for Appomattox Court House.

To resume my point of time and place, I was most of this day and the next adjusting relations in my changing commands, and with a part of my men, in picking up abandoned guns and munitions of value along the track of the Confederate march. I also had some thoughts which, as this is a personal narrative, it may be permitted to recall. For those who choose, the passage may be passed by. Some people have naturally asked me if I knew why I was designated to command the parade at the formal surrender. The same query came to my mind during the reflections of this day. I did not know or presume to ask those who perhaps would not have told me. Taking the assignment as I would any other, my feeling about it was more for the honor of the Fifth Corps and the Army of the Potomac than for myself. In lineal rank the junior general on the field, I never thought of claiming any special merit, nor tried to attract attention in any way, and believed myself to be socially unpopular among the "high boys." I had never indulged in loose talk, had minded my own business, did not curry favor with newspaper reporters, did not hang around superior headquarters, and in general had disciplined myself in self-control and the practice of patience, which virtue was not prominent among my natural endowments.

Some of my chief superiors had taken notice of this latter peculiarity apparently, as, when the recommendations for my promotion to brigadier-general after Gettysburg were ignored by the "delegation" at Washington, I found myself very soon assigned to command of a brigade. When, after the sharp tests of the Bristoe and Culpeper campaign, I was sent disabled to hospital from Rappahannock Station, and found on returning to duty that General Bartlett, of the Sixth Corps, sent over to relieve the dearth of generals in the Fifth, had chosen to take my brigade, I cheerfully returned to my regiment. Having in the meantime been applied for to command the Regular Brigade in Ayres' Division, I declined the offer at the request of General Griffin, who desired me to remain with the First Division. So remaining, I was often put in charge of peculiarly trying ventures, advance and rearguard fights, involving command of several regiments, from Spotsylvania to Cold Harbor. Immediately after this, being still Colonel of the 20th Maine, I was assigned in special orders by General Warren to the command of a brigade of six Pennsylvania regiments, made up of veterans of the First Corps, who had distinguished themselves at Gettysburg by their heroism and their losses, with a fine new regiment of full ranks,—mostly veterans also. I devoted my best energies to the perfecting of this command during the campaign before Richmond and the opening assaults on Petersburg, but in the first battle here was severely wounded leading a charge, after rather presumptuously advising against it. Here General Grant promoted me on the field to Briga-dier-General in terms referring to previous history. Returning to the front after months in Annapolis Naval School Hospital, I found my splendid brigade broken up and scattered, and its place filled by two new regiments, one from New York and one from Pennsylvania, both of finest material and personnel, but my command was reduced from the largest brigade in the corps to the very smallest. Although offered other highly desirable positions, I quietly took up this little brigade and with no complaints and no petitions for advancement went forward in my duty with the best that was in me. The noble behavior of these troops was the occasion of the brevet of Major-General, and no doubt in consideration of meekness in small things General Griffin placed under my orders for all the active engagements of this campaign, the fine Second Brigade of the division,—thus giving me a command equal to my former one, or any other in the corps.

So I had reason to believe that General Griffin had something to do with General Grant's kind remembrance, and negative merits appeared to stand for something. *Tout vient d point pour qui sait attendre*—"Everything comes in good time to him who knows how to wait."

On the morning of the 11th our division had been moved over to relieve Turner's of the Twenty-fourth Corps, Army of the James, near the Court House, where they had been receiving some of the surrendered arms, especially of the artillery on their front, while Mackenzie's cavalry had received the surrendered sabers of W. H. F. Lee's command.

Praises of General Grant were on every tongue for his magnanimity in allowing the horses of the artillery and cavalry that were the property of the men and not of the Confederacy, to be retained by the men for service in restoring and working their little plantations, and also in requesting the managers of transportation companies in all that region to facilitate in every way the return of these men to their homes.

At noon of the 11th the troops of the Army of the James took up the march to Lynchburg, to make sure of that yet doubtful point of advantage. Lee and Grant had both left: Lee for Richmond, to see his dying wife; Grant for Washington, only that once more to see again Lincoln living. The business transactions had been settled, the Parole papers made out; all was ready for the last turn,— the dissolving-view of the Army of Northern Virginia.

It was now the morning of the 12th of April. I had been ordered to have my lines formed for the ceremony at sunrise. It was a chill gray morning, depressing to the senses. But our hearts made warmth. Great memories uprose; great thoughts went forward. We formed along the principal street, from the bluff bank of the stream to near the Court House on the left,—to face the last line of battle, and receive the last remnant of the arms and colors of that great army which ours had been created to confront for all that death can do for life. We were remnants also: Massachusetts, Maine, Michigan, Maryland, Pennsylvania, New York; veterans, and replaced veterans; cut to pieces, cut down, consolidated, divisions into brigades, regiments into one, gathered by State origin; this little line, quintessence or metempsychosis of Porter's old corps of Caines' Mill and Malvern Hill; men of near blood born, made nearer by blood shed. Those facing us—now, thank God! the same.

As for me, I was once more with my old command. But this was not all I needed. I had taken leave of my little First Brigade so endeared to me, and the end of the fighting had released the Second from all orders from me. But these deserved to share with me now as they had so faithfully done in the sterner passages of the campaign. I got permission from General Griffin to have them also in the parade. I placed the First Brigade in line a little to our rear, and the Second on the opposite side of the street facing us and leaving ample space for the movements of the coming ceremony. Thus the whole division was out, and under my direction for the occasion, although I was not the division commander. I thought

this troubled General Bartlett a little, but he was a manly and soldierly man and made no comment. He contented himself by mounting his whole staff and with the division flag riding around our lines and conversing as he found opportunity with the Confederate officers. This in no manner disturbed me; my place and part were definite and clear.

Our earnest eyes scan the busy groups on the opposite slopes, breaking camp for the last time, taking down their little shelter-tents and folding them carefully as precious things, then slowly forming ranks as for unwelcome duty. And now they move. The dusky swarms forge forward into gray columns of march. On they come, with the old swinging route step and swaying battleflags. In the van, the proud Confederate ensign—the great field of white with canton of star-strewn cross of blue on a field of red, the regimental battle-flags with the same escutcheon following on, crowded so thick, by thinning out of men, that the whole column seemed crowned with red. At the right of our line our little group mounted beneath our flags, the red Maltese cross on a field of white, erewhile so bravely borne through many a field more crimson than itself, its mystic meaning now ruling all.

The momentous meaning of this occasion impressed me deeply. I resolved to mark it by some token of recognition, which could be no other than a salute of arms. Well aware of the responsibility assumed, and of the criticisms that would follow, as the sequel proved, nothing of that kind could move me in the least. The act could be defended, if needful, by the suggestion that such a salute was not to the cause for which the flag of the Confederacy stood, but to its going down before the flag of the Union. My main reason, however, was one for which I sought no authority nor asked forgiveness. Before us in proud humiliation stood the embodiment of manhood: men whom neither toils and sufferings, nor the fact of death, nor disaster, nor hopelessness could bend from their resolve; standing before us now, thin, worn, and famished, but erect, and with eyes looking level into ours, waking memories that bound us together as no other bond; —was not such manhood to be welcomed back into a Union so tested and assured?

Instructions had been given; and when the head of each division column comes opposite our group, our bugle sounds the signal and instantly our whole line from right to left, regiment by regiment in succession, gives the soldier's salutation, from the "order arms" to the old "carry"—the marching salute. Gordon at the head of the column, riding with heavy spirit and downcast face, catches the sound of shifting arms, looks up, and, taking the meaning, wheels superbly, making with himself and his horse one uplifted figure, with profound salutation as he drops the point of his sword to the boot toe; then facing to his own command, gives word for his successive brigades to pass us with the same position of the manual,—honor answering honor. On our part not a sound of trumpet more, nor roll of drum; not a cheer, nor word nor whisper of vain-glorying, nor motion of man standing again at the order, but an awed stillness rather, and breath-holding, as if it were the passing of the dead!

As each successive division masks our own, it halts, the men face inward towards us across the road, twelve feet away; then carefully "dress" their line, each captain taking pains for the good appearance of his company, worn and half starved as they were. The field and staff take their positions in the intervals of regiments; generals in rear of their commands. They fix bayonets, stack arms; then, hesitatingly, remove cartridge-boxes and lay them down. Lastly,—reluctantly, with agony of expression,—they tenderly fold their flags, battle-worn and torn, blood-stained, heart-holding colors, and lay them down; some frenziedly rushing from the ranks, kneeling over them, clinging to them, pressing them to their lips with burning tears. And only the Flag of the Union greets the sky!

What visions thronged as we looked into each other's eyes! Here pass the men of Antietam, the Bloody Lane, the Sunken Road, the Cornfield, the Burnside-Bridge; the men whom Stonewall Jackson on the second night at Fredericksburg begged Lee to let him take and crush the two corps of the Army of the Potomac huddled in the streets in darkness and confusion; the men who swept away the Eleventh Corps at Chancellorsville; who left six thousand of their companions around the bases of Culp's and Cemetery Hills at Gettysburg; these survivors of the terrible Wilderness, the Bloody-Angle at Spottsylvania, the slaughter pen of Cold Harbor, the whirlpool of Bethesda Church!

Here comes Cobb's Georgia Legion, which held the stone wall on Marye's Heights at Fredericksburg, close before which we

piled our dead for breastworks so that the living might stay and live.

Here too come Gordon's Georgians and Hoke's North Carolinians, who stood before the terrific mine explosion at Petersburg, and advancing retook the smoking crater and the dismal heaps of dead—ours more than theirs —huddled in the ghastly chasm.

Here are the men of McCowan, Hunton, and Scales, who broke the Fifth Corps lines on the White Oak Road, and were so desperately driven back on that forlorn night of March 31st by my thrice-decimated brigade.

Now comes Anderson's Fourth Corps, only Bushrod Johnson's Division left, and this the remnant of those we fought so fiercely on the Quaker Road two weeks ago, with Wise's Legion, too fierce for its own good.

Here passes the proud remnant of Ransom's North Carolinians, which we swept through Five Forks ten days ago,—and all the little that was left of this division in the sharp passages at Sailor's Creek five days thereafter.

Now makes its last front A. P. Hill's old Corps, Heth now at the head, since Hill had gone too far forward ever to return: the men who poured destruction into our division at Shepardstown Ford, Antietam, in 1862, When Hill reported the Potomac running blue with our bodies; the men who opened the desperate first day's fight at Gettysburg, where withstanding them so stubbornly our Robinson's Brigades lost 1185 men, and the Iron Brigade alone 1153,—these men of Heth's Division here too losing 2850 men, companions of these now looking into our faces so differently.

What is this but the remnant of Mahone's Division, last seen by us at the North Anna! its thinned ranks of worn, bright-eyed men recalling scenes of costly valor and ever-remembered history.

Now the sad great pageant—Longstreet and his men! What shall we give them for greeting that has not already been spoken in volleys of thunder and written in lines of fire on all the riverbanks of Virginia? Shall we go back to Gaines' Hill and Malvern Hill? Or to the Antietam of Maryland, or Gettysburg of Pennsylvania!—deepest graven of all. For here is what remains of Kershaw's Division, which left 40 percent of its men at Antietam, and at Gettysburg with Barksdale's and Semmes' Brigades tore through the Peach Orchard, rolling up the right of our gallant Third Corps, sweeping over the proud batteries of

Massachusetts-Bigelow and Philips,—where under the smoke we saw the earth brown and blue with prostrate bodies of horses and men, and the tongues of overturned cannon and caissons pointing grim and stark in the air.

Then in the Wilderness, at Spottsylvania and thereafter, Kershaw's Division again, in deeds of awful glory, held their name and fame, until fate met them at Sailor's Creek, where Kershaw himself, and Ewell, and so many more, gave up their arms and hopes,— all, indeed, but manhood's honor.

With what strange emotion I look into these faces before which in the mad assault on Rives' Salient, June 18, 1864, I was left for dead under their eyes! It is by miracles we have lived to see this day,—any of us standing here.

Now comes the sinewy remnant of fierce Hood's Division, which at Gettysburg we saw pouring through the Devil's Den, and the Plum Run gorge; turning again by the left our stubborn Third Corps, then swarming up the rocky bastions of Round Top, to be met there by equal valor, which changed Lee's whole plan of battle and perhaps the story of Gettysburg.

Ah, is this Pickett's Division?—this little group left of those who on the lurid last day of Gettysburg breasted level cross-fire and thunderbolts of storm, to be strewn back drifting wrecks, where after that awful, futile, pitiful charge we buried them in graves a furlong wide, with names unknown!

Met again in the terrible cyclone-sweep over the breastworks at Five Forks; met now, so thin, so pale, purged of the mortal,—as if knowing pain or joy no more. How could we help falling on our knees, all of us together, and praying God to pity and forgive us all!

Thus, all day long, division after division comes and goes, surrendered arms being removed by our wagons in the intervals, the cartridge-boxes emptied in the street when the ammunition was found unserviceable, our men meanwhile resting in place.

Meantime many men had been coming in late in the day, complaining that they had been abandoned by their officers and declaring that they preferred to give their parole in surrender, rather than encounter all the difficulties and hardships of an attempt to escape.

There are incidents of that scene which may be worth repeating. There was opportunity for converse with several Confederate generals. Their bearing was, of course, serious, their spirits sad. What various misgivings mingled in their mood we could not but conjecture. Levying war against the United States was serious business. But one certain impression was received from them all; they were ready to accept for themselves and for the Confederacy any fate our Government should dictate. Lincoln's magnanimity, as Grant's thoughtfulness, had already impressed them much. They spoke like brave men who mean to stand upon their honor and accept the situation. "General," says one of them at the head of his corps, "this is deeply humiliating; but I console myself with the thought that the whole country will rejoice at this day's business." "You astonish us," says another of equally high rank, "by your honorable and generous conduct. I fear we should not have done the same by you had the case been reversed." "I will go home," says a gallant officer from North Carolina, "and tell Joe Johnston we can't fight such men as you. I will advise him to surrender." "I went into that cause" says yet another of well-known name, "and I meant it. We had our choice of weapons and of ground, and we have lost. Now that is my flag (pointing to the flag of the Union), and I will prove myself as worthy as any of you."

In fact that was the whole drift of the talk, and there is no reason to doubt that it was sincere. Equally so but quite different was the strain of another. I saw him moving restlessly about, scolding his men and being answered back by them instead of ordering them. He seemed so disturbed in mind that I rode down the line to see if I could not give him a word of cheer. With a respectful salutation, calling his attention to the bearing of the men on both sides, "This promises well for our coming good-will," said I; "brave men may become good friends." "You're mistaken, sir," he turned and said. "You may forgive us but we won't be forgiven. There is a rancor in our hearts [here came in an anatomical gesture] which you little dream of. We hate you, sir." "Oh, we don't mind much about dreams, nor about hates either. Those two lines of business are closed," was the quiet reply. Then as if a little sorry for his opening, fixing his gaze on two ungainly looking holes in the breast of my coat and a much-abused sleeve, he exclaimed in a milder tone: "Those were ugly shots, General. Where did you get these?" Unfortunately I had to admit that this happened on the first day of the campaign in an afternoon I had the honor of spending with him and his party on the Quaker Road, where there were plenty of quakers and shakers also, and some few runners who left me a parting souvenir. "I suppose you think you did great things there," he burst in. "I was ordered to attack you and check your advance; and I did it too with a vim, till I found I was fighting three army corps, when I thought it prudent to retire." I was really sorry to have to re-assure him that there was no more than the third part of one corps present on our side. "I know better," he cries; "I saw the flags my-self." I think that he did stop to count three before he left us, leaving his cap behind. But I could not resist saying: "You saw the flags of three regiments; steady eyes could see no more." One of his staff officers corroborates this, and for a moment he subsides. Then he breaks out again: "It's a pity you have no lawyers in your army,"—I did not know what was coming now, unless he wanted to make his will,—"you don't know how to make out paroles. Who ever heard of paroles being signed by any but the parties paroled?" I tried to explain to him that this was a matter of mercy and humanity, for if we should keep all their men there till every individual could sign his parole, half of them would be dead of star-vation before their turn came. "Nonsense," he rejoins; "ah that is *spargere voces*; every law-yer knows such a parole as this is a mere *brutum fulmen*." "Sir," I answer, "if by brute thunderbolts you mean a pledged word to keep the peace accepted and adopted by the recipient of the favor, I don't believe your peo-ple need any lawyer to instruct them as to the word of honor." I was about to turn away; he catches the suggestion of the motion and is-sues a parting order. "You go home," he cries, "you take these fellows home. That's what will end the war." "Don't worry about the end of the war," I answer. "We are going home pretty soon, but not till we see you home." "Home!" he snatches up the word. "We haven't any. You have destroyed them. You have invaded Virginia, and ruined her. Her curse is on you." "You shouldn't have invited us down here then," was the obvious reply. "We expected somebody was going to get hurt when we took up your challenge. Didn't you? People who don't want to get hurt, General, had bet-ter not force a fight on unwilling Yankees."

By this time the thing grew comic. The staff officers both in blue and gray laughed outright; and even his men looked around from their somber service and smiled as if they enjoyed the joke. He turned away also to launch his "brute thunderbolts," not waiting to receive my thanks for instruction in Law and Latin. "The wise man foreseeth the evil and hideth himself, but the foolish pass on and are punished," says the old proverb. If there are no exceptions to this rule, then this gentleman was not rightly named.

With this comedy ends, in classic fashion, the stern drama of the Appomattox. A strange and somber shadow rose up ghost-like from the haunts of memory or habit, and rested down over the final parting scene. How strong are these ties of habit! How strange the un-dertone of sadness even at the release from prison and from pain! It seems as if we had put some precious part of ourselves there which we are loath to leave.

When all is over, in the dusk of evening, the long lines of scattered cartridges are set on fire, and the lurid flames wreathing the blackness of earthly shadows give an un-earthly border to our parting.

Then, stripped of every token of enmity or instrument of power to hurt, they march off to give their word of honor never to lift arms against the old flag again till its holders re-lease them from their promise. Then, their ranks broken, the bonds that bound them fused away by forces stronger than fire, they are free at last to go where they will; to find their homes, now most likely stricken, de-spoiled by war.

Twenty-seven thousand men paroled; seventeen thousand stand of arms laid down or gathered up; a hundred battle-flags. But regiments and brigades—or what is left of them—have scarce a score of arms to surren-der; having thrown them away by road and riverside in weariness of flight or hopeless-ness of heart, disdaining to carry them longer but to disaster. And many a bare staff was there laid down, from which the ensign had been torn in the passion and struggle of emo-tions, and divided piece by piece; a blurred or shrunken star, a rag of smoke-stained blue from the war-worn cross, a shred of deepened dye from the rent field of red, to be treasured for precious keepsakes of manhood's test and heirlooms for their children.

Nor blame them too much for this, nor us for not blaming them more. Although, as we believed, fatally wrong in striking at the old flag, misreading its deeper meaning and the innermost law of the people's life, blind to the signs of the times in the march of man, they fought as they were taught, true to such ideals as they saw, and put into their cause their best. For us they were fellow-soldiers as well, suffering the fate of arms. We could not look into those brave, bronzed faces, and those battered flags we had met on so many fields where glorious manhood lent a glory to the earth that bore it, and think of personal hate and mean revenge. Whoever had enlisted these men, we had not. We had led them back, home. Whoever had made that quarrel, we had not. It was a remnant of the inherited curse for sin. We had purged it away, with blood-offerings. We were all of us together factors of that high will which, working often through illusions of the human, and following ideals that lead through storms, evolves the enfranchisement of man.

Forgive us, therefore, if from stern, steadfast faces eyes dimmed with tears gazed at each other across that pile of storied relics so dearly there laid down, and brothers' hands were fain to reach across that rushing tide of memories which divided us, yet made us forever one.

It was our glory only that the victory we had won was for country, for the well-being of others, of these men before us as well as for ourselves and ours. Our joy was a deep, far, unspoken satisfaction,—the approval, as it were, of some voiceless and veiled divinity like the appointed "Angel of the Nation" of which the old scriptures tell—leading and looking far, yet mindful of sorrows; standing above all human strife and fierce passages of trial; not marking faults nor seeking blame; transmuting into factors of the final good corrected errors and forgiven sins; assuring of immortal inheritance all pure purpose and noble endeavor, humblest service and costliest sacrifice, unconscious and even mistaken martyrdoms offered and suffered for the sake of man.

Now on the morrow, over all the hillsides in the peaceful sunshine, are clouds of men on foot or horse, singly or in groups, making their earnest way as by the instinct of the ant, each with his own little burden, each for his own little home. And we are left alone, and lonesome. We miss our spirited antagonists in the game, and we lose interest. The weight is taken out of the opposite scale, and we go down. Never are we less gay. And when we took up the long, round-about march homeward, it was dull to plod along looking only at the muddy road, without scouts and skirmishers ahead, and reckless of our flanks. It was tame to think we could ride up to any thicket of woods we pleased, without starting at the chirrup of those little bluebirds whose cadence was so familiar to our ears, and made so deep a lodgement in our bosoms too, sometimes. It was dreary to lie down and sleep at night and think there was no vigilant picket out on the dubious-looking crests around to keep faithful watch and ward. And it seems sheer waste of opportunity and mark of military incapacity, when we emerge from some deep wood or defile and no battery belches destruction upon us from so advantageous a position as the commanding heights beyond.

But slowly these lingering images of memory or habit are lost in the currents of a deeper mood; we wonder at that mysterious dispensation whereby the pathway of the kingdom of Love on earth must needs be cut through by the sword, and why it must be that by such things as we had seen and done and suffered, and lost and won, a step is taken in the homeward march of man.

ALSO SEE

"Anniversary of Appomatox," *Bangor Daily News,* 10 April 1901, p. 5.

"Closing Scenes of War: Signal Honor to General Chamberlain," *Portland Sunday Telegram,* 14 April 1901, p. 9.

"The Dawn of the Morning at Appomattox," Military Order of the Loyal Legion of the United States, *War Papers: Read Before the Commandery of the State of Maine* 3, 1908, Portland, Maine: Lefavor-Tower Company, pp. 263–78.

"Honor Maine at Appomattox," *Lewiston Journal Illustrated Magazine,* 10 April 1965, pp. 1, 4.

"Personal Memories of Appomattox and the Impressive Scene of Lee's Surrender," *Lewiston Journal Illustrated Magazine,* 29 May 1915, p. 4.

"The Way It Was: Gen. Joshua Chamberlain's Part in the surrender at Appomattox, Virginia, April 12, 1865," *Maine Sunday Telegram,* 14 January 1979, p. 21A.

PERSONAL EXPERIENCES

★ Past personal ties between northerners and southerners meant little when the Irrepressible Conflict erupted. Colonel James T. Small, of Lewiston, Maine, was a salesman traveling through Tennessee and Texas when secession took place. His escape from New Orleans to the North by train and boat makes a thrilling story.

A slave state before the war, Missouri stayed with the Union but constantly had to fight against secessionist raiders. On September 3, 1861, Lewiston, Maine's, Stephen C. Cutler was conductor on a train heading over the Platte River. But guerrillas had set the trestle on fire—they thought the train carried Union soldiers— and Cutler and all but one passenger, plunged to their death. John A. Hodgdon, also from Lewiston, was one of the 4th Missouri cavalry raised to track down the bushwhackers. Ten months later, he and his comrades caught these border ruffians near Dogtown and almost completely exterminated them.

During the Civil War, medical problems were paramount. Inoculations and preventive health procedures were virtually unknown. Many more soldiers died from disease and dysentery than combat. Dr. S. C. Gordon, of the 13th Maine regiment, writes vividly of the war from a surgeon's point of view. He provides interesting insights into medical practices, prevalent diseases (measles, diphtheria, and diarrhea), and the physiognomy of disease. For example, he says the phrase "He doesn't have the guts for it." derived from the fact many northern soldiers had to be dismissed from the service because their systems could not adjust to soldierly life in the deep South.

In 1862, John H. Nichols, a teenage slave, made his escape to Union lines across Dismal Swamp in North Carolina. The details of this dangerous flight, in which he lost his father, illustrate the hurdles Blacks faced in their search for individual freedom. Maine doctor Alonzo Garcelon, who was in the medical corps, brought Mr. Nichols and several other Blacks back to Lewiston, Maine after the war. (Dr. Garcelon, incidentally, was the outgoing governor who dumped the snarled 1880 election problem into Joshua Chamberlain's lap. [See pages 261–71.])

★

William Winchester, Jr., of Columbia Falls, Maine, was a resourceful self-appointed spy who clearly possessed a wry sense of humor. He penetrated Confederate lines and quickly sought and received Federal credentials as a United States Spy. To gather information, he would purposely loiter aimlessly in southern neighborhoods to invite capture. At the military camps he would brilliantly practice his disguise as simpleton while snooping around. Eventually, he was suspected, chased, and wounded, before escaping back North.

In the spring of 1863 Captain Andrew Curtis got his naval commission, partly because of then-Congressman James G. Blaine's Washington advocacy. Curtis spent much of his time blockading the South Carolina coast. He chased blockade runners, shelled enemy forts, and conducted coastal commando raids. At war's end, he returned his command to Philadelphia and went home to Maine to help his brother harvest hay before resuming to his merchantman career. (Interested parties can find Curtis's complete biography serialized in the *Lewiston Journal Illustrated Magazine*.)

During the last two years of the war, Mary K. (Lynch) Kneeland, of Canton, and Dixfield, Maine, demonstrated exemplary service for the union cause—as volunteer nurse and part-time "spy"—in her adopted home of Rogersville, Tennessee. She carried out several dangerous missions and provided safety for Union Army officers and men. Indeed, Joe Haskell (a neighbor arrested by Union officers through her intelligence) had predicted she "would do more damage to the Confederacy than a half dozen regiments of Union soldiers!" Through wit and ingenuity, Kneeland was never arrested.

A. H. Hutchinson, of the 10th Maine Infantry's only Aroostook County company, languished in military prison for nearly a month after the war's end. He was captured in the spring of 1864 and sent to the Camp Ford stockade in Tyler, Texas. He and several friends broke out, but were recaptured during the last months of the war. Transferred to Camp Ford's "hell hole," they survived only because Lee surrendered and Confederate General Kirby Smith's troops refused to continue fighting.

This section ends with Joseph W. Wilber's February 18, 1865, meeting with Abraham Lincoln. The Lisbon Falls native was disabled at the Battle of Rapidan in Virginia and then enlisted in Hancock's Veteran Reserve Corps, where he was assigned to camp work near Washington. When an officious paymaster wouldn't pay him, Wilber went directly to Lincoln for redress. And after engaging in a friendly contest to see who was taller, Lincoln provided Wilber with a letter resolving his problem.

AWAY DOWN SOUTH IN DIXIE

L. C. BATEMAN

Everyone who is familiar with the history of the Civil War knows how intensely bitter was the feeling in the South just previous to the commencement of hostilities. When the states began to secede it was almost as much as a man's life was worth to be recognized south of Mason and Dixon's line as hailing from the North. Even if no outrage was perpetrated upon him, he was made to feel the utter loneliness of his situation, and that past friendships counted for nothing when weighed in the balance of political prejudice and love for the institution of slavery. It was an experience which once endured could never be forgotten, and was calculated to make the victim rejoice in the final overthrow of the old South.

Lewiston had one citizen who was in the South after the declaration of war, and the tale which he tells is one of interest. Colonel James T. Small, the well-known real estate dealer, had this experience, and the recollection of it is one that he delights to recall as he sits in his cozy library and entertains some friend or neighbor. Colonel Small was born in Bowdoin in 1840, and at the age of seventeen he shipped on the *City of Bath* for New Orleans. It was his first attempt to go down to the sea in ships, and Captain James Carney proposed to make him proficient in the ups and downs of a sailor's life.

The *City of Bath* proceeded to New Orleans to load with cotton for Mediterranean ports, and it was while here that he met his brother who induced him to leave the ship and enter into business with him. He had been but thirty days on shipboard, but the time was long enough to satisfy him that some other business would be fully as congenial to his nature as plowing the trackless deep. His brother was in the stencil plate business, which was a new one in that section, and together the two young men traveled over Louisiana, Alabama and South Carolina, and established a most lucrative trade. This was in 1858, and even then the evil passions of men were being aroused over the danger which threatened their pet institution of slavery, and frequent were the tirades to which the brothers were obliged to listen against the North and its people.

After remaining in the South for several months Colonel Small came home where he remained until 1859. As his business in the South had been a very profitable one he soon determined to return to that section. The only way to reach Alabama in those days was by way of St. Louis (Missouri), Cairo (Illinois), or Cincinnati (Ohio), and thence down the river. From those points there was no railroad leading south until Memphis, Tennessee, was reached. Colonel Small accordingly purchased his ticket to St. Louis and then took one of the Mississippi steamers down the river. Gambling was then in all its glory, and the rich planters going up and down the rivers devoted their whole attention to this pastime. Those old river boats were splendid ones, and the service and the living were all of the very best.

At Memphis the railroad to Chattanooga was taken, and from the latter place Colonel Small journeyed across Mississippi to Texas. He first went to Austin and from there to Houston, all of his traveling being done by stage. The plains swarmed with buffalo, and the immense herds of these animals could be seen on all sides. One thing that particularly caught his attention were the great salt licks that had been cut out by these animals

ORIGINALLY PUBLISHED IN *LEWISTON JOURNAL ILLUSTRATED MAGAZINE*, 1 MARCH 1902.

through countless generations. The utmost caution had to be used by the travelers to prevent a stampede of the buffalo, which would have ended in the certain death of every living thing in their wild rush.

Again Colonel Small returned to New Orleans, and thence up the Alabama River to Mobile, Alabama. He then went to Montgomery, Atlanta, and Macon and Augusta, Georgia. From this last place he crossed over to Washington, and a few days later was once more at his old home in Bowdoin.

The next year Lincoln was elected. The rumbling of war could be heard even before this event, but except by a few it was passed unheeded. For the third time Colonel Small had started for the South, and had reached Munsey, Indiana, on the day of the election. Here he sat up all night to hear the returns, and when the final result was reached he determined to continue his journey south at once. Even then he did not realize the magnitude of the danger before him, and as he had been treated with personal courtesy and respect in his former visits he seemed to have nothing to fear. John Brown had been hanged, and the evil passions of men were surging backward and forth. The dreaded tocsin of war had not sounded, however, and our traveler, in common with so many others believed that this catastrophe would be averted.

From Munsey, he went to Cairo, and here took [a] steamer for Memphis, being three weeks on the route. At Memphis he found everything was changed. Nearly every man he met wore a cockade on his hat as a sign of his sympathy for secession. War was in the very air, and agitation and discussion ran high.

At Memphis the Rebels had already taken a frontier fort, and were rapidly making preparations to extend their hostile operations on a wider scale. Finding the atmosphere too hot for him at this place he continued on down to New Orleans and from there through to Texas by the way of steamers on the Gulf of Mexico. Again he went to Galveston and Houston, but still he found the sentiment for secession strong and bitter. The next day after reaching the later place, Texas pronounced the fatal words and declared herself severed from the Union. The die was cast, and the soil of that state was no longer a place of refuge for a Northern man.

Colonel Small at once took [a] steamer back to New Orleans. Wherever they touched, he could hear the booming of cannon, cele-

brating the secession of that state. Louisiana went out the same day that he reached New Orleans, and the atmosphere was still more murky with hatred and revenge. Let Colonel Small tell his own story:

"When I reached New Orleans and found that the State had just seceded, I came to the conclusion that I must get out of the South at once. State after state was going, and the feeling was rising higher day by day. I knew that it would not do for me to be known as a Northern man, and I was equally certain that my identity could not long be hidden. For the first time the danger of my situation burst upon me with full force. I realized that if I was discovered I would probably be hung as a spy, but how to get out now became the question.

"While I was in New Orleans, General Twiggs came there. He was a United States officer, but he at once surrendered all the frontier gulf forts under his command, and then cast his fortunes with the South. His arrival at New Orleans was the signal for a great burst of disloyalty and Rebel enthusiasm. He was taken through the streets in an open barouche, and thousands of people cheered him on the way to the St. Charles Hotel.

"At that time I was stopping at the Girard Hotel in that city. Paul Warren was the proprietor, and he was one of the very few Union men in New Orleans. There was a recruiting office in the house where Rebel soldiers were being recruited, and as luck would have it the recruiting officers' room was next to mine, so you may judge that I heard plenty of disloyal talk. The captain, seeing that I was young and active, offered me the position of first lieutenant if I would enlist. I knew that it would not do to refuse point blank, so I put him off with an evasive reply. I promised to go with him, however, and I followed the troops to all the gulf forts that were now in the hands of the Rebels, selling stencil plates and saying nothing by which they could learn that I was a Northern man. I went with the soldiers to Mobile, and from there up the Alabama River to Selma and Montgomery. At that place I saw Jeff Davis when he reviewed the troops. I got a station near the stand, and heard the speech which he delivered. It was bitter in the extreme and among other things he promised them that the South would conquer and have the North prostrate at their feet within six months. There were fifteen regiments in front of him at the time and he promised them that they soon would be victors, and the heroes of their countrymen.

"I had the sense to know that the time would soon come when every man in the South would be forced to shoulder a musket, and I knew that if I ever was to get out it must be done at once. Then I began to make my preparations.

"The next day I started for Macon, by rail, and finding that place too hot for comfort kept on to Atlanta and Milledgeville, the capi-

COLONEL. J. T. SMALL

tal of the state of Georgia. From there I went to Augusta, Georgia, but still found no place where a Northern man was safe. While on the train to that place I learned of the fall of Fort Sumter, and a few minutes later came the news that the 6th Massachusetts regiment had been cut into pieces in Baltimore.

"All of this did not serve to quiet my fears, but when I reached Augusta, matters had grown still worse. A vigilance committee had been formed to examine every stranger coming into the city and find out the nature of his business. I now saw that it was a case of life or death. The only way out of Augusta was by steamer down to Savannah, and these had been stopped. The only way I could get out was by going back to Atlanta, and this I did at once.

"At Atlanta I was held up and a pass demanded. Of course I had none. I was in the car at the time, and was half asleep when the officer demanded to know where I was going. Before I realized what I was doing I said, 'To New York.' It was well nigh a fatal admission, and it brought me to my senses quickly. He then asked me where I belonged and I at once

replied, New Orleans. As luck would have it I had some checks and bank drafts on New Orleans, and this gave a plausible color to my story that I was going there to collect the money.

"I was taken to the same hotel where I had before stopped, and the landlord corroborated what I had said. He thought that I lived in New Orleans, and he told the officers that they were making a mistake in holding me. Then I was released.

"I was acquainted with a conductor, who was a Pennsylvania man, on the line from Atlanta to Chattanooga and Nashville, and to him I went for help. He did not dare to assist me, as he said they would hang him if he did. I then told him that I had got to get out or they would soon hang me for a spy. I promised if he would help me I would make it right with him, and finally he said he would see what could be done.

"In one end of his car there was a little room, or closet, where the conductor hung his clothes. He said to me: 'When my train starts, you jump on the rear car, from the opposite side and get into that little closet.' You may rest assured that I lost no time in doing as he told me to do. I crowded myself into the little den and there remained until Chattanooga was reached.

"At that place he handed me over to another conductor who had Union sentiments, and who was also anxious to earn a big fee, and in his closet I went through to Nashville. Then still another conductor was found who agreed to take me through to Bowling Green, Kentucky. It was a sort of underground railroad method of escaping, and I was paying roundly for my cramped quarters.

"At Bowling Green everybody had to be examined. It was near the Union states and every precaution was taken to catch spies. I had taken no baggage, so when we reached Bowling Green I stepped off the train quickly and walked around like a citizen. It was done so quickly that the officers did not detect me, and I carelessly walked around to where the train of Louisville was standing, and just as it started, swung myself on the end car like a brakeman. The ruse worked to a charm, and in a few minutes we were away from the city and the officers.

"On the train I soon found a Northern man who had a pass out of the country and who was making his way North. We sat together in the seat, and when I commenced to tell about my experiences, he quickly said: 'Don't talk about that. Talk about the weather, the rivers, anything but that.' He was frightened for fear that even his pass would not save him.

"The next morning we were in Louisville. I asked about a boat up the Ohio River, and found that they were running. I also found a curious state of affairs in that city. They were enlisting men there for both the Rebel and the Union armies, and sometimes the recruiting offices would be side by side. The Union sentiment was so strong that I no longer had any fear and the tremendous strain of the last few weeks was taken off my mind.

"The next day I went from my hotel to the boat, and there for the first time in months I saw the Stars and Stripes waving from the masthead. About two hundred men and women were on the wharf, and before realizing what I was doing I took off my hat and called for three cheers for the old flag. Before that moment not one of them had dared to cheer, but now they all shouted in concert, and from that crowd there went up a mighty roar.

"The crowd then appointed a committee to hunt up some more flags. The captain of the boat told us that there were only two that he knew about, and I at once went out and hunted them up. To get one of them I had to cross the river, and with the two on the boat we now had four in all, and started away with all of them flying.

"In going up the river, it was a curious sight that we saw. On the Indiana side, the Stars and Stripes could be seen everywhere, while on the Kentucky side, the Confederate Stars and Bars were just as plenty. On one side of the river the sentiment was for the Union; on the other side it was for secession. Between the two was a sort of armed neutrality, as each side knew that if any attack was made it meant the murder of both friend and foe. As the people on both sides knew each other and were neighbors and friends they simply contented themselves by floating their respective flags and going no further.

"We reached the city of Cincinnati Sunday noon just as the people were coming out of church. The news rapidly spread that a steamer loaded with refugees was coming, and by the time we drew up to the wharf there were fully ten thousand people there to receive us. Newspaper reporters were there by the score, and we had to answer all sorts of questions relating to our experiences.

"I was the only man in the crowd from Maine, and had to be pumped more than any of the others. On the whole it was a merry meeting, and vastly different from what I had been having to do for so long a time while dodging and hiding for [my] life.

"As soon as [I was] rested, I started for Pittsburgh, Philadelphia and New York. Reporters followed me wherever I went, and there was no end to the questions I answered. The parties dropped out one by one as they reached their homes, and at last I found myself alone once more. The last one who left me was a Massachusetts man, who switched off at Springfield.

"As soon as I got home and the fact became known, Governor Washburn sent for me to come to Augusta. Our leading men knew little or nothing of the feeling and condition of things in the South, and the Governor made me tell the whole story, and all that I had seen and heard. Lincoln had called for three hundred thousand men, and when Washburn asked me how many it would take to conquer the South, I replied: 'Governor, the people of the South are united, women and all, and Lincoln's call will have to be repeated many times before this war shall end.'

"Mr. Washburn then told me that I had given him more information and a clearer idea of the situation than he had ever before received from any source."

Many of our people are familiar with Colonel Small but some may have wondered just how he came by his title. In 1859 and 1860 there was a great revival of the military spirit in this State. The old musters that had fallen into disuse were again started, and militia companies were formed in almost every town of any size. It was one of the signs of approaching war, and military spirit seemed to be in the air. It was during one of his first visits home from the South that a company was organized in Bowdoin, and Mr. Small at once became a member. General Rodgers, who commanded the Maine militia, commissioned Mr. Small as a Lieutenant Colonel.

After ten companies had been formed in the surrounding towns a big muster and review of the troops was held at Higgins Corner in the town of Lisbon. A few weeks later the soldiers were again called together at Moody Hill in the same town, and before the summer was gone still another one was held in Bowdoinham. Of course Colonel Small figured as a field officer, and hence the title that has stuck to him ever since.

Since the close of the war Colonel Small has made several trips to the South, and visited the familiar scenes of antebellum days. In 1881 he organized a party of influential people such as Nelson Dingley and Frank Dingley, Jr. and made an extensive tour of the South, all of the principal points being visited. At Little Rock, Arkansas, the legislature was in session, and a special invitation was extended to the travelers to visit that body. They were received and entertained in fine style by the representatives, and many were the expressions of good will between the North and South that were uttered on that occasion.

Colonel Small expects to go South once more. The old love for roaming and for adventure is still upon him, and it would not be surprising if another and similar party was organized in the not distant future. In the meantime if anyone wants to hear about life in the South back in the old war days they should visit and draw out this genial gentleman. He will charm them with his vivid descriptions of life in a slave land, and with the incidents and tales of his journeyings away down on the Suwannee River.

Border Ruffian Warfare in Missouri— Two Interesting Stories

L. C. BATEMAN

Stephen Cutler was born in Lewiston in 1826, and here he remained until he was fifteen years of age when he went to Lowell, Massachusetts, where he remained for the next seven years.

The discovery of gold in California in 1848 had caused an immense excitement throughout all of the New England states, and hundreds of our young men were fired with an enthusiasm to make the pilgrimage to that distant Eldorado. Cutler was among the number, and was also one of the first to start. In those days there were but two ways of reaching the Pacific coast. One could take passage around Cape Horn in a sailing vessel, or he could cross the plains and Rocky mountains by ox team. Between the hardships of these two modes of traveling there was but little to choose. The father of the writer went by the Horn route, the same year, and suffered incredible hardships during his six months' passage. Cutler chose the overland route, and fared but little better. No one here can now fully realize the dangers that had to be encountered in making a trip of that kind in 1849. The entire country west of the Great Lakes was given over to wild beasts and dangerous warriors. Ox teams were the only conveyance, and every mile of the journey had to be contested. Buffaloes roamed the plains in herds of countless thousands, and this of itself constituted a danger of no small proportions. The stampede of a buffalo herd was even more to be dreaded than the sudden onslaught of a hostile band of Indians.

It was in one of those caravans that young Cutler made his way to the Pacific coast—having first secured passports from James Buchanan, then Secretary of State, and the Mexican authorities, since Cutler's intention was to swing south through Mexican territory.

The dangers of the journey were many, and some of them of a terrible nature. Time and again he and his companions were attacked by the Indians who were continually hovering around them. Only a few miles could be made each day. At night they slept under the wagons, while guards were posted and ever on the alert for approaching danger. Thus the long months dragged wearily on, while the dangers that beset them in crossing the mountain ranges were even greater than those which had surrounded them on the plains. Cold, hunger, fatigue and dangers of all kinds were continually theirs. At last the passage was made, and eight months after making the start the living members of the party had reached California.

After remaining in the mining region of California for nearly three years, Mr. Cutler again crossed the mountains and returned to Lewiston, where he remained for the next two years, and where he was married. But again the old-time spirit of adventure came upon him, and once more he returned to California by the overland route, enduring the same hardships and facing the same dangers as before. This time he remained in California for one or two years, and once more recrossing the Rocky Mountains he took up his residence

Originally published in *Lewiston Journal Illustrated Magazine*, 15 February 1902.

in Hannibal, Missouri, where he soon secured a situation as conductor of a passenger train running between that place and St. Joseph. His family, then in Lewiston, at once joined him, and for the next six years their home was in that place.

In the summer of 1861 Mr. Cutler came to Lewiston on a two weeks' visit, and while here he and his sister, Mrs. I. C. Peck went up to Riverside Cemetery for the purpose of selecting a family lot. Passing to the left, Mr. Cutler

STEPHEN CORODON CUTLER

went up on top of the high knoll, and after noting the magnificent view from that point, he turned to Mrs. Peck and said: "Right here I want to be buried."

Little did he think that in two weeks from that time his body would be resting beneath the sod where he then stood.

The next morning Mr. Cutler started for Missouri, reaching his home in Hannibal some two or three days later. Resuming his duties on the train he soon learned that there was a serious danger ahead, of which no man at that time could foresee the end.

The dread tocsin of war was beginning to be heard in the land. For several years the struggle known as the border warfare had been going on and had steadily grown in intensity and bitterness. The region around Hannibal and "St. Jo." was the very heart and center for the Border Ruffians to gather, and here many of their worst crimes were concocted and executed.

A few days after returning to his train he was making his usual trip and had neared the bridge that crossed the Platte within a few miles from St. Joseph. Word had reached the public that an attempt would soon be made to destroy this bridge, as the Border Ruffians believed that Cutler was carrying Union soldiers on his train. He had investigated the matter as much as possible and neither he nor the other officers of the road believed that there was any immediate danger. On this occasion he held up when within four miles of the bridge but soon received telegraphic orders to go ahead. No sooner had the engineer pulled the throttle and started the train than a lady passenger left her seat and, coming up to him, asked: "Do you think there is any danger, Mr. Cutler?"

Turning to the lady the conductor replied: "Madame, if I thought there was any danger I should not obey the order to go ahead, as life is just as dear to me as to you or any other person."

These were the last words that he ever uttered. A moment later the train was on the bridge and Mr. Cutler discovered when too late that the Border Ruffians had fired the structure from underneath, and the center was nearly burned through. Before the train could be stopped the fatal spot was reached, the bridge bent beneath the weight of the engine, and in less time than it takes to tell the story the entire train was precipitated into the river one hundred feet below.

Out of the seventeen passengers and a dozen or more train hands only one man was saved to tell the tale. It was a regular Thermopylae and the one lucky passenger, at once started on foot for St. Joseph, six miles away, where he gave the alarm.

The disaster had been complete. One of the first bodies found was Conductor Cutler's, and it was found that the head was completely severed from the body. The remains were immediately taken to Lewiston, and his widow and sister at once purchased the lot that had so impressed him in Riverside cemetery, and there by the murmuring waters of the river he loved so well he sleeps today.

The disaster of the Platte River bridge aroused the Unionists of St. Joseph to determined action. It was decided that the Border Ruffians must be exterminated at all hazards, and to best accomplish this result the fourth Missouri cavalry regiment was raised, and mounted on the best and swiftest horses that the government could purchase. This regiment was made up of the most daring men who could be found, and to them was assigned the dangerous duty of hunting down and destroying the worst set of cut-throats that this country has ever produced.

A member of this regiment was John A. Hodgdon, now the liquor agent of the city of Lewiston, and to him the writer went in quest of further information regarding the death of Cutler.

"I did not know Stephen Cutler," said Mr. Hodgdon, "as I did not get there until after the disaster which ended in his death. The Border Ruffians, or bushwhackers, were then in full swing around St. Jo. and it was a hard place. The life of no man who held union sentiments was safe for a moment. Men would be shot down in cold blood simply on suspicion that they were Union men.

"By the time of the Platte River bridge affair this condition of things had become intolerable. The Fourth Missouri Cavalry was made up to hunt down the outlaws and I became a member of Company 'B.' We were splendidly mounted and heavily armed, and our instructions were to take no bushwhacker prisoners. If we caught regular Confederate soldiers we treated them kindly, but the bushwhackers we looked upon as a set of assassins and shot them down without mercy wherever found.

"Platte River bridge was twice destroyed by them. The last time it was burned we were ordered there, and reached the spot and several of the injured were in farm houses and other buildings close by. Captain Cannon came to me and said 'Hodgdon, there is a man over in that building by the name of Cutler, who says that he is from Maine.' I immediately crossed over and found the man with a broken backbone and helpless. I learned that his name was George Cutler, but before I could find out more, word came that Rebels were in sight and I had to leave immediately and join my column. At that time I knew nothing about the Stephen Cutler matter, and when I first came to Lewiston and heard about it I supposed that the man I had seen with a broken back was he. I afterwards learned my mistake. Stephen was killed in the first bridge disaster, and my man was in the second.

"Well, from that time on things were hot. The country was full of bushwhackers and we had all we could do in hunting them down. We took no prisoners, but killed them the same as we would wild animals. Of course they did the same by our men when they could get a chance. It was war to the death, and quarter was neither asked nor given.

"St. Jo. was the jumping-off place for Pike's Peak and California, in those days, and it was filled with the most desperate characters. It was from this class that the bushwhackers were recruited, and as you might guess, they were no slow fighters themselves. In the early part of June, 1862, our battalion was in a wild section of the country and one day we saw a man coming on the run into camp. He was bareheaded and very excited, and told us that a party of fifteen bushwhackers had just murdered a man a few miles away. Major Kelly, then in command, ordered Captain Cannon to call for fifteen volunteers to go out after them. We proposed to make the fight an equal one, and the major thought that an equal number of our men would be a match for them.

"I was one of the volunteers accepted for the fight. We started off, and found that an old man had been killed and a young one mortally wounded, just as our informant had told us. The murderers had got the start of us by some two or three hours but we pushed on as fast as possible. After riding twenty-five miles we came to a place called Dogtown, and here we learned while eating our dinner that the bushwhackers had left only twenty minutes before we entered the town.

"We immediately mounted our horses and started after them. They tried to throw us off the track by dividing and going in different directions, but part of our boys were old scouts and knew they would come together again in a short time: so we stuck to the middle trail, and found it worked exactly as the scouts had said. We tracked them over a piece of prairie, and then into the woods and followed them for fifteen miles in this way.

"At last we came to a lane, and after following to its end we came to a schoolhouse. The teacher was standing outside and crying. She asked if we were Union soldiers, and when answered in the affirmative she told us that she had been assaulted by the bushwhackers and they were close by murdering a man whom they had found at the schoolhouse. She begged us to go after and kill them.

"Again we wheeled our horses and ran in the direction the teacher pointed, and came suddenly upon the gang. They had the man stripped and were about to kill him when we burst in upon them. They were heavily armed and fought like demons, but our sudden onslaught demoralized them, and soon we had them nearly all killed. The leader of the gang was a man named Montgomery, and he fought like a lion, but went down at last with a bullet crashing through his head.

"Only one man of the whole gang begged for mercy. I had chased him about one hundred rods and fired three times at him without bringing him down. Just then one of our men, named McNulty, rode up to my side. McNulty's father had been killed by the bushwhackers and he had begged the privilege of coming on this raid, hoping that he might find the murderer. Just as he reached my side the man at whom I had been shooting turned around and throwing up his hands said: 'I surrender, don't shoot!' McNulty gave one sharp look into his face and then fairly yelled: 'You are the man who murdered my father!' The next instant his revolver went *crack, crack, crack,* three times in succession, and the man dropped dead at our feet. His father was avenged!

"Only two or three of the bushwhackers escaped, and this lesson broke their power in that section. They realized for the first time that a remorseless foe was on their track and it took the courage out of the whole of them. After that a Union man could express his sentiments most anywhere without being murdered for his opinion. I have no doubt some of the gang we killed that day were the same men who fired the Platte River bridge where Cutler was killed. If so, they received their punishment, even if justice was a trifle tardy. I was the only man in our party who was hurt in that battle. A bullet struck me in the face, but it did no great damage. I was able to ride back to camp with the boys and am alive to tell you something about the wild days of border warfare."

All this makes interesting reading, but it marks the close of our story. When any of you chance to be in Riverside Cemetery again, it will be a fitting sequel to walk around to the big knoll on the left and see the grave of Stephen C. Cutler, who fell a victim to southern love for the accursed system of slavery.

REMINISCENCES OF THE CIVIL WAR FROM A SURGEON'S POINT OF VIEW

MAJOR S. C. GORDON

The beginning of the war found the nation ill-prepared for carrying on such a long and desperate struggle as it proved to be. Few men fully, or even approximately, appreciated the magnitude of the undertaking. When the prime minister of the administration announced that sixty days would surely end it, he little realized how much in earnest were the men who inaugurated the Rebellion, or at how much disadvantage the aggressive army was in comparison with the army of defense, working on their own soil with a full knowledge of the country.

With this general feeling, that armed with pop-guns and headed by a brass band the three months' troops could march "unvexed" to the capital of the Confederacy, it was no wonder that thousands of our best young men should enroll themselves in the battalions. Many believed that no fighting at all would take place and that it would be a good holiday excursion.

But few men in our regular army had been trained or disciplined by practical war experiences, so that from commander-in-chief to the newest recruit, with few exceptions, they had only the theory of war. Theoretical warfare, like theoretical law, medicine or science in any form, is quite another thing from the practical application.

The Bull Run disaster put a new phase on the matter. Affairs began to look more serious and enlisting was more a patriotic sentiment than before. Three years' men, enlisted during the last half of 1861, looked the issue squarely in the face. It was business with them,—no illusions of military "pomp and cir-cumstance of war," no large bounties of money,—nothing but the desire to preserve intact the union of the states.

To comparatively few men, however, were the stern realities of war apparent until they came to actual camp and field life. The great change from the comforts and regularity of home, however humble, tried the strongest constitutions, and disease and death began their ravages early in the history of every regiment, felling more men than battles ever did.

Medical officers, as a rule, were better fitted in their branch of the service than were most other volunteers. We at least had some experience to back us in the same line that we were called upon to serve in camp. Early in the war, however, the chief of the medical department was suspected of having an itching palm and dividing the profits with our purveyors. Certainly, requisitioning was very difficult initially. By persevering we succeeded in getting ordinary medical supplies, but "hospital stores" were so grudgingly doled out that we scarcely ever received enough on a month's requisition to supply the moderate demands of the field and staff, to say nothing of the sick. Later on the thing was much better managed: we were, for example, able to draw stimulants by the barrel and of a better quality than commissaries ordinarily furnish. But, of course, with Colonel Neal Dow as our noble example, the I3th Regiment remained a model of sobriety and temperance. Our med-

FROM WAR PAPERS. READ BEFORE THE COMMANDERY OF THE STATE OF MAINE, MILITARY ORDER OF THE LOYAL LEGION OF THE UNITED STATES 1, PORTLAND, ME., 1898.

ical officers were careful in the use of stimulants, often testing the medicine themselves before making poor privates swallow it.

The first troublesome illness my regiment, like most others, experienced was the common childhood disease of measles. It is surprising to find, as we did, how many adults there are in the community who have never had this disease. One hundred and twenty-five cases in my own regiment; and *such* measles! the like was never known! Why, some of those cases have lasted until now and the sufferer bears the trouble, as best he can, by the government paying him thousands of dollars back pay and twelve dollars a month the remainder of his life. Apparently, army measles like army itch never gets well.

On our way South, however, this same disease served me a good turn. Many of the men had congestion of the lungs and pneumonia following measles, as often happens. So that when we left the state on the eighteenth of February, 1862, with [the] thermometer at zero and three feet of snow on the ground, it was serious business for the poor fellows. We took the new steamer *Mississippi* at Boston, having on board four companies of my regiment and Colonel Goodings's entire 31st Massachusetts. Orders were to proceed to Fortress Monroe for General Butler, who was to command the Nineteenth Corps in the Department of the Gulf, and his staff. Dow, being senior colonel, took command of the troops, and having an eye for creature comforts, occupied the best stateroom, the one that had been assigned to General Butler. I suppose Dow fully intended vacating it before the general came on board, but through some mistake he had not removed his pennies and Butler found everything in confusion. In a rage he said, "Orderly, tell Colonel Dow to report to me." The colonel was not a graceful figure as a military man in those days, but he came tip-toeing along and with a salute said, "General Butler, I have the honor to report." But he was not allowed to make any further report, for Butler, in that peculiar, savage tone for which he was so noted, cut him short with, "I understand you have been occupying my stateroom from Boston. Get your things out of there damned quick and then apologize." Chaplain Moore and myself were standing near and hearing Butler nearly scared the poor chaplain out of his wits. Turning to me, he said, "Doctor, he is a awful man."

A few days afterward we were nearly shipwrecked in a furious gale off Hatteras. The hatches were closed for twenty-four hours and the fifteen hundred men nearly suffocated. Two days after, on a bright, calm, sunny morning, we went hard aground on Frying Pan Shoals, struck an anchor thrown to leeward and stove a hole in the forward compartment, which instantly filled with water. Every soldier's blanket was taken to stop the leak, until a gunboat came to our relief by taking off a portion of the troops and pulling us off when the tide served. While we were sending off these troops, the chaplain attempted to get into one of the boats and was stopped by General Butler with, "Here, you long-haired chaplain, come back; if we are going down we want you to pray for us." Moore remained for a little while but when the general relented and allowed him to go off to the gunboat, he sent back his resignation, which General Butler accepted with Colonel Dow's endorsement of approval. Several months afterward we finally replaced him with a man recruited from the ranks—a Baptist minister, who had enlisted from pure patriotism, I think. He became a very useful man in many ways, including nurse and postmaster. And I am very sure that he was an above average chaplain, although the strictly religious services were not often attended by many members of the regiment. (My observations of other regiments led me to believe that as a rule the chaplain who "went about doing good" in a practical way, served the Lord and his country best.) The religious sentiment was somewhat in abeyance with the average soldier during the stirring times of war. I am sorry to say that in not a few instances the chaplain himself lacked in "saving grace" to an extent that led us to think that many of these officers' salaries were out of proportion to their services—that it was good pay and "poor preach." But everything else in those days was only relative and not absolute.

Why we ran on to Frying Pan Shoals in broad daylight, with bright sunlight and a calm sea, no one knew and probably never will. The captain was accused of being a rebel and trying to put us where we would be captured. He was promptly arrested by General Butler, put in close confinement, and afterwards tried by court martial, but I think he was finally released, the charges "not being proven."

We went to Hilton Head with eighteen

feet of water in the forward compartment, and landed there the evening of March 2, 1862, just at sundown, having lost one man from diphtheria. This was the beginning of a most terrible scourge which prevailed in all the Maine regiments on Ship Island for the next three months.

As soon as we dropped anchor in the bay, the order went round to disembark and bivouac on the sand that night. It would have taken until midnight and then the men would have been obliged to sleep on the beach without blankets or tents, for nearly everything of that kind had been used in trying to stop the leak. The men were feeble and exhausted from hard work, confinement below the hatches and badly cooked rations, which were eaten from hand to mouth. I was the senior medical officer on the ship (the surgeon of the Massachusetts regiment dying from brain fever), and I determined that if the men went ashore it should be against the strongest protest I could make, and so informed Colonel Dow. "Why," said he, "if you dare to protest General Butler will place you under arrest." "Nevertheless," I replied, "I shall try it." So marching along to the stern where the general was, I saluted and said, "I understand that an order has been issued for the troops to land and sleep on the beach." "Yes, sir; and what have you to say about it?" "Simply, sir, that I protest against it as a very dangerous thing to do. These men have just come from an extremely cold climate. Many of them are now convalescing from measles and the sequences, and a large number will be rendered ill and doubtless die in consequence. They have neither blankets nor shelter, and after the labor of getting ashore, they will be in bad condition for lying down on the sand by the water's edge."

By this time the general was white with rage. "Well, sir;" said he, "any man who cannot sleep out there without getting sick, the quicker we get rid of him the better. I can do it myself with only the clothes I have on now." I remarked quietly, "I do not understand that it was for this purpose that these men enlisted. It is my duty to prevent them from getting ill and dying, if possible. Besides, General Butler, I do not think you could do it with safety, although you have not suffered the exposure that the soldiers have." Cooling a little the general continued, "My experience in army life so far has shown that whenever any movement is ordered there is always some-

one to protest. The quartermaster will swear there are not any means of transportation; the commissary that the stores are not ready; the ordnance officer that we have no ammunition; and now comes the surgeon, who swears the men are not in condition." "I have done what I think is my duty in protesting against this order," I added, touching my hat in salute. Within half an hour the order was countermanded.

I had occasion to meet General Butler many times afterward and always found him reasonable and courteous. He was a strict disciplinarian to be sure, but not so black as painted. His general and special orders in the Department of the Gulf were models of terse logic, quaint and unique as literary curiosities. His designation of the Negro as "contraband" expressed the true condition of things, and had the administration and all the departments acted upon the idea expressed in the word, it would have solved the Negro question during the war much more simply than did the course pursued. "Contraband of war" meant that they were to be used for any purpose that would aid us. Had we adopted the policy of using the Negroes in the climate, for all fatigue duty, we could have saved thousands of our New England boys who died from the effects of it. Wherever we took possession of any new section of country, thousands of Negroes flocked to our camps to eat our rations and give us trouble in many ways. "Ladies fever" broke out and ran its course, leaving as a result strictures and bladder troubles from which many a poor fellow suffers to this day, with the only consolation that he can have a pension. Well, it was "acquired in service" and why shouldn't he be remembered by the government? A case like that is good enough for the ordinary pension agent, especially as the applicant may not know or remember just how it was caused and the examiner is required only to state what he finds and the rate for it.

But this diversion has left my regiment on Hilton Head where we remained a week. The steamer was repaired, but our troops separated, my own going on the steamer *Matanzas* to Ship Island, where we found the Nineteenth Corps gathering. It was a desolate sand island covered at its northern end by a few straggling pines, which the soldiers cut and floated down for firewood. This was hard work, involving exposure to water as well as bearing heavy burdens. And here began the first real disease of the Department of the Gulf, viz., homesickness, or nostalgia. Many a poor fellow suffered to an extent scarcely to be believed. Several were discharged from my own regiment for this alone, for this was a well recognized disease in the government table. A severe case was indeed pitiful in the extreme. Next came Diphtheria, a most direful scourge, which almost decimated the four Maine regiments on the island. It began in my regiment, as I before said, on the passage out. We buried the first man at Hilton Head, and the second in the Gulf of Mexico. By the time we landed, many others had the germ implanted and it soon spread to the 12th, 14th and 15th Regiments. I do not exaggerate when I say that not less than a thousand cases occurred in these four regiments. Our hospital accommodations and medical supplies were extremely limited, for the Sanitary and Christian Commissions had not yet commenced their noble work.

This type of the disease was malignant and the men died like victims of the plague. What remedies we had seemed of no avail, for many were deathstruck from the first symptoms. My own regiment buried sixteen in the month of June, 1862, from this disease alone and, even more remarkable, it seemed to select the finest, most able-bodied men. Other Maine regiments suffered equally with ours. The dead march could be heard at almost any hour of day or night. That mournful roll of the drum with fife accompaniment became so dismal and doleful, adding to the deadly homesickness the fear of death, that the men became so demoralized, that a general order forbade any music at a funeral. It was estimated that nearly five hundred men, in the four Maine regiments, either died or were disabled to a great degree from diphtheria alone. It was a long and difficult struggle for convalescents to regain health again and afterwards when sent to Forts Jackson and St. Philip and the swamps of Louisiana, fever and ague found them easy victims.

The news of the surrender and the simultaneous occupation of the city of New Orleans changed the whole aspect of things. No amount of medication could equal the tonic effect of this victory. The terrible demoralization was over and nostalgia was practically eliminated from our list of causes for discharge. Surgeon's call was more a pastime than at any time before or after in the history of the regiment. It was no uncommon thing before that to have two hundred appear in a single morning and the difficulty of sorting out the bummers from the real sick men and sending them to "duty," taxed the diagnostic powers of our brightest surgeons to their utmost capacity. One had to learn to think quick in order to do anything like equal justice.

It was a rare school for the study of the physiognomy of disease, and he who was most apt in this direction made the least enemies, both among the soldiers and officers. These latter were oftentimes more difficult to deal with than the soldier himself. When large details for fatigue and guard were made, each captain was anxious to report as many "fit for duty" as possible, and if the surgeon excused none that the captain thought ought to be, oftentimes a complaint would go up to headquarters and the colonel would call a council consisting of surgeon and captain. At one time when we were suffering terribly from fever and ague, diarrhea, etc., these complaints came so thick and fast from the line, that Colonel Rust was made to believe that there was really some foundation for the complaint and questioned me very closely in regard to it. Our interview became rather animated, I defending myself as best I could, until finally the colonel said, somewhat hastily, "I admit, Doctor, that you have command of the sick, but I want you to remember that I command the regiment, sir." "Suppose, Colonel," I said, "that I put them all on the sick list, who will command them?" He appreciated the joke and adjourned the council. This was the only interruption to our otherwise extremely pleasant and friendly relations, for many years, both during and after the war. Indeed, in his last days I ministered to his sufferings within our own city by the sea. A more conscientious or braver soldier or truer friend never lived than Harry Rust.

In the Department of the Gulf, the death list from disease was a fearful one. Fever and ague and diarrhea, the former disabling and the latter killing, were worse foes than bullets, ten to one. It was estimated that at least ten thousand soldiers died and were buried in the Department of the Gulf, from disease of the bowels alone, from 1862 until the end of the war. It was a standing joke in our department that to be a good soldier here bowels are of more consequence than brains.

The slang phrase in regard to the soldier

who was discharged, was "He hasn't got the guts to stand it." The marches were long, the water poor (except on the banks of the Mississippi), the weather torrid, and the rations often times of poor quality, owing to the long distance from base of supplies. Fatigue duty under such circumstances, to Northern men especially, was deadly. The bones of the best young men of New England lie in unknown graves all over Louisiana. That terrible march of the Red River Expedition, in 1864, from Brashear City to Sabine Cross Roads, the fighting there and at Pleasant Hill, and afterward when "we all skedaddled from Grand Ecore," will never be forgotten by any member of the Nineteenth Corps. There was much, to be sure, that was ludicrous about it, viewed in the light of subsequent events, but few of us hardly saw "where the laugh came in" at the time. It was a long and lonely retreat, fighting by day and by night. To be sure we got some cotton, but it was mostly used to make bonfires and beds for our ambulances and wagons, to transport sick and wounded soldiers on. At Cane River we made operating tables of the bales, all marked C.S.A., which the soldiers interpreted as Cotton Stealing Association.

I shall never forget the heroism displayed by one of our Maine companions at the battle of Cane River. The Third Brigade of the Second Division was commanded by General Francis Fessenden, then colonel of the 30th Maine. He was shot on the open field leading his brigade, and it so happened that he was brought to me, where I had established hospital headquarters. As he lay on the ground with only a blanket under him, while I was dressing his leg, he was apparently unmindful of any suffering, but rubbed his hands with delight exclaiming, "Oh, Doctor, you ought to have seen that Third Brigade go in."

When I told him that he was in no immediate danger he said, "Now, Doctor, let me lie here for a while and you attend to those other poor fellows who are groaning around here." What fears he may have ever had were certainly now turned to a satisfaction which beamed from his animated face.

My own observation as well as experience leads me to believe that no man ever faced bullets flying thick and fast, or heard the sounds of "bombs bursting in air," with unqualified feelings of pleasure. I freely confess to being a most arrant coward under these circumstances. I have a strong sympathy with the officer who, when he was taunted with being scared in such a battle, replied, "Yes, I was scared; and if you had been there and had been half as scared, you would have run like the devil." It is the courage that stays through. It is said that most battles are lost by fear, rather than by being outnumbered and actually whipped. I have seen many a man actually paralyzed by fear, so he could not hold his gun. I remember so well a delicate young fellow at the beginning of this same battle of Cane River, who came to me saying, "Doctor, please tell me what is the matter with my heart. It beats so it seems as if it would come through my chest wall." He was pale and had evidently lost all strength. I took his gun, made a bed with his blanket under a tree, and told him to lie there until he felt better. I think he did not move until the battle was over. He was unlike the real skulker who coolly and deliberately shirks before the action and hides until danger is over. He meant to do his duty but the flesh was too weak.

The responsibility of deciding as to malingerers was thrown upon the medical officers and it was a trying condition many times. We always had a certain number of dead beats and the ingenuity displayed by them would have made them professionals in almost any calling in life. No species of lying was too subtle for them, although it might be difficult to detect the trick. In one company of my regiment were two brothers, Tom and Bob, who were skilled in that direction. On one occasion Bob came to surgeon's call with the usual complaint—diarrhea. I put him on light diet and sent him back sick in quarters. About ten o'clock that morning a message came from Company G, that Bob was very ill and wanted me in a hurry. I found him with a severe colic, which I suspected was due to overeating; but he swore roundly he had taken nothing but bread and coffee. I sent for an emetic and the result was a pint or more of beans, evidently taken for breakfast. Bob's life was made miserable ever after, for a practical joke was fun for the average soldier.

The last two years of the war gave us nearly everything we needed in the way of hospital stores and delicacies for the sick. The two great organizations, the Sanitary and Christian Commissions, with their able and efficient nurses, were a blessing which none but men in our department could properly appreciate. Thousands were saved by this beneficence.

I was detailed by General Franklin, after the Red River campaign, to fit out steamers at Alexandria to convey the sick and wounded to New Orleans. I loaded five steamers with the poor fellows who were more dead than alive, having been more or less neglected on account of our rapid retreat from Grand Ecore. On each steamer was a corps from each of these commissions, and the amount of milk punch distributed by them among the invalids would have put to shame a Maine prohibitionist. The delight and animation expressed upon their faces as they felt its genial influence would have warmed the cold heart of the most rigid ascetic. For all these things we were truly thankful, and the blessings bestowed by the sick and dying upon the heroic men and women, who were so unremitting in their attentions and labors for the benefit of such poor suffering wrecks of humanity, must have risen like grateful incense from the altar. These were among the bright reminiscences of a long and cruel war, during which humanity seemed as the beasts of the fields, to be sacrificed as necessity might demand. Such wars certainly are a disgrace to civilization, a blot upon the fair fame of a republic like ours, but out of the terrible struggle has come a higher and holier patriotism, which we may hope will be enduring.

Escape from Slavery Through The Dismal Swamp—The Experience Of John Nichols, a Lewiston Citizen

L. C. BATEMAN

How many of our people know that a former North Carolina slave is now living in Lewiston as one of its highly respected citizens? This is John H. Nichols of Central Avenue. Mr. Nichols made a wonderful escape in the early months of 1862 and crossed the entire Dismal Swamp without chart or compass, reaching the lines of the Union armies when but fourteen years of age. Born and reared a slave, he had an instinctive love of freedom and when yet but a child made his way through the horrors of the famous swamp immortalized by the genius of Tom Moore and reached a freedom of which he had hardly dared to hope.

The great body of southern slaves were made free by the Emancipation Proclamation of Abraham Lincoln and remained on the old plantation, but here was a young lad taking the most dangerous chances in a vast swamp of which he knew but little beyond the fact that it was as pathless as the sea, reeking with poisonous vapors and inhabited only by wild animals and venomous snakes. For nearly three days and nights he worked his way through the tangled underbrush, much of the time crawling on his hands and knees and listening to the hissing vipers that he disturbed. It is difficult at this distance of time to fully realize what this meant. No wonder that he values the liberty that he gained by such a desperate adventure.

But what are we to think of the causes that lead to such a condition of affairs? A so-called Christian nation dealing with human beings as with cattle and swine! And yet there are those around us today who believed and supported such an infamous system, and who are still obdurate in opposing every God given movement to benefit mankind! Thank God for such men as William Lloyd Garrison and Wendall Phillips who dared to brave the storms of hatred in breaking down a system so vile and inhuman.

Mr. Nichols was born in Paspatance County, North Carolina, at the foot of the Dismal Swamp. His parents were slaves, but his mother had died while he was yet a child, while the father had been sold to another man who owned a plantation but a short distance away, and this was but another infamous feature of the system of slavery. Parents were separated from their children and from each other and sent where they could never again meet in fraternal and parental clasp. It was a terrible system and one upon which the curse of God was bound to descend.

It was a short time since that the writer visited Mr. Nichols in his home and heard, from his own lips, of his early life as a slave, a story that no romance could surpass.

"The name of my master was Dempsey Richardson, and as a slave I took his name while I was on his plantation. That was the custom among the slaves. I had formerly been the property of his father, Ivory Richardson,

Originally published in *Lewiston Journal Illustrated Magazine*, 16 April 1921.

but when he died all the slaves went to the son with the other property. I can remember back to a few years before the war, but when father was sold I began to realize that slavery was the greatest curse on God's earth. And yet my case was not one of the hardest by any means as my master was really a kind man.

"Father was on a plantation but a mile or two away and I could see him now and then on Sunday or during the evening. Mother was dead and all the relatives I had were two uncles who were owned several miles away.

"I want to do my master full justice and I will say that he was reasonably kind to his slaves of whom he owned about thirty in all. The slave owners were much like the cattle owners here. Some were kind and others were cruel. The man who took care of his slaves got the most work out of them. You know there are men here who lick their cattle and horses but the horses do not do as much work and the cows do not give as much milk when they are beaten.

"We did not raise cotton on our plantation. It was wheat, corn, and potatoes. I was too young to do the hardest work but was compelled to learn all kinds of work on the plantation. I was an active and willing boy and for that reason got but few whippings.

"I was never whipped but once severely, and I have still got a scar on my side where the lash fell. The boss of the farm did it and used a hickory stick. They also used rawhide whips and these were even worse when laid on the bare flesh.

"The slaves all lived in little cabins of two rooms each and were huddled closely together. We were compelled to work from sun to sun but had our evenings for amusement when not too tired. I used to hire out now and then to work evenings and got a little money in that way. Some of the older ones earned enough money in this way to buy their freedom when they grew older but these cases were rare. The average price of a slave was nearly $1,000, but this depended upon his strength and ability to work.

"It was said that I was worth $600, as I was young. My master was offered that amount for me but refused to sell as I was a promising boy. It was something terrible to be always expecting to be sold and go farther South.

"In those days a slave had no way to learn what was going on as they could neither read nor write and only knew what was told them.

About 1862 we found out that a war was going on between the North and the South but we did not know what it meant. We were told by the whites that the Yankees were coming to take us to Cuba to work on sugar plantations but we did not want to go there. Some of the white men did not believe this but they did not dare to tell us. A few of these whites did not believe in slavery but they had to keep still if they valued their lives.

"After a time the war was known to everyone, but my master said they would whip the Yankees in a very few weeks. Six months was the very longest it would take to do this. Of course we didn't know but that he was telling us the truth."

As it came to be understood that Northern armies were on the other side of the Dismal Swamp it was whispered around among the slaves that there was a chance to escape. The father of young Nichols was one of the men who planned the scheme to cross the big swamp. Of course all the plantations for miles around had . . . slaves. Says Mr. Nichols: "I lived in a cabin just back of my master's home and there were twelve or fifteen of these cabins in all. Father lived only a short distance away and he made it his way to see all the slaves in that vicinity. All were so anxious to escape that they kept the secret very closely. News came to us now and then of the great armies less than 50 miles away and that only gave us courage to make the attempt.

"A colored man in the vicinity was familiar with the Dismal Swamp and he agreed to guide the party through for $300. This amount was raised among the Negroes who were in the scheme and paid over to the Negro guide. All kept quiet until all the plans were made and the time had come to make the attempt.

"It was a dark night, and we were assembled on the edge of the swamp. We were to start at midnight and follow a lumberman's trail until the following morning. One by one the slaves silently left their cabins and by twelve o'clock nearly 300 men and women were ready for the plunge into the swamp but our guide was not there according to promise.

"A hurried council was held among the men and it was decided that the guide had played us false. As father had planned the whole scheme and knew something about the swamp he was chosen the leader and he at once advised making the start without the guide to whom the money had been paid. If the colored guide had merely played false but kept his mouth shut we would have made the escape a success but at the last moment he had told my master and the alarm was at once sounded. All the white men in the vicinity gathered and arming themselves started on our track.

"By the time the whites reached our starting point we had a start of several hours and were a long distance on our way. We were following an old canal that had been used to bring lumber out of the swamp and the first night was easy traveling. By morning the whites were up with us and then all was confusion. We were unarmed and the trail was growing worse. A parley was held and the slaves decided to return rather than be shot. A few of the boldest refused and plunged into the thicket. I was among them, and never did I run faster in my life.

"As the whites had captured the greatest number they had no relish to follow us into the deep forest. In all, there were seven of us, and these were soon separated and I found myself alone. It was a terrible experience for a boy of my age. All trace of a road was lost and I was compelled to crawl on my hands and knees in order to get through the tangled jungle.

"It was 30 miles across the Dismal Swamp but I had a little hoe cake that I had brought with me and this kept up my strength. At night I laid down to sleep and so exhausted I was that I actually did sleep a little. I could hear the hissing of snakes and the scream of a panther and perhaps you can judge of my feelings. Moccasin snakes and vipers were around me and I could hear them although it was too dark to see them. I saw a few wild cats but these kept shy of me.

"Perhaps what terrified me more than all else was the fear of ghosts. The Negro slaves had been kept in ignorance and were very superstitious. They all believed in ghosts, good and bad, and I as a boy had been taught to believe in them. That first night in the darkness of that terrible swamp was something that I remember only with a shudder but cannot describe. In the morning I started on again as best I could.

"I always had a keen sense of location and a knowledge of the sun and stars. I knew that the settlement of Deep Creek was ahead of me and if I could make the so-called shingle bridge on the way the rest would be easy.

This was a bridge over which shingles were taken across a stream by the lumbermen. I had heard that Yankee soldiers were at Deep Creek and I had faith to believe that I could reach there before my strength failed.

"It was an awful journey and if I had to live it over again I doubt if the trip would be made. I knew, however, that if caught I would be sent to Georgia to wear my life away, as the song goes. My father's name was Jim Hinton, that being the name of his master, and I knew that he must be somewhere near me and that only added to my agony. As a matter of fact I never heard from him again and supposed that he must have perished in the Dismal Swamp. He was one of the seven who broke away from the whites after being captured in the swamp.

"We were told that we would be taken to Georgia in great hay racks each drawn by four or six mules, and we made up our minds that we had rather die and it seemed like death to cross that Dismal Swamp. Father was a strong man and I was a child but God smiled on me! Our masters thought if they could get us to Georgia that we would be safe until after the Yankees were whipped.

"I have always felt more bitter against that colored traitor than against our masters. They were after us the same as you would go after your cattle if they broke out of the pasture, while this Negro guide was a slave himself, and yet didn't want to see us escape after taking $300 to guide us to the foot of the shingle bridge. He promised faithfully to guide us to safety and then notified the whites when we started.

"Well, I fear that I may tire you with this story, as I am tiring myself. I had slept a little, but the next night got no sleep at all. I was sort of delirious. I was constantly expecting blood hounds on my track but fortunately these did not come. The whites seemed to have no hounds with them and probably thought that as they had captured most of their property it was not worthwhile following the few who fled into the jungle.

"I had got so accustomed to snakes that I had little fear of them. The moccasins were more dangerous than the rattlers but I was not attacked by any of them. The rattler never chases a person and only strikes when you come near to him when coiled up. I would like to see all the snakes in the Dismal Swamp gathered in one spot big enough to hold them. It would be a wonderful sight, but I saw enough on that journey to last me through my life.

"To make a long story short, much of my trip was traced by the old canal, and I knew that would bring me out somewhere in time. After nearly three days in the wilderness I came out near a settlement called Portsmouth and there found some Union pickets on guard.

"One by one the other slaves came straggling in until there were six of us who had started on that fearful journey. The soldiers told us to go into the woods and build a fire and they would give us something to cook. After that we must report to the Provost Marshal. This we did and he gave us a permit to go on a boat to Harrison Landing. There we entered government service driving mules and doing other service work like handling ammunition.

"That gave us two great advantages. It first gave us security from our former masters and it also gave us plenty to eat and better than we ever had in our old slave cabins. I remained in the service until the close of the war working between Portsmouth, Virginia, and Deep Creek, North Carolina. We were virtually right on the line of the two states and at times went as far as Culpepper Court House.

"I told you that I thought father died in the swamp but there is some doubt about that. One of my uncles afterwards told me that father was in Norfolk and wanted to have me come to him, but I refused as I felt safer with the army.

"I came to Maine at the close of the war with a party of colored men brought by Dr. [Alonzo] Garcelon [who had been an army surgeon]. He was in Lewiston at the time and was anxious to get a colored man and woman to work on his farm. Some of his friends also wanted to get colored men. These were Dr. Kilborne and Dr. Oakes of Auburn, Dr. Martin and Dr. Bradford of Lewiston and Dr. Garcelon undertook to bring on several ex-slaves from the South.

"This he did as he had the power to get them a free pass North. Garcelon was very kind to us when we reached Lewiston. He picked Bill Davis and his wife himself while I went to Colonel Ham and later to Dr. Martin. It was a good thing for us all to come to Lewiston although I should like to go back to the old plantation once more before I die. I have

an idea that I should see some of my old slave friends and it would be a wonderful meeting.

"Yes! I should like to visit my old home once more. My master is now dead but no doubt other members of the family are still living and I should have a pride in showing myself to them as a man and not as a slave. I do not know how they now feel about the system of slavery but I have no hard feelings towards them. They were brought up and educated to the system as something sacred and were sincere in their belief and willing to defend it with their blood. I would like to see the old plantation where I worked as a child, and would even like to go once more in the Dismal Swamp.

"Here are two hickory canes from the very road that we started in when escaping. Ex-Mayor Frank Morey owns a farm near the spot and when he was last down there he went into the swamp and cut these canes for me. He brought them back home and presented them to me in person. You cannot realize how much I value them or how grateful I feel to Mr. Morey. There are but few men who would have been thoughtful enough to do such a thing. To me they are dearer than the finest ebony gold headed cane. Mr. Morey owns a fine plantation there and has been on the same place where I lived as a slave. His place is nearer to Norfolk than where I lived."

Mr. Nichols married Miss Marguerite Brooks of St. Andrews, New Brunswick, and to the couple thirteen children have been born. Of these but three are now living. Some of these died in early childhood and never realized the hardships of their father in slavery. There are six grandchildren and one of these, Elmer Russell has been brought up by his grandparents. He is now eleven years of age, a student in the Lewiston schools and a very bright boy.

For many years Mr. Nichols has earned a living doing housecleaning and other odd jobs for people, and has won the good opinion and friendship of all he has served. He is a man of strong religious feeling and a constant attendant of the United Baptist Church, where he and his family are highly regarded members.

In speaking to the *Journal* he said: "I thank God that my children were all born in freedom. Of all the horrors of slavery the selling of children from their parents was the worst. My usage as a slave was heaven [compared] to what some others endured. I have witnessed scenes so pathetic that they would move the heart of a stone. And yet when a child was torn away from its mother she never dared to show her grief. Do you wonder that I love the North with its glorious air of freedom? I can never be too thankful that I was brought to Lewiston by Dr. Garcelon. He was a noble man and I revere his memory."

And who could believe that but a half century ago there were men here in Maine who would have consigned John H. Nichols to perpetual slavery? Truly, truth is stranger than fiction!

Also See

"Atticus, the Slave," *Courier-Gazette,* 19 January 1945, p. 4.

"From Slavery to Salt Making," *Portland Sunday Telegram,* 12 November 1967, p. 16A.

"A Fugitive Slave Case," *Rockland Courier Gazette,* 30 January 1945, pps. 1, 8 ; 2 February 1945, p. 1 ; 6 February, p. 6 ; 9 February, p. 5.

"North Monmouth Man Only Person Living in Maine Born in Slavery," *Portland Sunday Telegram,* 17 August 1930, p. 3D.

"Varied Life of Portland Woman Who was Born a Slave," *Lewiston Journal Illustrated Magazine,* 24 August 1912, pp. 1–2.

THE SPY FROM COLUMBIA FALLS

ANONYMOUS

To save their country from disruption and make it in reality the home of the free classes and colors, women and men of Revolutionary and Civil War days toiled and sacrificed as we of this world-war period have not yet begun to realize.

The makeshifts of the women, in the matter of respectable dressing alone would give pointers to those of us that complain of the pinch occasioned by bread and sweetening substitutes. Mrs. William Winchester of Columbia Falls was the mother of girls and boys, and the oldest son answered the challenge to patriots. The mother used her wool in spinning and weaving him an entire "dye-pot blue" with indigo, nor yet letting him go in white fustian or "natural colors," for she had but one black sheep, and that one grew a light fleece. But a friend south of Mason and Dixon's line sent her butternut dye, prepared by her own sympathetic fingers, for her heart was with the North though she was united to a man whom she was obliged to see march her two sons away to fight against the Yanks.

And in that butternut suit, in that handsome suit of gray—young Winchester took the trail for Southern lines, all by his lonesome, too, for his comrades enroute wore the blue, and his was an errand he was loath to share with even loyal brethren. The point where he sought to cross the Confederate lines was in the vicinity of Mrs. Hollbrook, his mother's friend. Contrary to his own inclination, he yielded to his mother's advice, and called upon that lady before entering upon his self-imposed duties.

It was fortunate that he did, for the raw northerner knew nothing of the country or the ways of its people. Too, his notion of a spy was that a deaf-mute would be ideal for the game. So it would, could one be sure he would be proof against all camouflage, but Mrs. Hollbrook dissuaded him from that hardest of all parts to act. It was her prompting that induced him to play the fool, the easiest of all, he told the home folks in later years, to carry out when you are fitted by nature for defective's cue. He fell into the spirit of it perfectly, and despite the danger, he declared he never took such keen delight in mere living, such zest in "doing the graycoats," as in the epoch of his existence just following. It assisted him much to have Mrs. Winchester's home for a sort of headquarters when in the immediate locality, as the Confederate soldiery at large, when they noted him come and go, supposed him to be her son or other relative. And those who knew better, supposing her leal to Southern hopes, merely believed him some Southern lad, befriended by the Southern woman. To forestall possible doubts, though, she cautioned him to make his visits after nightfall whenever possible, and to observe wary methods. And, again, she sent him first, to report to the Federal camps, that they might believe his story when he brought in valuable information, whereas, if he pursued his first plan of spying on his own initiative only, they would question his motives.

So Will Winchester, Jr., was duly established as U.S. spy and entered upon a career so gratifying to his humorous and adventurous soul that he would gladly have continued it as life vocation.

He was too wily—or Mrs. Hollbrook was—to think of entering alien lines at once. He loitered aimlessly in the neighborhood, and let them capture him and take him in.

He practiced letting his jaw hang down

ORIGINALLY PUBLISHED IN *LEWISTON JOURNAL ILLUSTRATED MAGAZINE*, 29 JUNE 1918.

and his mouth hang open and guarded against surprises that might startle him into an alert expression. They tried a kind of rude third degree on him, and when stern measures failed they resorted to the other extreme by shamming extreme friendliness. One magnetic fellow, in particular, tested him with chumminess, and finally pretended to treachery against the Cause in Gray and proposed delivering the army by piecemeal up to the enemy. He even asked him where he got his clothes, "Marm made um," the pretended half-wit returned, and when pressed for particulars said, "She made um outa cloth." This was as irritating as it was lucid, and when the nature of the dye was demanded, he said she colored "um" with "dirty water." A would-be wag slopped water over him, and Winchester made the only show of anger allowed himself within the Southern lines. He sputtered and wiped off the spatters, and at length waxed tearful over the damage done.

He schooled himself to sleep with his mouth open, to emphasize the simple look, and managed to acquire a resounding snore. A tent-mate became wrathful over the disturbance, and poked him in the ribs, with the admonition, "Wake up, you razorback, you-uns keeps we-uns all awake."

The offender promised not to offend again, and turned on his side, but after a little was making the echoes again, whereupon the other rolled him out upon the ground, pummeled him rather roughly, and bade him see if he could be any quieter. He crept to a far corner and sat up until daybreak, and, contrary to expectations, instead of following his persecutor around, cringing and fawning upon him, he evinced an aversion to him, dodged him when he came his way, avoided meeting him, and exhibited real fear whenever he approached. The coming night he recommenced his snoring, and when the same man undertook to thrash him for it, he raised a screaming so unearthly they drove him out under the stars. It was coolish, and he convinced them all of his foolishness by taking off his coat and spreading it over himself as he curled in a heap where all might see, when they looked out in the morning. They ordered him off the premises, and when he showed reluctance to obey, they showered him with stones, so he took to his heels like a hound, and troubled them no more for a long time, as he had learned what he wanted.

In another camp he practiced the same tactics, and added drooling when nobody was looking. He stuttered, too, when excited, but was careful not to indulge in this except on extraordinary occasions, for he understood that his fame, accompanied by a list of his characteristics would spread, and he must fit his part. All through his adventure he kept thinking up new marks of folly, but added them with caution. Only once in a while did he fall into a fit, and then when apparently badly scared,—rolled over and over, coughed, turned red in the face, strangled, became rigid as to limbs, but halted on the right side of unconsciousness lest someone would think to throw cold water in his face, and he doubted if he could resist a tremor under that ordeal. One of his facetious schemes was to play tricks on the boys in gray,—hide their belongings (guilelessly unearthing them when the joke had been carried to the extreme of desperation), telling lies in a harmless way,—lies that could be seen through on the face of them,—substituting salt for sugar, and the like.

Once he made a regulation Yankee scarecrow by stuffing a fellow's coat with swamp grass, setting it up against a tree, with the hat atop the effigy. Everybody thought it was a stranger sitting out there in the shade, and when the ruse was discovered the owner of the coat was wroth. But such kittenish capers misled his captors into believing in his genuineness as a half-witted tramp, and he had the run of a series of camps unchallenged. "Bandy-legged Bob," was the nickname they gave him, in honor of the hitch he cultivated in his walk, while others called him "Stuttering Steve" and "Foolish Freddie." So he lived chiefly among the gray uniforms, fetched water and split wood and drudged for them whenever he could not avoid it, but invariably shirking and betraying only shiftlessness and lack of ambition.

In one camp he got wind of their plan of attack and left suddenly on the eve of departure, to make mischief for them within Union lines. But he never dared return to that contingent in his old guise, so had to "make up" in another way. He was fair-haired, blue-eyed, as light as any Teuton, so decided to turn brunette for the time being. With his friend's assistance and a wash of her magnificent butternut dye, he tinted skin and hair a swarthy brown, and even colored his eye lashes so they cast a shadow over the sky blue tints beneath them.

Under cover of this mask he went, purporting to be on a quest for his Uncle George, a mythical person whose mother—his own grandmother—wanted to see once more before she died. He practiced a drawl of his own, for that of different Southern states differs as much as Pennsylvania accent contrasts with Maine's, and the place he pretended to hail from—Witche-he-he Crick (creek) was on nobody's map but his own. Of course he didn't find anybody's Uncle George, but the hunt got him through the Rebel lines.

Although he reckoned out the Negroes when he undertook his mission, he found them often his best Allies. In fleeing from Rebel pursuers he once had to leap over the bank of a river, into the sand jutting shore. An old Negro was cutting refuse grass and bushes just where he disappeared, and he was mortally certain the old fellow would be forced to give information, whether he willed or no. But the old man never flinched. Taking the cue instantly, he kept on cutting brush, only now chucking it overside by the armful, entirely concealing Will's retreat. When the pursuers came up, without waiting to be asked, the gentleman pointed to a rocky bend ahead, and told them, "I expect you've got rid of your job this time. I saw a head bob up once when he struck that ledge. It's surprising how mighty quick your breath leaves when you try not to get drowned."

They hastened ahead and surveyed the rocky projections in the river, and retraced their way.

At another time, "Auntie," a Negro matron, hid him for days in her cabin, feeding him corn pone and bacon and bringing him tidings of movements made by the enemy. At present he was a suspect with a price on his head, but it was important that he obtain certain secrets, and he implored his host to get said secrets for him. She made the supreme sacrifice; she took into favor a "no account" Negro man, Jim Johnsing, and insinuated that her ebony hand might be the prize bestowed on whomsoever was astute and heroic enough to extract the desired information according to directions and by subtle means.

Jim Johnsing consumed the bait and landed the object desired, and let us hope received his reward, though Auntie implied she would treat him like a doormat ever after.

Will Winchester brought back North a bonus of malaria and a real hitch in his leg, due to a too-impassioned bullet from a chasing guerrilla, together with a fund of memories to entertain his age, and anecdotes to amuse his neighbors.

For reasons of his own, he has never applied for a pension, nor received any Federal aid whatever. He disclaimed any patriotism in this matter, though, simply stating, when pressed to stand by his rights, that he had not been disqualified from self-support, and that the fun he derived from the experience more than compensated him for the trifling injuries sustained.

That is heroism.

Blockading the Confederacy—
The Romantic and Adventurous Life of
A Maine Sea Captain

CAPTAIN ANDREW CURTIS

Captain Andrew Curtis was born on July 3, 1835 in Bowdoinham, Maine. His father was a schoolteacher, and two of his three brothers also went to sea. His career began at the age of fifteen, when he sailed on his uncle's ship, the Mobile, to the port of New Orleans, in the spring of 1851. In 1862, after eleven years of working his way up the ranks, he became engaged to Rachel O. Wilson, a Maine woman, and in the spring of 1863, his voyages took him to New Orleans once more—to deliver a load of ice.

When we arrived there, [he says] I met several acquaintances belonging to the 15th Maine Regiment, Captain J. H. Whitmore, Lieutenant (now Major) H. A. Shorey, Lieutenant Plummer, formerly of the *Aroostook Pioneer*, Charles Graves of Bowdoinham and many others.

In company with Lieutenant Shorey I attended General Grant's reception, just after the taking of Vicksburg, and saw a number of famous generals. The guests were introduced by General Grant and General Thomas.

When I arrived home, I found that I had been drafted into the army. So I went to Lewiston to report to the provost marshal, Captain John S. Baker of Bath, an old friend. He put me in the way of getting a substitute, John Brooks from New Brunswick, for whom I paid $300. I then made an application for a position in the U. S. Navy, secured a good many recommendations and went to Washington.

There I met a great many who were ready to help me, the Honorable L. D. M. Sweat of Portland, the Honorable A. H. Rice of Boston, and the Honorable James G. Blaine of Augusta. Mr. Blaine invited me to call to see him so I went once or twice and had an interesting and enjoyable call each time. He was one of the most sociable men I ever met and I thoroughly enjoyed his conversation.

In a few days I was told that my papers would be attended to, soon, and that I could go home and await orders. I soon after received orders from the navy department to proceed to New York and report to Rear Admiral Paulding. I did so and was ordered to report on the U. S. Frigate *Savannah* for examination. I passed the examination and was given a week in which to get my uniform and to report on board for duty. Lieutenant Commander W. D. Whiting was in command, with George W. Jenkins, as executive officer, and J. A. Robinson as sailing master. We were drilled in the care of small arms and naval gunnery, with sword practice every day. Our instructor in small arms and sword exercise was an old German, Major Taff. We used to have a great deal of fun with him, for he was very irritable and we enjoyed plaguing him. When he was drilling the squad with muskets, he would become excited and stand close in front. When the command, "Ground Arms," was given, the one nearest the Major would watch his chance and bring the gun down

ORIGINALLY PUBLISHED IN *LEWISTON JOURNAL ILLUSTRATED MAGAZINE*, 22 APRIL TO 13 MAY 1905.

with a thump on the old Major's toes, just where he had plenty of corns, of which one or more was certain to be hit. Then the tears and oaths would flow in mixed English and German and he would curse the offender for "an awkward lout."

One of our acting ensigns was very tall and when he reported on board, the officer of the deck entered on the long slate, "Reported on board at 9 A.M., ensign W. H. Starbuck, 6 feet 11 inches, or 11 feet, 6 inches. I am not certain which." Starbuck wanted to go ashore, one night, after all had been piped down. So he spoke to the acting executive officer. Hepburn told him he might walk, for he was long enough. When Starbuck instantly replied, "Thank you! Thank you! Your kindness and condescension are only excelled by your large feet and ears!" Hepburn was large featured at both ends so the shot told, and he said no more; but we all laughed heartily.

I was attached to the *Savannah* for some time before I received orders to proceed to Baltimore and report to Commodore Thomas A. Dorrin for duty on board the U.S.S. *Potomska*. Acting Ensign William H. Millett of Salem was ordered with me, also Acting Ensign Watson. When we reported we found that our commander was acting volunteer Lieutenant Robert P. Swan of Maryland, with Homer E. Rand of St. Albans, Vermont, paymaster, and Edwin Vaughn of Taunton, Massachusetts, second assistant engineer.

We boarded with Mrs. Peters on St. Charles street, where a great many officers and others stayed. Madame Bonaparte boarded there also. She was a very fair looking old lady, and liked to talk of old times. I used to go into the parlor, where she sometimes invited me to sit down and have a long chat, when she told me about the days when she was in Europe. She had a great deal to say about her brother-in-law, Napoleon the First. Her conversation interested me very much. She was inclined to be a secessionist, but she did not say much on that subject.

We were in Baltimore some time, with very little to do except to report daily, as the steamer was refitting; but as I was executive officer I had a little more to do than the others. We finally got our crew from the receiving ship and sailed. For some reason which I do not recall we came back and passed July 4th in Baltimore.

When we left again we were ordered to report to Rear Admiral Dahlgren for duty in the South Atlantic blockading squadron. Very soon he ordered us to St. Simon's Sound, the entrance to the port of Brunswick, Georgia. We lay there a long time, with very little to do except to get under way and run outside to look around, once in a while.

There was a plantation very near where some soldiers, in the spring, had planted watermelons, cucumbers, sweet potatoes, peanuts, etc. Just then the melons were in their season, and we had all we wanted.

We used to fish and hunt for turtle's eggs, of which we found a great many. Every day, up Back River, we could see the smoke of some salt works which were in full operation. I used to ask Lieut. Swan to allow us to go to destroy them. He refused for a long time, from an idea, as he afterwards told me, that volunteer officers would not stand fire. However, he came to me, later, and said: "If you would like to go on an expedition to destroy these works, we will start tonight."

I said I would be delighted. So about 1 A.M. we set out. Capt. Swan had the third cutter, with five men, and I had the first cutter, with ten men, exclusive of the coxswain. Capt. Swan had a pilot to show us the way up Back River and into the creeks to the mainland. We reached the works about daylight, blew up the furnaces, destroyed the salt on hand, but found no one.

Close Encounter in a Georgia Creek

Hearing that there was a picket guard at Belle View, about five miles away, we started to try to capture them. On our way we passed a plantation, where there were an old man, his wife and a son about ten or twelve years old. The old man was terribly scared, and wanted to take the oath of allegiance. I believe, for some reason, it was not given him. We did not molest them, but went on, and in passing the cornfield I saw a young fellow trying to escape. I sent two or three men after him. In going through the field I came to the house, where I found a woman and her daughter, just sitting down to breakfast. They were much alarmed, but I calmed them as well as I could, asking them for a cup of coffee. They were much pacified by this, so I took some eggs, coffee, corn dodgers and bonnyclabber.

In the meantime my men returned with the young fellow whom they had caught. Finding that he was young and quite harmless, I promised to let him go when we came back. I then went on to Belle View, where Capt. Swan already had arrived. The guard had skipped!

We stayed there a little while and then started on our way back. When we passed the plantation where we had seen the old man in the morning, no one was to be seen but the old woman. When we reached the boats it was about noon. We started down the creek. It was then low water, and, my boat being the heavier, had not water enough to float her. So I had the men wade and pull her along part of the way. Capt. Swan, with the lighter boat, had no difficulty.

Before we had gone half a mile, his boat then being out of sight, ahead, our ears were saluted with a discharge of rifles and a splatter of water around us. My coxswain, sitting close beside me, said: "I am shot!" Others said the same.

I immediately ordered the wounded to the bottom of the boat and the rest to jump outside to pull the boat along, keeping under cover as far as possible. With the paymaster's clerk to assist me, each of us with a Spenser rifle, I opened fire on the rebels. The banks of the creek were very steep and about ten to twelve feet high. They were covered with tall grass to the very edge, making an excellent cover for the enemy.

The rebel's first fire was from a point a little astern, and could not have been more than fifteen yards distant. We heard the bullets strike the boat and "zip" as they flew past our ears. But we opened such a hot fire that the enemy soon began to fall back and the bullets whistled over our heads. After a while their fire slackened, and we waited a little to try to find out where they were.

I found out, for I saw a puff of smoke and felt a bullet touch my ear, so I fired at the puff and was rewarded by hearing a yell. I concluded he had all he wanted.

At one time during the fight, I received a wound through the right hand, but fortunately it did not disable me, and, in fact, I did not know just when I received it.

Their fire, soon after this, began to slacken and grew more distant. We did not have much more firing. When we got into the main river I saw the Captain's boat coming back. Just then I also detected two or three rebels and fired back at them. Capt. Swan at once turned and pulled for the ship, I following. When we got alongside, we were received as though rescued from the dead. Capt. Swan said that when he saw us come out of the

creek and fire he made up his mind that the rebels had captured us and were in pursuit of him. I told him I had no intention of letting them have the boat, as I needed her to come back on board in.

Serious Casualties for Both Sides

On counting casualties, I found that I had five wounded besides myself, one of them having a small ball lodged in his brain, from which he eventually died. Two others were badly wounded, and two others besides myself slightly.

The boat had nine holes entirely through her and 14 through the sail (a small one which we had set), besides many more which had struck, but did not go through, the hull.

The captain had three men badly wounded, one of whom died that night.

We expended two hundred cartridges during the fight, all of which were fired by myself and L. C. Millington, the paymaster's clerk. He was a cool hand and I hardly know what I should have done without him. A ball struck the visor of his cap and plowed a furrow along the scalp, taking the hair off.

In a few days we had a visit from Admiral Dahlgren, when he complimented me very highly on my conduct. So I felt pretty well over it.

We were soon relieved and ordered to Winyaw Bay off Georgetown, So. Carolina. I should mention, here, that after the evacuation of Charlestown I met Capt. Macbeth, who was a captain in the regiment stationed at Brunswick, where we made our raid. He told me that the old man, whom we saw that morning, sent his boy on to tell them of our raid and 35 men started out to lay for us. How they succeeded I have told, but 15 of them were killed or wounded in action.

Blockade Runner's Narrow Escape.

We lay in Winyaw Bay, in the mouth of the river just above the lighthouse to keep watch of the river and surroundings. We had our outlook posted in the tower of the lighthouse all day. About four or five miles up the river was a fort, on which 14 guns were said to be mounted. We went up in boats one night to reconnoiter and fired guns, but received no indication that anyone was there, although we knew well enough a considerable force was stationed in the fort.

One Sunday, the outlook reported a steamer, burning two-foot coal, (showing black smoke), standing in towards North Inlet, about six miles up the coast. Capt. Swan and I went into the tower with field glasses and saw that she was the type of blockade runners, showing no flag. She stood in near the inlet and anchored, as it was nearly low tide. Of course, we decided she was "contraband," as she appeared not to belong to our squadron; and no others had any right there without first reporting to us. So we decided if she attempted to enter, we would endeavor to capture her.

There was an inland passage to North Inlet, and as the steamer got underway and steamed into the inlet, we took two boats, the third cutter, Capt. Swan commanding, and the first cutter, myself commanding, with about 25 men in both boats. We were fully armed with rifles, cutlasses, revolvers; and in addition, each boat carried about ten or twelve hand grenades.

The plan was for Capt. Swan to board her on the starboard bow. At the same time I was to board on the port quarter, throwing our grenades on deck, immediately following them, overpowering and beating down the crew, thus capturing the steamer.

We arrived at the inlet about 9 P.M. Much to our disappointment we saw the steamer underway about 300 yards distant, heading out of the inlet. We pulled hard to catch her, but she had too much headway and soon disappeared.

We had anticipated an easy capture and a rich prize, feeling sure that she was a blockade runner. We pulled back to our ship, sadder if not wiser. A few days after we learned that a steamer of the North Atlantic squadron had been chasing another off the coast, and, running short of fuel, that she had put in there for a supply of coal, which she had a right to do without reporting to us. I have often thought what a desperate fight there would have been had we arrived ten minutes earlier, or had she been ten minutes later in getting underway. Her crew would have thought they were being attacked by rebels trying to capture them, while we, feeling sure she was a blockade runner, would have done our best to get her. Anyhow, there necessarily would have been considerable loss of life, as hand grenades are not healthful articles to throw among a body of men.

One evening, we heard a terrible uproar in the woods on the island and we sent a force to find out the cause. It proved to be two Southerners who were endeavoring to escape. They had forced some Negroes to ferry them over to the island and as they threatened to inform their masters when they got back, the Southerners shot them and took to the woods. They claimed the rebels were close after them, but we saw none.

They proved to be important persons, one being W. W. Ward of Kingstree, So. Carolina, a beef contractor in the rebel army, and the other Mr. McDonald, one of the chiefs in the rebel torpedo service. We kept them on board a few days and then sent them to the Admiral at Charlestown.

Capture of a Picket Guard

One day we heard that a picket guard of eight men and a sergeant was stationed at the Shoolbred plantation, 12 or 15 miles up the South Santee. So I volunteered to go after them. During the day we moved the steamer three or four miles down the coast to the mouth of the North Santee and lay there. About dark I started with the first cutter and ten or twelve men. We went up the North Santee four or five miles and then took one of the numerous bayous and crossed into the South Santee and proceeded up the river.

About 9 P.M. we arrived at the place, landed, and surrounded the house, but all was silent. Soon we heard the "sound of revelry by night," proceeding from one of the Negro houses. The men were drilled to separate before reaching a house and to pass around it on either side, so that by the time I reached the door the house was completely surrounded and no one could get away. With two men I burst in the door and ordered them to surrender. The men were taken by surprise and gave in at once. I could see but six and inquired where the others were. The sergeant said one was hunting turkeys and the other had gone to McClellanville. But I told him there was another, and on looking around I found the man pressed between two posts with his rifle all ready for use. I at once took it and told him that he might hurt someone if he was careless.

I put them all under a guard and started for the other plantation, as the Negroes wanted to leave. Just before, one of the men had seen and fired at a man who ran to the woods and escaped. I was sorry, for I suppose it was either the hunter or the other one. I posted guards while the Negroes were getting ready and I soon saw a man striding through the place. I immediately called out to stop him. He was caught, placed under guard, and we started on our way back. In five minutes this man was helplessly drunk. I had the Negroes help him along and we soon reached the boat with all our prisoners. I sent the Negroes on an old rice scow to pull down the river, while I went ahead with the boat.

The moon was shining very brightly and everything was still. I soon noticed an increased sadness on the countenance of the sergeant. He began to mourn and said he would not live to reach the ship. Finally I persuaded him to tell me the cause of his anxiety. It seems that there was an unused battery at the mouth of the South Santee, from which the guns had been taken to McClellanville, about five miles away, and about the same distance from where we captured the guard. The sergeant told me that the man at whom we fired was the one who had gone to town and that their orders, in case of a surprise, were to get the news to the battery at once. Then they could put the guns in the old battery and be ready to take us when we came down the river.

"The moon is bright," mourned he, "and the river narrow, so that we shall all be blown out of the water!"

I let him worry a while and then told him to "rest easy," as I did not intend to go near the battery. This information seemed to take a heavy load from his mind and he became quite cheerful. After going down the river some distance we crossed to the North Santee, and before daylight we were on board, with our prisoners. We permitted the Negroes to camp on the beach. The whole party were soon sent to the admiral at Charleston and I lost sight of them.

A few days after, I went, one night, in search of a battery which was said to have two guns. This was up the Santee, but the pilot became confused and lost his way. I doubt if ever he knew just where it was. When we came back, as we were passing a plantation, some of the men asked leave to go ashore to get some mess supplies. I gave them leave and half a dozen started on a foraging expedition. They soon returned, loaded with chickens, ducks, turkeys and other stuff. One old Negro followed, cursing and threatening, saying that they had taken all his things and that he would inform the Rebels.

I inquired and found that all the fowls belonged to his master, a notorious Rebel, so I took the Negro along too.

When we asked any of the Negroes their names, they would reply, "I Shoolbred nigger," or "Butler nigger," always giving their master's name. . . .

We were soon relieved and reported to Admiral Dahlgren, off Charlestown. He sent us to Port Royal for some small repairs. While there, Acting volunteer Lieutenant Swan was detached and ordered to command another steamer; while Captain (then Lieutenant) Mahan was ordered to us. We were then sent to Charleston for blockade duty. Our night station was off Swash channel with St. Michael's Steeple in line with Fort Sumter. Lieutenant Mahan was soon detached and Acting Master F. M. Mantell was ordered to us. We remained there all winter, except at short intervals.

We had great fun at night, when it was dark, for someone was likely to be fired into. We had a system of challenging with colored lights. For instance, one night the challenge would be "one red, followed by two white flashes," answered by perhaps "two red and two white flashes" or by some other combination. The list was made on the first of each month for every day that month.

Admiral Dahlgren issued strict orders to challenge at once and if not answered immediately, to fire at the ship challenged. Often, in foggy nights, a blockade runner would come upon us suddenly and then there was hurrying and scurrying!

"Beat to quarters!"
"Slip the chains!"
"Rake open the fires!"
"Fire into her as soon as possible!"

One night we fired into a steamer which came out of the fog close to us. She was not more than fifteen or twenty yards distant. The shell went through the pilot house, stove the wheel to pieces and killed the helmsman,—as we learned afterwards. She made a turn about and cleared out to sea in the fog. The steamer was furnished with patent floats on the paddles, so that these made no noise to speak of.

A Challenge Unanswered

There were times, when the weather was clear for several nights with a bright moon, when we had nothing to do. The regular army officers liked to hector Capt. Mantell, for if he was found fault with he took it exceedingly to heart. One day, when he went on board the *Vanderbilt* to make his daily report to Commodore Patterson, the senior officer, the latter began to find fault with him and told him that no blockade runner would ever come near him, as his ship was a floating lighthouse which could be seen all over the bay. He advised Capt. Mantell to keep fewer lights burning, etc.

Commander Preble, Commander Balch, and Commander Thompson were all present, as well as one or two others, and Captain Mantell came back feeling very sore over the interview.

I knew they were chaffing him and told him so, but he could not get over it, and he said he wished we could get even with them. I told him if he would leave it to me it would come out all right. He said I might do as I liked, if I did not get him into any trouble.

During the day I called the second boatswain's mate, who always had been in the navy and who would obey orders at any risk, and asked him how near he could put a shell to a steamer half a mile off and not hit her. He hesitated but a moment and then said: "Pretty near, sir."

"Fryer," said I, "if I order you to fire into a vessel tonight, put the shell as close as possible, but do not hit her."

"All right, sir," said he.

I think he understood what I intended to do, for he wore a queer expression for a moment. He knew we often challenged and received no answer, but, knowing that the ship was one of our own, that we took no notice. We used to think that they had sort of a contempt for us and that we dared not do anything.

That night, after the hammocks were piped down, about 9 P.M., as I was sitting on deck, the officer of the deck reported "A steamer outside, standing to the north!" I had seen her for some time and knew her to be the *Vanderbilt,* but was waiting for her to be reported.

I at once ordered, "Challenge her!" This was done, but we received no answer. I called to quarters, we cast loose the guns, slipped the chains and reported to Captain Mantell, who said: "It is the *Vanderbilt."* I said: "It cannot be, for she did not answer our challenge!" He ordered the men to challenge again, and still we received no answer.

So I ordered "Fire!" No. 2 gun was at once fired and I watched the shell by the burning fuse and saw that it went over and very close. At once, there flashed out answers to our challenge.

We returned to our anchorage and piped down. I said to Captain Mantell: "It must have been the *Vanderbilt* after all." No more was said until morning. After all the divisions had reported and the time had arrived to report to the senior officer, Captain Mantell sent for me and said: "I wish you would go on board the *Vanderbilt* and report. Tell Captain Patterson I am sick."

I went on board. The executive-officer of the *Vanderbilt* was Lieut. Gilbert S. Wiltse, afterwards captain of the U.S.S. *Boston* during the revolution in Honolulu. As I went up the side I met him, and, after sending up word that I had come to report, I waited till the sentry came back to tell me I could see Captain Patterson. Mr. Wiltse said: "You fired into us last night!" I said: "Why did you not answer our challenge?" He laughed and said he couldn't answer everyone's challenge. Then I grinned and said: "You must expect to be fired into!"

"Well," said he, "don't fire so close another time!"

I asked how near the shell came, and he replied that it passed between the smokestack and the mainmast, not fifteen feet above the deck.

Captain Patterson then sent for me to make my report, so I went into the cabin, where Commanders Balch, Preble and Johnson were with him. Captain Patterson said: "Good morning, sir; what report have you to make?"

With a solemn face, I began to tell him of seeing a blockade runner standing to the north, at such and such a time, which gave no answer to our challenge, so that I fired into her, when she at once answered; and that I supposed she must have gotten hold of our system. I went on to say that she had disappeared to the north and that we saw no more of her.

When I finished my story, Captain Patterson said nothing but looked at the others, and they all laughed, so I knew I was not fooling them. Then Captain Patterson turned to me. "I am glad," said he, "that you are obeying orders so well, but, when you fire into me again, make a little wider shot!"

Captain Patterson never forgot the incident, for he remembered it at Rio Janeiro more than a year afterward.

Encounter with a Blockade Runner

One night during the winter we chased a blockade runner and drove her ashore at the point opposite, about 300 yards from Fort Marshall, on the eastern end of Sullivans Island. It was very dark and somewhat thick. In the morning, when it grew light enough, we could see the rebels taking the cargo out of her. It was low water and there was a line of people all the way across the channel to the fort, carrying goods ashore.

We got under way and ran down to the senior officer, who, just then, was Captain Stephen B. Ridgeley of the U.S.S. *Shenandoah*. Captain Mantell asked permission to go in and shell her. He received it readily, with the order that if they opened fire on us we should leave at once. There was a light mist falling and considerable sea was on. But we steamed in to 18 feet of water, which was as shoal as we dared to go. Then we opened fire with the long 32's and 20 lb. Parrott. I gave the elevation at 1,500 yards, and ordered a 10-second fuse.

The first shells burst short, so I changed it to 1,800 yards and a 15-second fuse. The second shot from each gun struck her fairly, one amidships and one near the bow. Of the fifteen or twenty shells fired at her, four out of five struck her. When the first hit her, it amused us to see the people scatter, like a flock of sheep. There were fourteen guns in the fort, but there was only one to be afraid of, and that was a 7-inch Brooks rifle, around which they began to cluster. We kept on shelling, and soon saw that the fort was afire.

Soon a shot came from the gun in the fort. It fell nearly a quarter of a mile short. They fired again, and I saw the shell burst a little short, but in a direct line with us. so I kept watch for the next, and, when I saw they were ready to fire, I rang the bell for the engineer to go ahead fast. We had not gone our length when the shell fell directly in our wake.

This was a little too near for comfort, and we left and reported to Captain Ridgely that the fort was afire.

One morning, as the weather was very foggy, the *Pawnee,* which had been chasing a steamer and had run into shoal water, anchored in only about twelve feet of water and lay there until the fog cleared, when she found herself right under the guns of Fort Marshall. They started to weigh anchor, but the fort opened fire and a shell burst on deck, killing and wounding twelve men. They were not more than 300 to 400 yards from the fort, so they at once slipped their chain with a buoy on it and left.

We were away at the time, but one morning, a few days after, we saw something floating inshore toward the fort that looked like a boat. Captain Mantell asked me to take the gig and pull in to find out what it was, whether a boat or torpedo. I agreed, and with two men pulled in towards the fort. I didn't like the job, but I didn't like to back out! I could see the men clustered around the guns, and of course I could not tell what moment they might fire upon us. If they did, it would be "Goodbye, John," for one shell would have blown us out of the water. I finally reached the object, which proved to be the buoy of the *Pawnee*'s chain. As soon as I was sure what it was, I at once pulled back, unmolested.

Fort Moultrie and the Monitor

Such was our life off Charleston during the winter of 1864–65, varied by occasional trips up or down the coast.

I was sitting on deck, one morning, just after breakfast, looking toward the city and forts, when Fort Moultrie suddenly opened fire on the advanced Monitor. The Monitor lay only 300 yards distant from the fort, and it was said that there was a tacit agreement that neither should open fire upon the other. How that was I do not know, but the Monitor was still flying her meal pennant, signifying that the men were at breakfast. The people on board her took not the slightest notice of the shower of shot and shell that came upon them. I could see the shells strike the turret and glance off or fall on the deck, till I should think as many as a dozen had struck her.

When the breakfast hour was up, they hauled their meal pennant down and the turret began slowly to revolve. All at once a burst of flame and smoke came from her big 15-inch gun. We saw the shells burst inside the fort. Their fire was instantly silenced. But this one shot was fired from the Monitor, and it was a 15-inch Shrapnel. We learned afterward that it burst on the parade ground and killed and wounded thirty-five men. We also learned that the officer commanding the battery fired on the Monitor without orders, and that he was cashiered for it.

Sherman's army had taken *Savannah* before this, and we were kept busy going from one place to another, sometimes concerned in little skirmishes and sometimes carrying dispatches.

On Feb. 17, 1865, we left Winyaw Bay and during the night came down to Charleston Bar, reaching there in the morning. Many of the outside fleet were away. The senior officer outside was Acting Volunteer Lieutenant Fred Nichols in the U.S.S. *Cambridge*.

About 9 o'clock we discovered that the Stars and Stripes were flying from Fort Marshall. A few minutes later we saw them on Fort Moultrie. A dispatch boat was at once sent to the admiral, who was at North Edisto, for we could not go in until he came. While we were waiting and looking towards the city. I noticed a cloud of smoke arise from the upper end, near the wharves, followed by timber and rubbish. Then we heard a terrible explosion.

The admiral came about 10 o'clock and we went inside, signaling the *Potomska* to follow. We procured a pilot inside and followed Admiral Dahlgren past Forts Moultrie, Sumter and Castle Pinckney, and anchored off the upper part of the city, near Town Creek.

There we found that the explosion in the morning was the blowing up of the buildings on the N.E.R.R. wharf, which had been set afire, containing a large quantity of powder. Several were killed and wounded. Fires were burning in all parts of the city, guns were being fired, and everywhere were uproar and confusion.

After anchoring, Captain Mantell went on board the flagship to report, and I saw no more of him for the day. About 7 P.M. an officer came from the flagship with orders. I told him Captain Mantell was away, but I would try to find him. So I went ashore. The officer came on board two or three times before Captain Mantell returned. At last the latter came in ill humor. The orders were to proceed about six miles up the river to Stevens' Ferry, to protect the outposts. We got underway and proceeded through Town Creek, but had to keep clear of the wharves and other places where torpedoes had been laid.

On our way through Town Creek we ran into a burning wreck of the ship *Mackinaw*, and stuck there for some time before we could back clear. Our magazine was in the bow and at one time we feared the *Potomska* would take fire and be blown up before we could get clear. However, we finally got away and proceeded, anchoring at Stevens' Ferry, where we lay for three days.

Soon, we received orders to proceed up Cooper River and we went 50 miles to Dean Hall mills. This was at the junction of the East and West branches of the river. A large quantity of rice was stored there, about 40,000 bushels.

We went to the plantation of Peter Gourdin, to regulate matters, and soon there came word from a place on Back River, owned by Mrs. Tennant, that there was trouble brewing in that vicinity. We found the Negroes had decided to have a ball and that the white ladies must play the piano for them and serve then in other ways. We nipped that scheme in time, for we found that the originator was a Negro named Stevens, who claimed to be a Captain in a Negro regiment. We found that he had been in jail considerable and that he had stolen, or had given him, a United States uniform. Thus he posed as captain.

We postponed the festivities, arresting Stevens and sending him to Charleston. There were some threats made, so we left engineer Vaughan, with three or four men, to guard the place.

On our return, we found a visitor, Dr. Edmund Ravanel, with his daughter, Miss Emma. They had come on board to beg protection. So I went to his place, "The Grove," and found a lawless state of affairs. I remained there, with four of five men, for some days, looking out for that and other places.

Dr. Ravanel wished to move to town, so I had the Negroes assist him in all that was necessary. Threats were made by some of the lawless Negroes that when Dr. Ravanel went to the city they would take the schooner and plunder her. So, when they were ready, I went with him. There was no trouble on the way, as the Negroes probably decided it would not be safe to interfere.

After having his furniture carried to his house, I went up the river again and on my way seized a cargo of wood, sent it down, and delivered it to the authorities. When I returned to the steamer, I found an application from Mr. Elfe, near Stevens' Ferry, stating that the Negroes had tried to burn his buildings and had shot his brother-in-law in the arm. They expected more trouble that night.

I at once took four or five men and went down by land from the East branch. Before starting, Col. Ball of "Coming T" plantation nearby informed me that he had stolen from him the night before a very valuable, imported Spanish jack. He wished me to recover it as soon as possible.

He told me the plantation the thieves had come from, and as I was to pass that way I called and mustered the Negroes and inquired for the jack. They denied having seen the animal. But I knew better and told them if he was not brought out in fifteen minutes I should hang every one of them. In less than ten minutes, the jack was brought in and I ordered three of the Negroes to take him back to Col. Ball with my compliments, and to get there before eight o'clock that evening. They understood that they had better not trifle and so the animal was returned safely.

I then went down the river and stopped at "The Grove" to secure fresh horses. While there, a Negress came to me and wanted me to make her husband come back to her, as he had gone off "with another gal." I told her I could not make him love her unless he wanted to but that I could punish him, and I told her that I would take him out and hang him if she wanted me to. But she did not want him hung, although she did not object to any less severe form of punishment.

When I arrived at Mr. Elfe's, I found that the Negroes, numbering nearly a hundred, had set fire to the house and burned through one corner of it. Three of them had entered the room where Mrs. Elfe and her two daughters were, evidently intending to assault them, and tried to blow out the lights. Mrs. Elfe was plucky, and by good right, for she was a direct descendant of Col. Prescott of Bunker Hill fame. She placed the lights on the hearth behind her and dared the Negroes to touch either them or her. After awhile the Negroes left the room, vowing vengeance, and, being opposed by Mrs. Elfe's brother, they had shot him in the arm. Mrs. Elfe and daughters recognized many of the Negroes, most of them belonging to neighboring plantations. She gave me the names of about a dozen of the worst.

I called Fryer, the boatswain's mate, and giving him the list told him to take what men he needed and get them. In less than two hours he had captured them all and Mrs. Elfe and her daughters identified them. We locked them in an empty smokehouse that night and on the next morning I gave orders to get the prisoners ready and go back to the steamer.

Fryer lashed them all together with a hitch around each one's neck and the end of the rope held in one man's hands, behind.

They were fastened so that they had to walk pretty straight or choke.

When we reached the *Potomska* they were quartered in a scow, moored astern at night, and by day drawn up alongside where they could work scrubbing paint. They had a tarpaulin for shelter in the night and a quantity of biscuits to eat, besides all the water they could drink from the river.

At this time we had a number of prisoners, among them being three or four who had been concerned in the murder of an overseer some days before. This overseer was a Scotsman, and bore an excellent reputation. He was about 65 years old, and lived with two daughters, both unmarried. These Negroes came to their house one evening and demanded admission. On his opening the door, they stepped into the room and deliberately shot him dead in the presence of his daughters. I always wished I had been there when they were first taken. Later they were sent to the city, and I never knew what became of them.

Adventure with Dr. Mott

A complaint was made one day of the doings of the guerrillas, and that Dr. Mott, who lived above Strawberry Ferry, had harbored three. I was sent with orders to arrest him and take him to the U.S.S. *Cimarron* and deliver him to Commander Thompson, who was at Dean Hall.

I went to Dr. Mott's house with a boat's crew and found him at home. I informed him of my errand. There was an old gentleman with him who objected and who claimed that Dr. Mott could not go. I told him Dr. Mott could ride. He said there was not a horse on the place. I sent a man to find one, which he soon did, and I asked the man what he meant by that remark. He said that Dr. Mott could not sit on a horse. I said I would have him held on, for I had been sent to arrest Dr. Mott, and that he would go anyhow, and since this man had so much to say I would take him also, on my own responsibility. He seemed taken back at this, but I told him to get ready.

I had some of the Negroes hold Dr. Mott in the saddle and lead the animal, as the doctor was lame. He was a gentleman, and on the way down the river in the boat he talked a great deal, telling of his experiences as a surgeon in the U.S. Army in the Florida wars. He spoke of General Grant as captain in his regiment, who, he said, no one thought of anymore than average ability. He related many anecdotes of Grant which came under his own personal observation. He was a brother of Dr. Valentine Mott, so famous in New York.

I delivered the doctor to Commander Thompson and told him how I came to arrest the other man. He said he was glad I did so. Commander Thompson made Dr. Mott comfortable while he was on board, and in a few days took the men to Charleston to the admiral. The latter soon released Dr. Mott, but kept the other some days longer.

Chasing Rebels in the Swamp

Soon after this the U.S.S. *Jonquil* came up the river and reported to me at Strawberry Ferry, Capt. Mantell being away much of the time, leaving me in command. He gave me permission to go up the river as far as a plantation called "Richmond." While there, I told the officer in command not to permit anyone to go far from the steamer, as there were many guerrillas about. But he and three or four of his men took some horses and went off for a ride, with the result that before they had gone half a mile away the whole party was scooped in by the rebels. I suppose the men thought that because I had been going anywhere I wished and remained unmolested that it was safe for them to do the same. Dr. Ravanel had said once, when I asked him how it chanced that I was never molested: "God bless you, there isn't a man in this part of South Carolina who would ever trouble you. You are doing too much good on Cooper River!"

Word was brought back by the *Jonquil* of the capture of the officers. We took about forty men and started to try to recapture them. We stayed at Richmond that night, and about 11 P.M. I went out with two men and a guide to explore the country and try to find out something about the guerrillas.

We stopped at several places but could not find out much until we came to Monk's Corner, where lived a peculiar character, Miss Mary Von Hagan. She was of Dutch descent and was an educated woman. She taught school and understood Latin and Greek. She was very well spoken of by the neighboring planters. As there were no common schools for her to teach, at that time, she used to go around the neighborhood calling and visiting, and whenever she met any of the Negroes with guns she would take the arms from them and carry them home and destroy them.

She gave me a great deal of information about the people who were in sympathy with the guerrillas and said that the captain of the gang was a young man named Stevens, whose father-in-law, or step-father, was second in command. She said they had taken the prisoners to Hog Swamp, which is almost inaccessible, and in the midst of which is an island. She said Stevens lived near there with his mother and that there were about forty in his band.

After securing all the information I could, I went back to Richmond, arriving there about daylight. In the afternoon, we started for Hog Swamp, some 40 or 50 miles off. The most of us were mounted and I rode ahead with about 15 of my own men.

Near dusk, we came to a house where it was said one of the guerrillas lived. We surrounded the place, as usual, and I went in, but was told no one was at home except the lady, who was ill with a fever, and her two daughters. I told them I must see her. I found a very sick looking woman, who was much frightened by my call. After assuring myself there was no sham, I made an apology for my intrusion and told her we should do her no harm.

We took our leave just as the main body, under Capt. Mantell, came up. In a short time, I heard a great uproar and sent two of my men back to find out the cause. They reported that the former slaves were breaking into the smokehouse to steal bacon. This did not particularly concern us and we kept on and arrived at the Stevens' house about 9:30 P.M. We found no men at home, but Mrs. Stevens was there. (I call her Stevens, after her son's name, as I do not know her husband's.) With her was a young son of 10 or 12 years and two daughters. I asked Mrs. Stevens where her husband and son were and she said she did not know, but that they would soon be in.

I asked her where the prisoners were and she said she thought they were in the swamp. I informed her that if her husband and son did not come in before morning or if she could not show us the way to the swamp I should feel obliged to burn the house.

She was much frightened and after waiting until about midnight for them to come in she said she would try to find the way and take us to the swamp. Very few of the white people knew this route. Not many of the Negroes knew it, and, besides, they did not dare to go there.

We started off with about fifteen men, she leading the way. We had torches, but it was very dark and the road was blind. Soon the poor woman became confused and lost her way. She cried bitterly so that I pitied her and we went back to the house to wait until morning.

We sent for a Negro to take us into the swamp in the morning, but at 2 A.M. Captain Stevens and his step-father came in and delivered themselves up.

When morning came, Captain Mantell's courage seemed to be on the wane. He was determined to go back to the steamer, as he feared the large force of Rebels would gobble us up. No persuasion could alter his mind. He thought the capture of the leaders quite enough.

On the way back, we stopped at the house of Lieutenant Governor Cain and took a cup of coffee each. He was a fine looking man. Soon after leaving there I saw a landsman, one of the crew of the *Cimarron*, staggering under the weight of a mirror which he was carrying off. I asked him what he was going to do with it and he said, "I don't know, Sir, but I wanted to take something." I made him carry it back.

On our way, Captain Mantell fell out with some of the *Cimarron* officers, whom he accused of lagging behind. "If you don't attend to your duty and keep in line, I will have you all tried by court-martial," said he.

Soon after, one of the men had trouble with his mule, which balked. "If you don't do your duty and keep in line, I'll have you tried by court-martial!" said he. And that raised a shout! The remark became a byword among the *Cimarron*'s officers, much to Capt. Mantell's disgust.

In the course of the day, we arrived at Richmond with our prisoners, took them on board the *Potomska*, which then lay there, and delivered them to Com. Thompson, who sent them to Charleston. The captured men from the *Jonquil* were taken up country somewhere, and, after being kept awhile, were released, as then the war was over.

Sometime previous to this I learned that an attempt was to be made to burn Dean Hall mills, where 40,000 bushels of rice were stored. This rice was very much needed in the city, as the white and black people alike were drawing daily rations. As I had not enough men to guard the mill, in addition to my other duties, I went to Charleston to see Gen. John V. Hatch, to urge upon him the necessity of sending a vessel to get it and take it to the city.

I gave my name to the acting assistant adjutant general at the door of his private office, and he informed me that Gen. Hatch was busy. I waited for some time and then coolly walked in. I spoke to Gen. Hatch, who received me politely and I told him my errand. He said he would send a vessel up at once, as the rice was needed, and thanked me for letting him know about it.

When I came out, I was met by the A.A.A. general, who wanted to know how I got into the office without permission from him. I told him I walked in and that as I did not belong to the army I did not intend to cool my heels in anyone's anteroom. He did not seem at all satisfied with the answer, but it was all he received.

The schooner was not sent for the rice and two days later the mill was burned with all in it.

I had about all I could do to keep order on the plantations along Cooper River, So. Carolina. Just then I was busy making the Negroes plant rice for the next crop. I told them they would have to plant it or starve and that the crop would be divided between them and their former masters, so that they would get their share. Usually an order from me to this effect was sufficient. On a few of the plantations we had to make them work.

Northern vs. Southern Courtesy

Mrs. Simmons Lucas, a daughter of Judge Buist, came to me one day about some matter which needed attention from the provost marshal. That office was filled by Lieut. Col. Steward L. Woodford, afterwards governor lieutenant of New York. I went with her to Col. Woodford and introduced her to him. He listened attentively to her story and gave orders to have her wishes complied with. She thanked him and on leaving he said to her: "Mrs. Lucas, do all the ladies lift their veils when talking with Northern officers?" "All ladies do," she replied, and told him that she considered an officer a gentleman, whether of the North or South, and entitled to respectful treatment. He told her he considered her the first "real lady" he had met. She came away much impressed.

I stayed at Dr. Ravanel's house, while in town, and used to have many arguments, with Miss Emma Ravanel especially. At that time she was a thorough secessionist, but had no word of disparagement for Federal officers. Sometimes, in the midst of a heated argument, she would say, "But you are excepted, for you have saved all our lives." I had many pleasant talks with Dr. Ravanel, who was a learned man, having traveled all over Europe. He spoke often of the first Emperor Napoleon and King Louis Phillipe, to both of whom he had been presented. He was an eminent anchologist, having one of the best collections of fossil and marine shells in the country.

We attended the flag-raising at Fort Sumter, April 14th. I stood very near Major Anderson, when he raised the flag with his own hands. He was much affected.

Sent to Jupiter Inlet, Fla.

We did not stay in Charleston long after this, but were sent south to Jupiter Inlet to prevent the escape of Jefferson Davis, if he should try that way. We arrived there in a couple of days after leaving Charleston and anchored off the Inlet. It was a dreary looking place with not a thing to show any signs of having been settled except the lighthouse tower and buildings.

The next day I took a boat and went in to reconnoiter. We had some difficulty in going through the breakers into the Inlet. We went up the river several miles and then returned on board. Going out through the surf proved harder than going in, for we had to meet the breakers in going out. The situation may be imagined, with a wall of water, combing over, and coming with great speed, seven or eight feet high, and for the whole length as far as one could see filled with sharks, of which fifteen or twenty would be visible at one time. But we neither filled nor capsized and by good management shipped little water. We had been lying there several days, going in and out every day, when a United States steamer came down to assist us in keeping guard. The next day we made up an expedition, consisting of one boat from our vessel, with myself in command, and one from the other, with Acting Ensign Whittemore in command.

In going ashore, I suggested to Whittemore that he follow me, as I knew the way through the surf better than he, but he had no use for directions. In going through the surf, my own boat occupied my whole attention. We did not ship a drop, but when I looked around I saw the other boat coming through the breakers end over end. It landed, bottom side up, on the beach. Everything was soaked and we had the laugh on them.

After they had dried off, we went up the river and Mr. Whittemore, noting the number of alligators, asked me if I was a good shot

with a rifle. I told him that if I was shut up in a barn I might hit one side of it. He seemed disgusted and said no one could beat him at shooting. I saw an alligator about 30 yards beyond and remarked, "There is one, shoot him!" He fired twice and missed both times, so I said, "let me have a shot?" I fired at about 40 yards and the alligator gave one jump and turned over, shot in the eye. I said, "that is the way I always shoot alligators!" But the truth of the matter was that I was as much surprised as he, for I did not expect to kill the animal. But I did not let Whittemore know that fact and my reputation was made for a shot. Mr. Whittemore took the alligator on board.

Soon after, we stopped at a place to camp, where we built a fire and cooked our supper. Mr. Whittemore had portions of the alligator made into a stew. He invited me to partake, but I thanked him politely and declined. He pressed me to taste it and I did so, though I could not swallow it. However, if I had not known what it was, I should have called it excellent.

An Inland Excursion

We stayed there all night and the next day proceeded on our way to the Everglades. The river gradually narrowed, and about sunset we found we could not go farther in boats. We decided to camp there for the night and make our explorations by land. We were then in a part of the Everglades where the land was low and swampy, with shoal water, six or eight inches deep, covering one or two acres.

The place where we left the boats was a little higher, with a growth of tall pines from 20 to 50 feet to the lowest branches. We made our fires and cooked our supper, and at 9 o'clock rigged our tents and tried to sleep. But, oh, the mosquitoes! They came in clouds and seemed as large as birds! Some of the men said their bills were more than a foot long and that they stuck them through not only the canvas in which the men vainly wrapped themselves, but even through the boot leather! A few of the men climbed to the treetops seeking relief, but found none. Some made a smudge of smoke and got a little rest that way. It was a fearful night. Nothing would have induced us to endure another in that place. The next morning all were a horrible sight, with faces covered with smut and swollen from the mosquito bites.

That forenoon we spent in exploring the country. We found wheel tracks, as though someone had been trying to pass that way, but saw no other sign that anyone had ever been there or that the place was inhabited. We started down the river that afternoon, and on our way located a camping place free from the dreaded pest. The next day we returned on board, having seen no sign that Davis was attempting to escape that way.

Back to Charleston, in Command

We remained at Jupiter Inlet until we heard that he had been captured, and we were then ordered back to Charleston. We did not go up the Cooper River again, but lay off the city. I frequently visited Dr. Ravanel's and he expressed much sorrow that I could not have charge of the river again. He said the Negroes had become lawless, in spite of the officers who succeeded me, and related an incident which came under his own observation.

He, with George N. Saunders, owner of "The Flags," was going from Dr. Ravanel's to Mr. Saunders' place, one day. En route, they had to cross a creek. Some of the Negroes they found guarding the bridge, who refused to allow them to pass, even denying the officer. The latter parleyed with them for some time and then gave up, and the two were obliged to make a detour of two or three miles. Dr. Ravanel was indignant.

As Capt. Mantell wished to stay in Charleston, he was detached and I was placed in command and ordered to Port Royal for some repairs and a supply of coal preparatory to going North. We finished our repairs and began to load coal. I reported to Capt. John J. Almy when I began to take coal, and he told me to report an hour before I was ready to leave, as he wished to send dispatches home.

When I had nearly finished coaling, I went on board the *Juniata* and told Capt. Almy, "I shall be ready in an hour, sir!'

He flared up somewhat, remarking, "I told you to report four hours before you would be ready!'

"All right, sir," said I, "I shall be ready in four hours!'

He laughed, and in about an hour he gave me the dispatches to the Secretary of the Navy, and I took my leave with many good wishes on his part.

I sailed for Charleston and reported to Admiral Dahlgren, who ordered me to proceed the next day to Philadelphia and report to General John B. Hull, and to the Secretary of the Navy by letter.

I bade my friends in Charlestown "good-bye" and started for the North. On arriving in Philadelphia I was ordered to give my crew ten days' leave and to put the steamer out of commission, after removing to the navy yard all small arms, ammunition and other stores.

I had a small boat which had belonged to the old, first *Monitor*, of which I thought a great deal. To preserve her, I presented her to Lieutenant Commander Oscar O. Badger of the ordnance department, who had been very kind in assisting me in many ways. He seemed much pleased and said he would take good care of the boat.

The officers of the navy yard were all kind— Commodores J. B. Hull, Henry K. Hoff and others. When I was through, Commodore Hull gave me final orders from the navy department to take two months' leave of absence and at the end of that time to report to the department by letter. So I went home, arriving there June 25, 1865. My brother, Elias, also was at home, and he and I did the haying on the farm.

July 25th, Rachel Wilson and I were married by the Reverend Moses Hanscom. We took our wedding trip to Portland, then to Winterport and home by way of Waterville, visiting our many relatives on the way.

My discharge from the navy came soon after I reported when my leave was up. It was dated August 20th, 1865.

In December 1865, Captain Curtis resumed his career by signing on as mate for the Eastern Star *of Bath. His further adventures are serialized in subsequent issues of the* Lewiston Journal Illustrated Magazine *of May and June, 1905.*

In his old age, he moved in with his only surviving son, Minot W. Curtis, who lived in Lewiston and wrote his autobiography (we have presented most of chapters IV through VII) at the urging of family members, who were fascinated by the yarns he had told them.

Also See

"Blockade Life," Military Order of the Loyal Legion of the United States, *War Papers: Read Before the Commandery of the State of Maine* 2, Portland, Maine: Lefavor-Tower Company, 1902, pp. 1–10.

THE HEROISM OF A MAINE WOMAN IN THE CIVIL WAR

L. C. BATEMAN

The wearers of the United States uniform are not the only military heroes in this country. The records of the Civil War teem with noble deeds and brave actions accomplished by civilians who were prompted by no other motive than a love of country and a desire to serve its flag. Among those who were most distinguished in this line of work were many of the gentler sex, who in times of peace would never have been suspected of martial valor or the physical courage to perform daring deeds. Too often have these been overlooked in order to give all the glory to the sons of fortune who carried the sword rather than the knapsack and blanket. The soldier in the heat of battle recks not of danger or death as the excitement of the hour banishes all thought of fear. Not so with the tender woman who goes into the dark prison to minister to disease and suffering, or rides through the deep forests and swamps to carry messages which may mean weal or woe to an army. No roar of cannon nerves the heart and sustains the arm in those lonely hours. Such sacrifice and such deeds can only come from hands and hearts inspired by lofty patriotism and to them we can never accord the just need of praise.

Maine can justly boast of one character who deserves to rank among the brave. Mrs. Mary K. Lynch of Dixfield has a history which for daring patriotism can hardly be exceeded in the annals of war. Her form is now bent with age but the dark eyes light with a sudden flash as the memories of the long ago come sweeping back. Her share in the Civil War was one that called for bravery, intelligence and energy demanded by no other calling. Not only was she a volunteer nurse on the field of battle and in the hospital but she was frequently called upon for deeds that none but the bravest were selected to perform. In one sense she might be called a Union spy but so thoroughly did she win the respect of the Confederate commanders that she was never placed under arrest. They feared and watched her, but with true Southern chivalry they permitted her in no way to be harmed.

Mrs. Lynch was born in the town of Canton in 1829 and while yet a child went to Dixfield with her parents and in that town her girlhood days were passed. In 1854 she was married to Dr. John W. Kneeland of New Hampshire, who was a graduate of the New Orleans medical college. Being in a delicate state of health Dr. Kneeland was advised to go to a Southern climate and accompanied by his bride he at once went to East Tennessee and settled in the town of Rodgersville, Hawkins County. As he had enjoyed the advantage of several years practice in the marine hospital of New Orleans he had no difficulty in securing a profitable business in his new Southern home. This was not destined to last long, however, as he was soon prostrated by the disease that had fastened upon his system, and in eleven months, death came to relieve his sufferings.

The widow at once came North but in a short time returned to East Tennessee where she had property interests. In speaking to the *Journal* very recently of the times and scenes that followed Mrs. Lynch said:

ORIGINALLY PUBLISHED IN *LEWISTON JOURNAL ILLUSTRATED MAGAZINE*, 14 FEBRUARY 1907.

"It was about the year 1855 that my husband died in Rodgersville and I returned to my old home in Maine for a short visit. I then went back to my Southern home intending to live there in the future.

"At that time the anti-slavery agitation ran very high, and East Tennessee was a slave section. And right here I want to correct one false impression. There is an almost universal opinion in Maine that all the slave holding states were eager for rebellion. Nothing could be farther from the truth. East Tennessee was intensely loyal, and sent no less than 30,000 men into the Union armies. It was a slave state and the slave owners frankly told their Negroes that war would inevitably mean their freedom. They also told the slaves that when that result came they wished their former slaves to remain with them and share in the productions of soil.

"Of course there were some Rebel sympathizers in Rodgersville. There was Joseph Haskell, who was so bitter that he left his home and went further south and finally became a member of the Rebel congress. He was a personal friend of mine, and never alluded to his Rebel sympathies in my presence. As far as I could observe, there was never any bitterness between the loyal and the disloyal in that section. They lived side by side and in the most friendly manner. If there was any danger coming to a Rebel sympathizer some Union man would at once put him on his guard and the same held true when reversed. A Union man was certain to be notified if he was in any danger from Rebel troops. And it was the same with their Negroes. I lived there 20 years and never heard of one of them being whipped. There was the most friendly relations between all classes to the last. Of course in Middle Tennessee the Rebel sentiment was very strong.

"When the war broke out, I was in Rogersville and excitement was high. We saw but little of it until the winter of 1863 and 1864, and then we suddenly found ourselves hemmed in between two hostile forces. Burnside with his army was on one side of us and General Longstreet and the Confederates on the other. Burnside had his headquarters in the village, while Longstreet was four miles away and located in a three-story brick farmhouse owned by a Mr. Rice. Things were looking badly for the Union forces.

"Then it became necessary to send a message to General Woods, who was in Rutledge, forty miles away. To reach him one must run the gauntlet of Rebel forces nearly all the way, and it was thought best that a woman should undertake the job, as she would not be shot or caught. I had a reputation of being a fearless horseback rider, and also of intense loyalty, so the Union commander pitched on me to do the work.

"I was given a swift and strong horse, and at daybreak commenced the ride of life or death. I had to cross the mountains in order to avoid the Rebel pickets and this made my journey doubly hard. The journey was made, however, and at night I found myself in Rutledge. On attempting to deliver my dispatch to General Woods I found that officer drunk and utterly unable to transact any business. I had hoped to ride back home under cover of darkness but now had to wait for the general to sober off.

"The next morning I delivered my message and told him of the condition of affairs in Rogersville. Then I rode eight miles to the railroad and took the cars for Knoxville where I reported to General Sam Carter who commanded the forces there. After receiving assurance that reinforcement would be sent at once I took to the saddle again and started back to Rogersville. So many Rebel soldiers were on the road that I had to go the entire distance in hog paths over and through the mountains.

"When I got within a few miles of Rogersville I met a friend who told me that I had better turn back as the Rebel General Vaughn had discovered what I had been up to and had ordered my arrest. I told the man that Rogersville was the home of my adoption and I should go there in spite of General Vaughn or anyone else. I kept on and reached my home that Saturday night.

"The next morning General Vaughn and two aides came to my house. Of course I at once admitted them and then came a woman's wit in beating them. In my cellar I had a quantity of blackberry wine and I told my Negro woman to bring up a bottle and set it before my guests. I knew the weakness of Vaughn and felt certain that I could get him drunk. As soon as the bottle was empty I had another one before them together with some cake. It was powerful liquor and Vaughn kept on drinking until he was nearly upset. All this time he had not said a word about my arrest, but finally he said in maudlin tones: 'Madame, I came here to have you arrested but you have been so kind I shall not do it!'

"I asked him who it was that had inspired the arrest and he said it was Joe Haskell. Five days later I had my revenge by seeing Haskell arrested by the Union soldiers and marched by my house. Haskell had told Vaughn that Mollie Kneeland would do more damage to the Confederacy than a half dozen regiments of Union soldiers!

"For more than two years I had been secreting Union prisoners in my house. Among our forces my place came to be known as a sort of underground railroad. The Rebel and Union forces swayed backward and forth and with each turn of the tide I was in demand. Rogersville was depopulated of all its men and only women, children, and Negroes were left. In many cases the old men had been taken for ransom and those who could get away had done so. Both armies used the women well although I was looked upon by the Confederates as a spy and therefore was in greater danger than the others.

"Oh! You want to know something about my career as an army nurse. Well, that is an important chapter in my life. My first experience was a bit discouraging on account of the ingratitude displayed. A Negro was taken with the smallpox and there was no one to take care of him. When I learned the situation, I made a long horseback ride for medicine and then took him to my house and cared for him until he recovered. I burned tar and sulfur to kill the germs and did not take the disease myself. At that time I had a crop of oats growing and they were ripe just about the time he got well. I asked him to gather them, but he was too lazy to help me, I had saved his life and that was the gratitude he showed.

"Then came the big battle in our village in the early part of 1864. The Rebels were 25 miles above Rogersville and the night previous there was a tremendous rainstorm. Under cover of darkness and storm they made a forced march, reached Rogersville in the early morning and completely surrounded our troops. The battle was a fearful one and the Rebels won. One Ohio regiment was completely cut to pieces. The Rebel commander then issued a proclamation giving permission to the Union women of the place to care for the Union wounded. Many of these were

packed into the hotel and a Mrs. Johnson, Mrs. Netherland and myself volunteered to nurse them. We cooked their food, dressed their wounds, and cared for them in the best possible manner. Many died and many recovered. Strange to say.

"There had been fighting around Knoxville and many sick and wounded soldiers were sent from there for us to care for. I gave my entire time to nursing although I knew that

CAPTAIN T. W. ALLEN, RESCUED BY MOLLY KNEELAND

I should get nothing for it. We used our own money to buy food and medicine for the sick and it was done out of pure patriotism. History will record that the women of East Tennessee were as patriotic and self-sacrificing as the world ever saw. The women in Rogersville who were with me in that work are now all dead. I am the last link in the chain. The worst feature of our work was that as soon as a man recovered, the Rebels would take him and send him to Libby prison. To prevent this I hid many of them in my house until they could escape. We had all sorts of experiences.

"I remember once secreting a Captain Allen of an Ohio regiment who had been captured by the Rebels and escaped. He came to a Negro cabin and sent for me. You understand I was noted far and near for aiding such cases. I furnished him blankets and hid him in the woods. When I carried him food I took along some medicine bottles so if the Rebels stopped me I could say that I was going to visit a sick child. I kept a man watching the Rebel lines while I was taking food to Captain Allen. Once I hung out a piece of red flannel which was a signal for him to come to my house for breakfast. There was another escaped prisoner with him, and I managed to keep them hid until I could get a guide to take them across the river to a railroad. Years afterwards Captain Allen wrote me a very kind letter and sent me his photograph. Here it is, and you may have it to put in the *Journal.*

"At another time my house was surrounded by Rebels at three o'clock in the morning. They said that there were two men in my house who were trying to escape and demanded an entrance. I always slept with an ax and pistol by my side and I told the officer that if he attempted to come in before I was dressed I would kill him. I got the men up as quickly as possible and gave them some breakfast, while the Rebels outside were waiting impatiently. There was no escaping, that time, so after an hour I let the Rebels in and they took the two men away. They would have shot them but one of the officers objected and it was not done. The very next night the two men again escaped and were back at my house. I again hid them and then rode several miles on horseback for a guide to take them away. They finally escaped.

"One day I walked 28 miles to save a man by the name of Clint Mitchell. When the Confederates evacuated Knoxville they took all their prisoners with them. Mitchell made his escape and came to my house with a young lady who was his cousin. The Union forces were at Bull's Gap, 28 miles distant, and they wanted me to guide them to that place.

"The next morning I got breakfast early and before daylight took them over the Holsten River and from there on to Bull's Gap on foot. The Rebels were all along the way but by dodging into the woods and following hog paths we managed to prevent them from seeing us. At Bull's Gap we found Colonel Crawford in command of the Union forces and I explained to him about the case of Mitchell and he had him sent back to Knoxville. The young lady and I then trudged back to Rogersville. We saw the Rebels in several places but they did not attempt to arrest us although they watched us closely. A man took us over the river and by bedtime we were back in my house after our long tramp.

"The Confederates once took my house for their headquarters and kept it for four weeks. The officers were lousy, and I mixed a sulfur salve that rid them of the pests. One of the lieutenants had a wife in Knoxville and he wanted me to take a message to her but the commanding officer would not let me go as he smilingly said that I was a dangerous woman and a spy. He treated me with great politeness, however.

"I will say this for the Confederates, they were gentlemen one and all. Never did I receive the slightest indignity at their hands, but on the contrary I received very many kind acts and courtesies. I remember one instance of this in the closing days of the war. A Mrs. Kyle who was a strong Union woman, although she had lost 40 Negroes, was in Rogersville and out of food. I was in nearly the same condition as the Union soldiers had taken about all I had. We got a Negro to harness up an ox in an old cart and took some corn and oats and started to the headquarters of General Longstreet where there was a mill. There were 5,000 Rebel soldiers with him four miles out of Rogersville. Mrs. Kyle and myself got on the cart and let the Negro drive. As we were poorly dressed the soldiers did not suspect that we had food until we reached the headquarters of the general. Longstreet came out on the piazza and when he found out our mission he told us to both come into his house. He then ordered a guard to go back with us to my house in order that no one should take our meal. I shall always remember General Longstreet as one of the kindest and most perfect gentlemen that I ever met. He was always ready to do a favor to a Union woman.

"I continued to nurse the wounded soldiers until the war was completely over. Then I had other experiences. On one occasion I drove 200 miles to Salem, North Carolina, to get five young ladies who were there at school. Three of us made the trip in carriages. The country was in full possession of the Union forces and they would seize every horse they could find. As I was so well acquainted with the Union officers I was taken along to prevent the horses being taken. We had a Negro with us to drive an express wagon for the baggage. The reason they wanted me to go with them was that the family were Rebels and they expected little mercy in the way of saving their horses. As I was known to be Union, we were not molested. The trip was made and we got the girls and brought them back to Rogersville. It was a hard journey as everything was in a chaotic condition. We would get help at some farmhouse at night and our food we took with us. In one house I slept with the maid and found they had the curious custom of sleeping under the featherbed!

"In one place on the trip we stopped in a hotel where there were some twenty or more Rebel officers. When they found that we had some coffee they were crazy for it and we gave them some. They were delighted and were profuse in their thanks as they had not even smelled coffee for four years.

"Oh, yes! Those were stern old days and as I look back I can only wonder how I lived through them all.

"The work that we women did in East Tennessee was from pure patriotism. We expected nothing in return, but the government has used us badly. Many of the Union forces that remained after the Confederates were gone, cut down our fences and used them for fuel, took our corn, oats, and other property. The Rebels could do no worse. Years afterwards when Congress passed a bill to recompense us, Grant vetoed it!

"I lived in Rogersville until 1883. Soon after the war ended I was married to George W. Lynch and we lived near by. This gentleman, my second husband, died in 1879.

"I knew Governor Bob Taylor well when I was in Rogersville, as he lived at Jonesville, only 30 miles away. He and my husband were great friends. Years afterwards I heard him lecture in Kansas City, and after he was through, I went on the stage and asked how the folks in Rogersville were. 'Who are you?' he asked. Then taking a sharper glance, he said: 'God bless you, it is George Lynch's widow.'"

It is indeed a thrilling tale that has been told to us by a woman who was widely known through two armies as Mollie Kneeland, the spy and nurse. She is now back in Dixfield, the home of her youth, and resides with her sister, Mrs. Viola M. Chase. Honored and respected by all, no one would suspect from her gentle manners that she was possessed of an iron nerve and capable of the endurance and deeds of daring that she has so often shown.

In 1892 Congress passed a law to pension the volunteer nurses of the war. Her associates of that day are on fame's eternal camping ground but in her old age she deserves well of the country she so nobly served. Our delegation in Congress can certainly do no kinder or juster deed than to place on the pension list one who has suffered and sacrificed so much for the defenders of the dear old flag.

Lisbon Falls Veteran Relates His Interview with Abraham Lincoln

L. C. BATEMAN

The rolling wheels of time have again brought around the day that has been set apart to honor the memory of those brave men, who in the dark days of the Civil War, gave up their lives that their country might remain a nation of the people, by the people and for the people. As we scatter the flowers above the graves of those we love, we should not forget that there are those who took a part in that bloody conflict still with us, and these should also be remembered. The brave did not all die. Through shot and shell, on the weary march and around the nightly bivouac fire they nobly performed their part, and maimed and wrecked they are still with us. On the coming Memorial Day, their tottering footsteps will seek the spots where sleep will revive the memories of the long ago. For them the taps will soon sound and they will be called to pitch their tents on that unknown shore beyond the dark river of death. While they remain among us we should twine the laurel wreath for them and speak of their own heroic deeds.

A fine old veteran is Joseph W. Wilber of Lisbon Falls, and he is one of the few men who had a personal interview and experience with Abraham Lincoln, the martyred president. Mr. Wilber was born 81 years ago in that part of Minot now known as Auburn, but his parents, Benjamin and Mary Wilber, removed later to a farm at the head of No Name Pond, where the parents died and which continued to be his home for many years.

With the first rumblings of the Civil War Mr. Wilber grew uneasy and wanted to be in the conflict, as he came from a fighting race. His grandfather, John Wilber of Durham, had fought in the Revolution and his father in the War of 1812. One brother was in the Aroostook scrap and several more were in the Civil War. Sniffing the battle from afar he dropped his hoe one morning, and coming over to Lewiston enlisted in the 19th Maine regiment and was soon down in old Virginia getting a taste of real war. His service was not long, for at the battle of Rapidan he was severely injured and unfitted for further service at the front. His regiment had been sent on a flank movement to distract the attention of Stonewall Jackson, but in the retreat which followed the regiment reached the Rappahannock River, where some rifle pits had been constructed close to the edge of the water. Into one of these he fell, and the impact severely injured three of the vertebra and broke the base of his backbone. That ended further military operations for him for a time and he was sent to the hospital in Alexandria where he remained for a time and was then transferred to the convalescent camp in Virginia where several weeks more were passed. He was then discharged from the service and returned to his Lewiston home.

Mr. Wilber was not satisfied with this, He felt that he was still able to do some sort of service, and going to Massachusetts he enlisted again, but this time in Hancock's Veteran Reserve Corps. These were men unfitted for active field service, but yet capable of doing guard service and camp work and thus relieving able-bodied soldiers for more strenuous

Originally published in *Lewiston Journal Illustrated Magazine*, 29 May 1914.

service at the front. After being in camp for a time he was sent to Washington where he was assigned to the 7th Veteran Reserve Regiment doing guard duty in that city. It was while there that he met Lincoln, and the resulting interview and experience was of a nature never to be forgotten. Let Mr. Wilbur tell the story in his own way:

"After enlisting in the Reserve Veteran Corps it was several weeks before I was assigned to a regiment and during that time was posted around to several places, finally bringing up in Washington, where I was placed in the Seventh Reserve Veterans, of Hancock's Corps. I had been on Gallops Island and in the hospital before being assigned to the Seventh Regiment and when pay day came around the paymaster refused to pay me from the time of my enlistment. It was a matter of several weeks and as I had been mustered into the service I could see no justice in being denied my pay. It was no use to talk to the paymaster, as he only abused me for my pains. Then the Indian in my nature was aroused and I made up my mind to go straight to Lincoln.

"On reaching the White House I was shown into the waiting room next to the President's office and I sat in a chair made from the bones of animals with the seat of the tanned leather. People came and went and finally Lincoln spied me and as my uniform attracted his attention he inquired of the guard what I wanted. Without waiting for a reply, he said—'Let my son in.'

"'That paymaster is a servant, not an autocrat. I am the President here, and you are here to back me. You are just as good as I am and he will find it out.'

"Just at that moment Adjutant General Hedges of Maine came in and Lincoln said to him—'Here is one of your boys from Maine.' They then entered into conversation and Hedges noticing that I was very tall asked Lincoln to stand back to back with me to see which was the taller. We did this and Hedges exclaimed: 'Why, the President is a head taller than you!' Lincoln then asked me my height and I told him it was six feet two and one-half inches. He laughed and replied: 'Oh, I am six feet seven and a half inches!' And this he repeated several times.

"While I was there I saw one of the scenes that had made him prematurely gray and old. Two Southern women came in and asked him to allow their brother, who was a prisoner,

leave to go South. That was on the 18th of February, 1865, and a law had been passed by Congress and signed by him saying that no more prisoners should be exchanged. Lincoln took down a book and read the law to them and then said that it was out of his power to grant their request. They persisted and he gently refused. Then they turned on him with the most violent abuse and called him the vilest names. Lincoln turned red in the face and then deathly pale, but bit his lips and made no reply until they turned to go. Then he merely said: 'Good day, ladies, if I can call you ladies!' That gave me an idea of what he was obliged to go through and I no longer wondered that he was growing old. It was only a few weeks after that when he was assassinated.

"Then I took my letter from him and went over to the commanding officer. He read the note and turning to the aide gave some command. The officer disappeared and the general turned to me and said: 'You can report at your headquarters at once.'

"When I reached the headquarters I found the paymaster there and he had my money. He was angry and started in to abuse me, but I at once told him if he said another word I would go back and see Lincoln again. That shut him up for good, as I got my money and sent it home to my mother.

"I guess I must have come from fighting blood. My great-grandfather and his three brothers were in the English Army sent over here to subdue the colonies. With them were two brothers named Jones and after getting to Boston, the whole bunch deserted and joined the Continental Army. Later they were captured by the English, court martialled and sentenced to be shot. Before the day of execution they dug out of their prison, and by tramping nights and sleeping days they finally reached Scarboro, where they made friends with the Indians. Later this great-grandfather took up land and married an Indian woman. Still later they came to Durham. It is a singular fact that all the Wilber and Jones boys came from the same town in England. My father was born in Durham and of course was quarter Indian. Perhaps that blood is where I get my love of the woods and hunting from. The Jones boys also married squaws and their children were all great hunters and fishermen, like myself."

Mr. Wilber has been twice married. His first

wife died within a short time, and after a few years he married Miss Eleanor M. Merry of Garland. Five children have been born to the union, and one of these, William Wilber served in the Spanish War and was in the Philippines for twenty months of hard service. This son is now a resident of Portland while the others live away.

In speaking of the Civil War again, Mr. Wilber said: "It is a curious fact that my brother James Wilber and my wife's brother, William Merry, were both shot before Richmond and at almost the same moment. They were in the 8th Maine and in the same company and in the battle they both fell at the same moment, while standing side by side. Oh, yes, I often think of those old days, but cannot say that I would like to live them over."

ALSO SEE

"Called to Capital by Pres. Lincoln," *Portland Evening Express*, 11 February 1909 (Lincoln Centennial Supplement), p. 7.

"Civil War Veteran Met Lincoln," *Portland Sunday Telegram*, 21 September 1930, p. 2B.

"Her Father Guarded Lincoln," *Portland Evening Express*, 12 February 1959, p. 1.

"Livermore Falls Veteran Who Served as Lincoln's Bodyguard," *Lewiston Journal Illustrated Magazine*, 10 Jauary 1920, p. 10.

"Maine Hs Some Links with Abraham Lincoln," *Lewiston Journal Illustrated Magazine*, 7 February 1970, pp. 1, 4.

"Maine Woman Who Frequently Met Pres. Lincoln," *Lewiston Journal Illustrated Magazine*, 7 February 1925, pp. 1–2.

"A Personal Friend of Abraham Lincoln," *Lewiston Journal Illustrated Magazine*, 16 March 1907, pp. 1, 4–5.

"Rare Lincoln Relics and Pithy Maine Lincoln Writings Abound," *Lewiston Journal Illustrated Magazine*, 6 February 1960, pp. 1, 6–8.

"She Knew Pres. Lincoln," *Lewiston Journal*, 15 August 1906, p. 6.

"Tribute to Lincoln by Maine Member of President's Bodyguard," *Lewiston Journal Illustrated Magazine*, 8 February 1941, p. 4.

"Veteran of Twenty-Four Battles," *Lewiston Journal Illustrated Magazine*, 4 February 1906, p. 8.

WELL, WHY DON'T YOU SHOOT?

ANONYMOUS AND A. H. HUTCHINSON

One picture of War is often painted by storytellers. It brings out the roar of cannon, the charge of legions and the spirit of the battlefield. Here pain and bloodshed are necessary parts of glorious victory or valiant defeat. Conquerors' cheers conceal the wounded's cries.

That is the picture we prefer to look upon. But it is only part—a very little part—of the game called War.

The other picture that we don't often see consists of consequences. For example, there is the dull monochrome of those falling into the hands of the enemy and languishing in prison cells. This isn't a pleasant picture to gaze at, stripped, as it is, of glitter and tinsel. But it's a picture that will never fade, so long as there are veterans left to muse upon the days of their young manhood spent behind the dead-lines of southern stockades.

The story that follows is of this second kind. It consists of the words of a man who has suffered much and told but little. He rarely talks of his army life, and today's story is one that has never been printed, and appears almost against the will of him that tells it. It is the story of a southern prison the average reader will remember but little, for Camp Ford has not had the notoriety of Andersonville or Libby. Yet men died within it like sheep and conditions were so awful that men took every chance to escape its confines.

The man telling this story is Mr. A. H. Hutchinson, now a resident of Gardiner, Maine, and the prison of which the tale of escape and recapture is told was situated near Tyler, Texas.

Hutchinson had enlisted in the Tenth Maine Infantry in August, 1861, belonging to the one company in the outfit which came from Aroostook County. He served a year in that regiment, and on his discharge reenlisted in the Fifteenth Maine Infantry. He was thrice wounded, at Cedar Mountain, at Antietam and finally at the battle of Pleasant Hill, La., while serving General Banks' ill-fated expedition up the Red River. He lay on the field of battle, after this last mentioned engagement, until taken prisoner and hurried on to Tyler, Texas, where he was imprisoned on the 27th of May, 1864.

And it is of his escape from Camp Ford, and his subsequent recapture and confinement in the jail at Tyler, that this story deals. It begins on the 18th of March, 1865, at a time when Hutchinson had been some ten months in prison and was so weary and sick of the life that he and his companions were willing to take any chance to effect their escape. It is a story that holds one from its opening till its pathetic close, needing no embellishment to make it more interesting. I tell it much as it was told me, though much questioning was required to pry loose some details in which Hutchinson is most personally concerned. He does not like the idea of posing as the hero of even his own story, and very much deprecates the necessity of telling it in the first person.

"James Bickford of the navy, John Winship and Charles Decker of the Eighteenth New York cavalry, Tom Whislehurst of the Third Arkansas and myself had tried tunneling with the rest of the prisoners in a hopeless attempt at escape. But we gave that up and finally accomplished by strategy what we had been unable to effect by digging.

"Along toward the last of our confine-

Originally published in Lewiston Journal Illustrated Magazine, 30 May 1903.

ment the rebels had established what they called a hospital, over near the colonel's headquarters, outside the stockade. So far as being a hospital, it hardly deserved the name. It was a shack built of poles and brush, under which the sick and dying were carried to breathe their last. A detail of the prisoners was sent with the sick, to care for them as long as they lived and bury them when dead. The nurses had passes to go out and in the stockade anytime between roll-call in the morning and sundown.

"So far as I know, I originated the plan of escape by which we made our way from the prison. I talked with the nurses at different times and after awhile prevailed on them to assist us. Five of them were to come in from the hospital and give us their passes. As soon as the guard was changed at the gate we five were to go out as nurses, presenting at the gate the passes which we had borrowed.

"Everything worked as we had planned. The guard passed us without a word, though he looked at me so closely that I feared we were detected. My hand trembled so that I could hardly take the pass as he returned it. It was risky work at best, for there was the order nailed to the gate, commanding the guards to shoot any prisoners caught attempting escape. We made no unnecessary stop at the gate and on our arrival at the hospital sent the passes back by one of our officers, so that the nurses could come and attend to their duties. We stayed at the hospital till after dark and then began the work of threading our way between the guards that were thrown out to prevent escape from the hospital. We were two or three hours getting by the guard line and out of hearing of the sentries. Eventually, we came to a point of comparative safety, and, taking the north star for a guide, we struck out toward God's country.

"We tramped all night, giving farmhouses a wide berth, lest we should awaken the

Mr. A. H. Hutchinson

hounds. At daybreak we hid away in the woods until night should again lend us its friendly shade to continue our tramp. I think we had the worst scare of the trip this day. About noon we heard the baying of a pack of hounds, and, as the sound came nearer and nearer, we felt certain that they were after us from the fort. So close did the sound come that we took to the trees. It proved to be a false alarm, however, for the pack swerved off to one side, leaving us to come down and rest till night-fall.

"When the woods grew dark we started, pushing on through the tangled growth and keeping up as fast a pace as we could. Shortly before daylight we came to the Sabine River. We could hear the sweep of the waters, but we had to wait for daylight to find out how much of a river it was. And when the light came, what a sight met our eyes! The Sabine, swollen by the heavy rainfalls of the last few weeks, had overflowed its banks and the bottom land on each side of the stream was flooded. As far as the eye could see through the woods was nothing but one vast body of water. Here and there a high knoll made a small island among the trees. It was a dubious prospect at best, and Whislehurst, who came from Arkansas, and knew the kind of territory we were in, added to our misery by telling us that the bottom lands were often two miles in width on each side of the river. We found that he spoke the truth, for the Sabine was certainly four miles wide where we crossed it.

"It was a dreary outlook, but it was a case of cross the river or go back to the fort, and of the two evils we chose the first.

"To add to our troubles, Whislehurst could not swim. We did not wait for night here, for we knew that until we reached the other side of the stream we feared pursuit. We slept till we were somewhat rested and then began the crossing of the river. Sometimes we waded in water that varied in depth from waist to neck, and again we had to swim for it from one knoll to another. We hauled Tom along with the aid of a grapevine, torn from a tree. Most of the time when we hauled him in this way he was under the water, but he was so irrepressibly good-natured that when he came up at the end of the haul he was always on the broad grin.

"It was just before nightfall that we reached the main river. It was not over five rods in width, but the current was swift, and we decided to spend the night on a high knoll and wait for the morrow for the final crossing. We were beginning to realize what was staring us in the face—hunger. We had started with quite a quantity of parched meal which we had bought and saved for the occasion, but this had not only gotten wet but was now nearly gone. On the smallest possible allowance what we had left would last us but another day.

"It was a discouraging situation, but cold and wet and hungry we lay down and were soon asleep, guarded by a stretch of water two miles wide up on each side of us. At daylight we were up and planning to cross the main stream. It was Whislehurst that bothered us. The rest of us could get across, but the Arkansan was helpless. We finally built a sort of raft of logs and brush. We bound the brush together with withes, and, while it wasn't a very elaborate boat, we thought it would serve its purpose.

"To the raft we fastened a long grapevine and then cast lots to see who should be the first to try the current of the stream and carry the improvised cable to the other shore. The lot fell to me, and putting the slip-noose over my up-river shoulder I struck out. The men on the knoll were to play out the grapevine as fast as I wanted it. Things went all right till I reached the middle of the stream. Just then the slack of the vine caught on a snag. This prevented my going ahead, so, of course, I began drifting rapidly down the stream. When I got to the end of the vine the noose began to tighten, and for a few moments my life hung in the balance, with the chances all toward my never seeing another sunrise.

"The force of the current kept me under water most of the time, making the struggle all the more frightful. It was only by the most desperate efforts that I broke loose, and then I was too exhausted to swim further, but just managed to keep my head above water till I touched bottom at a bend of the river some distance below and on the same side from which I had started. Winship and Bickford were there to meet me and helped me to the shore, where I lay and gasped for a long time.

"I didn't relish the idea of trying the passage again, but there was not other way for it, and, after making a new cable, I plunged in once more. This time I reached the other side without difficulty and we hauled Tom over and went on our way. It took us till evening to reach dry land—two whole days to get across the river! We were now absolutely without anything to eat and must try for food at all hazards. Whislehurst left us as soon as it was light enough for him to find his way. He was gone so long that we feared he had been lost, and we were just on the point of going further into the swamp when he returned with some corn meal, some bacon and some corn dodgers already cooked. You may depend that we weren't long getting outside that corn dodger. Then, fearing that the Negroes who had given Whislehurst the food might give us away, we went further into the swamp and waited for dark to come.

"All that night we followed the north star, lying low till it gleamed again, and then taking up our march once more. We made slow progress now, for Winship, Decker and myself were barefooted and our feet were badly torn and bruised. The underbrush and briars were so close and thick at times that we could not force our way through them. Another day we lay in the swamp, and as darkness fell pushed on again. About midnight we came to what appeared to be another river. We waited for daylight and then found that we indeed had another river to cross. Off to our right we saw a clearing and a small cabin, from the chimney of which the smoke soon began to rise. Being again out of rations we decided to try our luck at the cabin. An old man answered our knock and invited us in. The household consisted of only the old man, his wife and a Negro girl. We told him who we were and offered to buy anything he had in the way of rations. He replied by telling us that he had served three years with the Confederate army, for which he had never received a dollar, and that all there was in the house to eat was a piece of ham and thirty or forty pounds of corn meal.

"The old woman had been eyeing us sharply.

" 'Be you-uns real Yankees?' she asked.

"We told her that we guessed we were a fair sample of live Yankees.

"'Shucks!' she exclaimed. 'You-uns don't look no diffr'nt 'n anybody else!'

"With which she went on with her weaving with a sort of look of disappointment.

"At last we prevailed upon the old man to take a dollar for all the rations he had, and he declared it was more specie that he had seen since the war began.

"He told us the stream was the Big Sandy and he volunteered to show us the ford, making us hustle for all we were worth, for he said that if he was seen aiding us to escape it would be as much as his life was worth. We waded and swum for about a mile till we found ourselves on the other side of the river, and then went into the swamp, where we ate a part of our provisions and lay down to sleep.

"That night we pressed on through fields and woods across slough holes, where the mud was often up to our waists. Our courage was good and we were beginning to believe that we were past the worst of our journey. We kept on and on in the same way, sleeping days and traveling nights, till we had been away from the stockade about two weeks. Tom thought we must be very near the Red River, and once across that he said we should be in Arkansas, where he knew the folks that could be trusted. We felt sure that we were going to see the old flag once more, and each day we took new heart.

"But we did not know what was just ahead of us. Deciding to come out of the swamp along toward the close of the day to try to locate some road that would lead up to the river, we came suddenly upon a white man, skinning a sow that had got hung in the fence we were cautiously skirting. Before we had a chance to turn back he saw us.

"'Hullo, boys!' he shouted. 'Out hunting?'

"'Well, no,' I replied, 'we belong to Hood's army and are on our way back from parole camp.'

"He grinned.

"'Well, boys,' said he, 'I have seen too many Yankee eyes to be deceived that way. I jes' reckon you-uns are from Camp Ford. I wuz down there guardin' you-uns fer awhile.'

"We owned up and he told us it was only fifteen miles to the Red River and directed us down a road that he said led direct to the river. The rest of the boys thought that he was all right but I had my fears and the further we went the more certain I seemed to feel that he was going to give us up. We found the road and then went into the woods to wait for dark-ness. We hadn't been there more than an hour when we heard the sound of hounds. The cry was a long ways off, but there was no mistaking the awful sound. The cry of the blood-hound strikes terror to the heart of the fugitive and as we lay there how we wished for a seven-footer, or even for our rifles. All we had between us was one little knife and we didn't like to think what that would be worth in a pack of blood-thirsty bloodhounds. We staid in the woods long enough to find that the hounds were undoubtedly on our trail. Then we broke for Red River. We had gone about half a mile when we came in sight of a house. We tried to get there ahead of the hounds and just succeeded. But it was a narrow margin for when we burst through the door, the dogs were but twenty rods away. Away behind them came Hicks (the man we met by the fence) and his son, a boy about twelve, both on horseback and each with a double-barreled shotgun slung across the pommel of his saddle.

"The house into which we had broken we found to be tenanted by an old man and an old woman who gave us their name as Pistole and promised that we should not be turned over to Hicks. Hicks rode up to the door and demanded us. The old man Pistole refused, saying that he should take us to the proper authorities at Clarksville and give us up properly but would never turn us over to the mercy of a pack of hounds. Hicks raved and swore for some time but the old man was game and Hicks finally called off his dogs and went home with his son.

"We found the old man to be a staunch Unionist at heart, and his eyes filled as he spoke of the flag. But he said that he could not help us, for if his neighbors so much as suspected that he was not Secesh to the core, they'd string him up without further notice.

"'All a man of my age can do,' said the old man, brokenly, 'is to join right in with 'em, cuss the Unionists and not let on even to his wife that his heart is true to the old flag.'

"He knew whereof he spoke for he told us that he had seen twenty-four men hung in a single day declaring that they believed in the Union.

"When we spoke of trying to reach the river, he said we could try it, though it would be sure [to be] an instant death to him in the morning. We could not permit this, so we gave up all hope of ever getting away and resigned ourselves to going to Clarksville with him in the morning. Hope died within us to think of giving up after going through all that we had suffered, risked and endured. It was a bitter moment for us all. Nevertheless, we shook it off and lay down and slept as though we hadn't a care in the world.

"The next morning, after a good breakfast, we started with Pistole for Clarksville, a distance of eight miles away. On our arrival we were turned over to the enrolling officer and used well until the next day when we started under a guard of five men from Camp Ford, the guards having been given their orders in our presence to shoot the first man that left the middle of the road.

"I wish I could pass over that march to the prison, that I might blot it from my mind forever. Picture, if you will, five half-starved, half-naked men, only two having shoes on their feet, marching over a hard road, their feet swollen and blistered, crippling along to keep up with the horses of the guard, being cursed and sworn at for not keeping up. If you can imagine this, you can judge my feelings on the second day of that march back to prison. Never but twice have I had such a feeling of utter despair.

"That morning my feet were so swollen and cracked that the blood started out at every step. I had crept along for two or three hours, being constantly sworn at for not keeping up. I grew so desperate that I have often wondered since if I was not insane.

"At last I deliberately walked over to the side of the road and sat down, determined not to take another step if I died for it."

The sergeant in charge of the guard ordered me back into the road, his cocked revolver being within a foot of my head.

"'Go back into the road,' he yelled. 'You heard my orders, and if you don't march, I'll shoot.'

"'Shoot then, and be damned to you!' I retorted.

"But he didn't shoot, and for five minutes I raved like a madman, damning the whole southern confederacy from Jeff Davis with every oath that I could lay my tongue to, and I had been in the army long enough to have heard a few. The guard kept his finger on the trigger all through my tirade but never pulled it, and when I finished cussing him out, I looked up at him.

"'Well, why don't you shoot?' I asked savagely.

"'I s'pose I'd oughter,' he drawled in a good-natured Southern way. 'I s'pose I'd oughter, but I haint er goin' to, fer I'll be dog-goned ef ye haint game, even ef ye be a Yank.'

"With that he called up one of his men and made him dismount, telling me to get on and ride for awhile. I took turns with the guards all the day, and they even went so far as to let Bickford and Winship ride part of the time. And when you know how bad a Texan hates to walk, you'll realize that them fellers had pretty good hearts.

"The next night we reached a parole camp, and there I had one of the most exciting bits of experience that came to me in the whole time we were on the march. There were four or five hundred soldiers present from different camps. One of them who was pretty drunk was riding up and down, firing his revolver and whooping for Jeff Davis. After awhile he spurred his horse through the crowd to where we were and got his bloodshot eye on me.

"'Look yeare,' said he, 'I'll bet a horse you're a Southerner.'

"I didn't think it was wise to contradict him and neither did I want to bring a hornet's nest round my head by saying I was a Southerner, so I compromised.

"'Maybe I am,' said I, 'but I was born in the state of Maine.'

"'That's a damned lie!' he snarled. 'You back up ergin that 'ere buildin' an' I'll damn soon find out whether you're a Southerner.'

"I didn't think my life was worth a picayune, for if I didn't do as he told me, he'd likely shoot me as I stood, and if I did as he told me, I had a very good idea that he was going to use me for a target.

"I kind of set my teeth together and allowed to myself that I could show that a Yankee didn't mind being under fire. I stood with my back to the building and stood there without flinching while he rode off about six rods and fired at me four times with his revolver. Some of the shots struck very near my head, but I never moved a hair, for I was bound that gang of rebels shouldn't see a Yankee show the white feather.

"After the fourth shot the fellow put up his revolver and rode off, swearing he knew damned well I was a Southerner.

"From the parole camp we were marched directly to the stockade and taken before Col. Brown. I shall never forget the look of devilish malignity with which he looked us over, saying: 'You have made your escape from the stockade. I don't want to know how you got out, but as you are too clever to stay in there I will send you up to Tyler, where you will be sure to stay and where you will have a chance to get the tan off and get bleached out before your government wants you.'

"With the grin still on his face, he called the guard and said: 'Take these men to Tyler and if one of them offers to step out of the road shoot him as you would a dog.'

"When we reached Tyler and were sent to our prison we realized then that the stockade with all its misery and suffering was a paradise upon earth beside what we now faced. The cell or dungeon into which we were thrust was in the corner of the building and partly under ground. It was about ten-by-twelve feet in size, all the light and air that entered coming from a narrow slit, two feet wide and six inches high, so near the ceiling that we could not see out of it.

"The walls were covered with planks driven as full of spikes as they could hold, the floor and ceiling being done the same way. The 'door' was about two-by-three feet in size, close to the floor, so that it was necessary to get down on one's hands and knees to enter. This door was a double one, one being made of wood and the other of iron. Inside this cell was an iron cage, six feet square, set up on blocks about a foot from the floor, with a door so that it could be locked if necessary. Our only chance to lie down was on the floor with our feet stretching in under the cage.

"In this miserable hell we found ten of our comrades who had been sent here for attempting to escape. Our own condition was pitiable enough, but it was nothing to that of the men we found in the jail. It was a case of systematic murder—fifteen of us confined in a room only ten-by-twelve feet in size. There we stayed for twenty-seven days, not being allowed out for any purpose whatsoever, save that one man was permitted to go outside for about an hour each day to cook the cornbread for us all. One pail of water per day and a little piece of cornbread no larger than one's hand was all we had for rations, and they would not allow us to clean out our cell at all. So awful did conditions become that when one of our number died his body had the appearance of smallpox.

"We tried to secure liberation on the strength of this and told the guard that it was smallpox. It scared the guard and he sent for a surgeon. The surgeon came. But he would not come inside our cell and made us drag the body to the door. He gave one look, said it was not smallpox, and went away. That ended that idea of getting out, and we settled back to suffer, day in and day out, much of the time, I think, being out of our right minds—the only thing to look forward to being the hour for one of our number to go out and cook the rations. Then to eat, then to sit back and wait for the hour to come again the next day.

"I have no question but that my own mind wandered, and I think it must have been much the same with the others. I can recall absolutely nothing of some days and there were visions that haunted me. One of them was the idea that I had a double. This duplicate of myself used to sit by my side hours at a time, and I could see myself just as plainly as though in a looking-glass. He would sit by me and we used to talk and talk, though what we said was never very clear to me afterward. That was one of the visions that came to me most often. Another was the picture of a log house in the woods and a mother praying for a son that would never return. This latter vision seemed to be a long ways in the dim and misty past, and I never got very near to the cabin—there always seemed to be something that kept me from getting very close. As for the future, that seemed an absolute blank and I could see nothing but cruelty, starvation and death.

"Better a thousand times a speedy death to the suffering that we endured! Some of us used to pray, but curses were oftener heard—curses for the rebel government—aye, even curses against our own government for leaving us there to die. How quickly at that time would we have seized the opportunity to have taken our guns and gone into the thickest of the hottest battle of the war!

"And yet there are some who will tell you that the men in these prisons were 'safe and out of danger'!

"Again, as we watched the days drag by, there came to me that feeling of utter hopelessness and we planned an exploit that we thought would lead—not to liberty, but to death and release. About sundown every day the guard came to give us our pail of water, and in order to do this he had to open the doors and come part way in. We planned to seize the guard as he set down the pail, drag him into the cell and then make our escape to the corridor. There was a guard on each side of the jail, one in the corridor leading to our cell, and right across the street, in an old church, was a full company of rebel cavalry. This will show you how utterly hopeless was our situation and to what desperation we had come.

"The appointed day came. Winship and a fellow named Potter were to seize the guard, while the rest of us made a break into the corridor. I suppose the man that went out to cook our rations must have betrayed us, for when Winship and Potter secured the guard the first man into the corridor met the volley of a passage-full of guards waiting for us. Only one man was hurt, and his wound was a shot through the arm. The guard fired too soon and too high to get the rest of us.

"We let the guard go and then it seemed to occur to us all at the same time that the cook must have betrayed us. We fell on him like savages and would have killed him in short order had not his cries for help brought the guards. They dragged him out, more dead than alive, and we never saw him after that.

"As a punishment we received nothing to eat or drink the day following. The next day we got our rations as usual and the guard told us that there was big news—that the war was over and that Lincoln was assassinated. We didn't believe it, but a few days afterward he threw in a piece of paper that proved to be a general order from General Kirby Smith, stating that the Confederacy had fallen and that Kirby Smith wanted to hold Texas against the Union and never surrender.

"It was good news, and at the same time it wasn't, for if Kirby Smith held out that meant long imprisonment, and long imprisonment meant the most horrible of deaths.

"The next day the guard told us that Smith could not hold his army, that it was breaking up and going home. Within a week we were on our way to Camp Ford. But such a spectacle! Of the fifteen men that had been thrown into that cell, six had died, one had been shot in attempting to escape, and, though he did not die, we never saw him again; and one had been taken away to save him from the men he had betrayed. That left only seven of us to walk forth to Camp Ford. Seven men, but what pitiable wrecks! Hollow-cheeked, sunken-eyed, with long, matted hair and beards, bare-footed and covered with indescribable filth and vermin. It was a sight to wring tears from an image of stone. Yet when we reached the stockade and were lined up before the colonel

in command, who had sent us away twenty-seven days before, the same fiendish grin was on his face as he surveyed his work.

"I wish my story might stop here, but the saddest part is to come. It is a part of the tale that makes me wince as I tell it. It concerns Winship, that brave, loyal heart who had stood beside me in all that we had undertaken, my comrade in all our attempts to escape, the man who was always cheerful, patient and full of courage under the most trying circumstances.

"For all his nerve, he could never bear restraint, and when brought face to face with the man that had sent us to that jail of living death, he broke forth and told him what he thought of his act. He told him that in the North they would not put swine in such a hole without cleaning them out and that he had murdered our comrades who lay buried at Tyler. This and much more he said to him in the heat of his anger, and the man to whom he spoke never showed that he heard him till he finished. Then, with that same smile on his face, he told the guard to take Winship back to Tyler and keep him there till he learned to hold his tongue.

"It sounded to me like a sentence of death, and so I think it proved for we never heard from Winship again. Winship pressed our hands in silence and walked away with bowed head, despairing, but too proud and too much of a hero to beg for quarter.

"His death, alone in that awful cell with never a hand reached out to him in the darkness, never the consolation of a comrade's cheer when the end came, has seemed and will ever seem to me the most awful picture of all the horrors of war that I witnessed."

Also See

"Auburn Veteran Relates Experiences in Rebel Prison Pens of the South," *Lewiston Journal Illustrated Magazine,* 31 May 1924, pp. 1–3.

"Civil War Prison Life Described by One of Maine's Two Survivors," *Lewiston Journal Illustrated Magazine,* 20 June 1964, pp. 5, 10.

"Horrors of Andersonville Prison Pictured by Men Who Survived Its Tortures," *Lewiston Journal Illustrated Magazine,* 15 Sepember 1906, pp. 8–10.

"In Battle and Dungeon," *Lewiston Journal Illustrated Magazine,* 24 May 1911, pp. 1–4.

"Jerry Foley—Survivor of Many Wounds and

Eight Months in Libby," *Lewiston Journal Illustrated Magazine,* 29 May 1914, pp. 1, 4, 16.

"Jottings from Libby Prison," *Lewiston Journal Illustrated Magazine,* 16 April 1904, p. 9.

"Leaves from Diary of Auburn Man Kept in Libby and Andersonville Prisons," *Lewiston Journal Illustrated Magazine,* 24 May 1913, pp. 4–5.

"Life in Libby," *Maine Farmer* 60, 15 September 1892, p. 4.

"Old Letters by Boothbay Soldier Who Starved in Andersonville Prison," *Lewiston Journal Illustrated Magazine,* 29 May 1914, p. 9.

"Our Escape from a Rebel Prison," *Lewiston Journal Illustrated Magazine,* 11 January 1908, p. 5.

"Out of Salisbury's Rebel Prison," *Lewiston Journal Illustrated Magazine,* 12 October 1901, p. 3.

"A Prisoner of Maffit," *Lewiston Journal Illustrated Magazine,* 21 August 1909, p. 2.

"A Prisoner of War at Seventeen Years," *Lewiston Journal Illustrated Magazine,* 6 September 1926, pp. 3 , 16.

"Starved in Libby Prison," *Lewiston Journal Illustrated Magazine,* 28 May 1921, p. 12.

"The Story Told by an Old Diary of a Union Soldier Who was in Libby Prison in the Days of the Tunnel Escape and in Other Rebel Pens," *Lewiston Journal Illustrated Magazine,* 1 March 1913, pp. 8–9, 11.

"A Survivor of Andersonville," *Lewiston Journal Illustrated Magazine,* 25 May 1912, p. 9.

"A Survivor of Four Rebel Prisons," *Lewiston Journal Illustrated Magazine,* 31 October 1903, pp. 1–2.

"Thomas Gould, Civil War Veteran, Lisbon Falls, was Taken Prisoner in Battle of Gettysburg," *Lewiston Journal Illustrated Magazine,* 25 May 1929, p. 1.

"Torture by Rebels Drove Him Insane," *Bangor Daily News,* 17 April 1901, p. 7.

"A Trip to Richmond," *Lewiston Journal,* 28 October 1871, p. 1.

"A Year in Rebel Prisons," *Lewiston Journal Illustrated Magazine,* 26 May 1917, p. 5.

AFTER THE WAR

After the Civil War ended, its effects lived on. For example, because of the war, John Wilkes Booth assassinated President Lincoln. Because Lincoln was killed, the South was probably treated more harshly during Reconstruction than it would have been otherwise. And because of this harsh treatment, Southerners' hatred simmered for generations.

Ironically, the brother of famous newspaper editor Charles Dana could have saved Lincoln's life. David Dana got wind of a plot, and had Booth and his co-conspirator Harold in custody on the day of the assassination, but was ordered to let him go. Notwithstanding, Provost Dana, having "authority over nearly all . . . parts of Maryland lying between the east branch of the Potomac and the Patuxent" Rivers, pursued both Booth and Harold after the fatal shot was fired. His intelligent actions ultimately foiled their plan for escape.

Several other Mainers, including Hannibal Hamlin's daughter, witnessed Lincoln's assassination on the evening of April 14, 1865. But Dr. O. K. Yates, a West Paris native, provides the most detail. An off-duty secret service agent, he was at Ford Theater merely for entertainment on the evening Lincoln was shot. Instead, Yates encountered a night of terror such as he never wanted to experience again. Years later, Yates earned a medical degree from Bowdoin—it had a medical school at the time—and settled down to practice in Maine.

In 1866, central Maine became the site of the nation's first home for disabled soldiers. At its heyday, the Togus home functioned as a small city, complete with opera house and band. Among its residents were such worthy personages as Richard Rowley, who served as a captain of the guns on the *Kearsarge* during its epic struggle against the Rebel raider *Albemarle*. More than 130 years later, a veterans center still exists at Togus.

Andrew Johnson succeeded Lincoln as President of the United States. A Democrat in political persuasion, he had enemies among the Radical Republican Reconstructionists, who attempted to impeach him in the spring of 1868 because of his

moderate policies. The impeachment might have happened if not for the cooler heads of Maine Senator William Pitt Fessenden and seven others. Fessenden was born in New Hampshire, but grew up in Maine and lived here for the rest of his life. Many considered him Maine's "ablest statesman" and the U.S. Senate's "ablest debater." Johnson's impeachment trial was Fessenden's finest hour, but unfortunately, that one vote ended his political career and possibly shortened his life.

In Ted Turner's movie *Gettysburg*, Jeff Daniels steals the picture as Joshua L. Chamberlain. But an even more impressive movie could be made of Chamberlain single-handedly defusing an incipient Maine rebellion in1880, when state election results were being bitterly disputed. He was an obvious choice to handle this type of crisis and bring reason to the State House, having been previously elected Major General "and assigned to the military command of the entire state." During the crucial twelve days, he had to force the disputants to submit to legal judgment, put down a riot, dodge kidnappers, and decline offered bribes.

Several North/South reunions took place at Gettysburg, scene of the Civil War's most famous battle. They provided a meeting place for old friends, and helped old enemies become new friends. Many stories were swapped, and, in the article we present from Henry M. Grigg, of Portland, an old Confederate tells of his participation in Pickett's charge. Chamberlain attended this reunion, looking as impressive as ever, but it was to be his last; he died little more than seven months later.

Loudville, a Maine island community if Muscongus Bay, may —or may not—have withdrawn from the United States because their 1860 Democratic votes were not counted by Republican Bristol. The anonymous article we include claims that loudville did, in fact, withdraw from the United States, the State of Maine, and the Town of Bristol. Its inhabitants paid no taxes, participated in no wars, and pelted invaders with potatoes. Indeed, they didn't decide to rejoin the country until World War I, when they felt they were needed once again. Another article that we have cited, however, takes a decidedly different view.

Finally, Adelbert Ames, a Rockland, Maine, native, was the original commander of the 20th Maine Regiment later led by Joshua Chamberlain. He served as senator from Mississippi after the war, and later was that state's governor. During the Spanish-American War he was recommissioned once more, shortly before his retirement, and served in combat. Ames became a wealthy man and lived until the age of 97. By the time of his death, in 1933, he was the last surviving Civil War General.

HE ALMOST SAVED LINCOLN

ANONYMOUS

Away down in a remote corner of New England, in the most easterly town in this broad country, dwells the man who alone had knowledge beforehand of the meditated assassination of Lincoln, and who tried by every means in his power to thwart the conspiracy, but all in vain.

This man, David Dana, brother of the late Charles A. Dana, lives in a small, one-story farmhouse in West Lubec, Me., on the ancestral farm of his wife's people. He came here some 20 years ago, when the opening of the lead mines in this vicinity promised to make Lubec famous the world over.

After a few years of extravagant expenditures on the part of the managers, work in the mines ceased, and Mr. Dana settled down to the quiet life of a farmer with his wife and his pets, of which he always has a great number.

Mr. Dana is 71 years old, yet strong and hale and capable of weathering a good many more of Maine's rough winters. In personal appearance he bears a striking resemblance to his noted brother, though somewhat shorter in stature. His face is as ruddy and his eye as bright and keen as a boy's.

Though [he is] somewhat stooped by the heavy labor of the farm, his step is brisk, and it would tire may a younger man to follow him through a day's work.

Though living nearly eight miles from the nearest village, he is by no means a recluse, but is well informed on all the events of the day, an omnivorous reader, and an ardent advocate of free silver.

In short, Mr. Dana is a most unique and interesting character, one who has seen his full share of life, and has been a part of the most stirring events in our country's history. It was the writer's good fortune recently to hear him tell of the part he took in the pursuit of the assassin, Booth, and his accomplice, Harold. Inasmuch as the story gives facts never before laid before the public, the recital cannot fail to be of great interest to everyone who has perused the story of these exciting times.

"In the spring of '65 I was near Washington," began Mr. Dana, "with my headquarters at Fort Baker, just above the east branch of the Potomac. It was within the lines of the 3rd brigade of Harden's division, 22d corps, commanded by General C. C. Augur, under whom I was provost marshal. I had authority over nearly all those parts of Maryland lying between the east branch of the Potomac and the Patuxent River. This part of the state was swarming with rebels, and I was commissioned to watch all their movements and learn if possible of any plots against the federal government.

"While patrolling this territory I learned that a plot was forming against the government, and that the blow would undoubtedly be aimed against the life of President Lincoln. I at once asked for a battalion of veteran cavalry, in addition to the regular provost guard, and the request was granted. I was ordered to establish a line of pickets from Fort Meigs on the left to Geisboro point on the right, with orders to permit none to enter the city of Washington during the day unless they could give their names, where they were from, and what was their business at the capital.

"From sundown to sunrise no one was to enter or leave the city except in case of sickness or death. All suspicious persons were ar-

ORIGINALLY PUBLISHED IN THE *BOSTON GLOBE*, 12 DECEMBER 1897.

rested and sent to the commanding general for examination.

"On Friday, April 14, 1865, two men appeared before the guard on the road leading into Washington from the east. Refusing to give their names or state their business, they were arrested and put in the guard tent, whence they were to be sent to headquarters. This was about 1 o'clock in the afternoon. In an hour or two they gave their names as Booth and Harold.

"The officers on guard under me had carried out my orders so strictly that it was very annoying to the rebel sympathizers who wished access to the city, so that many complaints were made by prominent citizens of Maryland.

"About 4 P.M. I received an order from General Augur to release all prisoners held by the guards, and to withdraw the guard until further orders. I sent an orderly to the officers on the line from fort Meigs easterly, with orders to release all prisoners, and to report to me at fort Baker. On the line from fort Meigs to Surrattville I went in person, and withdrew the guard to my headquarters.

"Booth and Harold were released as soon as the orders reached the guard, and they proceeded at once to Washington, reaching there about 6:30 in the afternoon. I had a guard at each end of the bridge on the eastern branch of the Potomac. One of the guards knew Booth and recognized him as he rode into the city and as he came out after the assassination, and had it been known that he had killed Lincoln, escape would have been impossible.

"I returned to headquarters about 11 P.M. and had dismissed the guard, and was eating supper, when an officer rode into camp with the startling intelligence that Lincoln was killed, and that the murderer, with another man, had ridden at a rapid pace into the country.

"I called out the guard and sent detachments in different directions, and then went to the bridge to learn what I could there. On my way I met a company of cavalry, the 13th New York, which I ordered to patrol the river to Guisi point and learn all they could, and then return to fort Baker.

"At the bridge I found an orderly from General Augur with orders from me to report to him at Washington without delay. I did so, and was ushered into his presence, where I found him standing by his desk, with streaming eyes. 'My God, Marshall,' he cried upon seeing me, 'if I had listened to your advice this terrible thing never would have happened!'

"After conversing with him a few moments, I was appointed adjutant general on his staff, and ordered to use my own judgment as to the best way of capturing Booth. The order read as follows:

To commanders of all divisions, brigades, regiments, companies and posts:

You will obey all orders emanating from Adjutant General and Provost Marshal D. D. Dana the same as though especially issued from these headquarters.

(signed)
Major General C. C. Augur,
Commanding 22nd corps
in Department of Washington

"While with General Augur and by his request I laid out the plan for the capture of Booth. First, one of the swiftest steamers which could be obtained should patrol the Potomac as far as the Patuxent River and seize all boats which could not give a good account of themselves. Then a steamer should be sent up the Patuxent, and all boats on this river were to be seized at all hazards to as far as Horse Head ferry.

"These orders were telegraphed to the boats on the Patuxent and were carried out to the letter. The reason was this: In scouting through Maryland I had learned that a boat would be used by the assassin, who would go by land to the Patuxent, thence across to the Albert River, from there to the Atlantic coast, and thence to Mexico. The only thing that prevented Booth's escape was the seizure of these boats.

"I returned to fort Baker, left orders for the cavalry, who were out scouting, took a small detachment of my own guard and started after Booth, taking the road by Surrattville to Bryantown. As we passed by the Surratt mansion all was dark as though it had never been inhabited, but I found an old man and woman who had a boy sick with the smallpox. Finding that no information could be obtained there from the old man or his wife, I took him along with us for a mile and a half to a secluded dell. [He still refused] to give the desired information, [so] I ordered him to be strung up to the limb of a big oak tree.

"It was a clear night, with the moon just rising, its silvery glints touching the tops of the trees in the dell and the flickering light of the campfire which the men had kindled casting fantastic shadows here and there. The rope was made fast about the old man's neck, and at a signal from me he was hoisted up and suspended between heaven and earth. It was a weird and gruesome scene, there in the light of the fire and the moon was the swaying body of the man struggling in his futile efforts to grasp the rope, while the spasmodic action of his body and the gurgling sounds from his throat produced an effect never to be forgotten.

"I ordered him to be cut down after a few moments and he was resuscitated. Rather than try a second pull on the rope he told me that Booth and Harold had been at the Surratt mansion, had had something to eat and drink, and that after supper, though Booth was badly hurt, they had mounted their horses and rode toward Bryantown.

"I pushed on after them, and a few miles from Bryantown I came to a detachment of 10 men under a sergeant as patrol guard to watch suspicious people in that section. I sent the sergeant to Port Tobacco at once, and ordered the troops to scout up the Patuxent River, to arrest all suspicious persons and to report to me at Bryantown. The patrol guard afterward acknowledged that they heard the clatter of Booth's and Harold's horses' feet, as they passed by on the road leading to Dr. Samuel Mudd's toward Bryantown.

"This came about from the fact that a short distance above the guard was a road leading to Dr. Mudd's, who resided about three and a half miles from the village, and that this road the pair had taken, reaching the doctor's house about 4 A.M., about two hours ahead of my troops.

"I arrived at Bryantown about 6, and at once placed guards at all the roads leading into the village, with orders that anyone might enter the town but that none were to leave it. About 2 o'clock that afternoon the detachment of troops from Port Tobacco reached me. In the meantime troops had been sent to Woodbine ferry and Horsehead ferry, all the boats had been seized and all crossing of the river had been stopped.

"By [our] taking possession of these positions and seizing the ferry boats and by closely guarding the line of the river, Booth's chances of escape this way were cut off. Could he have got across the Patuxent River into Calvert County, he would most certainly have reached Mexico in safety.

"After Booth and Harold arrived at Dr. Mudd's, Booth's leg was set, and after giving them their breakfast the doctor made a crutch for Booth and fixed him up ready to start at an instant's notice.

"Dr. Mudd came into Bryantown at 2 in the afternoon and stayed there until 8 or 9 in the evening, where a cousin of his, Dr. George Mudd, asked as a personal favor a pass for him through the lines. After closely questioning Samuel Mudd, and believing him to know nothing of Booth, and having confidence in what his cousin said, I let Dr. Samuel Mudd go.

"During the doctor's long absence Booth got uneasy and sent Harold on horseback to Bryantown. Learning that troops were in the town, he tied his horse in a large clump of willows that grew on the side of a stream near the road, and there watched for Dr. Mudd's return.

"When the doctor made his appearance, Harold came out and the two returned to the doctor's house. Booth was anxious to leave at once, but the good doctor assured him that there was no danger that night.

"George Mudd, let me say in passing, never intimated to me that his friend was a doctor, or was a relative of his. I learned the next day, when it was too late, that his cousin was a rank rebel, and I plainly told George Mudd what I thought of him.

"The fugitives left Dr. Mudd's early the next morning, and took the road for Horsehead ferry. When within 2½ miles of the ferry, they saw a man of about 60 years leaning of a fence in front of his house. Booth rode up and asked him if he had heard the news of Lincoln's being killed. He said yes, he had heard it from some troops that had arrived at the ferry. Booth then asked him if there were any troops then at Horsehead, and the man told him there were.

"Booth got a drink of water, and wanted a drink of whisky, but the old man had none. He asked the men who they were, and Booth answered: 'Detectives looking for Booth and Harold.' 'What are you doing with a crutch?' was the rejoinder. The assassin explained that his horse had stumbled and had fallen upon him, hurting his leg very badly. They asked the way to Woodbine ferry, and, being directed, set off at a brisk trot.

"When within two miles of Woodbine ferry they met an old Negro, and inquired: 'How far is it to the ferry?' Upon being told they asked him the news. 'Master Lincoln's killed, and Woodbine ferry's chock full of troops.' 'How many, uncle?' asked Booth. 'Golly, master, there's more than a hundred! They's swarming like bees!' answered the Negro.

"The horsemen rode on a short distance through a gate into a mowing field, and there all trace of their horses' footprints were lost. But they returned to the vicinity of Dr. Mudd's and entered the Sekiah swamp from the east. They made their way to a small island near the middle of the swamp, where they spent two days and two nights being supplied with food by friends near by.

"I had made arrangements for a detachment of troops to scour the swamp with a guide, when a heavy storm came on and made it impossible. Had I done so, I would certainly have caught them, as they did not leave until 2 or 3 o'clock that day. When my troops reached the island the next day, they found where the horses had been tethered, and the very moss where Booth and Harold had slept. They also found the pieces of blanket with which their horses' hoofs had been muffled. How they made their way from Woodbine ferry to the swamp is a mystery. It could only have been done by wrapping the horses' feet in blankets.

"The different movements they made from the time of the assassination to their reaching Sekiah swamp shows that they had their course all laid out beforehand. They knew where to go and who their friends were, and were only prevented from escaping by the rapid movements of the troops under my command.

"Sekiah swamp lies a short distance nearly west of Bryantown. It is full of quagmires and sinkholes, and is exceedingly dangerous to enter except by daytime. Even then great caution is required unless a person is acquainted with the swamp. Booth and Harold must have had a guide both in going in and coming out.

"They never could have got their horses there alone, to attempt it would have been the last of them.

"There is a small stream running through the swamp, but large enough to float a small boat. It discharges into the Patuxent River. After leaving the swamp, the fugitives went to a log cabin in a thick growth of pines and underbrush quite distant from any road. It was the dwelling of a man named Jones, who had a Negress for housekeeper. It was in that scrubby pine and underbrush, back of the house, that the two horses were killed and buried.

"Here Booth and Harold were kept three or four days, when they were taken by boat down the outlet of the swamp to a point below where the troops were stationed, and from there they were carried in a wagon to a point on the Patuxent, nearly opposite Aquia creek. From here they were taken across the Potomac and made they way across the Potomac and made their way to Garrett's, near Bowling Green, where Booth was killed."

ALSO SEE

"Lubec Man Told Strange Tale of Lincoln Tragedy," *Lewiston Journal Illustrated Magazine* 27 April 1963, p. 2A.

HE SAW LINCOLN SHOT

L. C. BATEMAN AND O. K. YATES

From a boy, Dr. O.K. Yates, of West Paris, has been possessed of strong will and originality of thought. For eight years previous to the Civil War he was in business in Auburn, and was the second man to enlist in the old Auburn Artillery when that company responded to the call of Lincoln. For a time he served in that organization and was then detailed in the secret service of the government. After the war he studied medicine with the late Dr. Tewksbury of Portland, and graduated from Bowdoin about 1870. For a time he remained with Dr. Tewksbury, and then came back to West Paris, where he settled and has been in constant practice for thirty-three years.

It was while acting as a government detective that Dr. Yates had an experience that can never be obliterated from his mind. He had been called to Washington as a witness, and while there he sought to while away the tedium of an evening by a visit to Ford's Theatre. In an hour and a half after he had taken his seat Abraham Lincoln was shot by the assassin Booth, and Dr. Yates was an eyewitness to that awful and tragic event. He is the only man in Maine who can tell that tale from personal experience, and for a time we will listen to his story:

"I was in Washington at the close of the late War of the Rebellion, and everybody was rejoicing at the close of the war, bands were playing and excitement ran high, and right here let me note a little instance.

"A crowd of enthusiasts gathered in front of the White House and loud calls were made for President Lincoln. When the President appeared upon the balcony, deafening shouts of applause greeted him while bands were playing stirring patriotic music. After a brief characteristic speech of congratulation of the close of the war, he remarked that our friends down South at the commencement of the war captured from us a piece of music and appropriated it to their own use recently. We had recaptured it and it was now legally ours. That was "Dixie." The remarks were greeted with loud applause and every band commenced playing "Dixie," which would have caused a riot a few moments before.

"It was announced on the morning of that fatal day, April 14, that the President, his cabinet and Gen. Grant would attend Ford's theatre that evening to witness the play of *Our American Cousin*. Feeling a great desire to see the assemblage of the distinguished dignitaries of our nation, I felt I would like to go to the theatre.

"Knowing full well if I waited until the doors were open my chances would be small in getting anything like a favorable seat, if lucky enough to get any, I suggested to my friend who accompanied me that we had better try a little strategy, so we started an hour earlier than the time appointed for the doors to open.

"We went to the theatre and with a liberal fee to those in charge we were admitted to the theatre and had the privilege of selection of our seats outside of the boxes. We selected our seats on the left-hand side near the boxes of that side. As we entered the theatre at the front door, exactly opposite of President Lincoln's box, we could see everything going on in that box.

ORIGINALLY PUBLISHED IN *LEWISTON JOURNAL ILLUSTRATED MAGAZINE*, 9 MAY 1903, AND SUPPLEMENTARY LETTER DATED 6 MAY 1903.

"We waited nearly an hour before the doors were opened. Oh, then what a rush! The house was soon filled to a crowding capacity. Soon after the house was filled and quiet restored, President Lincoln with his wife, his niece and Major Rathbone, entered the

Octavious K. Yates, M.D.

theatre. He was met with wild applause. I shall never forget his appearance. He was tall, lank and angular in form and apparently had no personal grace of bearing as he bowed his acknowledgement to the enthusiastic audience. When once [he was] seated in his box, the curtain was raised and the play of *Our American Cousin* was opened.

"As the play advanced we noticed that the President was deeply interested and laughed heartily at some portions of the play. Somewhere near ten o'clock I noticed a stranger with a military cloak and a soft hat walking toward the President's box, and when near the box seemed to stand with his hat in his hand looking down upon the stage. As he seemed to be a person of some distinction,I turned to a gentleman at my side and asked who he was. To this question I got no reply.

"Laura Keene was managing the theatre and was on the stage at the time. She saw the man about the same time that I did, and probably she knew him and divined his intentions, for I saw a look of anxiety sweep across her face as she suddenly turned and beckoned to some of the actors who were on the rear of the stage.

"Before they had time to step forward, I saw the stranger, who afterwards proved to be Booth, enter the President's box, and a moment later saw the flash and heard the report of the deadly pistol and heard Mrs. Lincoln scream. I saw Lincoln pitch forward. His face turned deathly pale, and there was an expression of agony on his features which plainly told that he had been mortally wounded.

"Booth attempted to spring over the balustrade in front of the President's box, but Maj. Rathbone caught him, and then I saw him swing a knife back to free himself from Maj. Rathbone's grip. In this he succeeded, and went over the balustrade and fell upon the floor of the stage and made his way off at the rear of the stage the best he could, and I know he never raised himself up and repeated, 'Sic Semper Tyrannis.'

"In a moment everything was in confusion. As I was a government detective I sprang over to the stage, but Booth had disappeared before I could reach him. I was satisfied that Booth could not go far, as he had struck the stage very heavily and I knew that he must have broken his leg in his fall upon the stage. Nothing but a tremendous will enabled him to make his way as far as he did to the rear of the theatre, where a horse was held in readiness for his escape.

"I then turned to the box, but found that I had sprained my ankle so that I could hardly walk. As soon as I was able I went across the stage, where I found some water in a dish, which I took up to the President's box. There I found Lincoln had been fatally shot. He was breathing very heavily. Laura Keene was there and holding Lincoln's head in her lap. She wore a magnificent white robe, and it was completely covered and stained with blood so that she presented a ghastly sight.

"They were pleased to receive the water and I hastened back to the stage to meet the mad fury of the people who were leaving the theatre. I saw one man from the upper gallery come down with a thud among the seats, but the excitement was so great that no one seemed to think or care for the unfortunate man. Everyone was trying to get outdoors, and the scene was simply indescribable. Men were cursing, and the cries of 'conspiracy' could be heard on every side.

"By that time officers had arrived, and

Lincoln was taken to a building across the street from the theatre. I then made my way out into the street, and the very air was stifling. Reports of other murders—that Seward, Grant and other members of the cabinet had been assassinated—were coming from all quarters. The excitement all around was something absolutely fearful.

"It was a night of terror such as I never want to experience again."

The above story is a fearful one, and coming as it does from an eyewitness of the entire scene is doubly interesting. It disposes of the "Sic Semper Tyrannis" story, which up to this time we have never heard challenged. Dr. Yates is a man of unquestioned coolness as well as veracity, and there would seem to be no possibility that he could have been mistaken. His story will be read with profound interest, and attract wide attention among all classes.

Also See

"Assassination and Funeral of Lincoln," *Portland Evening Express,* 11 February 1909 (Lincoln Centennial Supplement), p. 8.

"Damage Case in Maine Arising from Lincoln Assassination," *Lewiston Journal Illustrated Magazine,* 12 February 1938, p. 4.

"Darkest Hour," Military Order of the Loyal Legion of the United States, *War Papers: Read Before the Commandery of the State of Maine* 1, 1898, pp. 254–59.

"Hamlin's Daughter Watched Crime that Nearly Made Him President," *Portland Press Herald,* 11 April 1965, p. 10A.

"How Portland Received News of Death of Abraham Lincoln 63 Years Ago This Morning," *Portland Sunday Telegram,* 15 April 1928, p. 9B.

"James H. Taylor of Portland, Who was Serving in a Military Regiment at the Time of Lincoln's Assassination, Gives His Account of the Event," *Portland Evening Express,* 11 February 1909 (Lincoln Centennial Supplement), p. 6.

"Letter Found on Lincoln Assassination at Cape Elizabeth," *Portland Evening Express,* 12 February 1965, p. 1; *Portland Press Herald,* 13 February 1965, p. 7.

"Maine Man [Dr. Octavius K. Yates] Saw Lincoln shot," *Portland Evening Express,* 11 February 1909 (Lincoln Centennial Supplement), p. 7.

"Only surviving Member of World Wide Known Guards of Honor," *Portland Sunday Telegram,* 28 November 1926, p. 8A.

"Personal Recollections of the Funeral of Lincoln," *Portland Evening Express,* 11 February 1909 (Lincoln Centennial Supplement), p. 6.

"Some Recollections of the Assassination," *Portland Evening Express,* 11 February 1909 (Lincoln Centennial Supplement), p. 9.

THE FIRST NATIONAL SOLDIERS' HOME

DONALD W. BEATTIE

In 1810, locals discovered a sulphurous mineral spring in a swamp in the town of Chelsea, then part of Hallowell. The Worromontogus Indians called it *Togus,* meaning "strong medicine water." It was the age of medicinal springs, and, in 1858, businessman Horace Beals, who claimed the Togus waters had cured him of some strange malady, decided to build a luxury hotel and health spa to rival Saratoga Springs on his spring site.

Unfortunately, the project became known as Beals's Folly by the time of its completion in June 1859. Beals spent more than $200,000 to build a luxury hotel for 300 guests, with 134 rooms (many of them suites), spacious dining rooms, and dancing halls. But first he had to drain, clear, and beautify the land. In addition to his hotel and covered spring, Beals constructed gravel walks and avenues, a zoo, tennis courts, "stables, a bowling alley, a farmhouse, a bathing house, driveways, and a race track."

Beals's enterprise fizzled. The Civil War had reduced the tendency of the leisure class to spend money on travel and spas. He closed the hotel in 1862, three years after it opened, and died soon thereafter.

Founding of the Soldiers' Home

Before the Civil War, the Federal government provided few services for its less fortunate citizenry and took little responsibility for individual, social, or economic ills. But Federal compassion was stirred by the presence of thousands of disabled Civil War veterans, and on March 3, 1865, Congress established "Provisions for an Asylum for disabled soldiers."

Eventually, a network of thirteen "soldiers' homes" was established—collectively called the National Asylum for Disabled Volunteer Soldiers in 1866 and the National Soldiers' Home several years thereafter.

A Board of Managers oversaw these facilities. "Storming" Ben Butler, a Massachusetts Civil War major general, served as first president (from April 21, 1866, to June 16, 1880). Prominent civilians, politicians, and veterans staffed it. Their charge, which they accomplished fairly successfully, was to keep "dishonorable practices" from infiltrating any of the facilities.

The Beals heirs sold the closed facility at Togus to the United States Government for $50,000. On November 10, 1866, it became the nations' first "Soldiers' Asylum," providing "a home for veterans of the Civil War, who were in distress and suffering from wounds and illness." It was quite a feat, setting up "a miniature city where worn out and disabled heroes of Gettysburg and Appomattox" could "pass their last days in peace and comfort."

Soon the "Asylums" legislation was "extended to cover veterans of prior wars, such as . . . those of the War of 1812 as well as those of the Mexican War." Later laws permitted placing veterans of twentieth-century American wars at Togus.

Development of Togus

The Togus asylum's early years were tumultuous, evidenced by the fact that six different men held the leadership post during the first three years. Colonel Edward Hinks, who had scouted the site for General Butler, was appointed first "Governor of the Asylum" on July 13, 1866. He arrived in Augusta, Maine, in August and departed in early 1867 to assume directorship of a similar project in Milwaukee. Brevet Brigadier General Charles Everett, who had been serving as deputy Governor, took over for about ten weeks.

Major Nathan Cutler, who had been serving as Treasurer, Secretary, and Steward, became governor on an acting, then permanent, basis. But Cutler's health broke. He took a sick leave, returned briefly, then left for good. Dr. Bowman B. Breed, who had been working at Togus since September 1866, assumed the governor's duties on a temporary, then permanent, basis until late 1868.

Deputy Governor Captain Foster Kimball, who became manager of Togus in the spring of 1869, demonstrated great capability, but was soon replaced by Colonel E. A. Ludwick, who left a few months later, as had Hinks, for Milwaukee.

In 1868, just after the Togus Hotel had been remodeled for its new purpose, it, and many other Togus buildings, burned down.

Then it was discovered that new construction plans developed by Hinks never had been presented to the National Board of Managers for approval. Everett had been responsible, but Breed was blamed, and this was the reason Kimball replaced Breed.

Togus's era of stability began in November 1869, when General William Stowell Tilton was appointed Governor of the Asylum (1869–83). He supervised an extensive building program. Noted for excellence through discipline, Tilton "evolved order and regularity, and put the affairs of the institution in a condition that [met] the approval of the . . . managers, even after the most critical examinations."

Construction continued during the administrations of General Luther Stephenson, Jr. (1883–97) and Colonel Samuel H. Allen (1897–1905). During Stephenson's governorship, "Togus emerged from relative obscurity and grew into a well known and well respected landmark in the State of Maine. He established the Memorial Monument (Summer 1889)—proof of the Governor's personal concern for the veterans and the Home." Allen was noted for careful attention to details and had been, prior to his appointment at Togus, head of the Maine State Prison. In 1905 he reported having "over 2000 inmates" at Togus—the largest number in its history" (to date) and "up to its capacity."

General John T. Richards (1905–15) served almost until Togus's fiftieth anniversary. He was a modest, brave, and unassuming person with an especially impressive war record. He developed and managed the facility's resources effectively until being summarily dismissed, probably for political reasons, on February 16, 1915, and replaced by a Knox County Democratic State Committee member, Judge William P. Hurley, of Rockland, Maine.

Facilities and Grounds

Major Nathan Cutler had built one 50- by 100-foot brick building in 1867. Then, after the fire of 1868, Hinks's ambitious building plans were submitted for approval to the National Board of Managers. On July 1, 1869, board president Ben Butler visited Togus and gave approval for construction of several buildings: an amusement hall, a vocational workshop, a deputy governor/officers residence, a building for the three fire engines, and a brick stable (where bricks were made on site for the construction program).

By 1905 Togus consisted of some ninety buildings upon which millions of dollars had been expended. It was the third largest national Soldiers' Home in the country, "being excelled only by similar institutions at Dayton, Ohio and Hampden, Virginia."

Ten barracks and the hospital constituted the heart of the Togus complex. The barracks were 150 x 50 feet in size, each capable of accommodating 228 men. Large central rotundas, kept thoroughly warm and stocked with tables, chairs, and reading matter, served as lounging places.

Journalist L. C. Bateman, in an article for the *Lewiston Journal Illustrated Magazine*, described the layout of the first hospital (1914) at Togus. Offices of the chief surgeon and his assistants' offices were just inside the main entrance, on both sides of the hallway. Beyond them were the drug store and the dispensary, where men needing medical assistance assembled for 8 o'clock sick call each morning. Connected to the dispensary was a room equipped for minor surgical operations and dental work, and several dressing rooms. On the top story of the main structure was a "large, airy, well lighted and . . . scrupulously clean" operating room that Bateman called "one of the best and most up-to-date in New England." Across the hall was the etherizing room "where the patients are made ready for the operating table." Here, too, was the laboratory where the Togus dairy herd's milk was examined for purity. Elsewhere there was an insane ward where a few violent cases were kept; a blind ward, with a separate dining room; a ward for paralytic patients; and regular wards. Each ward was staffed by two orderlies and "a trained male nurse, who was deemed . . . necessary in this kind of work."

A three-story quartermaster's headquarters had been completed in 1869. During the early 1900s, this upgraded facility contained "great piles of clothing where the soldiers come to be fitted. . . ." The supplies were stored in several rooms, and the basement was "devoted to hardware and machinery."

The governor's residence was built in 1870. An amusement hall was dedicated on November 25, 1871. A chapel was constructed in 1887 to be used for veteran funerals (with flag-draped caskets) and as a place to meditate and hold worship services. It was replaced in the next century. Next to the first chapel was the headquarters building. The initial commissary storehouse was built during the early 1870s. An updated structure and the new bakery were combined into a single department in 1910. The bakery consumed up to five barrels of flour every fifteen minutes and could produce 650 loaves of bread at a time.

There were many other prominent buildings. A club house (with "card rooms and billiard tables in profusion") and a large attached library (with "many thousand volumes of literature as well as nearly all the leading magazines and papers of the country") opened in 1886. The assistant surgeon's residence was built in 1890. A hospital annex was completed in October 1899, and a greenhouse, completed afterward, supplied fresh flowers to the hospital daily. A "gasoline dry-cleaning plant" was introduced in 1912, where equipment steam-pressed, cleaned, and disinfected the clothes so professionally that they looked "nearly as well [as when] received from the manufacturer."

Additional architectural structures included a theatre—later an opera house—(with "nightly performances given by excellent companies") and a pavilion with a bandstand for the resident band—a renowned one at that!

Two large burial grounds, the "Old Cemetery" (West Cemetery) and "New Cemetery" (East Cemetery), were laid out over a fifty-acres area. Filled mainly by Civil War Veterans, these cities of the dead were arranged in long rows and eventually included over 5,000 graves. In 1961, nearly 100 years after August

Moller of the 103rd Volunteers became the first veteran to be buried there (March 3, 1867), the last lot was filled and both cemeteries were closed. The last Civil War veteran to be buried at Togus was William H. LeBaron, who died there February 26, 1938.

Many subsidiary facilities complemented the major buildings to ensure service, comfort, and safety for the veterans. Gardens and parks filled the grounds at Togus, including sporting grounds (for "the home's" several baseball teams and other outdoor sports), an artificial lake (filled with "graceful swans and other water fowl"), a zoological garden, and a park (with "bison, elks, Persian sheep, bears, pheasants and no less than 40 Maine deer . . . reasonably tame").

Togus became "a popular excursion spot for Sunday picnics" in the early 1890s, when two rail lines ended its relative isolation. The cities of Augusta and Gardiner were both "fully aware that whichever was the first to establish a system of rapid, efficient, all-weather transportation from the Kennebec River to Togus, would gain an enviable advantage over the other, commercially."

A 4½-mile narrow-gauge railroad (the Gardiner-based Kennebec Central Railroad) opened passenger and freight service between Randolph and Togus on July 1, 1891. Its Forney 0-4-4-T type locomotives were built in Portland and affectionately referred to as Elfins because of their "elflike look." Two passenger cars (with lengthwise seats and power brakes), six flatcars, and two boxcars painted battleship gray and lettered in black constituted the rest of this railroad's rolling stock. It was a financial success even when it ceased operating in 1929. The first regular passenger run to reach Togus station found "500 soldiers . . . in the vicinity of the station to welcome it" at an early hour. Several rode on its return trip to Randolph at 9:15 A.M. the same day.

Its competition, an electric trolley (built by the Augusta Electric Railway) opened its "street car line" to Togus almost simultaneously. Not as successful as the railroad, the trolley line closed, reopened in June 1901, and was ultimately discontinued in 1932.

During this period the first-rate Togus Home Hotel (built in 1905) enabled relatives and friends to enjoy extended visits with their loved ones at Togus. Nonetheless, in the fall of 1912 it was closed because of high heating costs.

Life at the Soldiers' Home

Over the decades, the United States Government and Togus's respective governors and their staffs took exceptionally good care of their wards. "The veterans at the Home . . . led a life very reminiscent of the service from which they had been discharged. A surplus Civil War uniform was issued to each new arrival and he wore this on the reservation only. The officials all had military rank and titles. . . and were assisted by non-commissioned officers in the running of the institution. The routine . . . [and] the nomenclature was military with such terms as 'Reveille,' 'Mess Call,' 'Tattoo,' 'Taps,' etc. as part of the everyday vocabulary. The bugle could be heard at regular intervals throughout the day until 9:30 P.M., when the old soldier would wrap himself up as 'Taps' was sounded. . . ."

Disabled veterans, who were at Togus for the duration, lived in barracks. According to Bateman, each building was filled by a company of men divided into four wards, and under charge of "a captain and assistant sergeant whose duty it is to look after their comfort and see that order is maintained." The men turned out "at 5:30 o'clock in the morning," aired their beds, and were " ready for breakfast in half an hour." There were certain rules to be observed, but much latitude prevailed. The men could come and go as they pleased providing they maintained proper decorum.

Bateman (1912) described the efficient meal service:

Visitors at the home like to watch the methods by which so large a number of men are fed in so short a time. In the wash room adjoining the dining hall, the dishes are all cleaned by machinery. Near by is the coffee room, where 275 gallons of coffee, 3,500 doughnuts, as well as other food are sent into the dining room on trucks. These trucks are three-deckers, and the coffee is poured only four minutes before the bugle call is given, in order that it . . . may be served hot. In the main kitchen the work goes on night and day, and here several relays of help are required. To feed more than 2,000 men three times each day . . . is a task of great magnitude, but it is carried out with military precision.

The officer of the day inspected every table before each of the three daily meals. A bell was rung, and the "troops" were then fed in 1,200-member increments. Each shift was given twenty minutes before tables were re-readied for the next group.

Typical 1912 meals, according to Bateman, were as follows:

For breakfast the men have scrambled eggs, potatoes, bread, coffee, and other eatables according to the season. Dinner finds a meal of salt cod, pork scraps, potatoes, soups, navy beans, bread, butter and coffee. The supper is made up of hominy and syrup with bread, butter and tea. This is the average day, but of course the menu is varied from time to time. In their season grapes, melons, oranges and berries are furnished in liberal quantities. The Sunday dinner is even more elaborate, as then roast beef, mashed potatoes, boiled onions, mince pie, bread and butter with other luxuries are furnished.

At holiday time the veterans' meals would "approach the dignity of a banquet." At the 1911 Thanksgiving Feast, "the following extras" were supplied: "700 lbs. apples, 300 qts. cranberries, 1120 lbs. sweet potatoes, 14 boxes oranges, [and] 2400 lbs. turkey."

The concept of work as a virtue was not absent at Togus. Occupational and recreational experiences were available to the veteran. For example, *Lewiston Journal* reporter M. R. Courchesne, researched the history of Togus during the early 1960s and remarked that because many of the veterans

. . . had come back from the war partially incapacitated, or were illiterate, efforts were made to educate them or teach them a trade. There were several shops—the shoe shop . . . [and] barber shops, the saw-mill, the laundry, the bakeries and kitchens, the farms, barns, and stables with their necessary blacksmith shops or forges. There was even a brick-yard, as well as the usual carpenter and plumber shops. In all of these the work was done by the veterans.

Veterans also manned fire, police, and post office departments. Pay ranged from $4.50 to $25.00 a month for these tasks.

Finally, Courchesne noted

Every effort was made to keep the

THE HEADQUARTERS BUILDING AT THE NATIONAL SOLDIERS' HOME, TOGUS

able [veterans] happy through activity. Cleanliness was of the utmost importance and bathing facilities were of the best and an integral part of every barracks. A review of all companies, headed by the Band, was held weekly, weather permitting. Furloughs, or outright discharges were permitted at the discretion of the board of directors and the Commandant.

Togus in the Twentieth Century

Togus's peak number of 2,793 residents, most of them Civil War veterans, was reached in June 1904. At that time, despite the excellent facilities and quality of care, there was an undercurrent of sadness because each year saw older and feebler entrants and more frequent deaths. Indeed, Bateman said in 1905:

> There is a pathos here that is most profoundly impressive, and whoever visits the place will come away with a feeling of sadness which even the lighter and more humorous features cannot wholly dispel. Shadows chase the sunlight in ever increasing swiftness and the solemn peal of the chapel bell tolling the death dirge of a departed hero mingles with the merry laughter

from the billiard rooms and the auditorium of the elegant theatre. It is a place of vivid contrasts, but where the gaunt spectre of death is the shadow of every feast.

From 1916 until 1930, despite gradual deterioration of equipment and buildings, Togus still maintained the level of service it had developed during the early decades of the post–Civil War period. But by the Great Depression, Togus's overall population had dropped dramatically. In 1920, approximately 1300 Civil War Veterans and 350 Spanish-American War Soldiers were being served; in 1929, only 119 Civil War Veterans remained.

Several other major changes took place during the 1930s. The Togus facility's name was changed from National Soldiers' Home to the Veterans' Administration Home on January 4, 1932. A consolidation of veterans' services took place in Maine in 1933–34. Togus opened a new hospital in 1933, which offered more modern health services, and Veterans' Affairs operations in Portland, Maine, merged with Togus in 1934. A number of the older buildings, such as the quartermaster's headquarters, were demolished in 1936.

In October 1945 Togus was renamed the Veterans Administration Center. In 1957 the VAC added a modern General Medical and

Surgical Hospital that offered extensive and up-to-date medical, surgical, and psychiatric inpatient and outpatient services for veterans. Currently (1996) the Department of Veterans Affairs Medical and Regional Office Center at Togus consists of a medical center, a regional office, and a national cemetery. Today, fewer than 200 inpatients (both male and female veterans) receive medical, surgical, or psychiatric services at Togus. The Regional Office Center provides compensation, pension, education, and related services for Maine veterans and their families.

Togus—the magnificent "miniature city" for disabled Civil War veterans between 1866 and 1915—is no more, and probably nothing like it will ever again be attempted. Still, when I read the inscriptions on the Soldiers Monument inthe West Cemetery, I felt a chill down my spine as I thought upon the glory that Togus once was:

EASTERN BRANCH NATIONAL HOME

FOR DISABLED VOLUNTEER SOLDIERS.

IN MEMORY OF

THE SOLDIERS AND SAILORS

WHO FOUGHT FOR THE UNION.

ALSO SEE

"A Friend of General Butler" *Lewiston Journal Illustrated Magazine,* 17 February 1906, p. 8.

History of Togus: First 100 Years, G. Heald, et al, eds., Chelsea, Me.: Dept. of Veterans Affairs (Togus), 1966. (Mimeographed and bound. Free.)

"Home for Indigent Soldiers and Sailors," *Portland Sunday Telegram,* 15 May 1901, p. 16.

"In the Barracks at Togas," *Lewiston Journal Illustrated Magazine,* 11 February 1905, pp. 8–9.

"Lone Woman Interred at Togus Veterans Facility Cemetery," *Lewiston Journal Illustrated Magazine,* 25 May 1963, pp. 6–7.

"Military and Official Career of Gen. John T. Richards, Governor of Togus Soldiers' Home," *Lewiston Journal Illustrated Magazine,* 29 May 1914, pp. 8–9.

"Togus, National Home of Veterans and Heroes, a Little City in Itself," *Lewiston Journal Illustrated Magazine,* 3 January 1912, pp. 8–10.

"Togus Veterans Facility—the Hospital that Emerged from a Lake," *Lewiston Journal Illustrated Magazine,* 18 May 1963, pp. 6–8.

"A Visit to Togus Hospital Where Nation's sick Veterans are Given Every Comfort," *Lewiston Journal Illustrated Magazine,* 18 April 1914, pp. 2 , 3.

"A Visit to Togus, the Eastern National Soldiers' Home, and Chats with the Veterans," *Lewiston Journal Illustrated Magazine,* 30 May 1920, pp. 8–10.

WILLIAM PITT FESSENDEN— A MAINE HERO

GEORGE LORING WHITE

Sixty years ago this spring, this country was excited beyond precedent by the attempted impeachment of Andrew Johnson, President of the United States. Seven Radicals whom the other Republican Radicals in Congress expected to side with them against the President, stood out in his behalf and refused to lend their names, influence and vote to the infamy.

How difficult it must have been to hold out is revealed by a pre-vote comment by Gideon Welles (Secretary of the Navy under both Lincoln and Johnson):

> As regards the seven Senators themselves, I have my doubts. They are intelligent, and I think conscientious, but it remains to be seen whether they will have the firmness and moral courage to maintain their position independently through the fiery conflict in the near future. . . . These Senators are marked and spotted men so far as the radicals are concerned.

These men were Senators Fessenden, Foss, Fowler, Grimes, Henderson, Trumbull, and Van Winkle. Had any one of them capitulated, impeachment would have occurred. But they did not—even though they knew they were signing their own political death warrants. And so it proved to be. But by courageously following their consciences, they stopped the United States Senate from performing a most unwarranted and disgraceful act.

Of these seven men, William Pitt Fessenden was in most respects the strongest, and therefore upon him fell the largest avalanche of vituperation and calumny. Sixty years have passed and still the name of this man, one of the heroes of the Civil War and of the 19th century, has never received the meed of praise and honor which his distinguished and valuable services deserve.

This article redresses that wrong: William Pitt Fessenden is entitled to the highest consideration. Former governor Nelson Dingley, Jr. referred to Fessenden as Maine's "ablest statesman" and his services to our Country were second to none.

The Fessenden stock reaches back in this country nearly to the landing of the Pilgrim fathers, and they were cultivated and well-to-do people. His father was one of the leading lawyers of Maine, born in Fryeburg July 16, 1784. He graduated from Dartmouth in 1806, taught school at Bascawen, N.H., and entered the law office of Daniel Webster as a student of law, remaining with him three years. In October of that same year, baby "Pitt," so-called all his life by his intimate friends and relatives, was born. So much did Mr. Webster think of his youthful student in law, he rode 20 miles through a snowstorm to be present as godfather at baby Pitt's christening.

Though Mr. Fessenden failed to be born in this State, he lived here all his life of 63 years except the first six months, for he was soon transferred to the home of his paternal grandfather, a minister, at Fryeburg. Not much is known about his time there, but, when nearly seven, he rejoined his father, who

ORIGINALLY PUBLISHED IN LEWISTON JOURNAL ILLUSTRATED MAGAZINE, 3 MARCH AND 10 MARCH 1928.

had begun to practice law in New Gloucester.

The writer knows what New Gloucester must have meant to Pitt sixty years ago. It is a pleasing spot of woods, hills, ponds, intervale, orchards, rocks. An active boy knows every apple tree within a radius of five miles. He knows where every spruce tree is located, and where gum to be distilled is drooping in resinous pendants. He is acquainted with every trout brook in town, particularly that of Lovell's brook in the backwoods of Gloucester Hill. He swims in numerous ponds in summer and skates on them in winter. And for adventure he sneaks-up on bear dens, snares rabbits, and shoots partridges.

When, at eleven years of age, he presented himself to the authorities of Bowdoin College for matriculation, though well fitted, they saw a slender boy in jacket and trousers, with a broad ruffle around his neck, so young in appearance that the President advised him to go back to his home for a year. Not discouraged he entered at twelve, being in the college at the same time as Longfellow, Hawthorne and Franklin Pierce.

After graduation he studied law in Portland, where his father had moved in 1822, until he became old enough to be admitted to the bar at 21.

He practiced law at Bridgton, Bangor and Portland, where he remained for rest of his life. His great merit attracted notice, and he began a career in politics which finally brought him to the Senate. Indeed, Nelson Dingley senior, who was then in Maine's Senate, years later said voting for William Pitt when he first ran for the U.S. Senate was one of the proudest acts of his life.

Fessenden arrived in the Senate in 1854 just before the vote for the Kansas-Nebraska bill was to be taken. He had been present less than one week, but being urged by the friends of freedom, he took the floor at one o'clock in the morning of March 4, and, without previous preparation or a memorandum of any kind, made for himself, by a powerful speech, a National reputation. It sent thrills of gladness through the hearts of all lovers of freedom the world over.

Senator Sumner wrote to a friend:

> Fessenden's arrival in the Senate was like a re-enforcement on a field of battle. Those who stood for freedom were no longer fourteen, but fifteen. He did not wait but entered into the debate with all

those resources which afterwards became so famous. Douglas, Case, and Butler interrupted, only to be worsted by one who had just ridden into the lists. . . . The Senator from Maine, erect, firm, immovable as a jutting promontory against which the waves of the ocean tossed in dissolving spray, there he stood. Not a Senator loving freedom who did not feel a champion had come.

Carl Schurz said of Mr. Fessenden:

> He would make an argument in a calm conversational tone, unmixed with the slightest oratorical flourish, so solid and complete that little more remained to be said on the subject in question. He gave the impression of having at his disposal a rich and perfectly ordered store of thought and knowledge upon which he could draw with perfect case and assurance. . . . Not one of his colleagues but held him in the highest esteem as a statesman of commanding ability and of lofty ideals, as a gentleman of truth and conscience, as a great jurist and an eminent constitutional lawyer, as a party man of most honorable principles and methods, and as a patriot of noblest ambition for his country.

Soon Mr. Fessenden came to be regarded as the ablest debater in the Senate. Stephen Douglas, renowned as a debater himself, said in 1858: "Henry Clay was the most fascinating, Daniel Webster the most powerful orator; John C. Calhoun was the logician of the Senate; but William Pitt Fessenden is the readiest and ablest debater I have ever known." And Sumner said: "This place (as a debater) he held to the end without a superior, without a peer. His words were swift, and sharp as a scimitar. He shot flying, and with unerring aim."

In 1864, Lincoln solicited him to take the place of Salmon P. Chase as Secretary of the Treasury. Mr. Fessenden suffered from ill-health during all his public life and felt that to do so might cost him his life. But it was at the darkest period of the war, and when Lincoln put his arms around Fessenden's neck and pleaded with him to accept that office, he consented, with the understanding that it would be for only a few months or to the end of the war.

About his effectiveness in this role, Herbert Quick says:

William Pitt Fessenden was the greatest man the state of Maine ever sent to Washington. I do not except James G. Blaine, or Tom Reed. Who was it stood by Lincoln's side all through the Civil War, and fought for the funds with which to pay the nation's bills? William Pitt Fessenden who, as Senator from Maine, was chairman of the Senate Finance Committee. Salmon P. Chase as Secretary of the Treasury takes second place as compared with Senator Fessenden.

How can that be said? Because when, under Chase's policies, the dollar went down to 34 cents in gold and the bonds of the Government could be sold no longer, Fessenden left the Senate, took the portfolio of the treasury and did a work worthy of Alexander Hamilton in straightening out the tangle left by Chase. . . .

After righting the nation's finances, Fessenden resigned, and, after a heated race against Hannibal Hamlin, regained his senate seat just in time to be ensnared by the Johnson mess.

In these days, so free from rabid, unreasonable party strife, it is difficult to realize the country's ferment shortly after the Civil War. Many Congressmen had lost sons, relatives, or friends in that conflict. Three of Senator Fessenden's four sons had been in the war, one killed in action, another severely wounded. A controversial figure, Vice President Andrew Johnson, had become president after Lincoln's assassination. Johnson had displaced Hannibal Hamlin as Lincoln's running mate because of the splendid work he had done during the war, in keeping the eastern portion of the State true to the Union, and acting as military governor. Prior to that, Johnson, a citizen of Tennessee, had been Governor of the State and served six years in the Senate. But Johnson was a bitter disappointment to the Radicals of the Republican party. He was obstinate, lacked tact and treated Congress contemptuously.

The Radicals had agreed with his attempts to find and punish those guilty of Mr. Lincoln's death. But they angrily denounced his attempts to follow Lincoln's conciliatory reconstruction policies. Even Mr. Lincoln, as shrewd and tactful as he was, could scarcely have escaped the bitterest opposition and calumny from such a lenient approach. And of course Lincoln's assassination only added fuel to the flames enkindled by the deadliest and costliest civil war the world had ever seen. Lincoln's theory was that the rebel states had never really been out of the Union and so Johnson, all that summer and fall following his inauguration, had been laboring assiduously to readmit the belligerent states, while disregarding Congress's role in their restoration.

WILLIAM PITT FESSENDEN IN 1868

However, much of the nation was inflamed by an hysteria of hate engendered by the war, the assassination of Lincoln, and the grave suspicion that, somehow, the South had conspired in his assassination. Many just and conscientious men were carried away by the huge ground swell of public indignation against Johnson for his high-handed measures for reconstruction, and his disregard of the rights of Congress as sharers in that work.

Great pressure was brought to bear upon Fessenden to vote for impeachment. He had consistently opposed the inauguration of such a movement, but when once [it was] inaugurated, the Radicals expected him to act with them. Party caucuses were held, and many were coerced who lacked the independence of mind and strength of conscience that characterized the Senator from Maine. The leading members of his party in this State besought him, on their very knees, figuratively speaking, not to fail them. Neal Dow, whom he greatly respected and loved, closed an urgent appeal in this way: "Hang Johnson by the heels like a dead crow in a corn field to frighten away all his tribe." And many like expressions were made by Republicans who ordinarily possessed their souls in peace.

Fessenden's principled decision is even more remarkable considering his dislike for Johnson and his *modus operandi*. In a letter home he wrote: "If he was impeached for general cussedness, there would be no difficulty in the case. . . . Whatever I may think and feel as a politician, I cannot and will not violate my oath. I would rather be confined to planting cabbages for the remainder of my days."

Many able men have subsequently supported the correctness of Fessenden's vote.

After the trial B. R. Curtis, a great jurist, wrote to Fessenden: "I say with entire sincerity that no man in my time has been in a position to render so great service to the Constitution of our country as you have been enabled to render."

Much later, in *Reconstruction and the Constitution*, Professor John W. Burgess of Columbia University wrote: "The country and the Republican party itself were placed under the deepest obligation to these men (Fessenden and the others) for their courage and independent action. They saved the country from the direst results of the great political scandal of the age, and they saved the Republican party from the commission of a deed which would have destroyed its hold upon the people."

Though the personal repercussions of his vote were terrible, Fessenden continued to comport himself with courage and dignity afterward. During Portland's Centennial celebration of 1886, Tom Reed, Maine's famous Speaker of the House, talked about Fessenden's facing down of opposition and hatred at the Portland Republican Convention of 1868:

The most impressive scene I ever witnessed took place in this very hall. Here, on almost the very spot where I now stand, William Pitt Fessenden stood before the constituency which had loved and honored him for so many years. The hall was black with the thronging multitude. It was at the begin-

ning of a great presidential campaign, the last he was ever to witness. The great problem of reconstruction was to be reviewed. Mr. Fessenden had been the master spirit in its solution. The war debt was to be assailed. Mr. Fessenden had been chairman of the Committee on Finance and Secretary of the Treasury. To all this was added the intense personal interest of his recent defeat of the impeachment of Andrew Johnson

With full knowledge of the storm about him, but with the courage of a perfect conviction, he faced the responsibility. The occasion was a great one but the man was greater than the occasion. Calmly ignoring, except in one sharp, incisive sentence, all that was personal, with his old vigor, terseness and simplicity, he explained to his townsmen the momentous issues of the campaign. From the moment he began, the party rage commenced to cease, and the old pride in his greatness and honesty began to take its place. How strong he looked that night! Although all the world might falter, you knew that calm face would be steadfast. To him had happened the rare good fortune of having the courage and character that matched a great opportunity. Few men would have been so brave and fewer still, successful.

A little more than a year later (September 9, 1869), shortly before his 63rd birthday, William Pitt Fessenden, Maine's greatest statesman, passed away rather suddenly, unappreciated and scorned by most of those in the state and nation he had served so well.

Also See

"Enter Pitt Fessenden," *New England Social Studies Bulletin* 14, May 1957, pp. 13–21.

"The Stirring Election of William Pitt Fessenden," *Lewiston Journal Illustrated Magazine,* 14 October 1905, pp. 3–4.

"William Pitt Fessenden of Portland, One of Pres. Lincoln's Most Valued Advisors," *Portland Evening Express,* 11 February 1909 (Lincoln Centennial Supplement), p. 3.

THE TWELVE DAYS AT AUGUSTA

ANONYMOUS

The year 1880 opened upon a violent demonstration over a contested election. According to the votes returned at the September election, there was no choice for Governor, but there was a majority of Republicans in the members elect for both houses of the Legislature. When the [current] Governor [Alonzo Garcelon] and Council came to canvass these returns, they took occasion, on account of various alleged irregularities, to throw out many votes, with the result that the members they "certificated" showed a majority for both houses to be of the "Fusionist" combination,—Democrats and Greenbackers.

This being so entirely at variance with the original returns, and with the belief in the localities affected and largely throughout the State, a protest arose at once with increasing excitement. Important issues were pending: there being no election of Governor by the people, the election devolved upon the Legislature,* and a United States Senator was to be chosen at this session. There was a widespread impression that the Governor and Council had yielded to the temptation, and had been controlled in their action by party motives.

In truth, political methods had got to a strange pass at that period. The intense greed,—not to say need,—of getting possession of the government led to practices not contemplated by the constitution, nor accordant with truth and right. Orders came, as in war times: "Win at all costs!" Hence distrust was easily wakened, and charges readily framed.

What made the difficulty serious now was

that the Governor and Council claimed, and doubtless believed, that they were within their legal rights in certifying members who, in their opinion, "appeared to be elected"; while on the other hand, the candidates and communities so overruled believed they were defrauded of their constitutional rights. In short, one side claimed to have with them the law; the other, to have the right. The feeling of the Fusionists was, however, supported by their belief in the abundant proof they had in hand of bribery and fraud practiced at the recent elections, which, if rightly investigated, would sustain their contention and substantially their majority. This sharp-edged issue perhaps led the contestants to think they could secure their rights only by appeal to the "primitive instincts." So the leaders started a line of "indignation meetings" in which the point to be made was that they must fight for their "rights";—a maxim which easily stirs the blood of a race of men like ours.

These demonstrations were so formidable, and the threats so violent, that Governor Garcelon was urged by his friends to call out the militia to resist attempts to capture the State House and control the proceedings at the opening of the session. This he wisely declined to do. But he felt compelled by the imminence of the danger to take a course which, however well-intentioned, was not wise. He assembled in the State House a force of men, —about a hundred,—with two leaders, all sworn to obey the Governor, fully armed and equipped, and, in fact, entrenched for desperate resistance. These men were not of very choice material; and, moreover, this body was not "known to the laws," either civil or mili-

* [According to Maine law at the time, when no gubernatorial candidate received a majority vote, the House forwarded two names to the Senate, and the Senate chose one as governor.]

A BOOKLET ORIGINALLY PUBLISHED IN PORTLAND, MAINE, BY SMITH & SALE, 1906.

tary, and hence was a dangerous instrument to handle, for the Governor or anybody else responsible for its existence, in case of a conflict of arms.

The effect, and presumably the intention, of such appeal to violence, was to rouse forcible outbreak and "mob law." Thoughtful men, who had the peace and good name of the State at heart, sought to avert this danger and have the question settled by lawful means, which the constitution must somewhere provide. The Hon. Lot M. Morrill, Ex-Governor and Ex-United States Senator, in a well-argued communication to the Governor, endeavored to induce him to submit the legality of the pending claims to the Supreme Court. General Chamberlain also disapproved the policy of violence. He sent a telegram to the Governor urging him to accept Mr. Morrill's advice, and bring the issue before a competent tribunal.[1] The Governor seemed impressed by these suggestions, but the questions he framed did not exactly meet the issue.

The recognized Republican leaders did not seem to favor this method, perhaps not quite liking to trust the issue to the opinion of a tribunal imbued with "legal" habits and ideas; so the "indignation" policy was pushed.

It was reasonable to suppose that Senator Blaine would favor peaceful measures. He seemed, however, not to ignore the other alternative, and so labored at the disadvantage of a "double objective." The General was not a little surprised to receive a message from Senator Blaine, asking him to get up an indignation meeting in Brunswick. He replied that he did not think such a demonstration wise, and wrote more fully to this effect.[2]

The dangers drew to a focus. The close, confronting condition was: no State government, legal or acting; a few outgoing, useless Department officers; no Legislature, but two rival bodies pretending to exercise its functions, or else a conflux of desperate claimants and champions fighting for their rights.

It happened that the General had been some time before, for reasons not apparent to him or anybody, elected major general by the Legislature, and quite recently assigned to the military command of the entire State. In the crisis now arising, the outgoing Governor, anxious to preserve the peace and promote the settlement of these difficult questions, just before his term expired, summoned the

General to the Capital by a formal order "to protect the public property and institutions of the State until my successor is duly qualified." This order discloses the state of things. At that moment the State House was barricaded and filled with armed men. Distinguished party leaders had left their duties elsewhere and gathered at the capital, where they summoned their fighting men. What they were prepared to do was precisely what the General was summoned there to prevent. He at once dismantled the State House as a military post, dismissed the unauthorized force then holding it, and sent the arms to the State arsenal. He then called on the Mayor of the city, Hon. Charles E. Nash,—a level-headed and independent man—reminding him that the duty was his to preserve the peace in the State House as well as in the city, as far as possible, and that the civil power should first be exhausted before calling on the military. He carefully pointed out the forms to be used in such an event, and drew up the papers. The Mayor entered at once on his part of this duty, while the General took prompt and effective measures, without the knowledge of the contestants, to put down with the strong hand any attempted violence beyond the Mayor's control.

In fact, this was a "three-cornered fight." There were three policies and three camps at the capital; one, the fighting wing of the Republicans, with headquarters, or, at any rate, point of departure, at the house of Mr. Blaine; another, the fighting wing of the Fusionists, at the office of Mr. E. F. Pillsbury and one of the downtown hotels; and the third, the modest combination of the General and the mayor, in one of the small offices in the State House. It will well be borne in mind that not a few, of all political parties, gave their sympathy and moral support to the General in the endeavor to have the question settled by peaceful measures, and that the real leaders in violent measures were not the candidates whose rights were in question but outside champions.[3]

It was a season when by law much matter came in from the towns and counties for the various executive departments. By reason of the confusion in these, many important matters were brought to [Chamberlain]. Resolving to keep himself aloof from doing or receiving anything pertaining to civil functions, he at once locked up the rooms of the Governor and Council, allowing nobody to enter them, placed a police guard over other executive rooms to keep out all unauthorized persons, and required important papers and documents to be placed in the vaults of the treasury. He called three members of his staff to keep his own records and papers in proper shape and see that his orders in other respects were carried into effect.[4]

Having been informed that the military organizations of the State had been advised from high quarters not to obey his orders, he did not allow this to be called in question, but required the assurance from every commanding officer that his orders would be promptly and loyally obeyed. The military power of the State being thus in hand, two or three nearest companies of infantry and a battery of artillery were directed to hold themselves ready at a moment's notice to repair to the capital for duty, and arrangements perfected with the railroads to forward troops under his orders with utmost dispatch at any hour of day or night, and with telegraph lines to give precedence to his dispatches. He also endeavored to calm the excitement of the people of the State by sending out public statements, assuring them of this purpose and ability to preserve the peace, and urging them to refrain from rushing to the capital.

[Chamberlain] soon became aware that there was a set purpose to put him in a false position before the public by reports of pretended "interviews" contradictory to his official statements, and he thereupon required every proposition made to him to be put in writing, and, with his answers, preserved in the files. Conversations, also, were carefully minuted. This was done to enable him to refute falsehoods cast abroad. He did not always bring these into use, and hence some wrong impressions are not even yet wholly removed, although the means of doing so are in his possession.

The General perfectly understood his duties,—both the point and the scope of them. And he took pains to make his position clear to others. He was on duty as a military officer; but it was at a crisis without precedent, and very many questions came up which military law and custom did not provide for, and which had to be determined by his judgment and discretion to meet the exigency. But he held strictly to the military line, not assuming to interpret the law, still less to serve political party, or allow such interest to affect him in the least.

Nevertheless, the attempt was made to undermine his authority and influence by trying to make it appear that he was acting as a partisan, with political motives and purposes. The charge was almost refuted in the very circumstance that it came from the "fire-eaters" in both parties. The "neat" thing about this tactic was that it was equally injurious to him, whether he was claimed or denounced by either.[5]

His orders left him to decide for himself what was a legal government, but he had no official power in the determination of that question. The initiative must be taken by the Legislature; it was for it to determine who are its members. But for reasons seen it was not permitted to organize until this question was somehow first settled. [Chamberlain's] opinion was well known that the only proper way to settle it was by bringing it before the Court. Any measures which would disturb the peace and endanger the institutions of the State it was his special duty to oppose. Hence he was antagonized from all quarters.

Each party was indignant with him because he would not at once recognize its paramount claim, and keep the contesting opponents out of the legislative chambers. None could be more anxious that he for the termination of this lawless condition of things, and release from the disagreeable duty placed upon him. But his yielding to either would not bring peaceful settlement. To the importunities of all he had one answer: "Take your case to the Courts." This they did not want to do, as if doubtful of the decision, but seemed to be restlessly studying some *coup de main*.

Among other things, a committee significantly selected from his old army friends was sent to him with the distinct proposal that he should permit an attack on the legislative chambers where the discordant elements mostly congregated, for the purpose of "pitching out" the falsely certificated members elect. His reply effectually stopped the movement, and greatly increased the animosity against him. It looked as if leaders in both parties were more anxious to remove him from the field than to settle the main question.[6] The situation was made even more difficult by the strange action of the protesting party in assenting to the formal organization of the Senate, when the very persons whose titles to sit as Senators,—which the Supreme Court afterwards declared void,—made the controlling majority. This not only weakened the contention of the protestants, but also made a serious embarrassment for the General, inasmuch as the President of the Senate so elected had a *prima facie* claim to the functions of Governor.

Mr. Lamson, the Senator so elected, was a sincere and honorable man, his spirit and manner at all times courteous. Had this not been so, more serious consequences would have ensured. he called at the General's office to learn whether [Chamberlain] would resist a demand from him as President of the Senate. He said the "fighters" in his party were driving him to demand recognition as Governor. To this the General replied that he recognized him as a Senator elect, and would respect him in all ways as such; but to recognize him as President of the Maine Senate upon present showing would settle nothing, but very much complicate existing difficulties.[7]

Mr. Lamson, however, made the formal demand. The General was entreated by careful friends, also good party men, to consult one of the judges of the Supreme Court, who was near at hand, as to the proper line of duty for him. He did so, and the judge said he had expected the question, and could say at once [that] in his opinion the only safe way for him was to recognize Mr. Lamson's claim. This was a grave addition to the General's responsibility; but he did not let it worry about his "safety," nor disturb his judgment. He could, however, better understand the hesitance of the party leaders about submitting the issue to the Court. He did not follow the judge's advice. He rested his refusal on the broad ground that as a public officer charged with a public duty in a critical situation he was bound to take notice of notorious facts, and in this case these would compel him to decline to vacate his trust. Several very able and eminent persons sought him to give similar advice. To these he gave similar answers.[8]

At this juncture, Hon. Nelson Dingley paid the General a visit, with a message from three members of the Supreme Court that they would answer questions put to them by the General affecting the present situation. He replied that as he had no right under the laws, as a military officer, to put such a question to the Court, their answer would not be sufficient warrant for any official action of his; that it would not be binding upon him, nor upon the members of the Legislature, so that the opinion of the Court given in answer to those expressly warranted by the Constitution in asking for it, although perhaps not legally binding, would have a moral effect compelling acquiescence.

Hon. Lot M. Morrill, who was trying to influence the gatherings at Mr. Blaine's to get the question before the Court, called on the General now and then, saying that "they" insisted on his coming, although for what reason or purpose he could not see,—at any rate, could not say. The General remarked that if the purpose was to find out what he was going to do, it was unnecessary, for his attitude was well known by his public acts and statements; that he had no secrets except as to his tactics as a military officer as occasion should require. These he believed were well organized and sufficient; but he did not propose to make them known beforehand for the benefit of those in any quarter who were endeavoring to thwart him.[9] However, Mr. Morrill was made quite welcome, as he was a reliable source of information which it was advantageous for the General to possess.

A diversion of interest now occurred in the appearance of Hon. Joseph A. Locke, with the information that he had been elected President of the Senate, and was about to assume the functions of Governor. This was a surprise to the General, for Mr. Locke had hitherto participated in the deliberations,—or, rather, discussions, —of the Fusion Senate. However, the General replied to him that even if the Republican members had chosen him president, such action could not but be irregular and was probably not valid. A similar answer was given to [Locke] as previously to Mr. Lamson.

Meanwhile the State House and the city were filling up with adventurers of all sorts from all quarters, some of them notorious characters from other states, ready for a "scrimmage."[10] Well-known champions commanded the formidable fighting lines training under the political leaders.[11] The General had means of knowing all that was going on. He became very anxious. He was in momentary expectation of bloody outbreak, and took his measures accordingly. He was ready to put down mob violence with a signal demonstration. An electric torch would cast a mighty change over the face of things. At this very juncture the short-sighted masters in politics were all straining to get him out of the way. Denunciation [and] detraction were not the only forces brought to bear upon the General. Others, quite different, but equally futile, were put in play.[12] If they had succeeded, there is not a doubt of the fierce conflict which would precipitate civil war. Those who persisted in bringing throngs of angry, armed men to the State House in defiance of his protest little comprehended the elements they were tampering with. They did not measure the sweep of passions, stirred in their followers, nor did they realize the possibilities of the lawless characters drawn by the expected opportunity for their own kind of profit, whom no simple-minded employers, nor dignified leaders, could control when once the demon of riot is let loose.[13]

In this pitch of excitement, the General, through the Mayor's "secret service," unearthed a plot of sworn renegades to assassinate Mr. Blaine and destroy his house. It was believed an assault was to be made on the Fusionists by the imported fighters of the Republicans. They were waiting the first outbreak of violence, even the smallest, to strike the blow. The General found the fact to be serious. He had not hitherto conferred with Mr. Blaine, but now informed him of the reality of this peril, and of the importance of discouraging violence. This made a decided impression upon Mr. Blaine. The leaders in the plot were arrested by the General's order, and the result was on all sides salutary.

Now, alarmed at the effect of their call to violence, the leaders begged the General to call out the troops. This he declined to do, because he was able to keep the peace without it; because a show of force would incite opposing force, and precipitate bloody conflict, perhaps civil war; and because such a move would imply a sense of weakness or fear on his part, and lessen the confidence of the people, on which he mainly relied. His very reserve seemed to impress the frenzied crowd around. They knew something of the General, and had also the proverbial awe of the unknown. This denial was not well received in other quarters. It was now proposed, or threatened, to call in the United States troops; but there were grave obstacles to this, in that there was no legal authority in the State to make such call, and no legal occasion to answer it; and the government authorities at Washington knew the General well, and had confidence in his assurance that such intervention was unnecessary, and would even be resisted.

The Republican members elect at last consented, under the skillful guidance of Hon. Eugene Hale, of the House, to get their case in shape to present to the Court, and much time was taken over it. Mr. Lamson also framed a submission of the question of his rights to the Court, which he did in good faith, and it would seem from the acquiescence of the Republicans in the existing organization of the Senate, with good right. But the turmoil, if anything, increased. Each party distrusted the other, and almost everybody else.[14]

The fighting Fusion wing now became very angry with Mr. Lamson because he did not overawe the General, but had been induced by him,—as they charged,—to submit the questions to the Court. They got their members together and elected a "Governor," Hon. Joseph S. Smith, one of the candidates for that office before the people. He was an able man, and a sensible man, and did not like to be so pushed forward. But they forced him to it, and to sharp measures. He published an order announcing his governorship and his military staff, and immediately thereafter another, revoking the trust placed in the General's hands by Governor Garcelon, also removing him from command of the militia of Maine, and forbidding anybody to obey his orders. There was a great stir, and no small scare. But the General declined to vacate his office, and gave his reasons in a formal communication. Thereupon an attempt was made to arrest him for disobedience of orders. It was not successful.[15]

In the very thick of the commotion around him, the General received dispatches from the mayors of three cities that they were unable to preserve the peace, and that riots were imminent. He replied that they must be held responsible for the peace and order of their cities; but at the same time he extended his frontier of observation, and strengthened his reserves, to be ready for the worst.

The tension was by no means lessened when the answers of the Court to the questions sent were received by the persons entitled to them. Bitter denunciation hardened into oath-clinched threats that the opinion of the Court should not take effect, and that the members recognized in it should not be allowed to organize. But the General took measures to preserve the peace, and no disturbance occurred. Upon receiving a certified copy of the answer of the Court, and shortly afterwards official notice of the election of a

Governor by the Legislature, the General, in a formal communication, declared his trust to be at an end, and at once withdrew from the scene.[16]

The stress and strain of those twelve days were most severe. He was glad when it was over. But in truth it was not over. Tokens of the hatred he had incurred by his course of duty seemed to multiply.[17] This did not surprise him. He knew well when he received this trust that in any case it was to his personal loss and injury. He well knew with what ill-favor the chief actors in these scenes looked upon his coming, and however they might have been profited by it, with what bitterness they followed his going. But the consciousness of a service rendered to his State overbore all this: the sense of duty fulfilled kept his spirit calm. The fact remained.

Amidst circumstances unparalleled in a New England state, and an opposition remarkable in violence and variety, he had carried through his purpose. Without calling out a single soldier or a single gun, but by his moral power, prudence, firmness, and, above all, his command of the confidence of the people, he had held the peace and honor of the State inviolate until at last the lawful measures he advocated were made effective.[18]

This case had drawn attention through the whole country and abroad, and been variously remarked upon. His course was appreciated by all dispassionate observers, and those who understood the situation regard this as by far the most important public service he ever rendered.

NOTES

1. (By telegraph.)
Brunswick, Dec. 25, 1879.

To Governor Garcelon:—The proposition to submit the disputed questions to the Court is eminently wise. Such a course would be honorable to you as Governor of the State, the highest officer of its peace. All good citizens would sustain you in it.

Joshua L. Chamberlain

2. Brunswick, Dec. 29, 1979
Hon. James G. Blaine:
Mr. Dear Sir:—I telegraphed Governor Garcelon the day Governor Morrill's letter appeared, urging him as earnestly as I could to submit the disputed questions to

the Court. I afterward wrote him a letter to the same effect.

As to the indignation meeting proposed here, it was my opinion that the demonstrations of that sort had already been sufficient to impress upon the Governor the state of public feeling; and that what we now need to do is not to add to popular excitement which is likely to result in disorder and violence, but to aid in keeping the peace by inducing our friends to speak and act as sober and law-abiding citizens.

In my opinion there is danger that our friends may take some step which would put them in the wrong. That would be very bad. If wrong is to be done, let the responsibility of it rest with those who do it, and do not let those who are aggrieved seek redress in a way to shift upon themselves the burden of wrongdoing.

I deprecate all suggestion of bloodshed in the settlement of the question. Not only would that resort be deplorable, but the suggestion of it is demoralizing. I cannot bear to think of our fair and orderly State plunged into the horrors of a civil war.

I hope you will do all you can to stop the incendiary talk which proposes violent measures, and is doing great harm to our people. I cannot believe that you sympathize with this, and I am sure your great influence can be made to avail much now to preserve peace and respect for the law.

Pardon me this, but I think circumstances demand of me to make these suggestions.

Very respectfully yours.
Joshua L. Chamberlain

3. It will be seen how incorrect it is to credit the General, as some of the popular cyclopedias do, with "adhering to the Republican party," as the character of his action and basis of his success in this matter,—which seems to be an "inspired" suggestion; and how utterly incorrect it is to represent him as coming "kindly" to the assistance of Mr. Blaine in this crisis, or that he and Mayor Nash were in anyway acting under his orders, as it has been the since prescribed and accepted way to put it. In fact, both these officers were together the head of the peace-keeping party awaiting the action of the Court, while the main thought of the other was some strategy or force as the only way out. Of course these parties were entirely antagonistic in their measures.

4. These were Colonel John Marshall Brown, Inspector and Chief of Staff; Major Joseph W. Spaulding, Judge Advocate; Major Frank E. Nye, Assistant General. Afterwards, Captain Henry E. Sprague and Captain Edward E. Small, of the Adjutant General's Department. The officer charged with the return of the arms from the State House to the Bangor arsenal was Captain John W. Berry.

The General's attempts to insure accuracy, however, were not wholly successful.

First, in a somewhat remarkable circumstance, in the "investigation" of the "count out" matters at August, though numerous witnesses were summoned, the General was not one of them. Thus making it easier to suppress not only his testimony but the history of his very active part in the interregnum. This makes it proper that some of the original and authentic evidence preserved in his files and memoranda should be given in these notes. (His official letters, orders and public proclamations are not, as a rule, inserted here, but only copies from such records as are not easily available.)

Second, the archives of the Adjutant General's office, where many of the papers belonging to this period were placed, have since been tampered with, and some of the most interesting have been taken from the files.

5. What claimed to be a leading Republican paper came out with daily headings like these: "The Republican Renegade," "The Fusionist Sympathizer," "Chamberlain the Most Dangerous Man in Maine." Then after days of denunciation, with equally malicious intent, so set as to seem commendatory: "Chamberlain Returned to the Republican Party." The General was not addicted to "returning" anymore than to turning.

At the same time, on the other hand, papers denouncing him as "The Lawless Usurper," "Traitor to His Trust," "The Serpent of Brunswick," and what was more widely absurd, "The Tool of Blaine."

All this while he was not influenced by party considerations in the slightest degree. Some people cannot understand this.

6. The General was wary about appearing in any gatherings to discuss the situation, desiring to avoid political complications. But on the day when his published reply to Mr. Lamson's demand appeared, as he was passing the door he was urged to step into a committee room in the State House, where the shining lights of statesmanship were exchanging reflections, when they all began to flatter him,—as they supposed. "That document will go down in history famous as the speeches of Cicero in the Roman Senate." and etc. All this was understood and duly appreciated by the General, who had not the habit of being moved even by sincere praise. With a bow he left the room. But no sooner had he stepped outside the door than the same speaker, with a flamboyant gesture, exclaimed, "What we want to do is to get rid of that Major General!"

At about this time he observed that when he left the State House, (which was seldom), a squad of policemen preceded and followed him. Upon inquiry he was told that this was by the mayor's order, who had reason to believe some plot was on foot to make way with him. He hardly gave credence to this, but stood more upon his guard when obliged to appear upon the streets.

There was a well-laid plot to kidnap him by night, and take him off to an obscure town in the "back country," and hold him until the game was over. This plot was awkwardly managed. He got word of it and foiled it by changing rooms at night, and also accepting the attentions of his son, who brought as part of his outfit two pistols that had been well tested in the "Civil" war, —having, in fact, been captured in a hot moment of battle,—and quite used to their business.

The next move was to arrest him on the charge of usurpation and treason. This was of course in the name of the party claiming the governorship: but "there were others" equally anxious to see the General removed, and it is highly probable that they connived at the plot. The persons in charge of this made no secret of it; they found him in the rotunda of the capitol, informed him of their purpose, and proposed to execute it on the spot.

He replied that he had usurped no civil functions, nor obstructed any civil process; and that as a military officer charged with the duty of preserving the peace against threatened violence he had not even called out the troops; and as to treason, he had not levied war against the State, nor adhered to its enemies. He then inquired upon whose complaint, and upon what authority this arrest was ordered; saying that he would submit to arrest upon warrant of any proper magistrate, and would go peacefully to the county jail, where it was proposed to take him. At this, a voice came out with some vigor from a crowd of bystanders, "Do it, and, by God, there'll not be one stone left upon another before morning!" So that plan wouldn't work.

7. *Conversation with Hon. Mr. Lamson, demanding recognition as Governor, January 11, 1880.*

Mr. L. I have come in to ask you if you will refuse to recognize me as acting Governor. I am President of the Senate, elected in accordance with the laws, which it is your duty to regard.

Gen. C. Your statement is correct in form. But this is an issue of fact. You must be aware that the contention here is that the laws have been misused to defeat a constitutional right of citizens.

L. But you do not set yourself above the laws, do you?

C. You will observe that my instructions are not exactly to see that the laws are executed, but "to protect the institutions of the State," one of which institutions is the electoral system as we have it, which is a part of the constitution. This is one of the things which it is my special duty to protect and preserve,—not only against violence, but against unfair pressure of adverse advantage. From the circumstances of the case I understand this to be in the purpose and intent of the order so entrusting me.

L. Has anybody a better right than I to assume the duties of this office?

C. Whoever is rightfully elected by the rightful Senate; you or anybody else. you are no doubt a Senator elect. There is doubt about several others. It is not my province to decide which of the candidates is elected to the Legislature, but to see that fair means are afforded for them to ascertain who is elected.

It is now gravely charged that you were elected by those not themselves elected. This is declared to be a known fact, capable of being shown upon opportunity. As a public officer, charged with peculiar responsibilities, I must take notice of this.

Your title to the authority you claim must go back one step farther than the election by members whose right to vote for you is gravely questioned by a large number of our citizens. The question must go to the Courts, or be decided by revolution,—an appeal to arms,—the arbitrament of war. That I am here to prevent. You see where we are?

I respect you much, and also your office, but cannot respect the authority you present until your right is made clearer.

8. *Memorandum of a conversation with the Hon. James W. Blaine, January 10, 1880.*

B. General, be careful not to make a mistake. There is not the shadow of a doubt that Lamson is Governor. The questions have been settled over and over by the Courts. He is Governor, and must be obeyed.

C. Your statement is very clear, but not the fact. This matter involves the whole contest now in issue. More than half the members elect of both Houses protest against the whole organization thus far made, on the ground that Mr. Lamson was elected President of the Senate by votes of gentlemen who themselves were not elected Senators,—as is known and notorious. I understand they never claimed to be elected, and do not now so claim, but stand entirely upon their certificates. The question is whether this is valid and legitimate ground.

B. The Senate organizes only on its certificates. It does not go into questions of contested votes until after organization.

C. Would it not be possible then for a Governor and Council to certificate men who had not right, scarcely a shadow of claim, who might thereupon proceed to elect a President or Governor? Would not that be very strange government of the people by the people?

B. That is the law, which presumes that the Governor and Council would do no violence to the rights of the people.

C. But what shall be done if by a possibility they did, nevertheless? Must we have a revolution? This is a very serious matter now. It goes to the foundations of our social order.

B. Is it not better to let this organization go on, and right itself later?

C. It might be too late; the case would be foreclosed, practically, after officers had been elected. It could only be righted by extraordinary and revolutionary measures, probably.

B. You seem to prejudge this case, which you have no right to do.

C. I should be prejudging it, first and finally, if I should recognize Mr. Lamson as Governor. I am here, not to pass upon the merits of parties or rights of candidates claiming under very doubtful authority. I am here to protect the institutions of the State.

B. But your own party leaders assented to this organization.

C. I have nothing to do with party leaders. I have my own responsibility. If the Legislature is in doubt, there is a civil tribunal which claimants should appeal to.

B. What right have you to intervene and demand it of them?

C. I think I have a clear right and a decided duty to know who has authority to give me orders. At present I know of no one so entitled. The claimant must show me his authority, and this must be clear, and not under protest and contest.

B. You are taking great risks.

C. I am aware of it. I have thought of it deeply. Not for fear, but to see my duty.

B. Your duty is to recognize the laws and the forms of law.

C. Let me ask a practical question. Ought not a "Senate," so certificated as this one now holding sessions is, to make its first organization a purely preliminary and pro tempore one, until it shall have determined the rights of members claiming seats, and actually seated the members in fact elected?

B. That would be a matter of honor; but the law would not require it.

C. Law that kills honor as well as right does not commend itself to me as fulfilling the purpose of law. Common sense tells me that election by the people is a more essential qualification for a Senator than a certificate of the Governor and Council. The fact of an election is more vital than a formal paper, and to suppress the ascertainment of that fact is bad policy.

B. I would advise you to escape serious trouble.

C. I shall not surrender my trust till I know what I am right in doing by all the tests our civil order affords. Certainly not to one elected by Senators who notoriously, or probably, were no more elected than you and I were. I must take that responsibility, or rather it is already upon me.

9. Nothing could be more open than the General's attitude in this whole affair. As to his tactical or strategic preparations, it would be ludicrous to charge his reticence to deceit. He always had a settled aversion to talking about what he was going to do, and in this critical situation he held to his old habit of keeping his own counsel; not giving away his plans, nor causing jealously by holding consultations. This gave opportunity to smart "publicists," whose business it is to find out everything before it happens, to make mistakes in their prognostications, which could be comfortably explained only by after-charges of indirection, or too frequent application of the "ruse de guerre." The party managers at Augusta were not scrupulous. A characteristic instance may be given:

When the General published his earnest protest against rushing armed men to the capital, endangering the peace he was endeavoring to preserve, this was immediately followed by a none-too-private dispatch to a "fire-eating" party in a neighboring city: "Come, and bring all you can get! J. L. C." Signed with his initials,—somebody having the same, perhaps allowing it. Here was an "item" passed round, with ready abuse or chuckling.

10. Many of those who came to the capital at the time for the opening of the Legislature were among the best and most trusted citizens of the State, and came with the purpose of helping to a peaceful establishment of the Government; but after the General's policy was known and his ability to sustain it recognized, they refrained from coming. Most of those who came later, in defiance of his public request to the contrary, bringing bodies of armed men conspicuously demonstrating their importance, and thereby aggravating the dangerous elements of the situation, were of a different class, but still influential representatives of the fighting wing. On the pressure of such in and about the capitol, the General took occasion to exclude from the Legislative chambers all persons except certificated members and those having well-grounded claims to seats therein. The rotunda accordingly presented quite a moving panorama, or what the boys call "a circus."

11. The Fusionist fighting column was headed by "Colonel" J. W. Blood, chiefly famous in New York, and Captain R. W. Black, a man of some prominence about the capitol. They were overmatched in force of character by Colonel A. G. Spurling of the 2nd Maine cavalry, a thorough soldier and a fearless man, who seemed to be chief on the other side.

12. *The following transcript from the memoranda made at the time may throw some light on the elements of the situation:*

In the midst of the dark doings to circumvent the General, or to be rid of him, two of the most influential members of the Democratic and the Greenback parties came to him with the formal proposal that if he would recognize an organization of the Legislature on its present certification, both these parties would waive all other considerations and elect him United States Senator. They added as justification or inducement, the remark: "Blaine and his drive are the bitterest enemies you have in the State." And one of them made the emphatic statement: "Distrust of Blaine more than anything is the origin and strength of the Greenback party in Maine." The General replied, of course, that aside from any other consideration he could not make use of a trust position for his personal advantage.

Curiously enough, Mr. Morrill came to him about the same time with a confidential message nearly in this language: "Mr. Blaine says he will give way, and leave the way clear for you to go to the Senate if you will recognize the Republican organization of the two Houses." There was but a short answer: "Mr. Morrill, they misjudge me. I am not here for self. I will recognize the right,—rightfully declared, and take the consequences."

They must have considered the situation desperate to be willing to pay such a price for it.

13. On one of the most frenzied days at the capitol, one of his staff rushed into his office from the rotunda with the outburst: "General, you are lost! There is a blood-thirsty crowd out there swearing they are sent to kill you and are going to do it!" The General buttoned up his coat, stepped out in front of this crowd,—twenty-five or thirty of them, evidently charged and maddened for their deed,—mounted two steps up the stairs and faced them. "Men, you wish to kill me, I hear. Killing is no new thing to me. I have offered myself to be killed many times, when I no more deserved it than I do now. Some of you, I think, have been with me in those days. You understand what you want, do you? I am here to preserve the peace and honor of this State, until the rightful government is seated,—whichever it may be, it is not for me to say. But it is for me to see that the laws of this State are put into effect, without fraud, without force, but with calm thought and sincere purpose. I am here for that, and I shall do it. If anybody wants to kill me for it, here I am. Let him kill!"

Here he threw open his coat, looking them in the eyes.

"By God, old General, the first man that dares to lay a hand on you, I'll kill him on the spot!" shouted a [grizzled] old veteran, pushing through them to the front,—a soldier still, in heart. A broken wave ran through the crowd, and it melted away, with various mutterings.

14. Doubts were freely expressed [about] whether the Court could properly receive and act upon questions presented by a minority of the certificated members of the House, and there was some delay. On the other hand, Mr. Lamson was informed that the Court would not recognize his right to present questions. He very naturally showed the General the questions he had prepared to submit to the Court, and stated his intention to abide by the decision. The case being fairly stated, and Mr. Lamson's sincerity manifest, the General, anxious to terminate this state of things and to miss no opportunity to secure the definitive opinion of the Court so long desired, informed the Chief Justice of his confidence in Mr. Lamson's purpose to acquiesce in the opinion of the Court, in the hope that they would find it proper to "recognize" [Lamson's] right to put these questions, sufficiently to give them an answer. Of course, nothing was intimated as to the nature of the answer to be given, as that would be an intrusion and impertinence.

The General's communication was immediately caught at by Mr. Boutelle and other assuming organs of the Blaine party, and falsely represented as an attempt to influence the Court to "recognize" Mr.

Lamson's right to the governorship,—quite a different thing from the right to ask a question concerning his claim and have it answered. No end of falsification and abuse was got up out of this.

15. One of these staff officers visited his room at midnight to make the bodily arrest. The General declined to be arrested, and the ensuing scene would have afforded a subject for a Hogarth or Zola.

16. When the new Governor was about to be inaugurated, he besought the General to remain and see him safely seated. This as a courtesy he would have cheerfully done. But learning that it had been determined to have a military force out, with a Gatling gun to command the approaches to the capitol, —which was against his judgment, as it was contrary to the spirit and aim of his whole struggle during the interregnum,—and especially as under military law he would be commander of these forces, unable to dissuade from this measure, he declined to be present; and it being intimated that he would be ordered to remain in the capital on military duty, he took occasion to meet an engagement out of the State.

Some of the outlaws, holding him responsible for the disappointment of their expectations of a chance for glory and loot, plotted to attack and destroy his house in Brunswick. This seems hardly serious, looked at from this calm distance; but it was quite in keeping with the temper of things at the capitol for days and nights past. The town officers of Brunswick thought it serious enough to keep a patrol about his house for some little time. Threats of assassination were renewed, and of bitter revenge in ways unknown to him.

17. For a long time after this, those who desired to secure office or contracts under the State or National Governments were obliged to represent themselves as not friendly to the General.

18. The person who first suggested and earnestly pressed the measure by which this question was finally determined was Mr. Lot M. Morrill, who appears to be ignored in the acknowledgments to and from headquarters. It is curious to note that this settlement was no sooner effected than the whole credit of it was characteristically claimed by the very persons who were largely responsible for the incitements to violence; and indeed, whose political methods had called, or driven, together as a protest the political combination known as "Fusionist," which carried the State the next year.

ALSO SEE

"Yesterday in Maine: The Slur that Cost Blaine the Presidency," *Kennebec Sunday Journal,* 29 September 1996, pp. 1D–2D.

In Front of Cushing's Battery

J. L. COBURN

The recent gathering of Federal and Confederate veterans of the Civil War on the battlefield of Gettysburg was an event alone in its class—the grandest exhibition of manly acquiescence to the march of progress the world has ever known. Therefore it was not at all strange that it was the occasion of the interchange of many personal experiences of the veterans who 50 years before exchanged shot for shot upon that historic field. One incident in particular, relating to Pickett's charge at the moment of its collapse in front of Cushing's battery, as related by an old Confederate seems of unusual interest.

The incident as related was retold to me by Henry M. Grigg, past commander of Thatcher Post, G.A.R., of Portland, who was present at the time the old Confederate described his experiences in front of one of the guns of Cushing's battery almost at the same moment that his heroic commander, General Armistead, met his death there—even as he laid his hand on the gun, claiming it as his own. But as that is familiar history we will let the old Confederate tell his own story, which in substance was as follows:

"I reckon you all know more about what transpired about that particular gun and the manner in which General Armistead met his death than I do, because you see it was this way: I didn't get quite so far as the gun when it was discharged directly into my face, hardly a rod distant. I reckon that there were not more than 150 of us with General Armistead when that last rush for the guns was made, and it was more an impulse for self-preservation that otherwise, as we were being made into mincemeat where we were by the spray of grape and canister from front as well as both flanks, and, the nearer the guns we could get, the safer we should be. There was not a man among us, I reckon, who did not know that the charge was a dead failure before we made that last rush from the Bloody Angle, and none knew this more truly than did General Armistead himself.

"You all can well understand that it was not time to hesitate, and General Armistead, with his hat raised high upon the point of his sword, shouted, 'Now for the guns, men!' and led off up the slope.

"There was a gun directly in front of me as we approached the battery, and, as we drew near, you may be sure I was keeping a sharp eye upon what they were doing about that gun. I saw but two men standing about it, one of them working frantically to recharge it before we could reach it and the other standing just outside a wheel of the gun carriage, leaning against it as he grasped it with one hand as if for support, while his other hand grasped the gun's lanyard.

"There has been a lot of gush written about that last charge of grape that the heroic Lieutenant Cushing discharged into the very faces of the Confederates before he fell back and expired, but I reckon that if that gun had been shot I should not be here now talking about it. The gunner had swabbed the gun and rammed the powder-charge, and, as he withdrew the rammer, he whirled toward us, raising his rammer high as though for a whack at our heads. I reckon he knew when he whirled toward us that he could not shoot the gun before we reached it.

"There was—it now seems to me—but the fraction of a second from the time the gunner whirled toward us and stood with his

Originally published in *Lewiston Journal Illustrated Magazine*, 6 September 1913.

rammer upraised, to the time the blood-besmeared man leaning against the wheel, yanked the lanyard, and yet during that short time the scene about that gun, even to its minutest details, was photographed upon my brain like a flashlight impression. There was the black muzzle of the gun, the gunner with his upraised rammer, the blood-besmeared face distorted with agony, the dead and disabled men lying about. One in particular was lying upon his side in front of the gun, partially raised upon his elbow, too weak to steady the aim of his revolver which he was trying to train upon us.

"It was one of those conditions of mental strain that comprehends every item of deadly surroundings instantly. I had experienced a sense of relief as the gunner whirled away from his gun facing us and had noted the things above described and more, for as the wounded man yanked the lanyard with one hand he had pushed himself away from the wheel he was leaning against as though to clear the recoil of the gun.

"Oh, I took it all in and it has remained a kind of nightmare with me ever since. I think of it by day, dream of it at night, and sometimes, while dreaming of other things with pleasant surroundings, there comes suddenly into the scene the agonized blood-besmeared face of the man who yanked the lanyard of that gun at the moment of discharge.

"Knowing what I did about artillery fire, it still remains a mystery to me why I should have experienced a sense of relief at the gunner's failure to shoot his gun. If I had had horse sense about me at the moment, I should have realized that so far as I was concerned the powder blast directly into my face at short range would have been about as fatal as canister. As it was, my only salvation so far as my eyesight was concerned was the fact that at the last instant, even after the lanyard was yanked, I instinctively shut my eyes tight—and that was the last glimpse I had of the battle of Gettysburg.

"As you all know, this happened late in the afternoon of July 3, 1863, fifty years ago about this very hour and minute, and upon about the very spot where I now am standing. Sometime after dark, I began to sense things. It was some time before I could understand what had happened, and, as consciousness became more complete, I began to suffer the most excruciating agony. The flesh about my face was hanging in shreds. You all can un-derstand what a godsend my partially filled canteen of water was to my lacerated, blood-and powder-besmeared face—my eyes especially—and to that alone was due my escape from the Federal lines during the night.

"As I lay there, trying to place things, I gradually took in not only my immediate surroundings but became convinced that the general condition of things had not been changed to any extent by Pickett's charge. There was but little firing. The sputtering fire of pickets in the distance, which soon subsided, in the direction of Little Round Top, to be repeated out toward the Peach Orchard or in the direction from which Armistead's brigade had advanced to the charge, satisfied me that there was no escape for me in that direction.

"The ground about me was pretty thickly strewn with the dead, but as I was nearly blind I could not in the semi-darkness distinguish one uniform from another. Evidently when the wounded had been removed I had been left for dead with the others. After awhile I succeeded in standing, half staggeringly, upon my feet and started up the slope, stumbling over dead men as I proceeded, hoping to find someone who could assist me, but the further I proceeded up the slope the less my chances seemed of finding relief, when suddenly, after I had passed over the crest of the slope I stumbled over a man lying asleep, and fell across another sleeper, only partially arousing them. I had stumbled into a Federal bivouac of men so exhausted that they might as well have been dead so far as danger to me was concerned; in fact, everybody was either dead of asleep, and I reckon, excepting the surgeons and wounded, they were. Anyway I was not even challenged by either Federal or Confederate pickets as I skirted about Culp's Hill to the southeast, and reached Gettysburg about daylight, where I received medical attendance. I was sent to Virginia with the wounded, where later on I rejoined my company and served to the surrender at Appomattox.

Also See

"At Gettysburg in 1863 and 1888," Military Order of the Loyal Legion of the United States, *War Papers: Read Before the Commmandery of the State of Maine* 1, 1898, pp. 49–57.

THE RESTORATION OF LOUDVILLE

ANONYMOUS

The United States of America is united again. Maine is united again, and citizens of Loudville are once more a happy people, for now they know that the government will be able to bring its full strength against the foes across the seas.

In other words, after a 57-year grouch, Loudville, which "seceded" from the United States in 1860, has returned to the fold, and will send its full quota of fighting men to the front. And will probably dig deep into its well-filled pockets and help out on the Liberty Loan. At least, that is the word that comes from that stubborn little town that has refused to "have anything to do with the United States, or Maine either," for so many years.

When the United States entered the war on the side of the allies, a *Boston Post* reporter made a journey to Loudville to find out what the attitude of that strangest of communities would be.

When he arrived there he found out that Loudville had lived apart from the United States ever since it got mad with the United States back in 1860. At that time it got mad with Maine, and got awfully mad with the town of Bristol in particular.

And for the last 57 years the people of the town have refused to pay taxes, town, state, or federal; refused to vote; refused telephone or telegraph connection with the world; refused to take part in the Civil War; and refused to become a town, village, plantation, or anything. They have just wanted to be let alone.

Loudville [Loud's Island] lies off Round Pond, which is part of the town of Bristol, which is half-way between Bath and Rockland. Imagine an island in the United States, settled way back in seventeen something, in the midst of civilization, yet refusing to be a part of the nation, refusing to help in its affairs, refusing to join in its government—and you have Loudville for the past half century.

There are about 140 persons in Loudville. Most of them are named Loud, Carter, Poland, and Thompson. Although they do much fishing, most of them have snug fortunes tucked away, and you can't buy the pine-covered rocks and woods on the island for love or money. It's as exclusive as Pride's Crossing or Bellevue Avenue.

Loudville's grouch began when Lincoln first ran for President, in 1860. That's when Loudville got mad. Up to that time Loudville had been a part of Bristol. Bristol was a Republican town, and Loudville was proud of being Democratic. They cast their vote at this election, and they all went Democratic, with the exception of one vote.

Bristol didn't like it. So Loudville's vote was contested and thrown out. Then Loudville got mad. But what could it do?

It did the only thing it could—it "seceded." It withdrew from Bristol, from Maine, and from the United States. And until now it has been "seceding" ever since.

The Civil War came on, and drafting began. Out of a possible 25 men, nine were drafted. Loudville thought it was unfair. It got mad, it got furious. But what could it do?

It did the only thing it could do—it refused to be drafted. When a United States officer came to Loudville to enforce the draft, the women of the town met him at the shore with a shower of boiled potatoes.

Later three men were again drafted—John Loud, John Thompson, and Henry McGray. They were determined not to help in the

ORIGINALLY PUBLISHED IN *Lewiston Journal Illustrated Magazine*, 27 OCTOBER 1917.

war, and so they hired three substitutes to fight for them, so that nobody could accuse Loudville of having taken a part in the war.

Since then they have lived apart. They never voted, not even for President, Governor, or for anything else. They have not paid a cent of taxes. They have had no town meetings, selectmen, or anybody. They did not keep up the streets, because they had no streets. They had no lights, no public buildings, no landings, no piers, no sewers, no nothing. There is only one community undertaking—the school.

They have received the United States mails three times a week—every day in the summer—for years. But they never asked for it. They just condescended to accept it.

The ancient name of Loudville is Muscongus, and it is often called so now. It is reputed to be the grave of the great chief Samoset. Many of the people are descended from the first settlers of Loudville, and they are a proud lot of folks.

There's Melvin Loud, one of the old Louds. The *Post* man met him on the way to his home: "There's no need of this war, as I can see," he said. "There's nobody here is interested in it. We were against war in 1865, and we are against it now.

"If they draft us, we won't go. We'll do as we did before. Bristol can't get us, nor nobody else, either. We are as set against it now as we were then. I don't see why we should help. Nobody has attacked us."

Then there's Everett Thompson, who keeps the grocery store. Both he and his wife are persons of education. But they are Loudvillettes to the core.

"We are all right as we are," said Mr. Thompson. "I see no need of our joining Bristol. Ever since we have been by ourselves things have been all right. We do not care who is to be President, or anything else that occurs in the country. We will stay out."

"Well, I am going to enlist," said Mrs. Luella Poland—she had been reading about women enlisting. She is a sister of Mr. Thompson and was visiting the island.

Charles Loud, who is 63, is another of the "old timers." "I'm frightened to death that they will come after my two boys," said his wife.

"Well, they shan't get them," said Mr. Loud, with a note of stubbornness in his voice. "We did not ask for the war, and we'll have nothing to do with it."

But now all is changed. Loudville has registered, and she has at last decided that the United States is good enough for her. And she is once more on the "inside" and will do her part.

ALSO SEE

"Muscongus Didn't Secede, but Its Status was Once Questioned by Bristol," *Lewiston Journal Illustrated Magazine,* 22 April 1944, p. 15.

"Secessionists had Active Support in Maine in 1860's " *Portland Sunday Telegram,* 31 July 1966, p. 12A.

"When Maine Towns Refused to Pay Civil War Bounties," *Lewiston Journal Illustrated Magazine,* 12 March 1938, pp. 2, 12.

ADELBERT AMES—LAST OF THE GENERALS

BOB MORRIS

During the First Battle of Bull Run in the Civil War, the green citizen soldiers of Maine and other northern states broke before the experienced country riflemen of the Confederacy. Many of the Union soldiers ran from the battlefield, but some didn't. One man who ranks high in New England's history earned the Medal of Honor for bravery there.

Adelbert Ames was born October 31, 1835, and died April 13, 1933. Encompassed within those 97 years was brilliant service in the Army, governorship of Mississippi, impeachment proceedings that forced him to resign that post, and later years of wealth among the wealthy in Tewksbury, Massachusetts and Florida.

Born in Rockland, Maine, Adelbert Ames was the son of a sea captain, Jesse Ames, who in later years owned and operated a successful flour mill business in Northfield, Minnesota. Del was educated in public schools, and in his teens followed his father to sea.

He was always interested in military affairs, so in 1856 he quit as first mate of a clipper and entered West Point.

Ames was graduated fifth in his class May 8, 1861. Among his classmates was George Armstrong Custer, and both earned generals' stars while still in their twenties.

At Bull Run

Eight days after graduation, Ames was promoted to first lieutenant and assigned to the 5th Artillery Regiment outside Washington, D.C. He drilled Volunteers for two months, until the regiment was ordered into the First Battle of Bull Run July 21. The battle was a catastrophe for the Union Army, which hoped to end the war in one major battle, but Ames earned the nation's highest military decoration there. Everywhere the Union troops seemed to collapse, but Ames's men did well in the battle. He was shot through the thigh early in the fighting, but insisted on staying with his section. Though bleeding badly, he sat on a caisson, directing his section's fire until he passed out and was carried away on an ammunition wagon.

For his bravery, Ames was given temporary rank of major in the regular army that day, and later [1893] Congress awarded him the Medal of Honor. Recovered from his wound in September, he rejoined his regiment, where he was made commander of a battery in October.

The Ames family was well known in Maine, and even in Massachusetts, where one member was elected to the General Court in 1636. While the new major drilled his men outside Washington during the winter, he had many socially and politically prominent visitors at his camp. One was another Maine native, Vice President Hannibal Hamlin. Ames always had an eye for business, and wrote his parents during this period that they should invest in real estate because the war was sure to drive up prices.

Heads 20th Maine

In March 1862, he was back in action. His battery provided supporting fire for troops until August as a part of the Peninsula Campaign in Virginia. The 5th was prominent in the siege of Yorktown, Virginia, in April and May, and later served at Gaine's Mill [on] June 27 and Malvern Hill [on] July 1. At Gaine's Mill, Ames's unit got within a few miles of Richmond before the Northern forces were finally forced to retreat. The Union forces weren't

ORIGINALLY PUBLISHED IN *TOWN CRIER*, 8 FEBRUARY 1973, AND (ROCKLAND, MAINE) *COURIER GAZETTE*, 8 MARCH 1973.

again to approach so near the capitol of the Confederacy until 1864. For his service at Malvern Hill, Ames was promoted to the temporary rank of lieutenant colonel in the regular army.

On August 29, 1862, he was promoted colonel of volunteers, whose units and ranks were separate from those of the regular army. Named commander of the Famous 20th Maine Volunteer Regiment, he engendered nearly universal hatred among green officers and men for his discipline, merciless drilling, and deep-voiced sarcasm as he honed them into an effective fighting unit.

The 20th Maine regiment saw service throughout the Maryland Campaign of September through November, including the Battle of Antietam on September 17. Then it joined the Rapahannock Campaign of December 1862 to June 1863, where it was severely tested during the Battle of Fredericksburg December 13.

MAJOR GENERAL ADELBERT AMES

Ames and The 20th Are Tested

General Ambrose Burnside's regiments failed repeatedly to capture a sunken, walled road in the area of the battlefield called Marye's Heights. Burnside finally ordered General Joseph Hooker to capture the road.

Hooker, who more than deserved his nickname of "Fighting Joe," viewed the objective through field glasses. The road lay uphill at the end of a 1700-yard open field, and was bristling with riflemen. Beyond the road, at the crest of the heights, was a tremendous concentration of artillery, all aimed at the field his men were supposed to storm uphill.

Hooker told Burnside the road was impregnable, and for one of the few times in the war, pleaded for an assault to be abandoned. Burnside repeated his order to attack, and Hooker told Ames to advance against the road.

Ames personally led the 20th Maine in the assault, the only regimental commander to do so at Fredericksburg. An officer from a regiment pinned down in the field later said Ames calmly led the 20th across the field to his position and told him quietly, "I will move over your line and relieve your men."

Hooker's belief in the road's impregnability proved correct. Colonel Ames, though six feet tall and a perfect target, escaped injury in the attack. Of the 36 men dead and wounded he lost, every one was behind him when hit. At nightfall the entire union army was pinned down without Ames capturing his objective, and before being able to withdraw, he and his regiment passed a freezing night pressed to the earth behind makeshift barricades of the dead.

After Fredericksburg, Ames's officers were so impressed with his leadership in the battle they gave him a $200 sword, sash and belt that at today's prices would be worth thousands of dollars.

Colonel Ames next saw service at the Battle of Chancellorsville, where he was aide de camp to General Hooker May 2–4, 1863.

Hooker, after constant requests to superiors, finally got Ames promoted to Brigadier General of Volunteers May 20, when Ames was only 27 years old. He thus became one of the Civil War's famous "boy generals."

The new brigadier almost immediately saw combat at the Battle of Beverly Ford [on] June 9. On July 1, the first day of the Battle of Gettysburg, he commanded a brigade and was given temporary promotion to colonel in the regular army. When his commanding officer was wounded in the fighting, Ames took command of the division [for] July 2 and 3. His division held the line at East Cemetery Hill, and was exposed to attacks from in front and on both flanks.

Earns Cheers from the Men

On the third day of the battle, Ames was riding with a general from General Meade's staff and found troops in one portion of the line cheering and waving their hats at them. Ames congratulated the general for drawing the response, but the general told him the troops were the 20th Maine, Ames's old unit, and were cheering him.

In the aftermath of their great triumph, even the men of his old unit had come to understand and appreciate him. One of them wrote to his father, ". . . we hated General Ames when he came to us in Maine, but when we found out the hard way what his training did for us, we loved him. . . ." Later, when their tattered regimental flag was replaced, they voted to present him with the old one, a gift he treasured all his life.

In the next 18 months Ames took part in the siege of Charleston, N.C., commanded a division in Florida and returned north. He saw action at Walthall Junction, Virginia, [on] May 7, 1864, and Cold Harbor [on] June 3. He led brigades and divisions in actions around Fredericksburg and Richmond until December, and was at Darbytown Road [on] October 13 and 27. During a brief leave in September, he sent his savings and everything be could borrow back to his father to invest in the family flour mill in Northfield, Minnesota.

His Greatest Battle

From December 7 [through] 28, 1864, Ames served in the unsuccessful attack on Fort Fisher. North Carolina, under Lowell's Maj. Gen. Benjamin Butler, who later became his father-in-law. Fort Fisher allowed Wilmington, North Carolina, to remain the Confederacy's last open port, and Ames was happy when his division was assigned to the second assault on the fort January 2.

General Alfred Terry, who now commanded the attack, tried for two weeks to capture the fort, but his troops failed in their attempts. Finally Terry turned the job over to Ames's 3rd Division, and left the job of planning the attack to Ames.

Ames attacked the fort at 3 P.M. January 16, eventually using a total of 3,000 men in the assault. He personally directed his troops into their positions, wearing his brigadier general's dress uniform, his brown hair, beard and mustache carefully groomed. The tall officer seemed unconcerned about repeated fire from sharpshooters he and his staff came under.

Col. Henry C. Lockwood, his aide de camp, later wrote, "Ames never hesitated to take desperate chances under fire. He seemed to have a life that was under some mystic protection." Lockwood described Ames as being cool, calm and gentlemanly throughout the attack.

"Under the heaviest fire, when men and officers were being struck down around him, he would sit on his horse, apparently unmoved by singing rifle ball, shrieking shot or bursting shell . . . and quietly gave his orders." Lockwood wrote.

During the night, Ames's division captured the fort, and took 2000 prisoners and 72 cannon. The attack cost him 650 men killed and wounded, including four of his staff officers he personally took into the fort during the assault.

Ames that day was appointed to the temporary rank of major general of volunteers. For his service at Fort Fisher, he was promoted February 22 to the permanent rank of captain in the regular army, and on March 13 was named to the temporary rank of major general in the regular army for his service in the war.

Terry Gets Credit

Although Ames was promoted, Terry took immediate credit for the victory at Fort Fisher. Terry later admitted Ames was responsible for the capture of the fort, but his admission was largely ignored.

Had it not been, Ames would probably have been known as one of the great generals of the Civil War, for the closing of Wilmington as a port meant the Confederacy was doomed.

After Fort Fisher, Ames's division moved up the Cape Fear River and helped capture Wilmington, North Carolina, February 27. General Ames fought in the Battle of Bentonville March 21, and also participated in the capture of Raleigh. North Carolina, before the war ended.

Serves in the Army of Occupation

After the war, Ames was mustered out of the volunteer army, and promoted to the permanent rank of lieutenant colonel in the regular army. He took 10 months' leave and traveled throughout Europe, where he was presented before the Court of St. James in England and that of Napoleon III in France.

In June 1867 he returned to the United States to serve with the army of occupation in South Carolina. He then served as deputy district commander in Mississippi and was named provisional military governor of Mississippi by General Grant, who gave him the temporary rank of major general in the regular army. Later Ames command was extended to the 4th Military District, one of the five districts that governed the occupied South.

Serves as Mississippi Politician

In 1869 Ames as elected to an unexpired term as U.S. Senator from Mississippi by the newly enfranchised blacks, unionist Southerners and Northern settlers. He resigned from the army before taking the post.

On July 21, 1870 he married Blanche Ames, the daughter of Major General Butler. Ames met Blanche in the senate galleries in 1868. Their wedding at St. Ann's Episcopal Church in Lowell was attended by 600 invited guests, and 10,000 persons cheered the wedding procession.

Ames's term in the senate was largely spent dealing with reconstruction acts. In 1873 he resigned from the senate when he was elected governor of Mississippi by the same reconstruction political elements.

The Ames Administration was a troubled one. Even before Ames took office, the former Confederates rioted in Vicksburg, and within months the State was in virtual anarchy. Blacks were lynched, police were rendered ineffective by the more numerous former Confederates, and state government almost ceased to exist.

Governor Ames called for help from Washington, but the Republican Administration there had made a deal with the former rebels not to block their reassumption of power in the South. In the November elections of 1875, the newly enfranchised former rebels captured a majority in the state senate and house of representatives.

When the new house and senate sat in 1876, the former Confederates immediately prepared articles of impeachment against Ames. The governor was accused of improper appointments to state offices and other technicalities, but his personal honesty and integrity were never attacked. Ames knew the former rebels would stack any jury against him, so he agreed to resign if the articles were withdrawn. The articles were withdrawn March 28, 1876, and Ames resigned the next day, the last Northern governor of a Southern state.

Subsequent Career and Retirement

For more than two decades, Ames functioned as a businessman, becoming wealthy through involvement in the family business and real estate, banking and other enterprises in Minnesota, New York and Lowell. But 62-year-old Ames again offered his services to the army when the Spanish-American War broke out in 1898. Appointed brigadier general of volunteers, he led a brigade in the trenches on Ft. San Juan Hill in Santiago, Cuba, an action which he described as making him feel like a youth again.

During his long retirement, Ames spread his time between Tewksbury and Ormand Beach, Florida, where he was a friend and golfing companion of John D. Rockefeller, Sr. He built a summer home on his 700-acre estate in Tewksbury in 1903, and called it The Castle. Built on a drumlin, the building appears to be a small mansion of 18 large rooms, a kitchen, seven bathrooms, two halls and a pantry.

The name stems from its construction materials. The walls were built of fieldstone, and all the floors, even those upstairs, were constructed of reinforced concrete.

Ames played golf winters in Ormand Beach until he was 94 years old, and, at the age of 87, [could still] to play 36 holes a day. He died in his Winter home at Ormand Beach on April 13, 1933, the last surviving union general in the Civil War, and one of the most prominent men in Civil War and New England history.

ALSO SEE

"Adelbert Ames: The Last General," *Maine Sunday Telegram,* 5 October 1980, p. 3D.

"The Capture of Fort fisher, North Carolina," *The Maine Bugle,* April 1987, pp. 167–87.

"A Man from Maine: A True History of the Army at Fort Fisher," *The Maine Bugle,* January 1894, pp. 29–71.

"Oldest of Surviving Civil War General [a] Maine Man by Birth," *Portland Sunday Telegram,* 20 November 1932, p. 1D.